Psychosocial Approaches to Negative Symptoms in Psychosis

Psychosocial Approaches to Negative Symptoms in Psychosis

Assessment & Intervention for Clinicians and Researchers

Edited by

TANIA LINCOLN
MARIE BROWN
AND
DAVID KIMHY

OXFORD
UNIVERSITY PRESS

OXFORD
UNIVERSITY PRESS

Oxford University Press is a department of the University of Oxford. It furthers the University's objective of excellence in research, scholarship, and education by publishing worldwide. Oxford is a registered trade mark of Oxford University Press in the UK and in certain other countries.

Published in the United States of America by Oxford University Press
198 Madison Avenue, New York, NY 10016, United States of America.

CIP data is on file at the Library of Congress

ISBN 9780197676790

DOI: 10.1093/oso/9780197676790.001.0001

Printed by Marquis Book Printing, Canada

The manufacturer's authorized representative in the EU for product safety is Oxford University Press España S.A., Parque Empresarial San Fernando de Henares, Avenida de Castilla, 2 – 28830 Madrid (www.oup.es/en or product.safety@oup.com). OUP España S.A. also acts as importer into Spain of products made by the manufacturer.

MIX
Paper | Supporting responsible forestry
FSC www.fsc.org FSC® C103567

Contents

List of Figures

List of Tables

List of Tables

List of Boxes

Preface

Marie Brown, Tania Lincoln, and David Kimhy

Negative symptoms are considered a core feature of schizophrenia and related disorders and have been consistently linked to low quality of life and diminished community functioning. Furthermore, negative symptoms have been found to have a greater adverse impact than positive symptoms across the areas of neurocognition and social and occupational functioning. Current antipsychotic medications have a low impact on negative symptoms, and at times may even mimic or exacerbate them. There is a growing body of evidence that psychosocial interventions show promise in improving negative symptoms; however, to date, no published book has focused exclusively on these interventions. This edited volume seeks to fill this gap by providing a comprehensive overview of psychosocial interventions for negative symptoms with chapters written by innovative and key leaders in the field. The book spans the areas of scientific and theoretical perspectives; clinical assessment; case formulation; and prominent psychotherapeutic interventions. Our aims for this collection are twofold. Firstly, we wished to create a book that could serve as a comprehensive reference guide for researchers in the field, particularly those interested in developing clinical trials for psychosocial interventions. Secondly, we designed the book to ensure practical relevance for clinicians actively engaged in providing care for individuals experiencing negative symptoms.

The editors of this book, Tania Lincoln, David Kimhy, and Marie Brown, have extensive clinical and research experience working with negative symptoms in psychosis. Their collective expertise spans psychological intervention, cognitive behavioral approaches, translational research, theoretical writing, and clinical practice. Tania Lincoln, PhD, is a Full Professor in Clinical Psychology and Psychotherapy at Universität Hamburg, Germany. Her research focuses on psychological intervention for psychotic disorders, with specific focus on the psychological processes that form and maintain negative symptoms. With her wealth of knowledge in this area, she brings invaluable insights into understanding and addressing negative symptoms from an evidence-based psychological research perspective. David Kimhy, PhD, is an Associate Professor and the Director of the Experimental Psychopathology Laboratory at the Icahn School of Medicine at Mount Sinai. With over 20 years of experience treating individuals with schizophrenia spectrum disorders, his research delves into behavioral/exercise approaches to psychosis, emerging digital practices, and translational research methodologies to illuminate potential mechanisms of recovery from serious mental illness. Marie Brown, PhD, is a Senior Psychologist and Team Leader of the OnTrack and Early Psychosis Treatment Program at Lenox Hill Hospital in New York City; and the current President of the International Society for the Psychological and Social Approaches to Psychosis, US Chapter (ISPS-US). Her extensive clinical experience working therapeutically with people experiencing psychosis across various settings, including in the public mental health system, enriches the practical aspects of this volume for clinicians.

This book is structured into three broad sections: Background, Assessment, and Intervention. Within each section, chapters draw upon material from empirical research, clinical practice, and theory. In order to ensure the book's relevance to clinicians, we have provided a "clinical pearls" section within each chapter with the aim of providing readily accessible key points for individuals to begin immediately incorporating into their practice. Part I of the book focuses on providing background on the construct of negative symptoms and situates these symptoms within neurobiological, interpersonal/social, and humanistic frameworks. In addition to the theoretical and research literature, Part I of this book also includes two chapters by people with personal experience of negative symptoms in order to provide readers with a more intimate engagement with the subject. Part II focuses on the assessment of negative symptoms, spanning standardized behavioral and clinical rating scales; self-report measures; digital technologies; and functional assessment. Our hope here to is expand the possibilities of assessment of negative symptoms to enrich clinical practice and research trials.

The last and most extensive section of the book, Part III, focuses on psychosocial interventions. From cognitive behavioral therapies and exercise interventions, to cognitive remediation and social skills training, each chapter explores a specific clinical intervention, detailing its theoretical foundations, empirical support, and practical applications. Our goal for this section is to provide readers with the most comprehensive listing of evidence-based and emerging practices within the contemporary domain of negative symptoms. Included in this section are two chapters addressing broader topics within the purview of intervention, specifically family and multidisciplinary team work and addressing negative symptoms in clinical high-risk populations. We hope this section brings about a recognition of the crucial role psychosocial interventions can play in addressing even the most persistent and debilitating aspects of psychotic illness.

Our goal is for this book to inspire further inquiry, innovation, and collaboration in the field of psychosocial interventions; working as an essential step toward improving outcomes, promoting recovery, and ultimately, enhancing the well-being of individuals affected by negative symptoms. We wish to thank all of our contributors for helping us craft an engaging and helpful text.

List of Contributors

Indrit Bègue, MD, PhD, Department of Psychiatry, University of Geneva, Geneva, Switzerland.

Kerem Böge, PhD, Department for Psychiatry and Psychotherapy, Charité – Universitätsmedizin Berlin, Berlin, Germany. Department of Psychology, Medical University Brandenburg, Neuruppin, Germany.

Marie C. Brown, PhD, ABSMIP, Department of Psychiatry, OnTrack and Early Treatment Program, Lenox Hill Hospital, New York, NY, USA.

Benjamin Buck, PhD, Department of Psychiatry and Behavioral Sciences, University of Washington, Seattle, WA, USA.

Ashby B. Cogan, BA, Department of Psychology, University of California, Berkeley, CA, USA.

Camille Delouche, MD, CHU, University Hospital, Caen, France.

Sonia Dollfus, MD, PhD, Prof, Health Department, University Caen Normandy, Caen, France.

Jérôme Favrod, CNS, Swiss Society of Social Psychiatry, Goumoens-la-Ville, Switzerland.

Ruth L. Firmin, PhD, Ruth L. Firmin, PhD, Department of Psychology, Gordon College, Wenham, MA USA.

Daniel Fulford, PhD, Departments of Occupational Therapy and Psychological and Brain Sciences, Boston University, Boston, MA, USA.

Mark van der Gaag, PhD, Department of Clinical Psychology, Vrije Universiteit Amsterdam, Amsterdam, Netherlands.

Helena García-Mieres, PhD, Industrial Researcher, Evidence-Based Behavior SL, Consultant Professor, Universitat Oberta de Catalunya, Gijón, Spain.

Richard Glisker, PhD, Department of Psychiatry, Icahn School of Medicine at Mount Sinai, New York, NY, USA and NY MIRECC, James J. Peters VA Medical Center, Bronx, NY, USA.

Lauren Gonzales, PhD, Department of Psychiatry, Columbia University Vagelos College of Physicians and Surgeons, New York-Presbyterian, New York, NY, USA.

Paul Grant, PhD, Beck Institute Center for Recovery-Oriented Cognitive Therapy, Philadelphia, PA, USA.

Kelsey Huling, PsyD, HSPP, Eskenazi Health, Sandra Eskenazi Mental Health Center, Indianapolis, IN, USA.

Ellen Inverso, PsyD, Beck Institute Center for Recovery-Oriented Cognitive Therapy, Philadelphia, PA, USA.

Pamela Jacobsen, PhD, Department of Psychology, University of Bath, Bath, England.

Sydney H. James, MS, Department of Psychology, University of Georgia, Athens, Georgia, USA.

Nev Jones, PhD, School of Social Work, University of Pittsburgh, Pittsburgh, PA, USA.

Stefan Kaiser, MD, Department of Psychiatry, Geneva University Hospital, Geneva, Switzerland.

David Kimhy, PhD, Department of Psychiatry, Icahn School of Medicine at Mount Sinai, New York, NY, USA and NY MIRECC, James J. Peters VA Medical Center, Bronx, NY, USA.

Matthias Kirschner, MD, Department of Psychiatry, Geneva University Hospital, Geneva.

Ann M. Kring, PhD, Department of Psychology, University of California, Berkeley, CA, USA.

Amanda Lister, PhD, Colorado Mental Health Hospital in Pueblo, Pueblo, CO, USA.

Lauren Luther, PhD, Department of Psychology, University of Alabama at Birmingham, Birmingham, AL, USA.

Tania Lincoln, PhD, Department of Clinical Psychology and Psychotherapy, Universität Hamburg, Hamburg, Germany.

Paul H. Lysaker, PhD, Department of Psychiatry, Indiana University School of Medicine, Richard L Roudebush VA Medical Center, Indianapolis, IN, USA.

Hilary Mairs, PhD, School of Health Sciences, University of Manchester, Manchester, England.

Alice Medalia, PhD, Department of Psychiatry, Columbia University Vagelos College of Physicians and Surgeons, New York-Presbyterian, New York, NY, USA.

Vijay A. Mittal, PhD, Department of Psychology, Northwestern University, Evanston, IL, USA.

Jessica Mow, PhD, Mental Health Service, San Francisco VA Health Care System, San Francisco, CA, USA and Department of Psychiatry and Behavioral Sciences, University of California, San Francisco, San Francisco, CA, USA.

Kim T. Mueser, PhD, Departments of Occupational Therapy and Psychological and Brain Sciences, Boston University, Boston, MA, USA.

Alexandra Nguyen, PhD, School of Nursing La Source, University of Applied Sciences and Arts, Lausanne, Switzerland.

Luz H. Ospina, PhD, Department of Psychiatry, Icahn School of Medicine at Mount Sinai, New York, NY, USA.

Shannon Pagdon, BA, School of Social Work, University of Pittsburgh, Pittsburgh, PA, USA.

Danielle N. Pratt, PhD, Department of Psychology, Northwestern University, Evanston, IL, USA.

Marcel Riehle, PhD, Department of Psychology and Psychotherapy, University of Witten/Herdecke, Witten, Germany.

Alice Saperstein, PhD, Department of Psychiatry, Columbia University Vagelos College of Physicians and Surgeons, New York-Presbyterian, New York, NY, USA.

Lauren P. Weittenhiller, PhD, Department of Psychology, University of California, Berkeley, CA, USA.

Lumi Winterson, Self-employed, Sydney, New South Wales, Australia.

Trevor F. Williams, PhD, Department of Psychology, Kent State University, Kent, OH, USA.

PART I
BACKGROUND

1

Negative Symptoms in Psychosis

An Introduction to the Construct

Richard Glisker

1. Introduction: Definition and Overview of Negative Symptoms

Negative symptoms are considered crucial targets in the treatment of psychosis due to their profound impact on psychosocial functioning and quality of life. Negative symptoms have been shown to significantly impact a person's ability to function in daily life, including the ability/desire to engage with others socially, maintain employment, and attend to personal care and hygiene. These symptoms are often chronic and enduring, and they can persist even when other psychotic symptoms are adequately managed. In addition, negative symptoms are often less responsive to (or even exacerbated by) psychopharmacological interventions, which can make treatment challenging. Additionally, negative symptoms also impact patients' motivation and ability to engage in mental health treatments, including psychosocial rehabilitation programs, and therefore should be an essential focus for intervention.

In contrast to positive symptoms, which are characterized by something "added" to a person (e.g., delusions and hallucinations), negative symptoms are often described as something "taken away" from a person, such as a reduction in their vitality, volition, or joie de vivre. Negative symptoms commonly take the form of a decrease in goal-directed activity, social behavior, speech, and emotional expression, as well as limited capacity to experience pleasure. They are considered a core aspect of schizophrenia spectrum disorders and can be seen across the psychosis continuum, including in people at ultra-high risk for psychosis, people experiencing first episode psychosis, and those diagnosed with chronic schizophrenia (Sauvé, Brodeur, Shah, & Lepage, 2019). In people diagnosed with schizophrenia, 60% have been found to experience prominent negative symptoms (Correll & Schooler, 2020). Negative symptoms can be seen not only in people diagnosed with schizophrenia, but also in substance-induced psychosis and mood/affective disorders (Correll & Schooler, 2020).

Richard Glisker, *Negative Symptoms in Psychosis*. In: *Psychosocial Approaches to Negative Symptoms in Psychosis*. Edited by: Tania Lincoln et al., Oxford University Press.
© Oxford University Press (2025). DOI: 10.1093/oso/9780197676790.003.0001

This suggests that negative symptoms are an important treatment target across the psychotic spectrum and continuum of illness.

This chapter provides an introductory overview for understanding the construct of negative symptoms, and will cover the historical development of the construct, specific subtypes, and current debates within the field. Importantly, this chapter will also explore the development of psychological models for negative symptoms, which occurred concurrently (but not necessarily in collaboration with) the broader development of the construct. The purpose of this chapter is to provide the reader with a foundation through which to understand this edited book as a whole.

2. Historical Development

2.1 Early Perspectives on Negative Symptoms

Negative symptoms have been recognized as a fundamental aspect of schizophrenia spectrum disorders since the early stages of defining the illness. The founding fathers of early psychosis research, Emil Kraepelin and Eugen Bleuler described behaviors that would later become called "negative symptoms" in their patients from the outset. Importantly, both of these researchers questioned the extent to which these symptoms were endogenous to the disorder or a reaction to environmental contexts, a line of thinking that would be further developed over time.

Kraepelin (1919/1971) coined the term dementia praecox to refer to what would later be termed schizophrenia by Bleuler. Kraepelin did not describe a firm distinction between negative and positive symptoms as different "types" of schizophrenia; instead, he discussed negative symptoms as essential features of psychotic illness more generally. For Kraepelin, dementia praecox represented an early, or precocious, onset of dementia, characterized by a deterioration of functioning across a wide range of domains. Although Kraepelin did not identify an organic etiology for dementia praecox, as in the case of the so-called organic psychoses like Alzheimer's, he hypothesized that there is ultimately some organic basis to explain the presence of negative symptoms. Thus, the diminished affectivity, interpersonal functioning, and other negative symptoms observed in the illness were viewed as only further abnormalities (along with hallucinations, cognitive and behavioral disorganization) associated with a general decline, ultimately attributable to some organic (e.g., brain) deterioration. Bleuler (1911/1950), who coined the term schizophrenia to emphasize the splitting of normal mental functioning characteristic of psychosis, held that schizophrenia could take on various distinct forms, for example, paranoid, catatonic, and hebephrenic. In addition, he posited four cardinal symptoms of schizophrenia, known as "four A's," to assist in diagnosis of the illness, including: disturbances in affect, loosening of associations, ambivalence, and autism. Although Bleuler himself also did not employ the distinction between negative and positive symptoms as separate symptom clusters, two of these cardinal features, namely, disturbances of affect and autism, would be considered in contemporary terminology as negative symptoms. Influenced by psychoanalytic concepts of psychic defense, Bleuler held that both the affective blunting and autistic withdrawal into the self are defensive reactions to, or ways of coping with, the primary symptoms of schizophrenia, that is, the cognitive and perceptual disturbances. Interestingly, this theory would later be re-discovered by contemporary cognitive behavior therapists as well as the later conceptualization of "secondary negative symptoms."

Taken together, analysis of early texts show that Kraepelin and Bleuler's descriptions of what would later be termed "negative symptoms" were murkier than they are today, and their descriptions did not fit into distinct subtypes or dimensions. For example, Kraepelin (1919) describes:

> Emotion—Very striking and profound damage occurs as a rule in the emotional life of our patients. The most important of these changes is their *emotional dulness* [sic]. The disorders of attention which have already been mentioned might be essentially connected with the loss of interest, the loss of inner sympathy, with the giving way of those emotional main-springs which move us to exert our mental powers to accomplish our tasks, to follow the train of thought. The singular indifference of the patients towards their former emotional relations, the extinction of affection for relatives and friends, of satisfaction in their work and vocation, in recreation and pleasure is not seldom the first and most striking symptom of the onset of disease.
>
> (Kraepelin 1919, 32)

Today, Kraepelin's description of negative symptoms would be even further subdivided, for example, into blunted affect ("emotional dullness"); avolition ("loss of interest"); and asociality ("indifference towards former emotional relations"), among others.

2.2 Emergence of Negative Symptoms as a Distinct Construct in Psychosis

The distinction between positive and negative symptoms originated in 19th century psychiatry and neurology (e.g., Reynolds, 1858; Jackson, 1889) to denote mental functioning that was either excessive or uninhibited (positive symptoms) or diminished (negative symptoms); the distinction did not apply to a specific diagnostic category but rather was more general in its application. The first use of the term "negative symptoms" was by British neurologist John Hughlings Jackson (1835–1911) as a general concept within the burgeoning field of neurology (inclusive of both neurodegenerative disease and psychiatric illness). Hughlings Jackson proposed a hierarchical model of cortical functioning, such that more basic functions are localized in the lower brain regions and more complex functions within the higher brain regions. He believed that "negative symptoms" in neurology were the symptoms that arise from a loss of functioning within higher brain areas (York & Steinberg, 2006). This term would later be adapted by psychiatric researchers to explain the functional impairments observed in their schizophrenia patients.

In the early 1970s, researchers began to understand negative symptoms as their own distinct process, with unique pathophysiology and/or psychosocial origin from positive symptoms. Strauss, Carpenter, & Bartko (1974) were among the first to separate positive symptoms from negative symptoms, suggesting that negative symptoms typically appear with gradual onset and are related to chronicity. These authors strongly suggested an environmental understanding of negative symptoms, such that institutionalization and social ostracism should be considered as causal factors of blunted affect, among other negative symptoms.

In the 1980s, American psychiatrist Nancy Andreasen became a key leader in the field of negative symptoms. Andreasen used the term "syndrome" to describe what she felt were opposite poles of a symptomatic continuum of disease, that is, the positive syndrome and the negative syndrome. Tim Crow similarly extended this idea, hypothesizing what he termed the "two syndrome concept" of schizophrenia. Specifically, he hypothesized that "type I" schizophrenia has a predominance of negative symptoms, whereas "type II" schizophrenia is defined primarily by positive symptoms (Mosolov & Yaltonskaya, 2022). Unlike Crow, Andreasen believed that people could experience mixed states, and there was not a firm distinction between different types of schizophrenia. As we will discuss later in this chapter, these theories contributed to the later delineation of "primary" and "secondary" negative symptoms. During this time Brian Kirkpatrick was also researching what he termed "deficit/non-deficit" categorization of patients. Specifically, Kirkpatrick's research focused on refining diagnostic criteria and assessment methods in order to identify those patients who could be considered of the "deficit syndrome subtype." The deficit syndrome subtype has a symptom profile that is primarily dominated by negative symptoms. Kirkpatrick suggested the following criteria (in addition to a schizophrenia diagnosis): (1) the presence of at least two negative symptoms; (2) these two or more symptoms must occur for at least 12 months and are always present during periods of clinical stability; and (3) the negative symptoms cannot be accounted for by a secondary factor, such as psychotic symptoms, antipsychotic medications, depression, or other mood disorder (Kirkpatrick & Galderisi, 2008). Recent understandings of the deficit syndrome suggest a distinctive genetic and neurobiological process underlying their presentation (Correll & Schooler, 2020). Estimates show approximately 15% of first-episode psychosis patients and 25%–30% of chronic psychosis patients can be categorized as "deficit syndrome" (Kirkpatrick, Buchanan, Ross, & Carpenter, 2001).

3. Development of Psychological Approaches and Treatments

Concurrent to the advances made toward understanding and measuring the construct of negative symptoms, psychological models and interventions were also being developed.

Beginning with Freud (a contemporary of Kraepelin and Bleuler), psychoanalytic theorists offered psychological conceptualizations of negative symptoms beyond viewing them merely as the consequences of illness deterioration. Freud held that the characteristic negative symptoms of general withdrawal into the self and a decreased interest in others and the external world can be understood as a regression into a more developmentally primitive state of narcissism (Arieti, 1974). In Freud's (1914/1957) model of narcissism, libido is withdrawn from investment in outer objects and individuals and redirected back into the self. This withdrawal into the self serves as a defense against some unbearable threat in the outside world. Although this theory has been largely unadopted by evidence-based practices, it laid the seeds toward later developments on the relationship between psychosis, trauma, and negative symptoms, as well as the concept that negative symptoms may serve a protective function for the individual. Later, the interpersonalist school of psychoanalysis (e.g., Fromm-Reichmann, 1960; Sullivan, 1962) further developed Freud's idea that psychosis involves a disruption in the individual's connection with their external environment, but instead of relying of Freud's libido theory, they viewed psychosis essentially as a disturbance in interpersonal relations. For the interpersonalists, early unpleasant experiences between caregiver and child, fueled by child's attempts to avoid increasing the caretaker's anxiety, influence distorted interpersonal interactions later in life. The child's failure to integrate dissociated parts of their personality, considered by the child to be undesirable/anxiety-provoking in the caregiver, contributes to intense interpersonal anxiety in social relations. In schizophrenia, this interpersonal anxiety can be understood to underlie the negative symptoms of psychosis such that the individual limits their social engagement. Again, this theory was later rediscovered by cognitive-behavioral (CBT) approaches, which explore the role of social skill deficits, previous negative social experiences, and internalized stigma on negative symptoms.

As the psychology field as a whole moved away from psychodynamic approaches and began focusing on behaviorism, so, too, did behaviorist principles become a focal point in the treatment of negative symptoms. This continued to occur prior to the development of a formalized construct called "negative symptoms." Behaviorism as a theoretical discipline was developed as a reaction to introspective approaches to psychology and was formed as a push toward developing psychology as an objective, measurable, and scientific practice by focusing on observable behaviors rather than on unobservable cognitions or thoughts (Watson, 1925/1970). Perhaps the most well-known behaviorist treatment for negative symptoms is the token economy, which rose to dominance in the treatment of negative symptoms (particularly in North America) during the 1950s and 1960s (Slade & Bentall, 1989). Token economies were developed based on the operant learning principles of B.F. Skinner, namely, the concept that an individual's behavior can be predicted and shaped through reinforcement or punishment. Token economies largely target the specific symptoms of low motivation, poor attention, personal hygiene, and social withdrawal (McMonagle & Sultana, 2000). The theory behind token economy presupposed that these symptoms/behaviors were subject to the same "laws of learning" as nonpathological behaviors and were therefore, able to be modified by preplanned prompts and reinforcers (Liberman, 2000). The emphasis on the token economy as a psychological practice was largely made possible due to the climate of the mid-20th century, just prior to deinstitutionalization, wherein people diagnosed with severe mental illnesses were often confined in long-term psychiatric facilities. As such, psychologists began to focus on the ways in which the milieu of the hospital itself could serve as the context for treatment. Specifically, to bring about positive behavior changes, patients would be rewarded through earning tokens for socially adaptive behaviors. These tokens could then be used similarly to money, in order to buy items (e.g., candy, soda) and/or privileges (e.g., ability to walk the grounds or take a field trip). The emphasis on this form of treatment was not in "punishment" (e.g., withholding/removing privileges in response to an undesirable behavior), but on positive reinforcement of socially adaptive behaviors. In this form of therapy, desirable behaviors were reinforced immediately through verbal praise and tokens, and staff would be careful to not inadvertently reinforce undesirable behaviors through, for example, offering increased attention or words of comfort to the patient. Maladaptive behaviors would be provided with direct feedback (e.g., "I can see you are having a hard time getting out of your room today. One of your treatment goals is to socialize more.") and alternative behavior prompts (e.g., "What are some things you can do to be more social today?). All staff within an institution (e.g., nurses, behavior technicians, doctors, therapists) would be trained specifically in behaviorist principles, to ensure consistency in the treatment. Examples of behaviors that would earn praise/tokens would be, engaging in solo leisure activities (e.g., reading, crossword puzzles), engaging in a conversation with a peer, verbally responding when prompted, and attending groups. Behaviors for which a patient may be "punished" (e.g., lose tokens or points), would be, for example, sleeping during the day, socially isolating, not eating food, inappropriate clothing, and so on. In addition to global punishment/reinforcement rules for the unit, personalized treatment programs would be constructed to address patient-specific problems.

Focus on token economies fell out of popularity mainly due to sociopolitical changes such as deinstitutionalization as well as ethical concerns regarding the practice. However, token economies are still considered to be an evidence-based practice in institutional/residential settings for people with psychosis, according to the American Psychological Association (APA) (American Psychological Association & Jensen, 2014). They were found to be one of the top evidence-based psychosocial treatment recommendations by the highly influential PORT Summary Statements (Dixon et al., 2009). Additionally, aspects of behaviorist principles and token economies were also rediscovered by outpatient CBT therapists in the form of behavioral activation, among other interventions for negative symptoms.

It was not until the 1980s and 1990s that CBT for psychosis became an intervention of interest for psychological researchers and practitioners (Mander & Kingdon, 2015). Treatment manuals and papers published during the early 2000s suggest that it was during this time that key leaders in the field of CBT for psychosis began strengthening their approach toward negative symptoms specifically. For example, it was during this time that Aaron T. Beck (2020), father of CBT, began publishing on the topic. In Rector, Beck, and Stolar (2005) a theoretical basis for a psychological approach to negative symptoms was first presented, challenging the assertion that negative symptoms are purely biologically derived and maintained. The authors hypothesized the importance of psychological variables, including preexisting personality traits, negative beliefs, and negative expectancies. For example, the authors suggested underlying appraisals for several negative symptom domains such as affective flattening ("If I show my feelings, others will see my inadequacy"); alogia ("I'm not going to find the right words to express myself"); and avolition ("Why bother, I'm just going to fail") (Rector et al., 2005, 252). This theory is significant, in that it presented a model of negative symptoms that could be modified through exploring a patient's thoughts and beliefs. As the rest of this volume will show, there have been a great many developments in the psychosocial treatment of negative symptoms since the early 2000s.

4. Evolution of Diagnostic Criteria and Measurement Tools

A significant step in the evolution of negative-symptoms research occurred with the development of measurement scales. In a recent analysis of historical research trends in negative symptoms, Sabe et al., 2023 found that an intellectual turning point occurred during the 1980s with two key papers: Andreasen's 1982 paper on the *Scale for the Assessment of Negative Symptoms* and Kay and colleagues 1987 paper on the Positive and Negative Syndrome Scale (PANSS). These two papers were the first to develop systematic scales to measure negative symptoms. As we will see later in this volume, these two scales continue to be used today, primarily in research on negative symptoms.

In 2005, the National Institutes of Mental Health (NIMH) held a Consensus Meeting on Negative Symptoms, the goal of which was to synthesize current scientific understandings of negative symptoms and to assess the state of the field and future directions for research. The Consensus Meeting led to the identification of eleven "agreements" on negative symptoms. Although this chapter does not allow for a full exploration of the 11 agreements, the majority having to do with pharmaceutical trials, some of the most important findings with respect to psychosocial interventions include: (1) a recognition that negative symptoms should be considered primary outcomes in clinical trials and a distinct area for intervention; (2) a distinction between negative symptoms and cognitive symptoms, as well as negative symptoms from social cognition deficits; (3) a concern that negative symptoms trials should control for secondary factors that may be contributing to their presentation or severity; (4) the identification of five separate subdomains of negative symptoms; and (5) a preference for the Scale for the Assessment of Negative Symptoms (SANS) for clinical trials.

5. Identifying Negative Symptoms

In terms of contemporary major diagnostic manuals and symptom check-lists, the *Diagnostic and Statistical Manual of Mental Disorders–Fifth Edition* (DSM-5; American Psychiatric Association, 2013) lists negative symptoms as inclusive of diminished emotional expression or avolition. The International Classification of Diseases (ICD-10; World Health Organization, 2016) lists negative symptoms as apathy, paucity of speech, and blunting or incongruity of emotional responses.

As mentioned previously in this chapter, the comprehensive list of negative symptom subtypes that was formalized by the NIMH Consensus Meeting includes the following: blunted affect, alogia, asociality, anhedonia, and avolition (Kirkpatrick, Fenton, Carpenter, & Marder, 2006). The summary statement of this meeting hypothesized that although substantial correlations exist across subtypes, these subtypes may nevertheless have separate neurobiological processes and may be considered separate treatment targets. The following section of this chapter reviews each subtype and related impact on functioning.

5.1 Avolition

Avolition refers to a profound lack of motivation and initiative. People experiencing avolition have difficulty starting and maintaining goal-directed activities, including daily tasks, participating in social interactions, or engaging in personal interests and hobbies. Avolition has been found to uniquely contribute to poor functional outcomes in people diagnosed with psychotic disorders, including in self-reliance and execution of tasks, such as self-care, meal preparation, engaging in recreational activities, and shopping for daily needs (Okada, Hirano, Taniguchi, 2021). Strauss and colleagues (2020) have suggested that avolition is a "central" symptom, the amelioration of which would in turn lead to improvements across other symptom domains.

5.2 Alogia

Alogia is often referred to as "poverty of speech." Individuals exhibiting alogia often use fewer words than is typical, have long speech latency, and show a decrease in spontaneous speech. In addition to psychotic spectrum disorders, alogia is also commonly found in nonpsychotic depression and autism. Thought blocking is considered a form of alogia, in which an individual will abruptly stop in the middle of an otherwise regular stream of thought. Cohen, Mitchell, and Elvevåg (2014) found that the pauses in speech, rather than the overall number of words spoken, were the driving factor in speech differences between people diagnosed with schizophrenia and control groups. Furthermore, Cohen, Najolia, Kim, & Dinzeo (2012) found alogia present across the psychosis spectrum, including in people diagnosed with schizophrenia, bipolar I, and major depression, and found it contributed to decreased social functioning.

5.3 Anhedonia

Anhedonia refers to a reduction in one's capacity to experience pleasure. Anhedonia has long been shown to contribute to lower social functioning among people diagnosed with psychotic disorders (Blanchard, Mueser, & Bellack, 1998). The concept of anhedonia is a complex one, as evidence suggests that people diagnosed with schizophrenia spectrum disorders do not report lower levels of pleasure as compared to controls when reporting on in the moment experiences, yet do report lower levels when asked to report nonconcurrently (Strauss & Gold, 2012). Therefore, it may be that people with schizophrenia do not actually lack the ability to experience pleasure, but instead have difficulty recalling past pleasure or anticipating future pleasant experiences.

5.4 Affective Flattening

Affective or "Blunted" affect is a decreased ability to exhibit emotions inclusive of facial expressions, bodily gestures, and tone of voice. In comparison to constricted affect, in which individuals are able to demonstrate some emotional reactivity, individuals with blunted affect do not exhibit emotional expression at all. Blunted affect has been found to negatively impact social functioning and the ability to maintain relationships, and has been found to evoke negative responses in others (Kring & Moran, 2008).

5.5 Asociality

Asociality is defined as a reduced participation in social activity as a result of diminished interest in and motivation for social interactions (Marder & Galderisi, 2017). Asociality is a concept that is also complex, because very real experiences of stigma and discrimination of people diagnosed with schizophrenia spectrum disorders may limit social opportunities. In fact, some studies have shown that people diagnosed with schizophrenia have intact experiences of pleasure when socializing with others (Kasanova, Oorschot, & Myin-Germeys, 2018). Therefore, there is likely a complexity undergirding asociality, inclusive of some of the concerns related to "anhedonia" as well as the social realities of stigma.

5.6 Two-Domains versus Five-Domains

The NIMH consensus of the domains or subtypes of negative symptoms has not been without debate. Factor analytic studies have suggested that instead of five-factors, negative symptoms can instead be understood as being composed of two-domains, specifically "diminished expressivity" (inclusive of alogia and blunted affect) and "motivation and pleasure" (inclusive of anhedonia, asociality, and avolition; Kaiser et. al, 2017). The two-factor model of negative symptoms has been a major influence in the field, including on the way negative symptoms are described in the *DSM-5*; the scoring of scales for statistical analyses; and conceptualization of biological mechanisms for research (Ahmed et al., 2019). Importantly, factor analytic studies have not supported the use of a single composite score for negative symptoms in research, instead supporting either a two- or five-factor model (Ahmed et al., 2022).

5.7 Differentiating Primary versus Secondary Negative Symptoms

Differentiating between primary and secondary negative symptoms has been considered imperative to the development of adequate case conceptualizations to guide future interventions. As mentioned, the question of negative symptoms being endogenous to a disease process, a defensive/protection from positive symptoms, or a product of environment was present in the discourse since the time of Kraepelin and Bleuler. This line of thinking became clarified and researchers began to distinguish between primary and secondary negative symptoms. This research was partially a development from the work of researchers such as Andreasen, Crow, Kirkpatrick, and Carpenter, positing that *primary* negative symptoms were largely caused by biological processes, inclusive of genetic or structural brain abnormalities (e.g., Pahl, Swayze, & Andreasen, 1990), whereas *secondary* negative symptoms were related to other factors, such as a response to positive symptoms, medication side-effects, or environment. Although a comprehensive list would be difficult to summarize, the main contributors toward secondary negative symptoms are thought to be: reactions to positive symptoms (e.g., social withdrawal due to paranoia); comorbid depression; antipsychotic medication side-effects; and extra pyramidal symptoms. In this volume, Chapter 6 offers a critique of the "primary" versus "secondary" divide.

6. Key Debates and Controversies

6.1 Validity and Reliability of Negative Symptom Construct

A key debate within the field of negative symptoms is whether negative symptoms are best conceptualized as a unified construct or multidimensionally as encompassing subdomains (i.e., blunted affect, alogia, asociality, anhedonia, and avolition). The unidimensional view maintains that negative symptoms are a single, unitary dimension of symptomatology. Supporters of this view cite evidence from factor analytic studies that often reveal a primary negative symptom factor, which suggests the individual symptoms and subtypes of negative symptoms are strongly interrelated and reflect a common underlying pathological process (Andreasen, 1982; Kay et al., 1987). In contrast, the multidimensional view posits that the subdomains of negative symptoms are distinct and provide individual targets for intervention (Blanchard & Cohen, 2006). Drawing on evidence from factor analytic studies (e.g., Kirkpatrick et al., 2006) that suggest a differentiation between negative symptom subdomains, supporters of the multidimensional view maintain that negative symptoms are, despite some commonalities among them, not interchangeable and may be linked to distinct neurobiological mechanisms (Chan et al., 2022).

6.2 Role of Culture and Societal Factors

Examining the influence of cultural and societal factors on how negative symptoms are conceptualized and assessed can help in the development of culturally sensitive treatment approaches. Discrimination and stigma associated with mental illness negatively impact individuals with schizophrenia, which limits social opportunities. As previously mentioned, the social isolation and ostracism caused by stigma can exacerbate negative symptoms such as asociality and avolition (Corrigan & Watson, 2002). In addition, poverty contributes to the limiting of opportunities, given that it restricts access to health care, housing, hobbies, and nutrition (Sarceno et al., 2005).

Systemic racism has a significant role in understanding and assessing negative symptoms. Brownlow's (2023) work discusses how racial threat leads to masking feelings, appearing aloof and distant, avoidance, all of which can be misinterpreted and/or further contribute to negative symptoms. Thus, what might appear as the negative symptoms of schizophrenia might be a misinterpretation of behaviors related to underlying social and racial divisions and dynamics. Strauss' work (Strauss et al., 2021) on environmental context suggests environmental factors such as location, daily activities, and social relationships influence the severity of negative symptoms (Luther et al., 2023).

6.3 Challenges and Limitations in Assessment

A further challenge to the assessment of negative symptoms is that defining the so-called normal threshold for more moderate expressions of these symptoms is difficult (Strauss, Bartolomeo, & Harvey, 2021). In addition, recent research suggests that widely used measures of negative symptoms, such as the

PANSS, might be outdated or not adequately reflect contemporary understanding of negative symptoms, potentially compromising the validity of these scales (Blanchard et al., 2011). Further, self-report and interview-based measures of negative symptoms might be limited insofar as they rely on subjective reporting and may be prone to recall bias (Luther et al., 2023). To address these limitations, recent work (e.g., Luther et al., 2023; Granholm et al., 2020) has implemented ecological momentary assessment (EMA) to provide more fine-grained, ecologically valid measurement of negative symptoms as they fluctuate according to changes in daily routine, environment (e.g., work, school), and social activity. This volume contains a full section on assessment to further illuminate these ideas.

7. Conclusion

The purpose of this chapter was to provide a general overview of the negative symptoms construct. This chapter discussed several key topics, including the impact of negative symptoms on psychosocial functioning and quality of life. In addition, this chapter reviewed the historical origins and development of the negative symptoms construct as well as several theoretical perspectives and clinical interventions. Finally, the chapter examined various symptom subtypes and highlighted important areas of debate in the current state of the research field.

References

Ahmed, A. O., Kirkpatrick, B., Galderisi, S., Mucci, A., Rossi, A., Bertolino, A., . . .& Strauss, G. P. (2019). Cross-cultural validation of the 5-factor structure of negative symptoms in schizophrenia. *Schizophrenia Bulletin, 45*(2), 305–314.

Ahmed, A. O., Kirkpatrick, B., Granholm, E., Rowland, L. M., Barker, P. B., Gold, J. M., . . . & Strauss, G. P. (2022). Two factors, five factors, or both? External validation studies of negative symptom dimensions in schizophrenia. *Schizophrenia Bulletin, 48*(3), 620–630.

American Psychiatric Association. (2013). *Diagnostic and statistical manual of mental disorders* (5th ed.). Washington, DC: American Psychiatric Association.

American Psychological Association, & Jensen, M. A. (2014). *Recovery to practice initiative curriculum: Reframing psychology for the emerging health care environment.* Washington, DC: American Psychological Association.

Andreasen N. C. (1982). Negative symptoms in schizophrenia. Definition and reliability. *Archives of General Psychiatry, 39*(7), 784–788.

Arieti, S. (1974) *Interpretation of schizophrenia.* New York: Basic Books Inc.

Beck, J. S. (2020). *Cognitive behavior therapy: Basics and beyond.* Guilford Publications.

Blanchard, J. J., & Cohen, A. S. (2006). The structure of negative symptoms within schizophrenia: implications for assessment. *Schizophrenia Bulletin, 32*(2), 238–245.

Blanchard, J. J., Kring, A. M., Horan, W. P., & Gur, R. (2011). Toward the next generation of negative symptom assessments: The collaboration to advance negative symptom assessment in schizophrenia. *Schizophrenia Bulletin, 37*(2), 291–299.

Blanchard, J. J., Mueser, K. T., & Bellack, A. S. (1998). Anhedonia, positive and negative affect, and social functioning in schizophrenia. *Schizophrenia Bulletin, 24*(3), 413–424.

Bleuler, E.P. (1950). Dementia praecox or the group of schizophrenias (J. Zinkin, Trans.). International Universities Press, New York (Original work published in 1911).

Brownlow, B. N. (2023). How racism "gets under the skin": An examination of the physical-and mental-health costs of culturally compelled coping. *Perspectives on Psychological Science, 18*(3), 576–596.

Chan, R. C., Wang, L. L., & Lui, S. S. (2022). Theories and models of negative symptoms in schizophrenia and clinical implications. *Nature Reviews Psychology, 1*(8), 454–467.

Cohen, A. S., Najolia, G. M., Kim, Y., & Dinzeo, T. J. (2012). On the boundaries of blunt affect/alogia across severe mental illness: Implications for Research Domain Criteria. *Schizophrenia Research, 140*(1–3), 41–45.

Cohen, A. S., Mitchell, K. R., & Elvevåg, B. (2014). What do we really know about blunted vocal affect and alogia? A meta-analysis of objective assessments. *Schizophrenia Research, 159*(2–3), 533–538.

Correll, C. U., & Schooler, N. R. (2020). Negative symptoms in schizophrenia: A review and clinical guide for recognition, assessment, and treatment. *Neuropsychiatric Disease and Treatment, 16*, 519–534.

Corrigan, P. W., & Watson, A. C. (2002). Understanding the impact of stigma on people with mental illness. *World Psychiatry: Official Journal of The World Psychiatric Association (WPA), 1*(1), 16–20.

Dixon, L. B., Dickerson, F., Bellack, A. S., Bennett, M., Dickinson, D., Goldberg, R. W., . . . & Kreyenbuhl, J. (2009). The 2009 schizophrenia PORT psychosocial treatment recommendations and summary statements. *Schizophrenia Bulletin, 36*(1), 48–70.

Freud, S. (1957). On narcissism: An introduction. In J. Strachey (Ed. and Trans.), Standard edition (Vol. 14, pp. 73-102). London: Hogarth Press. (Original work published 1914).

Fromm-Reichmann, F. (1960). *Principles of intensive psychotherapy*. University of Chicago Press.

Granholm, E., Holden, J. L., Mikhael, T., Link, P. C., Swendsen, J., Depp, C., Moore, R.C., & Harvey, P. D. (2020). What do people with schizophrenia do all day? Ecological momentary assessment of real-world functioning in schizophrenia. *Schizophrenia Bulletin, 46*(2), 242–251.

Jackson, J. H. (1889). On post-epileptic states: a contribution to the comparative study of insanities. *Journal of Mental Science, 34*(148), 490–500.

Kaiser, S., Lyne, J., Agartz, I., Clarke, M., Mørch-Johnsen, L., & Faerden, A. (2017). Individual negative symptoms and domains—relevance for assessment, pathomechanisms and treatment. *Schizophrenia Research, 186*, 39–45.

Kasanova, Z., Oorschot, M., & Myin-Germeys, I. (2018). Social anhedonia and asociality in psychosis revisited. An experience sampling study. *Psychiatry Research, 270*, 375–381.

Kay, S. R., Fiszbein, A., & Opler, L. A. (1987). The positive and negative syndrome scale (PANSS) for schizophrenia. *Schizophrenia Bulletin, 13*(2), 261–276.

Kirkpatrick, B., & Galderisi, S. (2008). Deficit schizophrenia: An update. *World Psychiatry, 7*(3), 143.

Kirkpatrick, B., Buchanan, R. W., Ross, D. E., & Carpenter, W. T. (2001). A separate disease within the syndrome of schizophrenia. *Archives of General Psychiatry, 58*(2), 165–171.

Kirkpatrick, B., Fenton, W. S., Carpenter, W. T., Jr, & Marder, S. R. (2006). The NIMH-MATRICS consensus statement on negative symptoms. *Schizophrenia Bulletin, 32*(2), 214–219.

Kraepelin, E. (1919). *Dementia Praecox and Paraphrenia*. Livingstone.

Kring, A. M., & Moran, E. K. (2008). Emotional response deficits in schizophrenia: Insights from affective science. *Schizophrenia Bulletin, 34*(5), 819–834.

Liberman, R. P. (2000). The token economy. *The American journal of psychiatry, 157*(9), 1398.

Luther, L., Raugh, I. M., Collins, D. E., Knippenberg, A. R., & Strauss, G. P. (2023). Negative symptoms in schizophrenia differ across environmental contexts in daily life. *Journal of Psychiatric Research, 161*, 10–18.
Mander, H., & Kingdon, D. (2015). The evolution of cognitive-behavioral therapy for psychosis. *Psychology Research and Behavior Management*, 8, 63–69.
Marder, S. R., & Galderisi, S. (2017). The current conceptualization of negative symptoms in schizophrenia. *World Psychiatry: Official Journal of the World Psychiatric Association (WPA), 16*(1), 14–24.
McMonagle, T., & Sultana, A. (2000). Token economy for schizophrenia. *The Cochrane database of systematic reviews*, (3), CD001473.
Mosolov, S. N., & Yaltonskaya, P. A. (2022). Primary and secondary negative symptoms in schizophrenia. *Frontiers in Psychiatry, 12*, 766692.
Okada, H., Hirano, D., & Taniguchi, T. (2021). Impact of negative symptom domains and other clinical characteristics on functional outcomes in patients with schizophrenia. *Schizophrenia Research and Treatment, 2021*, 8864352.
Pahl, J. J., Swayze, V. W., & Andreasen, N. C. (1990). Diagnostic advances in anatomical and functional brain imaging in schizophrenia. In A. Kales, C. N. Stefanis, & J. A. Talbott, (Eds.), *Recent advances in schizophrenia* (pp.163–189). New York: Springer-Verlag.
Rector, N. A., Beck, A. T., & Stolar, N. (2005). The negative symptoms of schizophrenia: a cognitive perspective. *Canadian journal of psychiatry. Revue canadienne de psychiatrie, 50*(5), 247–257.
Reynolds, J. R. (1858). On the pathology of convulsions, with special reference to those of children. *Liverpool medico-chirurgical journal*, 2: 1-14.
Sabe, M., Chen, C., Perez, N., Solmi, M., Mucci, A., Galderisi, S., . . . & Kaiser, S. (2023). Thirty years of research on negative symptoms of schizophrenia: A scientometric analysis of hotspots, bursts, and research trends. *Neuroscience & Biobehavioral Reviews, 144*, 104979.
Saraceno, B., Levav, I., & Kohn, R. (2005). The public mental health significance of research on socio-economic factors in schizophrenia and major depression. *World Psychiatry: Official Journal of the World Psychiatric Association (WPA), 4*(3), 181–185.
Sauvé, G., Brodeur, M. B., Shah, J. L., & Lepage, M. (2019). The prevalence of negative symptoms across the stages of the psychosis continuum. *Harvard Review of Psychiatry, 27*(1), 15–32.
Slade, P., & Bentall, R. (1989). Psychological treatments for negative symptoms. *The British journal of psychiatry. Supplement*, (7), 133–135.
Strauss, G. P., Zamani Esfahlani, F., Sayama, H., Kirkpatrick, B., Opler, M. G., Saoud, J. B., . . . & Luthringer, R. (2020). Network analysis indicates that avolition is the most central domain for the successful treatment of negative symptoms: Evidence from the roluperidone randomized clinical trial. *Schizophrenia Bulletin, 46*(4), 964–970.
Strauss, G. P., Bartolomeo, L. A., & Harvey, P. D. (2021). Avolition as the core negative symptom in schizophrenia: Relevance to pharmacological treatment development. *NPJ Schizophrenia, 7*(1), 16.
Strauss, Gregory P., & Gold, James M. A new perspective on anhedonia in schizophrenia. *American Journal of Psychiatry 169*,4 (2012): 364–373.
Strauss, J. S., Carpenter, W. T., & Bartko, J. J. (1974). Speculations on the processes that underlie schizophrenic symptoms and signs: III. *Schizophrenia Bulletin, 1*(11), 61.
Sullivan, H. S. (1962). *Schizophrenia as a human process*. W. W. Norton & Company.
Watson, J. B. (1970). *Behaviorism*. University of Chicago Press. (Original work published 1925)
World Health Organization. (2016). International Statistical Classification of Diseases and Related Health Problems (10th ed.).
York, G. K., & Steinberg, D. A. (2006). An introduction to the life and work of John Hughlings Jackson with a catalogue raisonne of his writings. *Medical History, Supplement, 26*, 3–34.

2

Interpersonal Risk Factors for Negative Symptoms

Marcel Riehle

Clinical pearls

- Negative symptoms, particularly asociality (i.e., low social motivation), may be maintained by expectations that others will distance or exclude.
- At the same time, asociality is likely to result in interpersonal behavior that makes others' distancing more likely, thereby reconfirming these expectations.
- An overarching goal for therapy should be to break these cognitive-interpersonal maintenance cycles by creating experiential counter evidence for the negative expectancies in the form of pleasant social interactions.
- Pivotal therapeutic steps are therefore: a tolerant and validation-providing therapeutic relationship, enhancement of social affiliation skills by training, and behavioral experiments that challenge negative expectations.

1. Introduction

Negative symptoms are in large parts "social" symptoms. Three out of the five symptoms by definition affect social interactions: Asociality is defined as diminished motivation for social contact and is typically associated with decreased social participation (e.g., Pillny et al., 2020). Diminished emotional expression and alogia describe reductions of nonverbal communicative behavior. Assessing these expressive negative symptoms requires behavioral observation of a patient who is engaging in social interaction, usually in an interview situation (e.g., Kirkpatrick et al., 2011; Kring et al., 2013).

But are "social" negative symptoms also caused by social risk factors? It seems natural to assume this, but other etiological paths highlighting the contribution of individual patient variables (e.g., explaining negative symptoms from reward

Marcel Riehle, *Interpersonal Risk Factors for Negative Symptoms*. In: *Psychosocial Approaches to Negative Symptoms in Psychosis*. Edited by: Tania Lincoln et al., Oxford University Press.
 DOI: 10.1093/oso/9780197676790.003.0002

processing deficits) have long dominated the field. However, in the light of limited progress having been made in the therapy of negative symptoms over the last decades, social risk factors are increasingly recognized as an important mechanism in the formation and maintenance of negative symptoms (Strauss, 2021). It is important to note that the broad term "social" usually encompasses interpersonal factors (e.g., family and peer relationships, dyadic interaction skills) and societal factors (e.g., welfare system, cultural norms). Even though both sets of factors have important ties to negative symptoms (for a review see Strauss, 2021), the focus of this chapter is on the interpersonal factors that contribute to the formation and maintenance of negative symptoms.

The goal of this chapter is to provide the reader with a framework that helps incorporate the interpersonal environments of patients in the individual working model of patients' negative symptoms (e.g., as a basis for functional analysis as presented in Chapter 13). This framework supposes that interpersonal risk factors are in dynamic interaction with intrapersonal patient variables over time. Some factors begin to exert their influence early in development (e.g., neglectful parenting), others come into play later (e.g., stigmatization). A common denominator for the various interpersonal risk factors is that they contribute to patients' ceasing to (or never developing an urge to) strive for belonging and being an active participant in the world.

First, I will briefly introduce the *Cognitive-Interpersonal Maintenance Model of Asociality in Schizophrenia* as a theoretical framework to guide through the chapter. Then, I will use this framework to show which interpersonal risk factors influence negative symptom formation and maintenance. Lastly, I will use a case example to illustrate where this model offers leverage points for various types of psychosocial interventions.

2. A Cognitive-Interpersonal Maintenance Model of Asociality in Schizophrenia

A recurrent theme of this chapter will be that negative symptoms should be thought of from both an *intra-* and an *inter-*personal perspective. With the term *intra*personal, I refer to processes that run "inside" a person. Examples relevant for negative symptoms are demotivating beliefs, diminished reward anticipation, and diminished approach motivation (for a review see Chan et al., 2022). With the term *inter*personal, I refer to processes that emerge when interacting with other people, such as receiving social support, social interaction dynamics, or adverse interpersonal experiences like social exclusion. Obviously, intra- and interpersonal processes are strongly interwoven, meaning that interpersonal

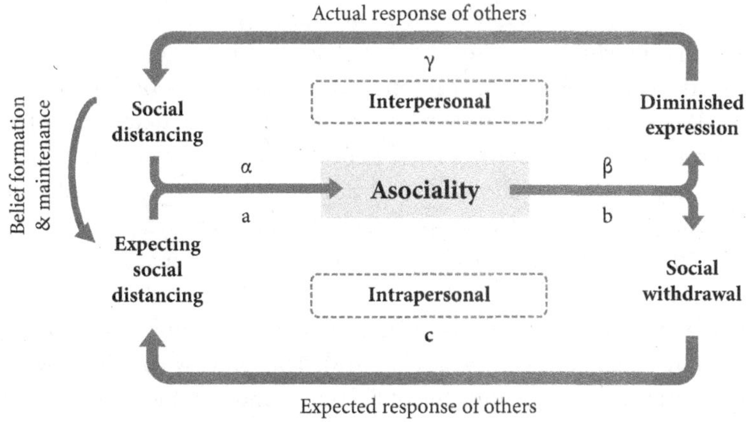

Figure 2.1 A cognitive-interpersonal maintenance model of asociality.

experiences are processed internally and that such intrapersonal processing shapes subsequent interpersonal behavior leading to new interpersonal experiences. For example, I may misinterpret someone else's remark as pejorative and feel so upset that I decide to never speak with them again, thus preventing me from being corrected in my misinterpretation. With the *Cognitive-Interpersonal Maintenance Model of Asociality in Schizophrenia*, shown in Figure 2.1, I propose a theoretical framework that applies this way of thinking about intra- and interpersonal processes to the negative symptoms of schizophrenia, specifically to asociality (i.e., diminished *motivation* for social interactions).

According to this model, asociality is maintained by two interacting cycles: an interpersonal cycle, whereby asociality is a response to others distancing themselves from the affected individual (path α), and an intrapersonal cycle, whereby asociality emerges as a consequence of *expecting* others to distance themselves (path a). Paths b and c of the intrapersonal cycle describe that asociality then manifests as actual withdrawal or avoidance of social interactions (i.e., the individual does not engage in social interaction, path b), which prevents them from having interpersonal experiences that challenge expectations that others will distance themselves (path c). The interpersonal cycle presupposes that within social interactions, asociality leads to diminished interactional engagement, most prominently noticeable as diminished outward expression and alogia (path β). Crucially, the diminished expression impedes creating affiliative bonds, which makes it more likely that others indeed distance themselves (path γ). Thus, not only do negative expectations about social interactions remain unchallenged (path c), they are also likely to get reconfirmed when social interactions take place (path γ).

The model's tenets are based on different strands of evidence and theory stemming from both clinical and social psychology. Similar cognitive-interpersonal frameworks can be found in theoretic conceptualizations of personality disorders (Pretzer, 2000) and in a model explaining the maintenance of social exclusion in psychotic disorders (Best & Bowie, 2022). The idea that exclusion and rejection deplete social motivation has been theorized in social psychology (Williams, 2009) and also specifically for negative symptoms (Pillny & Lincoln, 2020; White et al., 2013). That negative interpersonal experiences promote the development of asocial beliefs (e.g., "Making friends is not worth the effort") follows cognitive conceptualizations of negative symptoms (Beck et al., 2011; Pillny et al., 2018; White et al., 2013). This process (particularly path γ in Figure 2.1) will be a main focus of Section 3 and will therefore be detailed further there. Providing evidence for paths a and α, asociality has been shown to predict social withdrawal (e.g., Pillny et al., 2020) and diminished expressive behavior when communicating (e.g., Cowan et al., 2022; Riehle et al., 2018). This aligns with sociofunctional theories of expressive behavior (e.g., Keltner & Haidt, 1999; Martin et al., 2017) that state that communicative intent dictates expressive behavior. The idea that diminished communicative intent underlies diminished emotional expression has also been proposed for negative symptoms (Chan et al., 2022; García-Mieres et al., 2020; Jeganathan & Breakspear, 2021; cf. Chapter 19).

In the cognitive-interpersonal model shown in Figure 2.1, interpersonal risk factors are expected to be primarily relevant for negative symptoms that are proximally "social," thus, asociality and diminished expression. Nevertheless, avolition and anhedonia (i.e., more generalized amotivation) are also likely influenced by interpersonal factors and this, too, will be touched upon later in the chapter.

3. Interpersonal Risk Factors for Negative Symptoms

Building on the maintenance model shown in Figure 2.1, the following section will discuss interpersonal risk factors for negative symptoms. For this discussion, I will distinguish between premorbid (i.e., before the first psychotic episode) risk factors, implicated primarily in symptom formation, and risk factors that play a prominent role after the onset of the first psychotic episode, with implications in symptom formation and maintenance. Most of the risk factors discussed in this section are not specific to the negative symptoms of schizophrenia, but all have proven associations with negative symptoms. For example, low social functioning is an early precursor of negative symptoms that can be traced back as far as childhood (see following section), but is also an early risk factor for other forms of psychopathology (Leijdesdorff et al., 2022). Additionally, the literature recognizes some social risk factors for psychotic disorders in general (e.g., migration; Selten et al., 2020) for which it is less clear whether they relate to negative symptoms specifically. I will not discuss these further in this chapter (the interested reader is referred to Fett et al., 2019; Schalbroeck, 2020; Selten et al., 2013).

3.1 Premorbid Interpersonal Risk Factors: Childhood, Adolescence, and Early Adulthood

Given the typical onset of psychotic disorders in early adulthood, premorbid social risk factors for negative symptoms can be found primarily in childhood and adolescence. During this time, negative symptoms are likely to form as the result of early social interaction difficulties in combination with a social environment that lacks opportunities for compensating for these difficulties or overcoming them altogether. Early signs of negative symptoms include social withdrawal and diminished emotional expression (Baum & Walker, 1995; Bucci et al., 2016; Walker et al., 1993). These social behavioral precursors of negative symptoms appear to have a relatively stable trajectory, likely reflecting a trait-like component of negative symptoms (cf. Chan et al., 2022).

Such social behavioral aberrations can be expected to set a cascade of accumulating negative social experiences in motion. This process can be extrapolated from the two maintenance cycles of the cognitive-interpersonal model (Figure 2.1). During negative symptom formation, these cycles can be thought of as forming a downward spiral. Accordingly, the individual steadily internalizes negative social experiences and forms beliefs about their own social inability. These are not only maintained by missing out on disconfirming evidence (as a result of social withdrawal), but are additionally likely to be reconfirmed due to others' social distancing in instances where the individual interacts with other people.

Social interactions that are particularly relevant for children and adolescents with early signs of negative symptoms are those with family members and with peers (Gazelle & Rubin, 2019). These are highly frequent social interactions and can hardly be avoided even by socially withdrawn children and adolescents (e.g., peer contact in school). For these reasons, I will focus on interpersonal protective and risk factors stemming from interactions with peers and family members.

3.1.1 Peer Relationships

Children and adolescents with early signs of negative symptoms are at heightened risk for experiencing adverse interactions with their peers. The experience of ostracism (i.e., being excluded and ignored, typically by peers) appears to be particularly relevant. Social psychological theory (Williams, 2009) holds that chronic ostracism results in a resignation stage in which social contact does not seem to be worth any effort anymore (i.e., the social indifference characteristic of asociality). Some studies have shown that cumulative ostracism experiences result in increased negative symptoms (Jaya et al., 2016, 2022; Pillny & Lincoln, 2020), but these have not specifically looked into peer-relations in childhood or adolescence.

A concept that is related to ostracism and typically based in childhood and adolescence is bullying. How bullying victimization relates to psychosis has been primarily studied with an emphasis on childhood- and adolescent-onset of positive symptoms such as paranoia or hallucinations (e.g., Arseneault et al., 2011; Wolke et al., 2013). However, significant relationships between bullying victimization and negative symptoms have been repeatedly found (Catone et al., 2017; Jaya et al., 2016; Shakoor et al., 2015). This aligns with research in the school context that has shown that adolescent victims of bullies are particularly marginalized in their peer group and are rated as particularly socially withdrawn by their peers (e.g., de Bruyn et al., 2010; Pouwels et al., 2016). Being perceived as socially withdrawn by one's peers and becoming a victim of bullying have also been shown to form a vicious cycle over time (Gazelle & Rubin, 2019; Hodges & Perry, 1999; Laith & Vaillancourt, 2022).

Experiences like ostracism or bullying can be considered group-level marginalization processes given that they typically involve more than one perpetrator or bystanders (Saarento & Salmivalli, 2015). For people with early signs of negative symptoms, who become victims of ostracism or bullying, this can mean that their peer group as a whole does not emerge as a source of positive but rather negative interaction. This process may be similar to the process of developing social anxiety (Gazelle & Rubin, 2019). Indeed, social anxiety has been found to be associated with negative symptoms in adolescents and young adults with a clinical high-risk for psychosis (Kuhney et al., 2021). Forming a belief system that rationalizes and promotes diminished social interest and engagement (Beck et al., 2011; Pillny et al., 2018; White et al., 2013) then appears a reasonable strategy to protect the self from this adverse environment. Examples of such beliefs may be "Making friends is not worth the energy it takes" or "I am better off staying aloof from other people" (Grant & Beck, 2010; Pillny et al., 2018).

These beliefs pertain mostly to the aforementioned proximally "social" negative symptoms. However, ostracism and bullying may also affect more foundational beliefs about one's own capabilities in life resulting in generalized amotivation. For example, ostracized individuals may be picked last for a sports team, or others may not want to work with the individual collaboratively on group assignments. The affected individual may understand these instances of ostracism as indicating their lack of ability in performing these or even any activities. This could result in generalized defeatist performance beliefs such as "I am not able to do things as well as most other people" or "I feel useless at times" (Pillny et al., 2018). Such beliefs likely entail self-fulfilling prophecies, and it is therefore not surprising that there appears to be a bidirectional relationship between bullying victimization and low academic achievement (Laith & Vaillancourt, 2022). Overall, the belief system that can arise from these negative peer experiences provides a strong foundation for later negative symptoms.

3.1.2 Family Relationships

To the extent that negative symptoms or early signs thereof are a risk factor for negative peer experiences, those affected are likely to have to rely more strongly on family contacts. Strong familial cohesion and a caring, positive parental style can be expected to present important protective factors, guarding against the negative consequences of early signs of negative symptoms. In particular, parents' understanding of their child's needs and their ability to adequately respond to these (i.e., their ability to respond empathically) are the foundation of an autonomy-supportive parenting style that promotes exploration and curiosity (Roth et al., 2009), which are logical counterparts of negative symptoms. For example, parents need to consider whether their children benefit from being led to engage in more social activities (e.g., by enrolling children into a play group or a sports club). Indifferent familial environments (i.e., an environment lacking parental empathy) can be expected to support negative outcome expectancies for social interactions and thereby promote the formation of negative symptoms. Moreover, some parents may become hostile or criticize their children for early indicators of negative symptoms (e.g., not doing well in school, having few friends, preferring solitary hobbies). Particularly when the criticism becomes personal and generalizing ("I guess, you are just not smart enough!" "No wonder, no one likes you!"), the individual may form a belief system that rationalizes inactivity as a mechanism to avoid failure. ("If I can't do it right, I'm better off not trying.") Such beliefs have been found in association with generalized amotivation in people with schizophrenia (Pillny et al., 2018).

Providing evidence for the involvement of the family environment in the formation of negative symptoms, a study by Yung and colleagues (2019) found that negative symptom severity in a group of adolescents and young adults at ultra-high risk for psychosis was related to higher levels of parental emotional neglect. A meta-analysis showed that a history of parental neglect is also associated with the severity of negative symptoms among people with psychotic disorders (Bailey et al., 2018). Furthermore, more positive familial interactions are associated with a less chronic course of negative symptoms in people with a first psychotic episode (Dewangan et al., 2018; Halford et al., 1991; Otero et al.,

2011) and at clinical high-risk for psychosis (O'Brien et al., 2006, 2008). Low parental care has also been found to be associated with an avoidant attachment style in people with psychosis (Gumley et al., 2014). An avoidant attachment style is characterized by diminished emotional experience and social withdrawal and has been associated particularly with the experiential subdomain of negative symptoms (Degnan et al., 2022; Griffiths & McLeod, 2019, but see Carr et al., 2018). Together, these data support the idea that a lack of positive familial interactions (i.e., those that include warmth, soothing, and support) contributes to the development of negative symptoms.

Summing up this overview of premorbid interpersonal risk factors for negative symptoms, it seems that accumulating negative interpersonal experiences while lacking positive ones promotes negative symptom formation from childhood and adolescence to early adulthood and first psychotic episodes. If not interrupted, a result of the process is that the degree of social impairment can be expected to increase steadily until it reaches a clinically relevant level. Indeed, negative symptoms in early-course psychotic disorders are associated with a smaller number of friends and diminished friendship support (Gayer-Anderson & Morgan, 2013; Robustelli et al., 2017; Thorup et al., 2006). Moreover, a steeper decline of *social* functioning in the prodromal stages of the disorder has been found to be specifically associated with more severe negative symptoms after psychosis onset (Strauss et al., 2012; Yung et al., 2019).

It is important to note that "decline," as assessed in these studies, can, but does not necessarily, reflect a loss of normatively acquired skills and abilities (i.e., decline as illustrated in Figure 2.2, part A.). A decline like this would suggest that some incisive event has changed the developmental trajectory. Alternatively, a "decline" in social functioning could also reflect a growing discrepancy between the level of actual and normatively expected social functioning (i.e., growth as illustrated in Figure 2.2, part B.). The idea here is that with increasing age, social relationships become increasingly complex and

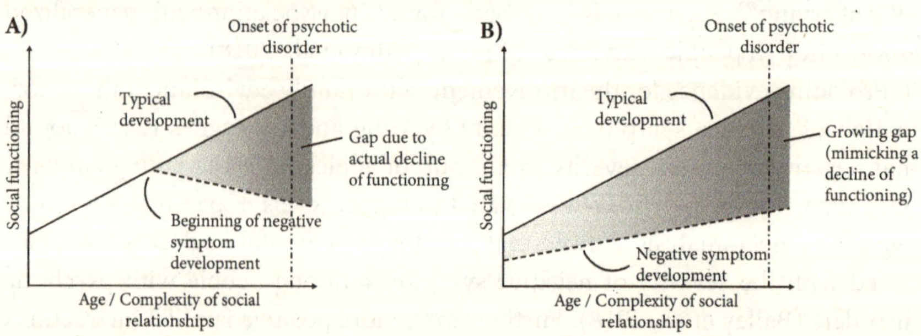

Figure 2.2 A decline (A) and a growth (B) model showing different developmental pathways to low social functioning in relation to negative symptom development.

increase in number (e.g., from parent-child interactions to the management of one's own position in a peer group). Accordingly, the adverse consequences of early signs of negative symptoms also increasingly exert influence on the social functioning level of the individual.

As we have seen, early precursors of negative symptoms can be traced back to early childhood and appear relatively stable. Additionally, the premorbid interpersonal risk factors for negative symptoms such as parental neglect or ostracism are normally long-term rather than single incisive events. The evidence available from research on negative symptoms specifically seems to point toward a growth model underlying symptom formation. There is evidence, however, for the existence of both pathways (decline and growth) in the development of more general social withdrawal in children and adolescents (Gazelle & Rubin, 2019), so it would be premature to dismiss a decline model altogether.

Even when assuming a growth model, it is, of course, not the case that all children and adolescents who show early signs of negative symptoms face an inevitable fate of social marginalization and staggering negative symptoms. As we have outlined, positive interpersonal experiences can be expected to push back against the further solidification of the early signs of negative symptoms. It rather seems to be the case that the early signs likely form the vulnerability aspect of a diathesis-stress model. They appear to be rooted in both genetic factors and early social learning experiences (Gazelle & Rubin, 2019). Negative interpersonal experiences with peers and in the family, which in part are consequences of these early signs of negative symptoms, are the stressors that cause negative symptoms to manifest in vulnerable children and adolescents. Positive interpersonal experiences such as experiencing parental warmth, experiencing friend support, or having positive role models, act as protective factors. It is unclear to what degree family- and peer-related factors such as parental neglect, ostracism, or bullying victimization interact in this process, or to what degree each of them explains unique portions of variance in the transition from early signs to clinically relevant negative symptoms. Either way, both the family and peer environment offer good leverage points for preventing negative symptom exacerbation in those who show early signs.

3.2 Postmorbid Interpersonal Risk Factors

Having discussed premorbid interpersonal risk factors in the previous section, this section will now focus on postmorbid interpersonal risk factors for negative symptoms, thus, those that exert their influence during or after a first psychotic episode of a psychotic disorder.

It is important to preempt that there is now good evidence showing that negative symptoms go into remission after a first psychotic episode in many people, although this typically takes longer than for positive psychotic symptoms (Häfner, 2019). For somewhere between 15 percent and 30 percent of people with a first episode of psychosis, negative symptoms remain stable (Mucci et al., 2017). In those with an early persistent course of negative symptoms, stability rates are as high as 67 percent after 20 years (Strauss et al., 2010). Overall, the data indicate that negative symptoms reach a somewhat stable plateau likely within the first few years after a first psychotic episode (Häfner, 2019). In those first years, however, negative symptoms are not necessarily stable phenomena. We can therefore expect that there are risk and protective factors modulating the level of their persistence after a first psychotic episode.

It may not surprise that the *premorbid* interpersonal risk factors that were discussed in the previous section also predict a more stable course of negative symptoms after the onset of a psychotic disorder (Mucci et al., 2017). A good example to illustrate the reach of premorbid risk factors into the early stages of a psychotic disorder (i.e., the first psychotic episode), is the time it takes until people with a first psychotic episode receive initial treatment (duration of untreated psychosis). A longer duration of untreated psychosis is a well-established early postmorbid risk factor for a stable long-term trajectory of negative symptoms (Mucci et al., 2017) and is associated with negative consequences of the premorbid social decline described in the previous section: People included in less supportive social networks were found to have longer durations of untreated psychosis (e.g., Mo'tamedi et al., 2014; Norman et al., 2005; Ruiz-Veguilla et al., 2012).

After people experience their first psychotic episode and enter mental health services, they are typically labeled as having a psychotic disorder. The psychosis label comes with severe stigma, and people tend to distance themselves from those they know to have a psychotic disorder (Best & Bowie, 2022; Nieweglowski et al., 2020). As we have seen, people with early signs of negative symptoms tend to already have relatively few close friends going into their first psychotic episode, so that for some the additional stigma of the psychosis label can result in total isolation. Stigmatization affects entire societies. Accordingly, stigmatization also occurs on the part of treatment providers, who endorse stereotypes of dangerousness and unpredictability of people with psychosis at a high rate and often communicate pessimistic outcome expectancies (Nieweglowski et al., 2020; Smith et al., 2017) that affected individuals are likely to internalize, creating or strengthening demotivating and self-stigmatizing beliefs.

For stigmatization to occur, the stigmatizing person needs to be aware of the disorder label (or at least of a broader mental health problem). Even in the absence of a diagnostic label, however, negative symptoms can lead to the rejection of people with psychotic disorders. Several studies, including our own work, have investigated responses of interaction partners toward people with schizophrenia, when these partners were unaware of the diagnosis (Krause et al., 1992; Lavelle et al., 2013; Penn et al., 2000; Raffard et al., 2015; Riehle et al., 2015, 2018; Riehle & Lincoln, 2018). These studies have generally found that negative symptoms and interpersonal behaviors associated with negative symptoms predicted an interaction partners' stronger desire for social distance toward the person with schizophrenia.

Similar to stigmatizing attitudes, these interpersonal distancing processes also affect treatment providers. For example, in our work, we have found that psychotherapists gave lower ratings of therapeutic alliance if their patients with schizophrenia had higher levels of expressive negative symptoms (Riehle et al., 2015). Therapists may grow frustrated with their patients over time if patients appear "hard to reach" or lacking in motivation for therapy (Jung et al., 2014). Therapists who communicate this frustration toward the patient without providing adequate validation for the patient's struggles may inadvertently (or carelessly) fuel the negative interpersonal expectations and further solidify the negative symptoms.

Summing up, a loss of social contacts, low motivation to and/or struggles to (re-)gain social contacts, and continued negative interpersonal experiences likely fuel beliefs of low social ability and low self-efficacy. These contribute to the formation and maintenance of negative symptoms as outlined in the cognitive-interpersonal maintenance model (Figure 2.1; cf. also Beck et al., 2011; Pillny et al., 2018; White et al., 2013).

3.3 Other Factors

Overall, there are many more negative consequences of having a psychotic disorder and of negative symptoms, such as difficulties in completing professional training, in getting hired, in finding a partner, or in starting a family. Together these factors lead to social isolation, financial struggles, and an overall monotonous life. Such environmental deprivation may also represent a risk factor for negative symptoms, given that the affected person has very limited opportunities to challenge the belief system that thwarts being an active participant in the world (Strauss, 2021).

4. Case Vignette

The following fictitious case vignette is thought to illustrate how interpersonal risk factors affect negative symptom formation and offer leverage points for intervention.

John is a 30-year-old man, who received a diagnosis of schizophrenia at the age of 22. With respect to negative symptoms, John has struggled for years with low motivation for being in touch with most other people and to finish his undergraduate university degree. When he engages in interactions with others, John is known to be rather quiet and to sit still. When talking his face remains neutral most of the time and others describe him as hard to read. John prefers solitary hobbies (and always has). These, however, now appear "dull" to him every so often. When asked about his most important struggles, he points to having to live with almost no spare money (German social security benefits); the fact that his studies at the university are put on hold and he sees no way how he could finish his degree; and that he feels lonely at times. He particularly yearns to have a romantic partner, much more so than to have friends, but does not see how he has anything to offer or would go about finding one.

When talking about his childhood and adolescence, John explains that he has had bad experiences with teachers and being bullied, starting in elementary school. He recounts one particularly incisive moment when he had overheard teachers talking about him ("It's sad how he gets picked on, but I can somehow see why the others don't like him. He's just odd."). From then on, "the case was pretty much settled" and he "tried to stand clear of the others as much as possible." He had not expected that moving to high school would be a fresh start. "It indeed just went on as before." He teamed up with "some other outsiders" at school, but he does not remember to ever have fully enjoyed their company ("I wouldn't necessarily say we were friends. In fact, I always thought they will cast me out one day."). John explains that these thoughts led him to withdraw more and more until he never met anyone outside of school. This was around the age of 16. At the same time, the others had formed a stronger bond, making it "hard to remain a part of that group."

John goes on to explain that his parents had split up when he was six and that he had stayed with his mother, who struggled with depression time and again. His father had been absent ever since the divorce. His mother, when not depressed, would have been occupied with work, so that he, an only child, was on his own a lot. Even though they never had been poor, he felt that they lived a "minimal life." John says that there also "were never any obligations, nothing to get me out of the house."

After finishing high school at age 19, John started a bachelor's degree at the local university and moved into a shared apartment with people he did not know and with whom he never felt any real connection. "I was always suspicious of them, did not feel comfortable with having to live with them." He said that he went to a party of other students once but sat around alone all night. "This showed me once more that I just won't fit in."

Toward the beginning of his third undergraduate year, his suspiciousness grew and generalized to fellow students and teachers at the university. Over the course of the following three months, he started to hear their voices and to feel persecuted more and more. Ultimately, out of desperation, he locked himself into his room for several days, until police, called by his roommates, forced the door open. John recovered from his severe psychotic symptoms in a psychiatric hospital over the course of three months. After this, he recounts that, "I had completely lost my motivation. I had been told that I would depend on medication, probably life-long, and that I was not able to handle stress well. I know that I am supposed to finish my degree, but what's the point when I can't handle work life after all?"

John's positive psychotic symptoms have remained in remission until now. His negative symptoms, however, have prevailed. He says they would now be responsible for him having to lead a socially isolated life. Of particular relevance are his demotivating beliefs that have formed in response to experiences of severe ostracism, parental neglect, failed attempts at socializing, and professionals' pessimistic recovery expectations. These were additionally strengthened by a lack of experiences of self-efficacy, self-worth, and belonging. Accordingly, John has a low expectancy of pleasure regarding social interactions and studying, leading to demotivated behavior such as social withdrawal.

Breaking the maintenance cycle(s) of John's negative symptoms requires several steps with the overarching goal of increasing the amount of pleasant social interactions to provide experiential counter-evidence for his negative interpersonal outcome expectancies. Most of the therapeutic interventions discussed in this book could be helpful for John at different stages of therapy. Certainly, an important first step is a constructive and validation-providing therapeutic relationship. For this reason, cognitive interventions challenging his beliefs (cf. Chapters 11), for example, Socratic dialogue, should be set aside until progress has been made behaviorally. To break the interpersonal maintenance cycle (cf. Figure 2.1), John would likely benefit from social skills training (cf. Chapter 17) that is focused on affiliative (not assertive) skills, such as learning to value smiling and overall expression to create more pleasant interpersonal encounters. Especially when delivered in a group format, this training may also be a source of initial positive social interactions. If successful, these interventions should also provide experiences of self-efficacy and self-worth, and we may expect John to become more motivated to try out interventions, both behaviorally and cognitively, that are increasingly challenging. Overall, factoring in both the intra- and interpersonal aspects that maintain John's negative symptoms helps his therapist to formulate an individualized treatment plan and helps John to gain hope and motivation for change.

References

Arseneault, L., Cannon, M., Fisher, H. L., Polanczyk, G., Moffitt, T. E., & Caspi, A. (2011). Childhood trauma and children's emerging psychotic symptoms: A genetically sensitive longitudinal cohort study. *American Journal of Psychiatry*, *168*(1), 65–72.

Bailey, T., Alvarez-Jimenez, M., Garcia-Sanchez, A. M., Hulbert, C., Barlow, E., & Bendall, S. (2018). Childhood trauma is associated with severity of hallucinations and delusions in psychotic disorders: A systematic review and meta-analysis. *Schizophrenia Bulletin*, *44*(5), 1111–1122.

Baum, K. M., & Walker, E. F. (1995). Childhood behavioral precursors of adult symptom dimensions in schizophrenia. *Schizophrenia Research*, *16*(2), 111–120.

Beck, A. T., Rector, N. A., Stolar, N., & Grant, P. (2011). A cognitive conceptualization of negative symptoms. In A. T. Beck, N. A. Rector, N. Stolar, & P. Grant (Eds.), *Schizophrenia. Cognitive Theory, Research, and Therapy* (pp.142–158). Guilford Press.

Best, M. W., & Bowie, C. R. (2022). Social exclusion in psychotic disorders: An interactional processing model. *Schizophrenia Research*, *244*(May), 91–100.

Bucci, P., Mucci, A., Piegari, G., Nobile, M., Pini, S., Rossi, A., Vita, A., Galderisi, S., & Maj, M. (2016). Characterization of premorbid functioning during childhood in patients with deficit vs. non-deficit schizophrenia and in their healthy siblings. *Schizophrenia Research*, *174*(1–3), 172–176.

Carr, S. C., Hardy, A., & Fornells-Ambrojo, M. (2018). Relationship between attachment style and symptom severity across the psychosis spectrum: A meta-analysis. *Clinical Psychology Review*, *59*, 145–158.

Catone, G., Marotta, R., Pisano, S., Lennox, B., Carotenuto, M., Gritti, A., Pascotto, A., & Broome, M. R. (2017). Psychotic-like experiences in help-seeking adolescents: Dimensional exploration and association with different forms of bullying victimization—A developmental social psychiatry perspective. *International Journal of Social Psychiatry*, *63*(8), 752–762.

Chan, R. C. K., Wang, L., & Lui, S. S. Y. (2022). Theories and models of negative symptoms in schizophrenia and clinical implications. *Nature Reviews Psychology 2022*, 1–14.

Cowan, T., Strauss, G. P., Raugh, I. M., Le, T. P., & Cohen, A. S. (2022). How do social factors relate to blunted facial affect in schizophrenia? A digital phenotyping study using ambulatory video recordings. *Journal of Psychiatric Research*, *150*(August 2021), 96–104.

de Bruyn, E. H., Cillessen, A. H. N., & Wissink, I. B. (2010). Associations of peer acceptance and perceived popularity with bullying and victimization in early adolescence. *The Journal of Early Adolescence*, *30*(4), 543–566.

Degnan, A., Berry, K., Humphrey, C., & Bucci, S. (2022). The role of attachment and dissociation in the relationship between childhood interpersonal trauma and negative symptoms in psychosis. *Clinical Psychology & Psychotherapy*, *29*(5), 1692–1706.

Dewangan, R. L., Singh, P., Mahapatra, T., & Mahapatra, S. (2018). Role of perceived family environment in the pathogenesis of schizophrenia. *Indian Journal of Social Psychiatry*, *34*(1), 69.

Fett, A. K. J., Lemmers-Jansen, I. L. J., & Krabbendam, L. (2019). Psychosis and urbanicity: A review of the recent literature from epidemiology to neurourbanism. *Current Opinion in Psychiatry*, *32*(3), 232–241.

García-Mieres, H., Lundin, N. B., Minor, K. S., Dimaggio, G., Popolo, R., Cheli, S., & Lysaker, P. H. (2020). A cognitive model of diminished expression in schizophrenia: The interface of metacognition, cognitive symptoms and language disturbances. *Journal of Psychiatric Research*, *131*, 169–176.

Gayer-Anderson, C., & Morgan, C. (2013). Social networks, support and early psychosis: A systematic review. *Epidemiology and Psychiatric Sciences*, *22*(2), 131–146.

Gazelle, H., & Rubin, K. H. (2019). Social withdrawal and anxiety in childhood and adolescence: Interaction between individual tendencies and interpersonal learning mechanisms in development. *Journal of Abnormal Child Psychology 2019, 47*(7), 1101–1106.

Grant, P. M., & Beck, A. T. (2010). Asocial beliefs as predictors of asocial behavior in schizophrenia. *Psychiatry Research, 177*(1–2), 65–70.

Griffiths, H., & McLeod, H. (2019). Promoting recovery from negative symptoms: An attachment theory perspective. In K. Berry, S. Bucci, & A. N. Danquah (Eds.), *Attachment theory and psychosis: Current perspectives and future directions* (pp. 62–83). Routledge/Taylor & Francis Group.

Gumley, A. I., Taylor, H. E. F., Schwannauer, M., & MacBeth, A. (2014). A systematic review of attachment and psychosis: Measurement, construct validity and outcomes. *Acta Psychiatrica Scandinavica, 129*(4), 257–274.

Häfner, H. (2019). From onset and prodromal stage to a life-long course of schizophrenia and its symptom dimensions: How sex, age, and other risk factors influence incidence and course of illness. *Psychiatry Journal, 2019*, 1–15.

Halford, W. K., Schweitzer, R. D., & Varghese, F. N. (1991). Effects of family environment on negative symptoms and quality of life of psychotic patients. *Psychiatric Services, 42*(12), 1241–1247.

Hodges, E. V. E., & Perry, D. G. (1999). Personal and interpersonal antecedents and consequences of victimization by peers. *Journal of Personality and Social Psychology, 76*(4), 677–685.

Jaya, E. S., Ascone, L., & Lincoln, T. M. (2016). Social adversity and psychosis: The mediating role of cognitive vulnerability. *Schizophrenia Bulletin, 43*(3), sbw104. https://doi.org/10.1093/schbul/sbw104

Jaya, E. S., Pillny, M., Lincoln, T. M., & Riehle, M. (2022). Does social defeat cause negative symptoms? A prospective study in a multi-national community sample. *Comprehensive Psychiatry, 113*, 152289.

Jeganathan, J., & Breakspear, M. (2021). An active inference perspective on the negative symptoms of schizophrenia. *The Lancet Psychiatry, 8*(8), 732–738.

Jung, E., Wiesjahn, M., & Lincoln, T. M. (2014). Negative, not positive symptoms predict the early therapeutic alliance in cognitive behavioral therapy for psychosis. *Psychotherapy Research: Journal of the Society for Psychotherapy Research, 24*(2), 171–183.

Keltner, D., & Haidt, J. (1999). Social functions of emotions at four levels of analysis. *Cognition and Emotion, 13*(5), 505–521.

Kirkpatrick, B., Strauss, G. P., Nguyen, L., Fischer, B. A., Daniel, D. G., Cienfuegos, A., & Marder, S. R. (2011). The brief negative symptom scale: Psychometric properties. *Schizophrenia Bulletin, 37*(2), 300–305.

Krause, R., Steimer-Krause, E., & Hufnagel, H. (1992). Expression and experience of affects in paranoid schizophrenia. *European Review of Applied Psychology, 42*(2), 131–140.

Kring, A. M., Gur, R. E., Blanchard, J. J., Horan, W. P., & Reise, S. P. (2013). The Clinical Assessment Interview for Negative Symptoms (CAINS): Final development and validation. *The American Journal of Psychiatry, 170*(2), 165–172.

Kuhney, F. S., Damme, K. S. F., Pelletier-Baldelli, A., Chun, C., Ellman, L. M., Schiffman, J., & Mittal, V. A. (2021). Prevalence and functional consequences of social anxiety in individuals at clinical high-risk for psychosis: Perspective from a community sample comparison. *Schizophrenia Bulletin Open, 2*(1), sgab025.

Laith, R., & Vaillancourt, T. (2022). The temporal sequence of bullying victimization, academic achievement, and school attendance: A review of the literature. *Aggression and Violent Behavior, 64*, 101722.

Lavelle, M., Healey, P. G. T., & McCabe, R. (2013). Is nonverbal communication disrupted in interactions involving patients with schizophrenia? *Schizophrenia Bulletin, 39*(5), 1150–1158.

Leijdesdorff, S. M. J., Bakker, J. M., Lange, I., Michielse, S., Goossens, L., Klaassen, R., Popma, A., Schruers, K., Lieverse, R., Marcelis, M., van Os, J., Wichers, M., Myin-Germeys, I., & van Amelsvoort, T. (2022). Home alone: Social functioning as a transdiagnostic marker of mental health in youth, exploring retrospective and daily life measurements. *Comprehensive Psychiatry, 115*, 152309.

Martin, J., Rychlowska, M., Wood, A., & Niedenthal, P. (2017). Smiles as multipurpose social signals. *Trends in Cognitive Sciences, 21*(11), 864–877.

Mo'tamedi, H., Rezaiemaram, P., Aguilar-Vafaie, M. E., Tavallaie, A., Azimian, M., & Shemshadi, H. (2014). The relationship between family resiliency factors and caregiver-perceived duration of untreated psychosis in persons with first-episode psychosis. *Psychiatry Research, 219*(3), 497–505.

Mucci, A., Merlotti, E., Üçok, A., Aleman, A., & Galderisi, S. (2017). Primary and persistent negative symptoms: Concepts, assessments and neurobiological bases. *Schizophrenia Research, 186*, 19–28.

Nieweglowski, K., Qin, S., Paniagua, D., & Corrigan, P. W. (2020). Understanding the impact of mental health stigma and the role of clinicians as allies. In J. C. Badcock & G. Paulik (Eds.), *A clinical introduction to psychosis: Foundations for clinical psychologists and neuropsychologists* (pp. 63–84). Elsevier Academic Press.

Norman, R. M. G., Malla, A. K., Manchanda, R., Harricharan, R., Takhar, J., & Northcott, S. (2005). Social support and three-year symptom and admission outcomes for first episode psychosis. *Schizophrenia Research, 80*(2–3), 227–234.

O'Brien, M. P., Gordon, J. L., Bearden, C. E., Lopez, S. R., Kopelowicz, A., & Cannon, T. D. (2006). Positive family environment predicts improvement in symptoms and social functioning among adolescents at imminent risk for onset of psychosis. *Schizophrenia Research, 81*(2–3), 269–275.

O'Brien, M. P., Zinberg, J. L., Bearden, C. E., Lopez, S. R., Kopelowicz, A., Daley, M., & Cannon, T. D. (2008). Parent attitudes and parent adolescent interaction in families of youth at risk for psychosis and with recent-onset psychotic symptoms. *Early Intervention in Psychiatry, 2*(4), 268–276.

Otero, S., Moreno-Iniguez, M., Payá, B., Castro-Fornieles, J., Gonzalez-Pinto, A., Baeza, I., Mayoral, M., Graell, M., & Arango-López, C. (2011). Twelve-month follow-up of family communication and psychopathology in children and adolescents with a first psychotic episode (CAFEPS study). *Psychiatry Research, 185*(1–2), 72–77.

Penn, D. L., Kohlmaier, J. R., & Corrigan, P. W. (2000). Interpersonal factors contributing to the stigma of schizophrenia: Social skills, perceived attractiveness, and symptoms. *Schizophrenia Research, 45*(1–2), 37–45.

Pillny, M., & Lincoln, T. M. (2020). The demotivating effect of social exclusion: An experimental test of a psychosocial model on the development of negative symptoms in psychosis. *Schizophrenia Research, 215*, 330–336.

Pillny, M., Krkovic, K., & Lincoln, T. M. (2018). Development of the Demotivating Beliefs Inventory and Test of the Cognitive Triad of Amotivation. *Cognitive Therapy and Research, 42*(6), 867–877.

Pillny, M., Schlier, B., & Lincoln, T. M. (2020). "I just don't look forward to anything." How anticipatory pleasure and negative beliefs contribute to goal-directed activity in patients with negative symptoms of psychosis. *Schizophrenia Research, 222*, 429–436.

Pouwels, J. L., Lansu, T. A. M., & Cillessen, A. H. N. (2016). Participant roles of bullying in adolescence: Status characteristics, social behavior, and assignment criteria. *Aggressive Behavior, 42*(3), 239–253.

Pretzer, J. (2000). Kognitive Therapie bei antisozialer Persönlichkeitsstörung. *Psychotherapie, 5*(2), 268–280.

Raffard, S., Salesse, R. N., Marin, L., Del-Monte, J., Schmidt, R. C., Varlet, M., Bardy, B. G., Boulenger, J.-P., & Capdevielle, D. (2015). Social priming enhances interpersonal synchronization and feeling of connectedness towards schizophrenia patients. *Scientific Reports, 5*, 8156.

Riehle, M., Jung, E., Wiesjahn, M., Mehl, S., Rief, W., & Lincoln, T. M. (2015). What's in an item? Predicting social outcomes in schizophrenia spectrum disorders from the PANSS item "Poor Rapport." *Schizophrenia Research, 168*(1–2), 593–594.

Riehle, M., & Lincoln, T. M. (2018). Investigating the social costs of schizophrenia: Facial expressions in dyadic interactions of people with and without schizophrenia. *Journal of Abnormal Psychology, 127*(2), 202–215.

Riehle, M., Mehl, S., & Lincoln, T. M. (2018). The specific social costs of expressive negative symptoms in schizophrenia: Reduced smiling predicts interactional outcome. *Acta Psychiatrica Scandinavica, 138*(2), 133–144.

Robustelli, B. L., Newberry, R. E., Whisman, M. A., & Mittal, V. A. (2017). Social relationships in young adults at ultra high risk for psychosis. *Psychiatry Research, 247*, 345–351.

Roth, G., Assor, A., Niemiec, C. P., Ryan, R. M., & Deci, E. L. (2009). The emotional and academic consequences of parental conditional regard: Comparing conditional positive regard, conditional negative regard, and autonomy support as parenting practices. *Developmental Psychology, 45*(4), 1119–1142.

Ruiz-Veguilla, M., Luisa Barrigón, M., Diaz, F. J., Ferrin, M., Moreno-Granados, J., Dolores Salcedo, M., Cervilla, J., & Gurpegui, M. (2012). The duration of untreated psychosis is associated with social support and temperament. *Psychiatry Research, 200*(2–3), 687–692.

Saarento, S., & Salmivalli, C. (2015). The role of classroom peer ecology and bystanders' responses in bullying. *Child Development Perspectives, 9*(4), 201–205.

Schalbroeck, R. (2020). The social defeat hypothesis of schizophrenia: a parsimonious explanation for multiple psychosis risk factors? *Psychological Medicine, 53*(1), 286–287.

Selten, J.-P., van der Ven, E., Rutten, B. P. F., & Cantor-Graae, E. (2013). The social defeat hypothesis of schizophrenia: An update. *Schizophrenia Bulletin, 39*(6), 1180–1186.

Selten, J. P., Van Der Ven, E., & Termorshuizen, F. (2020). Migration and psychosis: A meta-analysis of incidence studies. *Psychological Medicine, 50*(2), 303–313.

Shakoor, S., McGuire, P., Cardno, A. G., Freeman, D., Plomin, R., & Ronald, A. (2015). A shared genetic propensity underlies experiences of bullying victimization in late childhood and self-rated paranoid thinking in adolescence. *Schizophrenia Bulletin, 41*(3), 754–763.

Smith, J. D., Mittal, D., Chekuri, L., Han, X., & Sullivan, G. (2017). A comparison of provider attitudes toward serious mental illness across different health care disciplines. *Stigma and Health, 2*(4), 327–337.

Strauss, G. P. (2021). A bioecosystem theory of negative symptoms in schizophrenia. *Frontiers in Psychiatry, 12*, 655471.

Strauss, G. P., Allen, D. N., Miski, P., Buchanan, R. W., Kirkpatrick, B., & Carpenter, W. T. (2012). Differential patterns of premorbid social and academic deterioration in deficit and nondeficit schizophrenia. *Schizophrenia Research, 135*(1–3), 134–138.

Strauss, G. P., Harrow, M., Grossman, L. S., & Rosen, C. (2010). Periods of recovery in deficit syndrome schizophrenia: A 20-year multi-follow-up longitudinal study. *Schizophrenia Bulletin, 36*(4), 788–799.

Thorup, A., Petersen, L., Jeppesen, P., Ohlenschlaeger, J., Christensen, T., Krarup, G., Jorgensen, P., & Nordentoft, M. (2006). Social network among young adults with first-episode schizophrenia spectrum disorders: Results from the Danish OPUS trial. *Social Psychiatry and Psychiatric Epidemiology, 41*(10), 761–770.

Walker, E. F., Grimes, K. E., Davis, D. M., & Smith, A. J. (1993). Childhood precursors of schizophrenia: Facial expressions of emotion. *American Journal of Psychiatry, 150*(11), 1654–1660.

White, R. G., Laithwaite, H., & Gilbert, P. (2013). Negative symptoms in schizophrenia. The role of social defeat. In A. Gumley, A. Gillham, K. Taylor, & M. Schwannauer (Eds.), *Psychosis and Emotion* (pp.178–190). Routledge.

Williams, K. D. (2009). Chapter 6 Ostracism: A Temporal Need-Threat Model. *Advances in Experimental Social Psychology*, *41*, 275–314.

Wolke, D., Lereya, S. T., Fisher, H. L., Lewis, G., & Zammit, S. (2013). Bullying in elementary school and psychotic experiences at 18 years: A longitudinal, population-based cohort study. *Psychological Medicine*, *44*(10), 2199–2211.

Yung, A. R., Nelson, B., McGorry, P. D., Wood, S. J., & Lin, A. (2019). Persistent negative symptoms in individuals at Ultra High Risk for psychosis. *Schizophrenia Research*, *206*, 355–361.

3

Contemporary Understanding of the Pathophysiology of Negative Symptoms of Schizophrenia

Implications for Psychosocial Treatments

Indrit Bègue, Stefan Kaiser, and Matthias Kirschner

Clinical pearls

- Apathy may be related to difficulties in anticipating rewards (i.e., being unable to imagine a reward or pleasurable experience when thinking about engaging in a future event) and negative beliefs about one's abilities.
- Blunted or constricted affect may be related to difficulties with speech production and may be particularly challenging for people in high-demand social situations.
- Clinicians can learn about the neurobiological pathways of negative symptoms to help inform successful psychosocial interventions.

1. Introduction

Negative symptoms of schizophrenia are present from the early stages of the disorder (Lyne et al., 2012, 2015) to chronic phases (Galderisi et al., 2018, 2021) and persist in almost a third of patients with schizophrenia (Bobes et al., 2010; Sicras-Mainar et al., 2014; Szkultecka-Dębek et al., 2015). These symptoms have a considerable detrimental impact on functioning, long-term outcome, and quality of life (Fervaha et al., 2014; Galderisi et al., 2013; Rabinowitz et al., 2012; Strauss et al., 2013). The high prevalence and deleterious impact sharply contrast with the limited therapeutic options available at present, with interventions demonstrating moderate effects at best. Consequently, negative symptoms have been considered a major "unmet need" in psychiatric care for patients with

Indrit Bègue, et al., *Contemporary Understanding of the Pathophysiology of Negative Symptoms of Schizophrenia*. In: *Psychosocial Approaches to Negative Symptoms in Psychosis*. Edited by: Tania Lincoln et al., Oxford University Press. DOI: 10.1093/oso/9780197676790.003.0003 schizophrenia (Galderisi et al., 2018; Galderisi et al., 2021). In this context, research efforts can be particularly useful to investigate underlying mechanisms in the hope of identifying translational targets to treatment development.

Negative symptoms broadly map onto two dimensions with partly distinct neurobiological substrates (Bègue et al., 2020; Galderisi et al., 2021; Kirkpatrick et al., 2006): (1) apathy, entailing a loss of motivation (avolition), pleasure (anhedonia), and loss of motivation for social contact (asociality); and (2) diminished expression, corresponding to an impairment of affective expression (blunted affect) and speech production (alogia). Recent psychometric evidence has supported a more differentiated five-factor model of negative symptoms (Ahmed et al., 2022). However, most evidence on negative symptom pathophysiology stems from studies investigating the two dimensions of apathy and diminished expression, which will therefore guide the structure of the current chapter.

Before examining behavioral and neural correlates of negative symptoms, it is worth bearing in mind that considerable heterogeneity in research exists, derived from how negative symptoms are assessed (Galderisi et al., 2021). Furthermore, there is a lack of systematic distinction in the literature between primary (characteristic of schizophrenia per se) and secondary negative symptoms (as a consequence of psychosis, depression, medication effects, and so on (Kirschner et al., 2017), see Chapter 1 for detailed information. Most studies reviewed in this chapter have attempted to include negative symptoms with primary schizophrenia-inherent sources rather than secondary negative symptoms. However, the application of exclusion thresholds in these studies for psychosis, depression, antipsychotic parkinsonism, and so on has been variable. Therefore, it is probable that the evidence reviewed here also includes studies investigating secondary negative symptoms.

Another important caveat in pathophysiology considerations is that most studies apply cross-sectional assessments, which does not capture temporal fluctuations in the clinical evolution of negative symptoms (Lincoln et al., 2017; Savill et al., 2015), particularly, when it comes to apathy. So far, attempts to reduce heterogeneity *retrospectively* have allowed for the development of "deficit syndrome"—a syndrome whereby the presence of primary negative symptoms is required for at least 12 months duration (Kirkpatrick et al., 2017)—albeit with limited clinical application due to extensive training needs (Galderisi et al., 2021), though effort has been made to simplify these needs (Goetz et al., 2007). To address the problem of heterogeneity, the European Psychiatric Association (EPA) guidance group recently recommended the use of the "persistent negative symptoms" construct—that is, the requirement of an at least six-month persistence of negative symptoms (Galderisi et al., 2021). Another source of heterogeneity stems from clinical interviews, often prone to several biases due to the retrospective nature of the reports and the role of subjectivity. Thus, efforts are now being dedicated to develop digital phenotyping of negative symptoms (see Kimhy and Ospina Chapter 9, this volume; Cohen et al., 2020, 2021; Henson et al., 2020). Future research should clarify whether digital phenotyping will fulfill its promise of better characterization of negative symptoms and their associated neurobiology.

In the present chapter, we review the cognitive-behavioral and neural evidence for the two negative symptom dimensions: apathy and diminished expression. We then further outline potential avenues through which dimension-specific behavioral mechanisms and brain correlates may be modulated by psychosocial treatments. Overall, we aim to provide an overview of how behavioral and cognitive mechanisms of negative symptoms could advance the development of symptom-specific psychosocial treatment approaches. A comprehensive review of neural substrates would go beyond the scope of this chapter, and we kindly refer to recent reviews on this topic (Bègue et al., 2020; Collo et al., 2020; Galderisi et al., 2015; Mørch-Johnsen et al., 2018).

2. Apathy

Apathy in schizophrenia is currently conceptualized to result from deficits in processes linked to goal-directed behavior—the capacity to make a choice and select actions on the basis of desired goals (Bortolon et al., 2018; Husain & Roiser, 2018). When faced with a decision, goal-directed behavior entails a set of processes that enable individuals to generate options regarding potential ways to tackle an objective, then ponder these options for their costs (e.g., effort, time required, and associated risks) versus the anticipated benefit (internal or external reward), before choosing and selecting the actions to follow (see for a review Husain & Roiser, 2018). Monitoring of performance via metacognitive mechanisms may be important to ensure goal progression. Moreover, working memory may be relevant to maintaining the main goal and the intermediate subgoals. Finally, a learning process takes place to facilitate subsequent decision-making and optimize future choices. Several lines of research have examined impairments in different aspects of goal-directed behavior that we outlined above, in particular: (1) impaired anticipation of rewards, (2) aberrant cost-computation in effort-based motivation, (3) deficient reward-learning (see for a review on 2–3 Strauss et al., 2014), 4) metacognitive defeatist beliefs (Grant & Beck, 2009), but also (5) deficits in the preliminary stages of goal-directed behavior, such as option generation and planning (Faerden et al., 2009; Hartmann et al., 2015),

We detail these mechanisms in the following section and subsequently provide potential ways to tackle associated deficits with psychosocial treatments.

2.1 Behavioral and Cognitive Mechanisms of Apathy

2.1.1 Impairments in the Anticipation of Rewards

Research employing reward processing tasks have consistently shown an impairment of reward anticipation at the neural level. To our knowledge, no studies have reported behavioral correlates of reward anticipation equivalents in psychosis. A consistent finding is the negative association between ventral striatal (VS) activation during reward processing and negative symptoms in patients with schizophrenia (see for a meta-analysis Radua et al., 2015). Blunted ventral striatal reward anticipation activity seems to specifically relate to apathy and not diminished expression (Kirschner et al., 2015; Moran et al., 2019; Simon et al., 2010; Stepien et al., 2018; Waltz et al., 2010, 2018; Wolf et al., 2014) even at subclinical level in the general population (Simon et al., 2015), suggesting that aberrant reward anticipation processes underlie apathy pathophysiology.

2.1.2 Cost-Computation in Effort-Based Motivation

Several studies have suggested that motivational impairment in patients with schizophrenia is associated with impaired effort-based decision-making during physical or cognitive effort (Barch et al., 2014; A. Culbreth et al., 2016; A. J. Culbreth et al., 2020; Gold et al., 2013; Hartmann et al., 2015; Strauss et al., 2016; Wolf et al., 2014), impairments are, however, somewhat inconsistently related to the emergence of apathy (see for a review M. Hartmann-Riemer et al., 2018).

With respect to *physical* effort, a reduced motivation to produce effort (i.e., progressively incremental button presses) in order to obtain rewards has been found in schizophrenia and such reduction relates to negative symptoms (Strauss et al., 2016; Wolf et al., 2014). In our group, we also found that more apathetic patients were less willing to perform physical effort (i.e., squeeze on a handgrip to obtain rewards) to obtain monetary rewards (Hartmann et al., 2015). Concerning *cognitive effort*, a recent study examined incremental effort employing an *n*-back task (i.e., in a string of letters, subjects are asked to indicate when the current letter matches a letter appearing previously—the task is more difficult with increasing number of letters) and found that, similarly to physical effort, motivational impairment was associated with a decreased willingness to exert cognitive effort (A. J. Culbreth et al., 2020). Taking a slightly different approach, we employed a classic *n*-back task with two cognitive load levels modified by reward (reward vs. no reward) to examine the neural integration of cognition and reward across the psychosis continuum. We found that more severe apathy, but not diminished expression, was associated with hypoactivity in cerebellar-midbrain-striatal circuitry during the high load condition already in unmedicated individuals at risk for psychosis and those with first-episode psychosis (Bègue et al., 2022). This suggests that impairments of cognitive effort allocation also seen in chronic schizophrenia (A. Culbreth et al., 2016) may intervene early on in the pathophysiology of apathy (Bègue et al., 2022; Chang et al., 2020).

2.1.3 Deficient Reward-Learning

Current evidence points to selective deficits in learning from positive (e.g., reward) outcome (Gold et al., 2012; Waltz et al., 2007; Yilmaz et al., 2012) while learning from negative outcomes (e.g., punishment) seems to be relatively intact (Maia & Frank, 2017). Moreover, such impaired learning from positive outcomes may relate specifically to apathy (Dowd et al., 2016; Gold et al., 2012; Waltz et al., 2007); these findings, however, are not universal (M. N. Hartmann-Riemer et al., 2017). Further, it was shown that these learning deficits may in fact be linked to representation of expected values (Gold et al., 2012); in other words, more severe negative-symptom patients would fail to distinguish between rewarding and loss-avoiding stimuli. This suggests that people with schizophrenia may suffer from a dysfunction in expected value representation impacting positive-outcome actions (Waltz & Gold, 2016) and instead, may rely on rather "valueless" stimulus-response learning to guide decisions (Hernaus et al., 2018), ultimately invalidating goal-directed behavior associated with severity of apathy (Hernaus et al., 2019).

2.1.4 Dysfunctional Metacognitive Beliefs

Metacognition (i.e., thinking about thinking, or cognition about cognition) entails a broad set of competences (Frith, 2012) that engage distinct neural correlates in healthy controls and neuropsychiatric patients (Bègue et al., 2018; Bègue, Vaessen et al., 2019). A well-known element of metacognitive experience is confidence in one's own decisions. For example, low confidence in a financial decision may prompt the individual to reconsider the investment altogether. Over time, task-based metacognitive experiences create the basis to create and maintain general implicit and explicit metacognitive beliefs, ideas, or theories of self/others and cognitive performance (e.g., "I am good in math," "I am bad with remembering names/faces") necessary for self-knowledge. Defeatist performance beliefs—generalized negative self-knowledge beliefs, particularly, with respect to one's own performance in a given task, are a type of metacognitive belief. Defeatist performance beliefs are unhelpful beliefs about one's own success in goal-directed behavior, therefore limiting engagement with these behaviors (to illustrate in the social domain, but other domains are affected: "Why bother trying to socialize if I am bad with people anyway?"). Defeatist performance beliefs have been linked to the pathophysiology of negative symptoms, and apathy in particular (Grant & Beck, 2009; Staring et al., 2013), across the psychosis spectrum from preclinical to chronic schizophrenia (Clay et al., 2021; Luther et al., 2016). Furthermore, metacognition seems to be a key parameter that predicts the strength of the synchrony in self- and clinician-ratings of motivation.

2.1.5 Deficient Option Generation

Although a large body of research links deficits in goal-directed behavior to apathy, very little is known about how option generation—the capacity to generate representations of possibilities for goal-directed action (Kalis et al., 2013)—for achieving a particular goal may be impaired in apathy (Husain & Roiser, 2018). Hypothetically, more apathetic patients would generate fewer options for actions than less apathetic patients, thereby minimizing the set of choices for goal-directed behavior. To our knowledge only one study specifically examined the association between the capacity to generate options and severity of apathy in patients with schizophrenia. Hartmann and colleagues (Hartmann et al., 2015) examined the quantity of options generated in real world scenarios in patients with schizophrenia or schizoaffective disorder and healthy control participants. Their results indicated that patients generated significantly fewer options than control participants and clinical apathy ratings correlated negatively with the number of generated options. Option generation has been further linked to various cognitive functions, in particular, to working memory (Leder et al., 2018), raising the question of the extent to which working memory deficits contribute to the development of apathy. Working memory is critical for actively maintaining internal representations that are crucial for forming goals and subgoals to guide behavior. Several studies have linked impaired working memory to apathy in patients across the schizophrenia spectrum (Faerden et al., 2009; Foussias et al., 2015; Gold et al., 2019; Raffard et al., 2016), although others have found rather nonspecific associations between working memory and both negative symptom dimensions (Galderisi et al., 2018; see also our section on diminished expression). Although these findings support a relationship between impaired working memory and apathy, it remains to be established how deficits in working memory and other cognitive domains contribute to deficient option generation in patients with apathy. In this regard, the study from Hartmann and coworkers (Hartmann et al., 2015) found that only verbal fluency was partly mediating the effect of apathy on option generation, while working memory was not directly measured in this study. In sum, these results provide preliminary evidence that predecisional deficits in option generation contribute to impaired goal-directed behavior in apathy, but research on option generation in negative symptoms remains surprisingly limited.

2.2 Apathy: From Mechanisms to Psychosocial Treatment

Thus far, we have identified several mechanisms by which impairments in goal-directed behavior play a role in apathy pathophysiology. These disturbances in goal-directed behavior may be amenable to psychosocial treatments including cognitive remediation and cognitive-behavior therapy.

Reward deficits (including anticipation, effort, learning) can also be amenable to cognitive remediation and cognitive behavior therapy. One cognitive remediation trial has suggested that improvement in reward or punishment sensitivity is related to reductions in negative symptoms (Cella et al., 2014). Considering the complex relationships among motivation, effort, and cognitive function, Foussias and colleagues (Foussias et al., 2015) propose to differentiate treatment of cognitive deficits in patients with and without amotivation, such that in the former subtype, amotivation is tackled first.

With respect to metacognition, few intervention studies targeted defeatist performance beliefs to treat overall negative symptoms and improve functional outcome with promising results (Klingberg et al., 2011, Grant et al., 2012). In a multicenter study, Klingberg and colleagues observed improvement of negative symptoms through interventions tackling defeatist beliefs; however, to be noted, this group did not include a treatment-as-usual control group. Therefore, it is difficult to interpret the improvement over time as a specific result of an intervention addressing defeatist performance beliefs (Klingberg et al., 2011). Grant and colleagues found a specific effect of such interventions on apathy in a smaller single-site study (Grant et al., 2012). These preliminary results suggest that negative symptoms, and apathy in particular, may be amenable to psychotherapeutic interventions that address defeatist performance beliefs (Grant et al., 2012, Velligan et al., 2015). A recent meta-analysis found a positive association between defeatist performance beliefs and negative symptoms (Campellone et al., 2016), highlighting the potential for interventions tackling defeatist performance beliefs to improve negative symptoms. Recently, an intervention designed to tackle defeatist thinking, reward anticipation, and maintain positive symptoms was related to improvements in anhedonia and apathy specifically (no impact on diminished expression) compared to treatment as usual (Favrod et al., 2015; Favrod et al., 2019; Favrod et al., 2019) and the results were sustained at six-month follow-up (Favrod et al., 2019). This group intervention consists of eight sessions of one hour each applied to a group of five to ten participants using audio and visual materials and focuses on changing defeatist performance beliefs, savoring pleasant experiences, expressing emotions by increasing behavioral expression, sharing pleasant experiences with others, and anticipating pleasant moments in the future. We invite the reader to consult Chapter 18 for more information on this intervention. While such a promising domain-specific intervention requires replication in bigger cohorts, it suggests that mechanism-informed approaches may contributing to closing the therapeutic gap in negative symptoms.

Option generation and cognitive functioning (including working-memory) can be targeted with cognitive remediation therapy. To our knowledge, no study has examined cognitive remediation effects on option generation and effects on apathy. One study (Cella et al., 2017) aimed to empirically show cognitive remediation effects and found improvements in verbal working memory and apathy through such an approach. These improvements were relatively independent from each other; however, only verbal working memory was assessed, suggesting that therapeutic tackling of working memory to alleviate negative symptoms has still a long way to go.

3. Diminished Expression

Research in the diminished expression domain is limited and a comprehensive model for diminished expression is lacking. To date, diminished expression has been conceptualized primarily in the "limited cognitive resources" framework, postulating that in the context of overall insufficient cognitive resources, less resources are available for language and emotional expression, resulting in diminished expression symptoms (Cohen et al., 2012, 2014). Recently, additional models have been formulated conceptualizing diminished expression (García-Mieres et al., 2020) in a more complex cognitive model. In this model, diminished expression arises from the interaction between deficient cognitive symptoms, impaired metacognitive self-reflectivity, and higher-order language disturbances, which interfere with the capacity to understand and express emotions in a coherent manner. Overall, research in the pathogenesis of diminished expression has focused on dysfunction in emotion expression and emotion perception, cognitive function, and higher order functions outlined in the following sections.

3.1 Behavioral and Cognitive Mechanisms of Diminished Expression

3.1.1 Deficits in Emotion Perception and Expression

Research has focused on impairments in emotion perception, and preliminary evidence suggests a direct link between emotion perception deficits and flat affect (Gur et al., 2006; Lepage et al., 2011). It needs to be clarified, however, whether these observations reflect a more general deficit rather than a specific abnormal emotion perception as underlying mechanism of diminished expression (Kerr & Neale, 1993; Kohler et al., 2010; Kring & Elis, 2013). Blunted affect has been further linked with several motor aspects of emotion expression in patients with schizophrenia (Trémeau et al., 2005; Tron et al., 2016), such as deficits in motor cognition (Trémeau, 2006), facial mimicry (Varcin et al., 2010), and mirror neuron system dysfunction (Lee et al., 2014).

3.1.2 Deficits in Cognitive Function

Diminished expression, and in particular, alogia, may relate to impaired semantic memory organization (Sumiyoshi et al., 2005), and more broadly, to deficits in cognitive function (attention, abstract thinking, and cognitive rigidity) as conceptualized in the cognitive resource limitation model of alogia (Cohen et al., 2012, 2014). This model postulates that social interactions represent highly complex demands for cognition (requiring elaborated speech in open-ended situations, for example). Speech depends on multiple cognitive domains—including controlled retrieval during verbal fluency tasks (Docherty et al., 2011), semantic memory organization (Sumiyoshi et al., 2005), and verbal fluency (Joyce et al., 1996). In the presence of impaired cognitive functioning (Barch & Berenbaum, 1997; M. N. Hartmann-Riemer et al., 2015), people with schizophrenia display decreased speech production and impaired semantic and lexical speech (Chang et al., 2018; Foussias et al., 2014) in situations associated with high cognitive demands (such as during social interactions). Diminished expression is associated with cognitive impairments in patients with schizophrenia (Galderisi et al., 2014; M. N. Hartmann-Riemer et al., 2015; Sevy et al., 2020). In sum, according to this model, for people with limited baseline cognitive functioning, situations with high cognitive demands (e.g., social situations) may lead to an insufficiency of cognitive resources available for speech and, in turn, may cause symptoms of diminished expression, in particular, alogia.

3.1.3 Impairment in Metacognition, Cognition, and Higher-Order Language Function

In the previous section, we examined metacognition under the lens of generalization of self-knowledge about one's own efficacy in a given domain (defeatist performance beliefs). Metacognition, however, also has been defined more broadly, as a notion closer to self-conscious awareness and self-reflection. In this view, metacognition would involve the integration of different experiences to form a coherent and meaningful representation (integrative model of metacognition (Lysaker et al., 2020); for a full description see Chapter 19, this volume. A disrupted integration due to impairments in metacognitive capacity may cause patients with schizophrenia to perceive their emotions and thoughts as being fragmented and confusing, leading to expressive deficits such as blunted affect or alogia. A recent study (García-Mieres et al., 2020) examined the role of metacognition, cognition, and higher-order language structures in the diminished expression dimension. They employed a novel approach, *situation models*, which aims to examine higher order language structures linked to the causal, intentional, and temporal cohesion of the language extracted from patients' personal narratives. Their results showed that self-reflectivity impairment fully mediated the impact of cognitive deficits (and partly, that of higher language structures) on diminished expression. Even though this study focused on the diminished expression dimension, and no correlations with experiential symptoms were found, it is conceivable that metacognition-based self-reflection deficits would also generally impact the subjective experience of apathy (see Borda & Sass, 2015).

3.2 Diminished Expression: From Mechanisms to Psychosocial Treatment

Diminished expression has rarely been the specific therapeutic focus of cognitive-behavioral therapy (CBT)-based interventions, even though recently modules taking a mechanistic-based approach tackling deficits in emotional expression and speech production have been included (Klingberg et al., 2011).

Several studies have aimed to tackle emotion perception dysfunction, in particular recognition and expression of facial emotions (Sevos et al., 2018) and recognition of basic facial expressions (Marsh et al., 2016) via attentional-focused cognitive remediation (Gaudelus et al., 2016). The translation to improved diminished expression, however, remains to be established. Some preliminary evidence with relevance to diminished expression has shown improvement in facial emotion recognition and overall negative symptoms with cognitive remediation (Gaudelus et al., 2016; Wölwer & Frommann, 2011) as well as speech and language therapy to tackle discourse deficits (Joyal et al., 2016).

With regards to speech and communication deficits, few studies have reported specific outcomes for diminished expression (Turner et al., 2014). Small-to-medium positive effects have been found with social skills training focusing on communication (Rus-Calafell et al., 2013).

On the other hand, cognitive remediation has shown a positive effect on negative symptoms overall (Cella et al., 2017), possibly through improvement of the limited cognitive resources. Cognitive remediation effects on diminished expression have rarely been reported except in two studies by Ventura and colleagues (Ventura et al., 2019) who found improvements in the cognitive remediation arm for both negative symptom dimensions (apathy and diminished expression). This positive effect on the diminished expression dimension was confirmed by Sevy and colleagues (Sevy et al., 2020). Small improvements in expressive deficits were observed with body-oriented psychotherapy (Priebe et al., 2016), but no positive effects were observed with arts therapy (Crawford et al., 2012). Finally, expressive deficits can be tackled via metacognitive interventions such as Metacognitive Reflection and Insight Therapy (Lysaker et al., 2020) or Metacognition Oriented Social Skills Training (Inchausti et al., 2018) that may be useful to assist patients to better integrate thoughts and goals (Lundin et al., 2020).

4. Summary

The presented chapter outlined current concepts and recent advances in behavioral, cognitive, and neural mechanisms of the two negative symptoms dimensions in schizophrenia, namely, apathy and diminished expression. Apathy relates to various aspects of motivation and goal-directed behavior including deficient option generation, impaired anticipation of and learning from reward values, effort-based decision-making, and dysfunctional performance beliefs. Diminished expression is less studied than apathy; however, it is currently conceptualized as arising from insufficient resources for speech production and emotional expression, particularly in a high-demand social context, in the presence of globally limited cognitive resources in schizophrenia.

At the same time, progress has been made in developing symptom-specific psychosocial treatments such as psychotherapeutic interventions targeting apathy and anhedonia. In addition, more recently, efforts are being made to identify targeted cognitive remediation therapies for each negative symptom dimension. In this regard, advances in identifying specific pathogenetic substrates of apathy

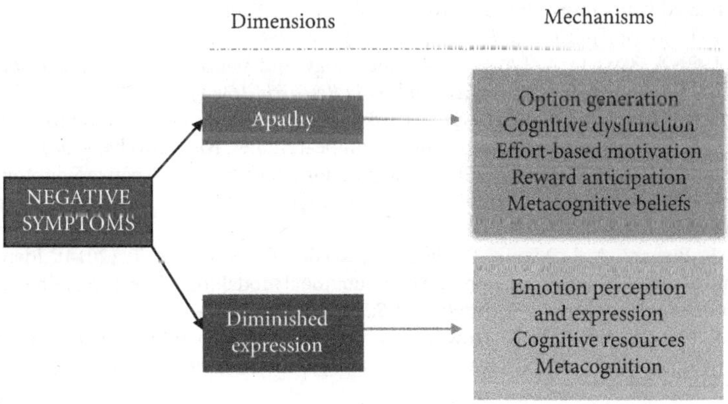

Figure 3.1 A schematic overview of mechanisms and potential therapies with clinical relevance.

and diminished expression could inform the development of psychosocial treatments by providing the basis for mechanistic targets as well as ways to quantify treatment efficacy (Figure 3.1). Altogether, an integrative understanding of apathy and diminished expression will be instrumental to providing individual and successful care of these debilitating symptoms in our patients.

References

Ahmed, A. O., Kirkpatrick, B., Granholm, E., Rowland, L. M., Barker, P. B., Gold, J. M., Buchanan, R. W., Outram, T., Bernardo, M., Paz García-Portilla, M., Mane, A., Fernandez-Egea, E., & Strauss, G. P. (2022). Two factors, five factors, or both? External validation studies of negative symptom dimensions in schizophrenia. *Schizophrenia Bulletin, 48*(3), 620–630.

Barch, D. M., & Berenbaum, H. (1997). The effect of language production manipulations on negative thought disorder and discourse coherence disturbances in schizophrenia. *Psychiatry Research, 71*(2), 115–127.

Barch, D. M., Treadway, M. T., & Schoen, N. (2014). Effort, anhedonia, and function in schizophrenia: Reduced effort allocation predicts amotivation and functional impairment. *Journal of Abnormal Psychology, 123*(2), 387–397.

Bègue, I., Blakemore, R., Klug, J., Cojan, J., Galli, S., Berney, A., Aybek, S., Vuilleumier, P. (2018) Metacognition of visuomotor decisions in conversion disorder. *Neuropsychologia, 114*, 251–265.

Bègue, I., Vaessen, M., Hofmeister, J., Pereira, M., Schwartz, S., Vuilleumier, P. (2019). Confidence of emotion expression recognition recruits brain regions outside the face perception network. *Social Cognitive and Affective Neuroscience, 14*(1), 81–95.

Bègue, I., Brakowski, J., Seifritz, E., Dagher, A., Tobler, P. N., Kirschner, M., & Kaiser, S. (2022). Cerebellar and cortico-striatal-midbrain contributions to reward-cognition processes and apathy within the psychosis continuum. *Schizophrenia Research.* 246, 85–94.

Bègue, I., Kaiser, S., & Kirschner, M. (2020). Pathophysiology of negative symptom dimensions of schizophrenia—Current developments and implications for treatment. *Neuroscience & Biobehavioral Reviews, 116*, 74–88.

Bobes, J., Arango, C., Garcia-Garcia, M., Rejas, J., & CLAMORS Study Collaborative Group. (2010). Prevalence of negative symptoms in outpatients with schizophrenia spectrum disorders treated with antipsychotics in routine clinical practice: Findings from the CLAMORS study. *The Journal of Clinical Psychiatry, 71*(3), 280–286.

Borda, J. P., & Sass, L. A. (2015). Phenomenology and neurobiology of self disorder in schizophrenia: Primary factors. *Schizophrenia Research, 169*(1), 464–473.

Bortolon, C., Macgregor, A., Capdevielle, D., & Raffard, S. (2018). Apathy in schizophrenia: A review of neuropsychological and neuroanatomical studies. *Neuropsychologia, 118*, 22–33.

Campellone, Timothy R et al. (2016). Defeatist Performance Beliefs, Negative Symptoms, and Functional Outcome in Schizophrenia: A Meta-analytic Review. *Schizophrenia Bulletin, 42*(6), 1343–1352.

Cella, M., Bishara, A. J., Medin, E., Swan, S., Reeder, C., & Wykes, T. (2014). Identifying cognitive remediation change through computational modelling—Effects on reinforcement learning in schizophrenia. *Schizophrenia Bulletin, 40*(6), 1422–1432.

Cella, M., Preti, A., Edwards, C., Dow, T., & Wykes, T. (2017). Cognitive remediation for negative symptoms of schizophrenia: A network meta-analysis. *Clinical Psychology Review, 52*, 43–51.

Chang, W. C., Kwong, V. W. Y., Or Chi Fai, P., Lau, E. S. K., Chan, G. H. K., Jim, O. T. T., Hui, C. L. M., Chan, S. K. W., Lee, E. H. M., & Chen, E. Y. H. (2018). Motivational impairment predicts functional remission in first-episode psychosis: 3-Year follow-up of the randomized controlled trial on extended early intervention. *Australian & New Zealand Journal of Psychiatry, 52*(12), 1194–1201.

Chang, W. C., Westbrook, A., Strauss, G. P., Chu, A. O. K., Chong, C. S. Y., Siu, C. M. W., Chan, S. K. W., Lee, E. H. M., Hui, C. L. M., Suen, Y. M., Lo, T. L., & Chen, E. Y. H. (2020). Abnormal cognitive effort allocation and its association with amotivation in first-episode psychosis. *Psychological Medicine, 50*(15), 2599–2609.

Clay, K. B., Raugh, I. M., Bartolomeo, L. A., & Strauss, G. P. (2021). Defeatist performance beliefs in individuals at clinical high-risk for psychosis and outpatients with chronic schizophrenia. *Early Intervention in Psychiatry, 15*(4), 865–873.

Cohen, A. S., Cowan, T., Le, T. P., Schwartz, E. K., Kirkpatrick, B., Raugh, I. M., Chapman, H. C., & Strauss, G. P. (2020). Ambulatory digital phenotyping of blunted affect and alogia using objective facial and vocal analysis: Proof of concept. *Schizophrenia Research, 220*, 141–146.

Cohen, A. S., McGovern, J. E., Dinzeo, T. J., & Covington, M. A. (2014). Speech deficits in serious mental illness: A cognitive resource issue? *Schizophrenia Research, 160*(1–3), 173–179.

Cohen, A. S., Morrison, S. C., Brown, L. A., & Minor, K. S. (2012). Towards a cognitive resource limitations model of diminished expression in schizotypy. *Journal of Abnormal Psychology, 121*(1), 109–118.

Cohen, A. S., Schwartz, E., Le, T. P., Cowan, T., Kirkpatrick, B., Raugh, I. M., & Strauss, G. P. (2021). Digital phenotyping of negative symptoms: The relationship to clinician ratings. *Schizophrenia Bulletin, 47*(1), 44–53.

Collo, G., Mucci, A., Giordano, G. M., Merlo Pich, E., & Galderisi, S. (2020). Negative symptoms of schizophrenia and dopaminergic transmission: Translational models and perspectives opened by iPSC techniques. *Frontiers in Neuroscience, 14*, 632.

Crawford, M. J., Killaspy, H., Barnes, T. R. E., Barrett, B., Byford, S., Clayton, K., Dinsmore, J., Floyd, S., Hoadley, A., Johnson, T., Kalaitzaki, E., King, M., Leurent, B., Maratos, A., O'Neill, F. A., Osborn, D. P., Patterson, S., Soteriou, T., Tyrer, P., & Waller, D. (2012). Group art therapy as an adjunctive treatment for people with schizophrenia: Multicentre pragmatic randomised trial. *BMJ, 344*, e846.

Culbreth, A. J., Moran, E. K., Kandala, S., Westbrook, A., & Barch, D. M. (2020). Effort, avolition, and motivational experience in schizophrenia: Analysis of behavioral and neuroimaging data with relationships to daily motivational experience. *Clinical Psychological Science, 8*(3), 555–568.

Culbreth, A., Westbrook, A., & Barch, D. (2016). Negative symptoms are associated with an increased subjective cost of cognitive effort. *Journal of Abnormal Psychology, 125*(4), 528–536.

Docherty, A. R., Berenbaum, H., & Kerns, J. G. (2011). Alogia and formal thought disorder: Differential patterns of verbal fluency task performance. *Journal of Psychiatric Research, 45*(10), 1352–1357.

Dowd, E. C., Frank, M. J., Collins, A., Gold, J. M., & Barch, D. M. (2016). Probabilistic Reinforcement Learning in Patients With Schizophrenia: Relationships to Anhedonia and Avolition. *Biological Psychiatry: Cognitive Neuroscience and Neuroimaging, 1*(5), 460–473.

Faerden, A., Vaskinn, A., Finset, A., Agartz, I., Ann Barrett, E., Friis, S., Simonsen, C., Andreassen, O. A., & Melle, I. (2009). Apathy is associated with executive functioning in first episode psychosis. *BMC Psychiatry, 9*, 1.

Favrod, J., Nguyen, A., Chaix, J., Pellet, J., Frobert, L., Fankhauser, C., Ismailaj, A., Brana, A., Tamic, G., Suter, C., Rexhaj, S., Golay, P., & Bonsack, C. (2019). Improving pleasure and motivation in schizophrenia: A randomized controlled clinical trial. *Psychotherapy and Psychosomatics, 88*(2), 84–95.

Favrod, J., Nguyen, A., Fankhauser, C., Ismailaj, A., Hasler, J. D., Ringuet, A., Rexhaj, S., & Bonsack, C. (2015). Positive Emotions Program for Schizophrenia (PEPS): A pilot intervention to reduce anhedonia and apathy. *BMC Psychiatry, 15*, 231.

Favrod, J., Nguyen, A., Tronche, A.-M., Blanc, O., Dubreucq, J., Chereau-Boudet, I., Capdevielle, D., & Llorca, P. M. (2019). Impact of positive emotion regulation training on negative symptoms and social functioning in schizophrenia: A field test. *Frontiers in Psychiatry, 10*, 532.

Fervaha, G., Foussias, G., Agid, O., & Remington, G. (2014). Motivational and neurocognitive deficits are central to the prediction of longitudinal functional outcome in schizophrenia. *Acta Psychiatrica Scandinavica, 130*(4), 290–299.

Foussias, G., Agid, O., Fervaha, G., & Remington, G. (2014). Negative symptoms of schizophrenia: Clinical features, relevance to real world functioning and specificity versus other CNS disorders. *European Neuropsychopharmacology, 24*(5), 693–709.

Foussias, G., Siddiqui, I., Fervaha, G., Mann, S., McDonald, K., Agid, O., Zakzanis, K. K., & Remington, G. (2015). Motivated to do well: An examination of the relationships between motivation, effort, and cognitive performance in schizophrenia. *Schizophrenia Research, 166*(1), 276–282.

Frith, C.D. (2012). The role of metacognition in human social interactions. *Philosophical Transactions of the Royal Society London Series B: Biological Sciences, 367*(1599), 2213–2223.

Galderisi, S., Kaiser, S., Bitter, I., Nordentoft, M., Mucci, A., Sabé, M., Giordano, G. M., Nielsen, M. Ø., Glenthøj, L. B., Pezzella, P., Falkai, P., Dollfus, S., & Gaebel, W. (2021). EPA guidance on treatment of negative symptoms in schizophrenia. *European Psychiatry, 64*(1), e21.

Galderisi, S., Merlotti, E., & Mucci, A. (2015). Neurobiological background of negative symptoms. *European Archives of Psychiatry and Clinical Neuroscience, 265*(7), 543–558.

Galderisi, S., Mucci, A., Bitter, I., Libiger, J., Bucci, P., Fleischhacker, W. W., Kahn, R. S., & Eufest Study, G. (2013). Persistent negative symptoms in first episode patients with schizophrenia: Results from the European First Episode Schizophrenia Trial. *European Neuropsychopharmacology, 23*(3), 196–204.

Galderisi, S., Mucci, A., Buchanan, R. W., & Arango, C. (2018). Negative symptoms of schizophrenia: New developments and unanswered research questions. *The Lancet Psychiatry, 5*(8), 664–677.

Galderisi, S., Mucci, A., Dollfus, S., Nordentoft, M., Falkai, P., Kaiser, S., Giordano, G. M., Vandevelde, A., Nielsen, M. Ø., Glenthøj, L. B., Sabé, M., Pezzella, P., Bitter, I., & Gaebel, W. (2021). EPA guidance on assessment of negative symptoms in schizophrenia. *European Psychiatry: The Journal of the Association of European Psychiatrists, 64*(1), e23.

Galderisi, S., Rossi, A., Rocca, P., Bertolino, A., Mucci, A., Bucci, P., Rucci, P., Gibertoni, D., Aguglia, E., Amore, M., Bellomo, A., Biondi, M., Brugnoli, R., Dell'Osso, L., De Ronchi, D., Di Emidio, G., Di Giannantonio, M., Fagiolini, A., Marchesi, C., . . . Italian Network For Research on, P. (2014). The influence of illness-related variables, personal resources and context-related factors on real-life functioning of people with schizophrenia. *World Psychiatry, 13*(3), 275–287.

Galderisi, S., Rucci, P., Kirkpatrick, B., Mucci, A., Gibertoni, D., Rocca, P., Rossi, A., Bertolino, A., Strauss, G. P., Aguglia, E., Bellomo, A., Murri, M. B., Bucci, P., Carpiniello, B., Comparelli, A., Cuomo, A., De Berardis, D., Dell'Osso, L., Di Fabio, F., . . . Italian Network for Research on Psychoses. (2018). Interplay among psychopathologic variables, personal resources, context-related factors, and real-life functioning in individuals with schizophrenia: A network analysis. *JAMA Psychiatry, 75*(4), 396–404.

García-Mieres, H., Lundin, N. B., Minor, K. S., Dimaggio, G., Popolo, R., Cheli, S., & Lysaker, P. H. (2020). A cognitive model of diminished expression in schizophrenia: The interface of metacognition, cognitive symptoms and language disturbances. *Journal of Psychiatric Research, 131*, 169–176.

Gaudelus, B., Virgile, J., Geliot, S., & Franck, N. (2016). Improving facial emotion recognition in schizophrenia: A controlled study comparing specific and attentional focused cognitive remediation. *Frontiers in Psychiatry, 7*, 105.

Goetz, Raymond R et al. (2007) Validity of a 'proxy' for the deficit syndrome derived from the Positive And Negative Syndrome Scale (PANSS). *Schizophrenia research, 93*(1–3): 169–177.

Gold, J. M., Barch, D. M., Feuerstahler, L. M., Carter, C. S., MacDonald, A. W., Ragland, J. D., Silverstein, S. M., Strauss, M. E., & Luck, S. J. (2019). Working memory impairment across psychotic disorders. *Schizophrenia Bulletin*, *45*(4), 804–812.

Gold, J. M., Strauss, G. P., Waltz, J. A., Robinson, B. M., Brown, J. K., & Frank, M. J. (2013). Negative symptoms of schizophrenia are associated with abnormal effort-cost computations. *Biological Psychiatry*, *74*(2), 130–136.

Gold, J. M., Waltz, J. A., Matveeva, T. M., Kasanova, Z., Strauss, G. P., Herbener, E. S., Collins, A. G., & Frank, M. J. (2012). Negative symptoms and the failure to represent the expected reward value of actions: Behavioral and computational modeling evidence. *Archives of General Psychiatry*, *69*(2), 129–138.

Grant, P. M., & Beck, A. T. (2009). Defeatist beliefs as a mediator of cognitive impairment, negative symptoms, and functioning in schizophrenia. *Schizophrenia Bulletin*, *35*(4), 798–806.

Grant, P. M., Huh, G. A., Perivoliotis, D., Stolar, N. M., Beck, A. T. (2012). Randomized trial to evaluate the efficacy of cognitive therapy for low-functioning patients with schizophrenia. *Arch. Gen. Psychiatry*, *69*, 121–127.

Gur, R. E., Kohler, C. G., Ragland, J. D., Siegel, S. J., Lesko, K., Bilker, W. B., & Gur, R. C. (2006). Flat affect in schizophrenia: Relation to emotion processing and neurocognitive measures. *Schizophrenia Bulletin*, *32*(2), 279–287.

Hartmann, M. N., Hager, O. M., Reimann, A. V., Chumbley, J. R., Kirschner, M., Seifritz, E., Tobler, P. N., & Kaiser, S. (2015). Apathy but not diminished expression in schizophrenia is associated with discounting of monetary rewards by physical effort. *Schizophrenia Bulletin*, *41*(2), 503–512.

Hartmann, M. N., Kluge, A., Kalis, A., Mojzisch, A., Tobler, P. N., & Kaiser, S. (2015). Apathy in schizophrenia as a deficit in the generation of options for action. *Journal of Abnormal Psychology*, *124*(2), 309–318.

Hartmann-Riemer, M., Kirschner, M., & Kaiser, S. (2018). Effort-based decision-making paradigms as objective measures of apathy in schizophrenia? *Current Opinion in Behavioral Sciences*, *22*, 70–75.

Hartmann-Riemer, M. N., Aschenbrenner, S., Bossert, M., Westermann, C., Seifritz, E., Tobler, P. N., Weisbrod, M., & Kaiser, S. (2017). Deficits in reinforcement learning but no link to apathy in patients with schizophrenia. *Scientific Reports*, *7*(1), Art. 1.

Hartmann-Riemer, M. N., Hager, O. M., Kirschner, M., Bischof, M., Kluge, A., Seifritz, E., & Kaiser, S. (2015). The association of neurocognitive impairment with diminished expression and apathy in schizophrenia. *Schizophrenia Research*, *169*(1–3), 427–C.

Henson, P., Barnett, I., Keshavan, M., & Torous, J. (2020). Towards clinically actionable digital phenotyping targets in schizophrenia. *Npj Schizophrenia*, *6*(1), Art. 1.

Hernaus, D., Frank, M. J., Brown, E. C., Brown, J. K., Gold, J. M., & Waltz, J. A. (2019). Impaired expected value computations in schizophrenia are associated with a reduced ability to integrate reward probability and magnitude of recent outcomes. *Biological Psychiatry: Cognitive Neuroscience and Neuroimaging*, *4*(3), 280–290.

Hernaus, D., Gold, J. M., Waltz, J. A., & Frank, M. J. (2018). Impaired expected value computations coupled with overreliance on stimulus-response learning in schizophrenia. *Biological Psychiatry: Cognitive Neuroscience and Neuroimaging*, *3*(11), 916–926.

Husain, M., & Roiser, J. P. (2018). Neuroscience of apathy and anhedonia: A transdiagnostic approach. *Nature Reviews Neuroscience*, *19*(8), 470–484.

Inchausti, F., García-Poveda, N. V., Ballesteros-Prados, A., Ortuño-Sierra, J., Sánchez-Reales, S., Prado-Abril, J., Aldaz-Armendáriz, J. A., Mole, J., Dimaggio, G., Ottavi, P., & Fonseca-Pedrero, E. (2018). The effects of metacognition-oriented social skills training on psychosocial outcome in schizophrenia-spectrum disorders: A randomized controlled trial. *Schizophrenia Bulletin*, *44*(6), 1235–1244.

Joyal, M., Bonneau, A., & Fecteau, S. (2016). Speech and language therapies to improve pragmatics and discourse skills in patients with schizophrenia. *Psychiatry Research, 240*, 88–95.

Joyce, E. M., Collinson, S. L., & Crichton, P. (1996). Verbal fluency in schizophrenia: Relationship with executive function, semantic memory and clinical alogia. *Psychological Medicine, 26*(1), 39–49.

Kalis, A., Kaiser, S., & Mojzisch, A. (2013). Why we should talk about option generation in decision-making research. *Frontiers in Psychology, 4*, 555.

Kerr, S. L., & Neale, J. M. (1993). Emotion perception in schizophrenia: Specific deficit or further evidence of generalized poor performance? *Journal of Abnormal Psychology, 102*(2), 312–318.

Kirkpatrick, B., Fenton, W. S., Carpenter, W. T., & Marder, S. R. (2006). The NIMH-MATRICS consensus statement on negative symptoms. *Schizophrenia Bulletin, 32*(2), 214–219.

Kirkpatrick, B., Mucci, A., & Galderisi, S. (2017). Primary, enduring negative symptoms: An update on research. *Schizophrenia Bulletin, 43*(4), 730–736.

Kirschner, M., Aleman, A., & Kaiser, S. (2017). Secondary negative symptoms—A review of mechanisms, assessment and treatment. *Schizophrenia Research, 186*, 29–38.

Kirschner, M., Hager, O. M., Bischof, M., Hartmann, M. N., Kluge, A., Seifritz, E., Tobler, P. N., & Kaiser, S. (2015). Ventral striatal hypoactivation is associated with apathy but not diminished expression in patients with schizophrenia. *Journal of Psychiatry and Neuroscience, 40*(5), 140383.

Klingberg, S., Wölwer, W., Engel, C., Wittorf, A., Herrlich, J., Meisner, C., Buchkremer, G., & Wiedemann, G. (2011). Negative symptoms of schizophrenia as primary target of cognitive behavioral therapy: Results of the randomized clinical TONES study. *Schizophrenia Bulletin, 37*(suppl_2), S98–S110.

Kohler, C. G., Walker, J. B., Martin, E. A., Healey, K. M., & Moberg, P. J. (2010). Facial emotion perception in schizophrenia: A meta-analytic review. *Schizophrenia Bulletin, 36*(5), 1009–1019.

Kring, A. M., & Elis, O. (2013). Emotion deficits in people with schizophrenia. *Annual Review of Clinical Psychology, 9*, 409–433.

Leder, J., Häusser, J. A., Krumm, S., Germar, M., Schlemmer, A., Kaiser, S., Kalis, A., & Mojzisch, A. (2018). The cognitive underpinnings of option generation in everyday life decision-making: A latent variable analysis. *Cognitive Science, 42*(8), 2562–2591.

Lee, J. S., Chun, J. W., Yoon, S. Y., Park, H. J., & Kim, J. J. (2014). Involvement of the mirror neuron system in blunted affect in schizophrenia. *Schizophrenia Research, 152*(1), 268–274.

Lepage, M., Sergerie, K., Benoit, A., Czechowska, Y., Dickie, E., & Armony, J. L. (2011). Emotional face processing and flat affect in schizophrenia: Functional and structural neural correlates. *Psychological Medicine, 41*(9), 1833–1844.

Lincoln, T. M., Dollfus, S., & Lyne, J. (2017). Current developments and challenges in the assessment of negative symptoms. *Schizophrenia Research, 186*, 8–18.

Lundin, N. B., Hochheiser, J., Minor, K. S., Hetrick, W. P., & Lysaker, P. H. (2020). Piecing together fragments: Linguistic cohesion mediates the relationship between executive function and metacognition in schizophrenia. *Schizophrenia Research, 215*, 54–60.

Luther, L., Salyers, M. P., Firmin, R. L., Marggraf, M. P., Davis, B., & Minor, K. S. (2016). Additional support for the cognitive model of schizophrenia: Evidence of elevated defeatist beliefs in schizotypy. *Comprehensive Psychiatry, 68*, 40–47.

Lyne, J., O'Donoghue, B., Owens, E., Renwick, L., Madigan, K., Kinsella, A., Clarke, M., Turner, N., & O'Callaghan, E. (2012). Prevalence of item level negative symptoms in first episode psychosis diagnoses. *Schizophrenia Research, 135*(1–3), 128–133.

Lyne, J., Renwick, L., O'Donoghue, B., Kinsella, A., Malone, K., Turner, N., O'Callaghan, E., & Clarke, M. (2015). Negative symptom domain prevalence across diagnostic boundaries: The relevance of diagnostic shifts. *Psychiatry Research, 228*(3), 347–354.

Lysaker, P. H., Chernov, N., Moiseeva, T., Sozinova, M., Dmitryeva, N., Alyoshin, V., Faith, L. A., Karpenko, O., & Kostyuk, G. (2020). Contrasting metacognitive profiles and their association with negative symptoms in groups with schizophrenia, early psychosis and depression in a Russian sample. *Psychiatry Research, 291*, 113177.

Lysaker, P. H., Minor, K. S., Lysaker, J. T., Hasson-Ohayon, I., Bonfils, K., Hochheiser, J., & Vohs, J. L. (2020). Metacognitive function and fragmentation in schizophrenia: Relationship to cognition, self-experience and developing treatments. *Schizophrenia Research: Cognition, 19*, 100142.

Maia, T. V., & Frank, M. J. (2017). An integrative perspective on the role of dopamine in schizophrenia. *Biological Psychiatry, 81*(1), 52–66.

Marsh, P. J., Polito, V., Singh, S., Coltheart, M., Langdon, R., & Harris, A. W. (2016). A quasi-randomized feasibility pilot study of specific treatments to improve emotion recognition and mental-state reasoning impairments in schizophrenia. *BMC Psychiatry, 16*(1), 360.

Moran, E. K., Culbreth, A. J., Kandala, S., & Barch, D. M. (2019). From neuroimaging to daily functioning: A multimethod analysis of reward anticipation in people with schizophrenia. *Journal of Abnormal Psychology, 128*(7), 723–734.

Mørch-Johnsen, L., Agartz, I., & Jensen, J. (2018). The neural correlates of negative symptoms in schizophrenia: Examples from MRI literature. *Clinical EEG and Neuroscience, 49*(1), 12–17.

Priebe, S., Savill, M., Wykes, T., Bentall, R. P., Reininghaus, U., Lauber, C., Bremner, S., Eldridge, S., & Röhricht, F. (2016). Effectiveness of group body psychotherapy for negative symptoms of schizophrenia: Multicentre randomised controlled trial. *The British Journal of Psychiatry, 209*(1), 54–61.

Rabinowitz, J., Levine, S. Z., Garibaldi, G., Bugarski-Kirola, D., Berardo, C. G., & Kapur, S. (2012). Negative symptoms have greater impact on functioning than positive symptoms in schizophrenia: Analysis of CATIE data. *Schizophrenia Research, 137*(1–3), 147–150.

Radua, J., Schmidt, A., Borgwardt, S., Heinz, A., Schlagenhauf, F., McGuire, P., & Fusar-Poli, P. (2015). Ventral striatal activation during reward processing in psychosis: A neurofunctional meta-analysis. *JAMA Psychiatry, 72*(12), 1243–1251.

Raffard, S., Gutierrez, L.-A., Yazbek, H., Larue, A., Boulenger, J.-P., Lançon, C., Benoit, M., Faget, C., Norton, J., & Capdevielle, D. (2016). Working memory deficit as a risk factor for severe apathy in schizophrenia: A 1-year longitudinal study. *Schizophrenia Bulletin, 42*(3), 642–651.

Rus-Calafell, M., Gutiérrez-Maldonado, J., Ortega-Bravo, M., Ribas-Sabaté, J., & Caqueo-Urízar, A. (2013). A brief cognitive-behavioural social skills training for stabilised outpatients with schizophrenia: A preliminary study. *Schizophrenia Research, 143*(2), 327–336.

Savill, M., Banks, C., Khanom, H., & Priebe, S. (2015). Do negative symptoms of schizophrenia change over time? A meta-analysis of longitudinal data. *Psychological Medicine, 45*(8), 1613–1627.

Sevos, J., Grosselin, A., Gauthier, M., Carmona, F., Gay, A., & Massoubre, C. (2018). Cinemotion, a program of cognitive remediation to improve the recognition and expression of facial emotions in schizophrenia: A pilot study. *Frontiers in Psychiatry, 9*, 312.

Sevy, S., Lindenmayer, J.-P., Khan, A., Ljuri, I., Kulsa, M. K. C., & Jones, O. (2020). Differential improvement of negative-symptom subfactors after cognitive remediation in low functioning individuals with schizophrenia. *Schizophrenia Research: Cognition, 19*, 100145.

Sicras-Mainar, A., Maurino, J., Ruiz-Beato, E., & Navarro-Artieda, R. (2014). Impact of negative symptoms on healthcare resource utilization and associated costs in adult outpatients with schizophrenia: A population-based study. *BMC Psychiatry, 14*, 225.

Simon, J. J., Biller, A., Walther, S., Roesch-Ely, D., Stippich, C., Weisbrod, M., & Kaiser, S. (2010). Neural correlates of reward processing in schizophrenia—Relationship to apathy and depression. *Schizophrenia Research, 118*(1–3), 154–161.

Simon, J. J., Cordeiro, S. A., Weber, M. A., Friederich, H. C., Wolf, R. C., Weisbrod, M., & Kaiser, S. (2015). Reward system dysfunction as a neural substrate of symptom expression across the general population and patients with schizophrenia. *Schizophrenia Bulletin, 41*(6):1370–1378.

Staring, A. B., Ter Huurne, M. A. B., & van der Gaag, M. (2013). Cognitive Behavioral Therapy for negative symptoms (CBT-n) in psychotic disorders: a pilot study. *Journal of behavior therapy and experimental psychiatry, 44*(3), 300–306.

Stepien, M., Manoliu, A., Kubli, R., Schneider, K., Tobler, P. N., Seifritz, E., Herdener, M., Kaiser, S., & Kirschner, M. (2018). Investigating the association of ventral and dorsal striatal dysfunction during reward anticipation with negative symptoms in patients with schizophrenia and healthy individuals. *PLoS One, 13*(6), e0198215.

Strauss, G. P., Horan, W. P., Kirkpatrick, B., Fischer, B. A., Keller, W. R., Miski, P., Buchanan, R. W., Green, M. F., & Carpenter, W. T. (2013). Deconstructing negative symptoms of schizophrenia: Avolition-apathy and diminished expression clusters predict clinical presentation and functional outcome. *Journal of Psychiatric Research, 47*(6), 783–790.

Strauss, Gregory P. (2014) et al. A review of reward processing and motivational impairment in schizophrenia. *Schizophrenia bulletin, 40*(2), Suppl 2: S107-S116.

Strauss, G. P., Whearty, K. M., Morra, L. F., Sullivan, S. K., Ossenfort, K. L., & Frost, K. H. (2016). Avolition in schizophrenia is associated with reduced willingness to expend effort for reward on a Progressive Ratio task. *Schizophrenia Research, 170*(1), 198–204.

Sumiyoshi, C., Sumiyoshi, T., Nohara, S., Yamashita, I., Matsui, M., Kurachi, M., & Niwa, S. (2005). Disorganization of semantic memory underlies alogia in schizophrenia: An analysis of verbal fluency performance in Japanese subjects. *Schizophrenia Research, 74*(1), 91–100.

Szkultecka-Dębek, M., Walczak, J., Augustyńska, J., Miernik, K., Stelmachowski, J., Pieniążek, I., Obrzut, G., Pogroszewska, A., Paulić, G., Damir, M., Antolić, S., Tavčar, R., Indrikson, A., Aadamsoo, K., Jankovic, S., Pulay, A. J., Rimay, J., Varga, M., Sulkova, I., & Veržun, P. (2015). Epidemiology and treatment guidelines of negative symptoms in schizo-phrenia in central and eastern Europe: A literature review. *Clinical Practice and Epidemiology in Mental Health: CP & EMH, 11*, 158–165.

Trémeau, F. (2006). A review of emotion deficits in schizophrenia. *Dialogues in Clinical Neuroscience, 8*(1), 59–70.

Trémeau, F., Malaspina, D., Duval, F., Corrêa, H., Hager-Budny, M., Coin-Bariou, L., Macher, J.-P., & Gorman, J. M. (2005). Facial expressiveness in patients with schizophrenia compared to depressed patients and nonpatient comparison subjects. *American Journal of Psychiatry, 162*(1), 92–101.

Tron, T., Peled, A., Grinsphoon, A., & Weinshall, D. (2016). Facial expressions and flat affect in schizophrenia, automatic analysis from depth camera data. *2016 IEEE-EMBS International Conference on Biomedical and Health Informatics (BHI), 2016*, 220–223.

Turner, D. T., van der Gaag, M., Karyotaki, E., & Cuijpers, P. (2014). Psychological interventions for psychosis: A meta-analysis of comparative outcome studies. *American Journal of Psychiatry, 171*(5), 523–538.

Varcin, K. J., Bailey, P. E., & Henry, J. D. (2010). Empathic deficits in schizophrenia: The potential role of rapid facial mimicry. *Journal of the International Neuropsychological Society, 16*(4), 621–629.

Velligan, D. I., Roberts, D., Mintz, J., Maples, N., Li, X. Medellin, E. Brown, M. (2015) A. randomized pilot study of MOtiVation and Enhancement (MOVE) Training for negative symptoms in schizophrenia. *Schizophrenia Research, 165*, 175–180.

Ventura, J., Subotnik, K. L., Gretchen-Doorly, D., Casaus, L., Boucher, M., Medalia, A., Bell, M. D., Hellemann, G. S., & Nuechterlein, K. H. (2019). Cognitive remediation can improve negative symptoms and social functioning in first-episode schizophrenia: A randomized controlled trial. *Schizophrenia Research, 203*, 24–31.

Waltz, J. A., Frank, M. J., Robinson, B. M., & Gold, J. M. (2007). Selective reinforcement learning deficits in schizophrenia support predictions from computational models of striatal-cortical dysfunction. *Biological Psychiatry: Cognitive Neuroscience and Neuroimaging*, *62*(7), 756–764.

Waltz, J. A., & Gold, J. M. (2016). Motivational deficits in schizophrenia and the representation of expected value. In E. H. Simpson & P. D. Balsam (Éds.), *Behavioral neuroscience of motivation* (pp. 375–410). Springer International Publishing.

Waltz, J. A., Schweitzer, J. B., Ross, T. J., Kurup, P. K., Salmeron, B. J., Rose, E. J., Gold, J. M., & Stein, E. A. (2010). Abnormal responses to monetary outcomes in cortex, but not in the basal ganglia, in schizophrenia. *Neuropsychopharmacology*, *35*(12), 2427–2439.

Waltz, J. A., Xu, Z., Brown, E. C., Ruiz, R. R., Frank, M. J., & Gold, J. M. (2018). Motivational deficits in schizophrenia are associated with reduced differentiation between gain and loss-avoidance feedback in the striatum. *Biological Psychiatry: Cognitive Neuroscience and Neuroimaging*, *3*(3), 239–247.

Wolf, D. H., Satterthwaite, T. D., Kantrowitz, J. J., Katchmar, N., Vandekar, L., Elliott, M. A., & Ruparel, K. (2014). Amotivation in schizophrenia: Integrated assessment with behavioral, clinical, and imaging measures. *Schizophrenia Bulletin*, *40*(6), 1328–1337.

Wölwer, W., & Frommann, N. (2011). Social-cognitive remediation in schizophrenia: Generalization of effects of the Training of Affect Recognition (TAR). *Schizophrenia Bulletin*, *37*(suppl_2), S63–S70.

Yilmaz, A., Simsek, F., & Gonul, A. S. (2012). Reduced reward-related probability learning in schizophrenia patients. *Neuropsychiatric Disease and Treatment*, *8*, 27–34.

4

Black Sun

A First-Person Account of "Negative Symptoms"

Anonymous

It wasn't like I just woke up one morning, "unmotivated" to shower or eat or do anything more than stare at the shadows on the wall. It was a journey. It was, in large part, the inexorable slow motion collapse of a tower of dominos. (That was my life.) There was the diagnosis (schizophrenia). There was the mind-fuck journey of googling schizophrenia, reading about schizophrenia; scrolling through page after page of medical tutorials, psychoeducation, journal article abstracts all saying the same thing: A chronic brain disease; a "devastating illness." "Requires lifelong medical treatment" the Mayo Clinic website tells us, still now; "a serious mental disorder in which people interpret reality abnormally." Healthline defines negative symptoms as "the absence of things present in most people. This includes things such as facial expressions, emotional response, and interest in the world." Everything that is normal is not "schizophrenia." Everything the world desires us to be.

On the social side, friends scatter like animals before an earthquake. Sensing that something is wrong, and something that leaves only discomfort. They're gone. What replaces them: psychiatrists, nurses, clinicians, case managers. One is no longer a person, really. One is thing-ified. You go to your appointments, sometimes you're hospitalized. Every last person you see is paid to talk to you, paid to ask checklist questions, paid to suggest more medications. Like your so called friends, everything that once mattered—school, careers, a family—either evaporates or fades. All these ideas you once had about yourself and your future; memories of the way that people used to talk to you. You miss them, you feel so much pain, also anger. At least at first. But nothing changes; nothing is going to change. Weeks turn into months turn into years. Change is a lie. Even the emotions make it all worse. The past will never come back.

There are so many reasons that the mind then begins to play tricks on you (tricks or defenses?): There's no reason to live. Really there isn't. All the different means of suicide play out a hundred thousand times in your head. The train a few blocks away; lying there on the hot rusty tracks, waiting. The bridges, the tall

Anonymous, *Black Sun*. In: *Psychosocial Approaches to Negative Symptoms in Psychosis*. Edited by: Tania Lincoln, et al., Oxford University Press. © Oxford University Press (2025). DOI: 10.1093/oso/9780197676790.003.0004 buildings. Jumping into the lake, off a pier. Over and over how amazing it would be to never again have to wake up to so much shame and brokenness. All those people who once upon a time said you'd be great, you'd do great things. You just can't live down how wrong they were. The images of death become a new kind of friend, a source of comfort. While you just "stare at the wall" during your appointments, while you're "unmotivated" to do anything, you're "disheveled," you're not "displaying appropriate emotions." Because you're somewhere else, free in your mind, waiting or already dead on those tracks. And who the fuck therefore cares about the clinicians, the questions, the treatment plan. Above all, your mind is desperate to escape it all. To keep your body alive, I suppose.

While they're there, explaining "negative symptoms," explaining that it's a "feature of the illness" (just like lack of insight, while *you* know that you've actually been buried alive by the pain of it all), and you don't blink. You stare at the floor. You dissolve into the arms of the chair. Now you're outside, in that tree, literally you flowed there.

Does it actually matter if you shower? No. Does it matter if you eat? No. Does it matter if you "take care of yourself"? No. Death is one outlet; "delusions"—what they call delusions—are another. Because there's another world where you are something—they want you dead, but that's something. That's something that's not a clinician paid to talk to you, that's not a psychiatrist paid to medicate you, that's not a nurse taking blood samples, blood samples, because you're on clozapine, because you have negative symptoms, because you're treatment resistant. Because it's been two years, three years, and you're "not improving." "We have to try other things. We want to help you. And it doesn't actually matter that those other things are vacant—clozapine, a temp job stuffing envelopes. They really mean well. They're trying to help. And they have no idea what's actually going on.

Back to the "delusions"—other worlds are better. And you know what? They unfold behind the "vacant" stare. The clinicians think that you not saying anything means you're not thinking, not experiencing. You are, but you've left them. And there's no point to talk about it. Endless useless therapy. Endless useless questions. There is in fact no reason to engage anymore.

But behind the walls, those other worlds open up. There are plots, conspiracies. The nature of reality bends. Surfaces that are supposed to be solid are porous. You just flow out from your hands, stuck in those waiting room chairs, your hands flow into the plastic, into the multicolored washable clinic carpeting. And those fragments of color, crystallize as a different, parallel universe. The clinicians are still there because they're pawns, in a way, they are pawns in a different kind of cosmic experiment. Do they know it or not? You spend a long time thinking about this. Do they know what they actually are? And maybe they're not human after all, all the assumptions being possibly entirely wrong. A deception in a deception. A Truman Show. While you're thinking all these things, flying, sinking, a fragment of a poem by Paul Celan—"So Many Constellations"—comes to mind:

> *. . . sometimes,*
> *comet-like an eye whizzed*
> *toward extinguished matter, in the canyons,*
> *there where it burned out, stood*
> *tit-gorgeous time, along*
> *which grew up and down*
> *& away what*
> *is or was or will be—*

Celan, Celan who killed himself in the Seine. Drowned. Because of death and human destruction—the murder of his parents, the Holocaust—that he could never get away from. You—you're trying. Your mind is trying. Is desperate to go somewhere else. Anywhere but here. To save your body, actually.

"Sophie," are you listening? "No." Or maybe you say nothing. Fire in the crystals in the rug. That's where you are—in those constellations. But you say nothing. You don't want to say anything. You don't want to talk. You want none of it.

***

I was hospitalized once for "alogia" (and being disheveled and "self-neglect"); another time a crisis team was called in. I was stuck, I would get stuck—that part is true, not a clinical fiction. Words just wouldn't come. Why the words wouldn't come—that's a real question. That's the real question, maybe even. And I think I'm going to stop there. But I will say—not for one fleeting moment did the label of negative symptoms or cognitive deficits or any of that help. The motivational interviewing, the CBTp, the "baby steps back" to school/work. Instead, I wanted to scream a thousand times "fuck all that." "Fuck you" to the motivational interviewers. But I never said it. I never said anything. Just sat there in those chairs, with their plasticized upholstery, while well-intentioned clinicians tried to help, using the tools they had, coming to the conclusions they came to. Having been taught what they'd been taught. I said nothing.

5

My Personal Experience of Negative Symptoms

Lumi Winterson

When people talk about schizophrenia and psychosis, they usually think of symptoms such as hearing voices, having delusions, or experiencing paranoia. These are what are known as "positive symptoms." There is another group of symptoms called "negative symptoms." They are probably more common, but less talked about and even less understood by the general population. With positive symptoms, we see an increase in the experience, such as hearing voices. With negative symptoms, it is usually a lack of something that is causing the experience. There are many of these symptoms, but they can include a lack of speech or thought processes, a lack of emotion and/or affect, lack of interest or joy in anything around an individual, lack of motivation in social activities, and inability to act spontaneously.

You would think that hearing voices or having delusions would be the hardest thing to deal with in psychosis, but for me the negative symptoms have been a lot more debilitating than the positive ones. Being unable to find joy or pleasure from anything gets very tedious after a while, it wears one down until there seems to be little left to live for.

I have schizoaffective disorder and was diagnosed at 19 years of age. Although the first symptoms I experienced were rapid cycling mood swings, I also suffered from the negative symptoms of psychosis. These are hard to differentiate from the depression as they look very similar, and the symptoms can overlap somewhat. It was only when I became very unwell that I experienced positive symptoms, such as delusions and hallucinations. Having lived with this disorder for 23 years, I would consider myself an expert by experience.

For me, there is a vicious cycle that occurs related to both my physical and mental health, side by side. The negative symptoms such as apathy, lack of motivation, and reduced social drive, affect my mood and can lead to depression. Further to this, my thought processes can become compromised, and I might find myself eating poorly, not engaging in exercise, and falling into a deep hole. This is exacerbated by the very lethargy and apathy that started the

Lumi Winterson, *My Personal Experience of Negative Symptoms*. In: *Psychosocial Approaches to Negative Symptoms in Psychosis*. Edited by: Tania Lincoln et al., Oxford University Press. © Oxford University Press (2025).
DOI: 10.1093/oso/9780197676790.003.0005

whole cycle in the first place, making it difficult to dig myself out of the poor mental health. The phenomenal effort involved in overcoming psychosis and its resulting effects needs to be understood further. And the overlapping of symptoms being shared by multiple diagnoses, makes the understanding a whole lot harder.

With negative symptoms of psychosis such as apathy and lack of motivation, it is easy enough to foresee a possible future with poor physical health. Add to this the side effects of many of the medications being prescribed, and you will very soon be looking at obesity and type 2 diabetes. Here again, I talk about the vicious cycle. It starts with apathy, which leads to inactivity, which leads to obesity, which leads to diabetes, leading to depression, and then back to apathy and so on. Apathy robs me of my desire to engage, which can result in social isolation and lethargy. Until you have both mental and physical health working side by side, life is like a carousel that you just can't get off.

Reduced social drive is also common in psychosis. I would become reclusive and hide from the world. The force that would normally have me spending time with my friends, engaging in enjoyable activities, or even going for a walk was lessened. I would limit myself to my apartment and decline all social invites. Social activities are an integral part of maintaining one's mental health, and yet these negative symptoms deny the person the energy needed to overcome feelings of hopelessness. This is another vicious web that psychosis likes to catch people in.

The negative symptoms experienced during psychosis vary from person to person. When I am in psychosis, one of the first things my psychiatrist notices are a look of anxiety on my face, a perplexed look, which she refers to as "scrunchy face." I have always thought that I was good at hiding my emotions, but apparently in psychosis, my face gives it away. This perplexed face reflects the confusion I am experiencing inside. I am beginning to experience both negative and positive symptoms, and I become unsure of what is real or not. It is a scary situation to be in, where I am lucid enough to know that things are not quite right, yet I am on my way down the rabbit hole faster than Alice.

The next thing I experience is what I call a "muddled head." It feels like my thoughts are hard to understand. I continue to lose all interest in everything that used to give me joy. I can't even do any artwork or play the piano, which would normally give me pleasure. The thought processes are just not working, as if the cogs in my brain have run out of oil to keep them moving smoothly. It upsets me that these creative outlets that usually support me are no longer available to me, that these colourful distractions which would normally help hold me up, have suddenly left. I feel numb and unable to express myself.

A common negative symptom of psychosis is a condition called alogia, sometimes called "poverty of thought and speech." Where there is poverty of thought, it is as though the mind were completely empty. There is nothing inside your head, just a black hole of darkness. Consequently, any speech that occurs is limited mainly to monosyllabic words. Sometimes, when the psychosis gets particularly bad, I find it hard to do anything at all. I lie in bed, or sit in a chair, and I cannot think of anything. I can interpret stimulus, I can understand language, I can tell where I am, but I am not able to engage or communicate properly. I understand what people are saying to me, but I can't necessarily compose meaning or words in order to answer. When I do answer, it does not make sense because the words that come out are jumbled. In my head they make some sense, but I do not seem to express the thoughts properly. When I try to, the lack of thought processes and speech are so strong that I begin to stutter. The whole thing is tiring, and my head again feels muddled. On several occasions when I was unable to express myself verbally, I would write down my thoughts on paper. Many clinicians who were looking after me at the time refused to read my notes. They thought that I was trying to get attention and didn't want to enable my behavior. This though could have had dangerous consequences. One such time, I felt like I was having a heart attack, and yet because the clinicians would not read my notes, I ended up getting the wrong medication. It's important for people to do all they can in an effort to communicate with the patient, no matter how frustrating it may be. It may not be the best way to get the point across, but at least the patient is doing what they can, and that needs to be acknowledged. When I am in this situation, one thing that really helps is my artwork and art therapy. It allows me to express what I am feeling inside when words won't do. I think that art bypasses the spoken and written language, it allows me to communicate using a different part of my brain, especially when I am nonverbal.

Another negative symptom sometimes experienced during psychosis is a lack of social contact. A person might find it hard to reach out physically to other people, to engage in social contact in the form of touching, hugging, or even acknowledging another's presence. This adds to feelings of isolation and loneliness, which in turn add to depression. Like I have said, the negative symptoms seem to affect me more than the positive ones, even when I am not in a deep psychosis. Most of the time, I am quick to think and am an intelligent person; however, even when I am relatively well, I still suffer the negative symptoms to some extent. In general, I do not find that much enjoyment out of things that would normally bring me joy, and I often find myself in a bit of a haze, a brain fog. I can't even do something as simple as read a book due to my poor concentration and working memory. This made studying at university as a mature-age student incredibly difficult and motivating myself to do anything at all productive made me feel stupid.

Being creative in any format has been exceptional in my recovery. I first connected with my creativity after being included in Art Therapy during one of my many hospitalizations. Although I have always liked art, music, and writing,

I had had bad experiences with my art teacher in high school and as a result I dropped out of art and refused to even pick up a pencil for many years afterward. In art therapy, I was given the opportunity to express myself through art without fear or judgment of those in a position of power. I didn't have to consider making a masterpiece, all that was asked of me was to express how I was feeling, whether it be with pencils, pens, paints, pastels, collage, whatever. I would not be judged.

As I continued with art therapy, I realized I had some talent, and was especially interested in crafts such as cross stitch, embroidery, crochet, and knitting. I found doing crafts very meditative, especially as I became better at it; it required less and less thought processes and left me able to relax. This was a powerful tool during my psychotic episodes, when I was suffering from the negative symptoms. I found solitude in my art and was able to express these feelings I was experiencing yet had so much difficulty verbalizing.

I also found writing to be therapeutic for me during the experiences of the negative symptoms. One form of writing that I found interesting to play with was called "Eraser Poetry." It is where you find an article in a magazine or an old book and with a pen, you mark over words that you don't want, leaving the article with just the words you have purposely left there. Following this, you can copy to a blank piece of paper all the words and sentences that were left, leaving you with an interesting piece of writing. I found this particularly helpful because although I wasn't really writing, I was able to somehow fit words together into a noteworthy piece of prose.

Although I play the piano, it has been years since I have seriously sat down to play. In hospital, we were also offered Music Therapy, and although I didn't find it exceptionally helpful, there were others who did, and it is for that reason that I write about it here. When experiencing negative symptoms of psychosis, I do find myself making a connection with the music that I listen to. My taste in music is varied, and I have many playlists put together for the sole purpose of feeling that connection with another person, especially when I can understand the meaning behind the lyrics.

Many different interventions are being offered these days for those experiencing negative symptoms of psychosis. For me, creativity and art are my saviors. They have pulled me out of the mud when nothing else, including meds, could touch me. Everyone has to find their own way to live with this illness, and what works for one person may not necessarily work for another. But I urge you to look with eyes wide open, because I am sure that as a consumer you will find your path, and as a carer/health professional you will learn more by listening to those you aim to help than you would from just reading a book.

It is my hope that what I have shared with you here will give you some insight into the complex nature of psychosis: While positive symptoms may be more visible to others, in my experience negative symptoms have just as great an impact. I can only tell you how I experience these symptoms, but everyone is unique, everyone is different. So do not be afraid to ask the questions you have in your head. It is only by communicating, having conversations, and asking questions for confirmation and advice, and by being honest and open that we will challenge the stigma, find the answers to unlocking the brain and unraveling the web of psychosis within.

6

Negative Symptoms

Meaning-Centered and Lived Perspectives

Marie Brown, Shannon Pagdon, and Nev Jones

Clinical pearls

- Clinicians may benefit from reframing their understanding of negative symptoms away from deficit models toward viewing these experiences as meaningful and purposeful phenomenon.
- It may be helpful to rename negative symptoms in nonclinical and experience-near language (e.g., alogia = silence; avolition = stillness).
- Negative symptoms may potentially be important forms of communication and may contain seeds of insight into a person's life history, social context, trauma history, and relationships.
- It can be helpful to formulate negative symptoms as embedded within a person's context (rather than existing solely within the isolated individual).
- It is okay to sit in silence with your client.
- Help family members reframe their understanding of negative symptoms as generative using imagery or metaphor (ecological—spring thaw, chrysalis and the butterfly) and storytelling (e.g., Tortoise and the Hair -"slowness"; The Six Swans—"alogia/silence").
- Connect negative symptoms to spiritual practices (if relevant to the individual and family).
- Be patient.

1. Introduction

The weeks, the months, or the years began to pass us by. Now our aging was no longer marked by the milestones of a year's accomplishments but rather by the numbing pain of successive failures. We tried and failed and tried and failed until it hurt too much to try anymore. Now when we left the hospital it was not a

Marie Brown, Shannon Pagdon, and Nev Jones, *Negative Symptoms*. In: *Psychosocial Approaches to Negative Symptoms in Psychosis*. Edited by: Tania Lincoln et al., Oxford University Press.
 DOI: 10.1093/oso/9780197676790.003.0006

> question of *whether we would* come back, but simply a question of *when* would we return. In a last, desperate attempt to protect ourselves we gave up. We gave up trying to get well. Giving up was a solution for us. It numbed the pain. We were willing to sacrifice enormous parts of ourselves in order to say, "I don't care." Our personhood continued to atrophy through this adaptive strategy of not caring anymore. And so we sat in chairs and smoked and drank coffee and smoked some more. It was a high price to pay for survival. We just gave up. And winter settled in upon us like a long cold anguish (Deegan, 1996, p.5).

An exception in a body of work dominated almost entirely by second-hand observation and theory, Pat Deegan's writing points us to a markedly different, experientially grounded understanding of "negative symptoms," or what are all too often taken to be them—a reflection of demoralization, engulfment, and psychological adaptation to life—and "chronicity"—at the margins of society. The standard, textbook definitions of "negative symptoms," explored throughout this edited volume, generally understands this construct to be multidimensional, spanning deficits or "deficiencies" in motivation (e.g., amotivation), language and communication (e.g., alogia), affect (e.g., blunted affect), and social functioning (e.g., social withdrawal). As operationalized in the research literature, these dimensions have in turn been strongly and consistently associated with worse functional outcomes. And yet—as Deegan's counter-narrative makes clear, critics of a deficit-oriented understanding are not necessarily disputing such outcomes or associations, but rather what is really behind them.

In contemporary psychiatry and psychological literature, negative symptoms are theorized as occurring within two domains: primary and secondary. Primary negative symptoms are thought to result from biological pathology, occurring as part of the disease process, whereas "secondary" negative symptoms are operationalized as reactions or responses to treatment (e.g., medication side effects) and/or social and psychological impacts of a diagnosis (social rejection leading to isolation; demoralization and depression stemming from the loss of structure and opportunities) (Kirschner et al. 2017). Within this literature, primary negative symptoms are consistently located at the level of the individual, involving both psychological deficits (e.g., maladaptive or self-defeating thoughts) and biological deficits, at the neglect of the social, political, and structural realities of people's lives.

In addition to the inevitable neglect of the extent to which social and structural conditions influence motivation and affect, mainstream theorizing regularly fail to call attention to the potential for the labeling of challenges of motivation, socialization, and connection as relatively fixed (primary) negative symptoms to negatively impact self-image and sense of self. Psychotherapist Tom Andersen in *Language is not innocent* (1996), an essay on the language of mental health services, talks about the ways in which clinical language works not so much as a *descriptor* of mental or behavioral health, but as an *influencer* in how people come to view themselves and their problems. His central thesis is that words (and ideas) are not innocuous, but have a profound power: the ability to limit the capacity to imagine oneself otherwise. He states:

> Through which language is the person to search in order to form him- or herself? What happens if we, the professionals, require the therapeutic talks to be in our professional language and our professional metaphors? What happens if that professional language is a so-called deficit or incompetence language, a language that comprises words that describe failures and shortcomings? What kind of persons are thereby formed?
>
> (Andersen, 1996, p.122).

As noted in the first person account published in this volume (Chapter 4), biopsychological framing of experiences as largely intractable "negative symptoms" can engender significant iatrogenic harm as patients come to think of themselves not only as unmotivated or socially disconnected but afflicted by primary neurobiological deficits of motivation, affect and empathy. In contrast, lived experience activists have long noted such iatrogenic harms, cautioning that language and narratives powerfully shape identity and expectations. Activists and critical scholars have also expressed serious concern with the hegemonic cultural assumptions baked into conventional individual-psychopathology-centric conceptualizations, as well as concerns—often intersecting—with class-driven discrimination. Allegations of lack of motivation, for example, have been widely applied to enslaved people and rationalized through the eugenic narratives of the 20th century (Appleman, 2018; Kühl, 2013).

While much has been written on the potential harms of myriad diagnoses (e.g., personality disorders, schizophrenia), as well as select symptom domains, negative symptoms specifically are largely absent from critical analyses and first person accounts, a gap also reflected in an extraordinarily small qualitative literature on the subjective experience of negative symptoms (Moernaut & Vanheule, 2021). This chapter seeks to address alternative ways of thinking about negative symptoms through an exploration of meaning-centered and lived experience conceptualizations and narratives. Firstly, we discuss how a framework for meaning-centered approaches to negative symptoms may be understood. Next, we describe lived experience perspectives on the phenomenon as gathered from our grassroots project "Rethink Negative Symptoms." Lastly, we will discuss the implications of lived experience and meaning-centered approaches to psychosis for clinical practice and research.

2. Meaning Centered Approaches

Meaning-centered approaches to psychosis prioritize service user/survivor's experiences and interpretation of their experiences and the contexts in which they are embedded, explicitly valuing collaborative processes of meaning-making that are in fact ubiquitous across human societies and relationships (cf. Jones & Shattell, 2013; Jones et al., 2016; Kalofonos, 2023; Schrader et al., 2013). This focus on meaning stands in sharp contrast to solution-oriented therapies that revolve around the assumed biological and/or psychological deficits of the individual. Where conventional approaches tend to identify problems, challenges, or sources of distress (typically assumed to be negative or undesirable), meaning-centered approaches instead seek to "open-up" conversations about experiences that may be good, bad, or polyvalent, and create opportunities for discussion and exploration of a range of meanings and interpretations that individuals may attach to their experiences and associated social, political, and cultural contexts. The goal is not solving problems or reducing symptoms but rather open processing, sense-making, and integration of complex experiences with identity and sense of self. Reduced distress is a byproduct of this approach.

Grace Cho's memoir *Tastes Like War* (Cho, 2021) illustrates some of the differences between meaning-centered approaches and standard conceptualizations of negative symptoms. The memoir follows Cho's experience of her mother's schizophrenia. Cho's mother grew up in Korea under Japanese colonial rule during World War II. She experienced catastrophic trauma during that time. Half of her family "disappeared" or were overtly killed by the time she was 20 years old, including her sister, brother, and father. She experienced the division of her country, such that Korea became occupied by the Soviet Union and U.S. Forces, dividing the country between North and South, splitting people off from one another and weakening Korean cultural practices. A familial secret was that her mother worked as a prostitute on an American base, where she eventually met Cho's father, a white merchant marine. Cho's mother later relocated to the United States to be with her husband. Cho describes the difficulty of her mother's immigration to the United States, where she first lived in a very white-dominated city in Washington state. Cho's mother was subject to social alienation, racism, and even further displacement from her Korean roots.

The memoir depicts her mother's development of schizophrenia during middle age, which in the book appears to be of a primarily "negative symptom" presentation, that is, her mother's life becomes very narrow, consisting of long hours watching television, social isolation, apathy, and self-neglect. A predominant issue in the book is her mother's inability/difficulty in consistently feeding herself.

Whereas standard psychiatric and psychotherapeutic practice may view Grace's mother's symptoms primarily as evidence of a neurological byproduct of a disease labeled as schizophrenia (medical model), or explain their maintenance as being stuck in a self-reinforcing "rut" (behaviorist model), Cho takes a more meaning-centered approach through connecting her mother's "symptoms" to her experiences of war and colonization. For example, in a passage from which the title of the book is derived, Grace's mother is refusing to eat. In particular, she is upset by the condensed milk that her son and daughter-in-law provide for her. Cho essentially sees her mother's food restriction not as self-neglect, but as a way of recalibrating to her past. Her mother does not want American food, yet does not have access to the Korean food from her childhood. Cho's mother refuses the condensed milk by stating, "it tastes like war," a phrase that (through research) Cho connects to her mother's experience of food deprivation during the course of the war, when condensed milk was a commonly provided ration. Both "symptoms," the food restriction and the seemingly nonsensical statement, "tastes like war" are openings for Grace to understand her family's long-hidden secrets of sociopolitical trauma.

Cho's mother begins to demonstrate improvements in functioning, as she begins to allow her daughter to cook and prepare meals from her childhood in Korea. Although behaviorists might be tempted to explain this change as resulting from "behavioral activation," Cho deepens the meaning behind this shift in her mother's presentation to be the result of a rekindled connection to Korea, and the opportunity to impart cultural traditions to her daughter, long suppressed by war, colonization, and later immigration. If taken within a teleological framework, Cho's mother's symptoms were not meaningless, but in fact, an unconscious catalyst toward deeper emotional intimacy with her daughter, and a remembering of "home." From a social justice perspective, Cho's mother's symptoms not only brought a sense of familial "healing" to herself and her daughter, but also brought forth a form of radical decolonization.

This potential relationship between so-called "negative symptoms" and colonization also appears in the work of Frantz Fanon and Jacques Azoulay, in their 1954 paper, "Social therapy in a ward of Muslim men: Methodological difficulties" (Fanon et al., 1954). In this paper the authors discuss their attempts to incorporate "social therapy" at Blida-Joinville in North Africa (Algeria), a psychiatric hospital that included both Arab and European patients. Fanon and Azoulay were interested in reforming the hospital by implementing social activities into the milieu, something that was unheard of in postwar France, where asylums were akin to prisons or concentration camps (Robcis, 2021). Fanon and Azoulay conceptualized psychosis as related to sociocultural alienation and therefore felt that healing was contingent on connecting patients back into the social world. They found that the instituting of activities such as movies, basket weaving, and a newsletter/journal writing club, was beneficial for their withdrawn and apathetic European patients, but these same activities had no impact on their Muslim patients, who remained disengaged and isolative. Fanon, himself a person who experienced the oppression and horrors of colonization in his youth in Martinique, recognized that they had been attempting to impose a Eurocentric view of social life onto the Muslim patients, thereby recreating the conditions of colonization experienced by their Muslim patients. In response, Fanon and Azoulay engaged with culturally relevant activities, such as establishing a Moorish café, engagement with Muslim celebrations, and rather than a written periodical, employing a storyteller. Adapting their intervention to the culturally specific interests of their patients led to significant changes on the unit, and their once withdrawn, amotivated, and apathetic patients began to collectively engage in social life. Again, this can be understood merely in terms of the benefit of adopting culturally informed behavioral interventions. From a more teleological or meaning-oriented approach, however, these patients' "negative symptoms" can be seen as *in themselves* bringing about a hospital-wide enactment of decolonization.

It may be easy to dismiss this framework as ungrounded in the empirical literature on negative symptoms; however, when looked at from outside the perspective of the West, so-called psychotic symptoms have often been vehicles of communication regarding otherwise "unspeakable" sociopolitical trauma. For example, anthropologist Jie Yang analyzed the content of voices heard by people diagnosed with schizophrenia in China, and found that the content of these voices specifically articulated a sense of dissent and divergence from dominant sociopolitical narratives (Yang, 2023), such that Yang conceptualizes psychotic symptoms as holding important messages for the collective, indicating evidence of the unspoken, painful ramifications of the sociopolitical landscape. (See also Kamens, 2023, for similar analysis focused on service users in occupied Palestine.) Of course, in addition to non-Western perspectives, this line of thinking has often been a part of consumer/survivor/peer discourse, such as the Hearing Voices Movement, which often frames "psychosis" as "the canary in the coal mine," that is, as an indication of something occurring in the environment that is noxious or amiss (e.g., Moynihan, 2016, *Healing Voices*). What makes examples such as Fanon's work and Cho's memoir particularly striking, is the application of this line of thinking to negative symptoms specifically.

3. Negative Symptoms Explored

When looked at from outside the field of psychiatry, experiences such as silence and stillness (arguably nonpathological ways of describing alogia and amotivation) are often understood as having generative potential. Our ability to view negative symptoms in this way is limited by the disconnection of these experiences from continuum theories. Although voices and visions are often presented as existing on a continuum (and often connected to spiritual practice), this is not often the case for negative symptoms, which instead are framed as organic, unfathomable, or "other." Periods of amotivation, social withdrawal, and alogia are, however, common human experiences—whether volitional, nonvolitional, or cultural. For example, silence/stillness is a central practice across a variety of religious traditions. Within the Quaker tradition, silence/quiet is the starting point toward a greater connection with God/the Creator. Likewise, in religious practices from both the Christian and Buddhist traditions, replacing extraversion for a more introspective life is a way toward greater self-improvement. As such, people willingly enter monasteries and cloisters, and in some cases, choose the life of a hermit or religious recluse, in the pursuit of a more meaningful life. Asceticism, seen across Islamic, Hindu, Judeo-Christian, and Buddhist traditions, among others, often involves the pursuit of enlightenment, inner peace, or connection to the Divine through withdrawal from worldly pleasures, material possessions, and modern life. In some ascetic traditions, this extends toward "self-neglect," such as India's *fakirs,* who may leave their hair long and unkempt, wear rags, and intentionally not cut their fingernails. Of course, individuals diagnosed with schizophrenia are different from those who *willfully* withdraw from society, remain silent, or unwashed. What is relevant here, however, is that the behaviors we view as "pathological" in the psy professions, in a different context, can be viewed as meaningful. Although stressful and difficult, these practices are attempts to bring a person closer to a culturally consonant form of "wellness." Applying this same logic to schizophrenia, experiences of withdrawal, silence, or inaction might be understood as involving periods of withdrawal, processing, or growth (rather than just as nonvolitional byproducts of an illness). Returning again to Grace Cho's mother, her self-neglect (i.e., not eating) and social withdrawal ultimately led to a type of decolonial healing, as she reconnected with the displaced culture of her youth and strengthened her bond with her daughter. In looking backward from the result back to the symptoms, we might speculate that had she never experienced such symptoms, this deep healing may never have taken place.

Few accounts exist that illustrate a first-person perspective of negative symptoms. However, psychologist Eleanor Longden's personal account of negative symptoms is one example. It shows great connection to the aforementioned religious traditions:

> Maybe I was just removing myself from things; maybe that was my idea of freedom, to purchase some cheap brand of absolution. (Cheap: an intriguing word—most assistance in my life was costly and medical and unexciting.) The possibility of escaping the world in this way (so simple and painless, so

> effective) began to consume me, lingering above my head like the raw-boned, rangy haloes of medieval saints.
>
> (Longden, 2012, p. 180)

What makes this passage pertinent, is Longden's acknowledgement that her "negative symptoms" were in some sense volitional, and, in fact, may have been intended as a means toward self-healing (i.e., in contrast to the "costly/unexciting" approach of the medical field, Longden searches for a new method of healing through the perennial practice of social withdrawal). It is interesting that she uses religious imagery, connecting her thoughts to the halos of saints. Within psychiatric or even psychological frameworks, negative symptoms most often appear as a dead-end, an obstacle to overcome, and are rarely, if ever, seen as methods for self-healing (conscious or not). Colloquially, however, people often subscribe to the belief that it is only after coming through a painful and difficult experience that we are able to see that it was somehow purposeful all along.

As Longden's autobiographical writings also relate, withdrawal can be defensive and/or self-protective in other ways. In the face of often tremendous social exclusion and stigma, for example, withdrawal, both physical and emotional, protects the individual from the pain they might be subject to from others. Similarly, withdrawal from the pursuit of activities such as work, school, or career may protect an individual from the potential for further repetition of failure, disappointment, or shattered dreams that frequently accompany the onset of psychosis.

As mentioned, many cultures/subcultures/world religions view silence ("alogia"), hermitage ("social isolation"), asceticism ("poor hygiene") as spaces of potential generativity. Are "negative symptoms" an end in themselves, or, if given the space/care, a needed pause, a "creative quiet"? Returning again to Pat Deegan (1996), we can see a similar distinction between looking at people in terms of "deficit" versus. "potential." She states, "[. . .] rather than seeing us as unmotivated, apathetic, or hopeless cases, we can be understood as people who are waiting. We never know for sure but perhaps, just perhaps, there is a new life within a person just waiting to take root if a secure and nurturing soil is provided" (Deegan, 1996, p. 8).

4. Rethink Negative Symptoms

The next part of this chapter is a description of our project *Rethink Negative Symptoms*. In order to understand more from the perspective of people with lived experience, the authors of this chapter created a grassroots project to seek first-person accounts of negative symptoms: The Rethink Psychosis/Rethink Negative Symptoms project (https://rethinkpsychosis.weebly.com/).

In the formal (i.e., peer reviewed) research literature on negative symptoms (in psychosis) internal literature searches did not yield a single coproduced or participatory research project. Meanwhile, while mixed methods of psychopathology research, including qualitative phenomenology and clinical ethnography, have been brought to bear on, and helped reshape contemporary approaches to the conceptualization of positive symptoms—particularly paranoia, delusions, and hallucinations—a 2021 systematic review of the qualitative literature on negative symptoms identified only a single study expressly focused on the lived experience of negative symptoms explicitly defined as such (Moernaut & Vanheule, 2021). As philosophers of psychiatry are often quick to point out, (a) subjective experience, (b) neuropsychological and neurocognitive measurement; and (c) functional neurophysiology constitute different and incommensurate levels of explanation. Simplistically explaining higher levels of experience (e.g., subjective experience) through simpler (lower level) component parts is inherently problematic and constitutes a "reductionist" fallacy (36; 40–41). In addition, such philosophical problems hold to the epistemic equity issues associated with an absence of direct lived experience/user involvement and leadership in conceptualization and interpretation.

Outside the formal literature, lived experience writings such as Deegan (1996), Longdon (2013), and Anonymous (this volume), help draw attention to the profound difficulties involved in separating what might be categorized as "negative symptoms" from the broader social and structural contexts of institutionalization and psychological/medical framing, social rejection, societal prejudice, and associated impacts on identity, as well as intersecting forms of social marginalization associated with psychosis (bullying and discrimination on the basis of race, sexual identity, appearance and weight, for example). In keeping with the criticisms suggested by Andersen (1996), Anonymous' account in this volume also foregrounds the problems inherent in observation-based determinations—that is, ratings of "negative symptoms" based on the observation and interpretation of clinicians (and sometimes family) rather than first-person experience.

A series of unedited first person accounts compiled in the Rethink Psychosis/Rethink Negative Symptoms project (https://rethinkpsychosis.weebly.com/) provides a further window not only into potential disjunctures between clinician observation and subjective experience, but also into the risk of harm through mislabeling and the overshadowing or foreclosure of alternative explanations. One respondent, for example, attests to the weaponization of the language of negative symptoms in their experience:

> *Many times during forced hospitalization this language [negative symptoms] was used about me as if I wasn't present and lacked insight and agency to make decisions or understand and interpret my own experiences. This language was also used to argue that I was severely impaired and that this warranted more severe treatment methods—like confinement, restraint (chemical, mechanical, physical, psychological and coercive measures), higher doses of antipsychotics and multiple antipsychotics (polydrugging), and "emergency ECT." In my experience this language was used to undermine my agency, undermine and argue that any attempt to accommodate different communication methods with me would be futile as I was likely completely impaired and unable to comprehend it, suggest there was no point trying to help me as I was "too far gone" and had a "poor prognosis," and ultimately violated my human rights.*

Even more directly attributing their experiences to medications, another participant explained:

> *Prescribers seem to deeply underestimate just how sedating and stifling antipsychotics are. At the time, on heavy doses of antipsychotics, I wasn't really sure what to attribute it to, but once I discontinued I realized just how much the mental fogginess, the perpetual lack of energy, the fatigue, and loss of vitality, was not due to psychosis but medications. It was like a veil was lifted when I finally stopped, and I could see the world in color again.*

Under each major "negative symptom" category (motivation, affect, social withdrawal), respondents pointed to alternative explanations of alleged negative symptoms that instead involve adaptation to rejection and internalized shame and perceived failure. It's easy to see how labeling these experiences as biologically based deficits risks significant psychological and epistemic harm to service users.

> *I believe the change in how my emotions are outwardly expressed and inwardly felt in "negative symptoms" is because I was experiencing a state of such profound threat to the safety of my being (emotional, psychological, physical, spiritual/existential, social/attachment/belonging and identity threat), I moved into an intuitive adaptive process to preserve life, one that aligns with some of the freeze-shut-down type trauma and threat responses. In this state, my communication changed, and my immersion and connection with my emotions and the experiences I was responding to (and therefore my expression of my emotions and associated behavior) adapted in order to rapidly reduce my distress in order to prioritize survival and functioning of my nervous systems to reduce the state of emergency.*

> *I think my sense of personal guilt and shame, which I can now recognize as disproportionate and catalyzed by several emotionally stressful situations, tipped over into worthlessness, leading to a desire for self-punishment resulting in the cessation of typical activities of daily care (regular eating schedule, sleep hygiene, personal grooming).*
>
> *I have been very hurt by the notion that self withdrawal or refusing to interact socially are "negative symptoms." For me, when I was in the hospital, my silence and social withdrawal was a positive method of survival. I needed to not talk, so I could focus deeply on my inner world. I needed to not interact, so I could cling to the silent connections I still felt with the natural world. Being silent and withdrawn was my way to protest the brutality of the psychiatric institution. Silence needs to be respected.*
>
> *I think psychosis is lonely. I don't like social withdrawal or self-isolation. It puts the responsibility for making friends solely on the survivor rather than acknowledging that relationships are 2 way. I think what others perceived as social withdrawal on my part was due to a lot of people avoiding me because I was always down about my mental health and they didn't want to spend time with someone who was always sad.*

To the extent that alleged negative symptoms may in fact function as psychological defenses against threat, or understandable responses to internalized oppression, perceived failure, and/or social rejection, as described here, framing them instead as relatively fixed biological or psychological deficits risks foreclosing the role of critical (nondeficit) psychological processes and sociostructural determinants. Similarly, these descriptions demonstrate an element of volition to these experiences, the person in question is not a nonagentic victim of their faulty biology or maladaptive thought processes, but an active participant in their own survival against oppressive forces (c.f. Jones et al., 2016).

Turning to the older literature on the effects of (literal) institutionalization, there was arguably much more acknowledgement of a causal relationship between the environmental context of mental institutions and motivation and social functioning (e.g., Goffman, 1961). Although not wholly unacknowledged in contemporary literature (e.g., Yanos, 2018), the reality remains that, even in the community, many adults diagnosed with schizophrenia continue to lead extremely marginalized and impoverished lives, with few opportunities for environmental enrichment and intellectual stimulation. Consider, for example, a typical inner city service user living in a single room occupancy hotel, whose only contact with others is their case manager, psychiatrist, nurses, and possibly peer specialists. Typically living well below the poverty line, car ownership is uncommon, and thus access to green spaces, nature, hiking. Even in a city full of culture—museums, theaters, music—the costs will generally exceed an

SSI-driven income by a large margin. The language of negative symptoms all too easily functions as an alibi for the refusal to acknowledge and address these underlying social and structural realities.

5. Conclusion

The purpose of this chapter was to expand our understanding of "negative symptoms" through an exploration of the phenomenon surrounding meaning-centered and lived experience perspectives. We began the chapter with a discussion of how negative symptoms may not be deficits at all, but in fact generative. First, we explored Grace Cho's interpretation of her mother's experience of negative symptoms as holding important meaning for herself, her family, and the sociopolitical world. Then, we considered some of the ways in which comparable experiences, defined outside of the mental health professions, instead view social withdrawal, isolation, and silence as processes tied to growth, healing, and spirituality. Lastly, we presented our grassroots project, *Rethink Negative Symptoms,* to engage with a few of the ways in which the first person narratives included here challenge and recontextualize the language of "negative symptoms." Our project found that many people resist such framing, instead calling attention to the social and structural roots of these experiences, their protective role, and the iatrogenic harm of reductionistic labeling (i.e., the medical-model language of mental health services and societal discrimination leads to a depleted life).

We believe that the mental health field has much more to learn about the subjective experience of phenomena labeled negative symptoms and the consequences of how they are conceptualized and explained by clinicians. We propose four critical future directions for the field: (1) engagement with and inclusion of service users in understanding "negative symptoms"; (2) a reorientation to social and structural context in which these symptoms occur; (3) a stronger recognition of antipsychotic side effects and their role; and (4) a reframing of "negative symptoms" outside of deficit models.

References

Andersen, T. (1996). Language is not innocent. In F. W. Kaslow (Ed.), *Handbook of relational diagnosis and dysfunctional family patterns* (pp.119–125). John Wiley & Sons.

Appleman, L. I. (2018). Deviancy, dependency, and disability: The forgotten history of eugenics and mass incarceration. *Duke Law Journal, 68*(3), 417–478.

Cho, G. M. (2021). *Tastes like war: A memoir.* Feminist Press at CUNY.

Deegan, P. (1996). Recovery as a journey of the heart. *Psychiatric Rehabilitation Journal, 19*(3), 91–97.

Fanon, F. & Azoulay, J. (1954/2018). Social therapy in a ward of Muslim men: Methodological difficulties. In J. Khalfa, R. J. C. Young (Eds.). *Alienation and freedom* (pp. 353–372). New York: Bloomsbury Academic.

Goffman, E. (1961). *Asylums: Essays on the social situation of mental patients and other inmates.* Aldine Transaction.

Jones, N., & Shattell, M. (2013). Engaging with voices: Rethinking the clinical treatment of psychosis. *Issues in Mental Health Nursing, 34*(7), 562–563.

Jones, N., Kelly, T., & Shattell, M. (2016). God in the brain: Experiencing psychosis in the postsecular United States. *Transcultural Psychiatry, 53*(4), 488–505.

Jones, N., Shattell, M., Kelly, T., Brown, R., Robinson, L., Renfro, R., . . . & Luhrmann, T. M. (2016). "Did I push myself over the edge?": Complications of agency in psychosis onset and development. *Psychosis, 8*(4), 324–335.

Kalofonos, I. (2023). Meaning in psychosis: A veteran's critique of the traumas of racism, sexual violence, and intersectional oppression. *Culture, Medicine, and Psychiatry, 47*(4), 1–23.

Kamens, S. (Ed.). (2023). *Reconceptualizing schizophrenia: The phenomenology of urhomelessness.* Taylor & Francis.

Kirschner, M., Aleman, A., & Kaiser, S. (2017). Secondary negative symptoms—A review of mechanisms, assessment and treatment. *Schizophrenia Research, 186*, 29–38.

Kühl, S. (2013). *For the betterment of the race: the rise and fall of the international movement for eugenics and racial hygiene.* Springer.

Longden, E. (2012). Negative symptoms: More, not less. In J. Geekie, P. Randal, D. Lampshire, & J. Read (Eds.). *Experiencing psychosis. Personal and professional perspective* (pp.179–186). Routledge.

Moernaut, N., & Vanheule, S. (2021). Experiencing negative symptoms in psychosis: A systematic qualitative review. *Psychosis, 13*(2), 175–187.

Robcis, C. (2021). *Disalientation: Politics, philosophy, and radical psychiatry in postwar France.* University of Chicago Press.

Schrader, S., Jones, N., & Shattell, M. (2013). Mad pride: Reflections on sociopolitical identity and mental diversity in the context of culturally competent psychiatric care. *Issues in Mental Health Nursing, 34*(1), 62–64.

Yanos, P. T. (2018). *Written-Off: Mental health stigma and the loss of human potential.* Cambridge University Press.

PART II
ASSESSMENT

7

Negative Symptom Assessment

Clinical Ratings and Behavioral Methods

Ann M. Kring, Lauren P. Weittenhiller, and Ashby B. Cogan

Clinical pearls

- A thorough and careful assessment of negative symptoms is an important step when developing treatment goals and evaluating outcomes.
- Clinical interview assessments are reliable and valid and can be readily adopted for use in clinical settings; the CAINS or BNSS may be particularly useful measures.
- Clinical interviews can provide a quantitative baseline at the beginning of treatment as well as at the end of treatment (i.e., outcome). These interviews can also provide meaningful information for the development of treatment goals.
- Clients may be less likely to raise negative symptoms as a focus for treatment (compared to positive symptoms), and thus having the structure of the questions in clinical interviews for negative symptoms can be valuable at the beginning of treatment.
- Sharing the results from clinical interviews for negative symptoms with clients can help elucidate areas of strength or areas for growth and can provide a forum for clients to identify the personal meaning of the experiences and symptoms they describe in the interview.
- Some behavior coding assessments are more useful in clinical practice than others given the time, resources, and equipment needed to implement these. Nevertheless, the literature reporting studies using these methods can inform clinical practice.

1. Introduction

Clinical interviews and rating scales are common methods for assessing negative symptoms and can aid in making a diagnosis as well as providing a roadmap

Ann M. Kring, Lauren P. Weittenhiller, and Ashby B. Cogan, *Negative Symptom Assessment*. In: *Psychosocial Approaches to Negative Symptoms in Psychosis*. Edited by: Tania Lincoln et al., Oxford University Press.
 DOI: 10.1093/oso/9780197676790.003.0007

for treatment. The clinical interview may also serve as a form of "therapeutic assessment" (Finn, 2007) given that discussion of the domains covered by negative symptoms—emotion, social relationships, and motivation—are ripe treatment targets. Clinical interviews focus on negative symptoms over a specified time interval (e.g., last week, last month) and provide information on the severity of individual symptoms and broader dimensions. Clinically, it can be beneficial to understand whether a specific person exhibits particular symptoms, as opposed to sole reliance on a global rating or total score that sums across all symptoms.

Indeed, with the current focus on "personalized medicine," we are at an inflection point whereby consideration of particular symptoms or dimensions can guide treatment decisions more effectively and efficiently compared to lumping symptoms together. To be sure, a focus on individual symptoms is not new (Neale et al., 1985; Persons, 1986), and symptom-based dimensional models represent the scientific state of the art (e.g., Kotov et al., 2020; Kotov et al., 2017). The past three decades of research have better pinpointed the mechanisms underpinning negative symptoms (see also Chapters 2 and 3 of this volume), such that more focused treatment approaches can now be effectively implemented (see Chapter 13, this volume).

At the outset it is worth noting one important challenge for clinical interviews and rating scales; these assessment methods can have the unintended consequence of privileging interviewer observations over first-person reports, particularly if an interviewer's observation is at odds with a client's report. Indeed, interviewers may mistakenly assume that someone with a severe psychotic disorder lacks insight into their symptoms or is unable to reliably report on their experiences (e.g., Selten et al., 1998). Reconciling two discrepant reports is never an easy task, but such discrepancies could reflect something other than lack of insight or limited self-awareness on the part of the person with psychosis. For example, asking people with psychosis whether they generally experience pleasure (or even to describe what kinds of things they find pleasurable) might elicit a different response than asking whether they derive pleasure from being with friends or going on a hike; that is, the context in which questions about emotional experiences are asked can lead to different responses.

Because there are strengths and weaknesses to any assessment approach, use of multiple measures and methods (see also Chapters 11 and 12 in this volume) is ideal to ensure comprehensive coverage of negative symptom domains that treatment needs to target (Aleman et al., 2017; Elis et al., 2013).

At the same time, some methods are more feasible in clinical settings than others.

2. Clinical Interviews and Rating Scales

A pivotal moment in negative symptom assessment was the publication of the National Institute of Mental Health (NIMH) consensus statement on negative symptoms (Kirkpatrick et al., 2006). This paper summarized the consensus development conference that included mental health professionals and scientists working in academia, industry, and government to evaluate the state of negative symptom research, and importantly, to provide future recommendations. One of the conclusions was that the evidence base supports five domains of negative symptoms: asociality, avolition, anhedonia, blunted affect, and alogia. Factor analyses of various negative symptom measures support a "behavioral" factor, which is typically referred to as expression or EXP as well as an experiential factor, typically referred to as motivation/pleasure or MAP (e.g., Blanchard & Cohen, 2006; Horan et al., 2011; Kaiser et al., 2017; Kirkpatrick et al., 2011; Kring et al., 2013; Liemburg et al., 2013; Messinger et al., 2011; Peralta & Cuesta, 1995; Strauss et al., 2012). Another conclusion was that the currently available clinical rating scales were not optimal for assessing these five domains or the two broader factors. Indeed, the first recommendation for the future was the development of a new clinical interview and rating scale that could be used in clinical trials to evaluate negative symptom treatments.

Here, we briefly describe two older, yet still used "first-generation" clinical rating scales, as well as measures for those with subthreshold psychotic symptoms who may be at clinical high risk (CHR) for psychosis. We then describe two newer, "second-generation" measures along with adaptations of these measures for CHR groups. For consideration of other clinical interviews and rating scales and more detailed comparisons among measures, we recommend the excellent and comprehensive reviews by Lincoln and colleagues (2017) and Strauss and colleagues (2020).

2.1 First Generation Measures

Although the consensus statement emphasized the need for a new negative symptom interview and rating scale, it also noted consensus that two first generation measures were appropriate for clinical trials: the Schedule for the Assessment of Negative Symptoms (SANS; Andreasen, 1982, 1984) and the Positive and Negative Syndrome Scale (PANSS; Kay et al., 1987). Although the SANS and PANSS are still used, their weaknesses render them less optimal compared to newer measures (Blanchard et al., 2019).

The SANS covers blunted affect (six items), alogia (four items), avolition/apathy (three items), and anhedonia/asociality (four items). Each of those four domains can also be scored with one global rating item. Psychometrically and clinically, it is useful to have more than one item per domain to provide more comprehensive assessment of a particular symptom. The SANS also includes two items on attention and one item on inappropriate affect; however, neither of these are considered negative symptoms (Blanchard & Cohen, 2006; Kirkpatrick et al., 2006). Items are rated on a 0 (none) to 5 (severe) rating scale, and the anchor wording for each point on the scale is somewhat descriptive. The original SANS did not contain interview questions for making these ratings, but other investigators have published questions and probes that can be used in research and clinical settings (e.g., Mueser et al., 1994). The time period assessed with the SANS is most commonly the last month. Importantly, the more retrospective the assessment period, the more difficult it is to accurately recall and therefore rate the symptoms. The psychometric properties of the SANS range from very good to very poor (Mueser et al., 1994).

There are additional conceptual difficulties with the SANS (Blanchard et al., 2011). For example, the anhedonia/asociality domain in the SANS conflates frequency of social contact and social activity, decreased interest, decreased pleasure, or even hostility. Thus, it is not possible to determine precisely which processes are impacted: pleasure, motivation, or relationships. It also does not assess a person's interest or desire for social relationships, which is core to asociality.

The PANSS was developed by adapting items from two existing general rating scales: the Brief Psychiatric Rating Scale (BPRS: Overall & Gorham, 1962; Ventura et al., 1993) and the Psychopathology Rating Scale (PRS; Singh & Kay, 1975). Because the BPRS and PRS were not designed to assess negative symptoms specifically, the items on the PANSS do not fully cover negative symptom domains. More specifically, the PANSS negative symptom subscale includes only three items covering consensus negative symptoms: blunted affect, passive-apathetic social withdrawal, and lack of spontaneity/flow of conversation. It also includes four conceptually distinct items (emotional withdrawal, poor rapport, difficulty in abstract thinking, and stereotyped thinking). Items are rated on a 1 (absent) to 7 (extreme) scale with fairly descriptive anchor ratings. Some researchers, however, have used a 0-to-6 scale, making comparisons across studies difficult. Internal consistency and test-retest reliability of the PANSS is moderate to high (Kay et al., 1987). The time period assessed with the

PANSS is most commonly the last week. Though the psychometric properties are generally strong, the PANSS contains fewer negative symptom items than the SANS.

The SANS and PANSS are related to each other (e.g., Rabany et al., 2011), and a metric to compare scores on the two measures has been developed (van Erp et al., 2014). Although these measures are still used, particularly in clinical trials, they both have additional weaknesses. The symptom rating anchors in both measures do not directly assess a person's experience. However, certain negative symptoms, such as anhedonia, are almost fully about *the experience* of pleasure and the *anticipatory experience* of pleasure (Kring & Elis, 2013). From a clinical standpoint, using these older measures may assess functional difficulties (e.g., employment, family conflict, difficulty in persisting with goals) but will miss key components of negative symptoms, including those that can be effectively targeted for treatment (e.g., emotional experience, desire for relationships, interest in goals). Neither the SANS nor the PANSS have systematic training materials (manuals, videos, workshops) readily available, and thus these are more difficult to use in clinical settings.

Neither the SANS nor the PANSS was developed with an eye toward those who may be at clinical high-risk for psychosis but are not yet exhibiting sufficient symptoms to meet a diagnosis. The North American Prodrome Longitudinal Study (NAPLS; Addington et al., 2007) and its follow-ups (NAPLS-2, NAPLS-3; Addington et al., 2012; Addington et al., 2020) identified participants as CHR using the Structured Interview for Prodromal Syndromes (SIPS; Miller et al., 2003). Although identification of CHR focuses primarily on positive symptoms and disorganization, negative symptoms can predate the onset of a psychotic disorder (e.g., Walker et al., 1993, 1994) and are also present among those at CHR (e.g., Piskulic et al., 2012).

Like the PANSS, some of the negative symptoms on the SIPS are (mostly) part of the consensus negative symptoms (i.e., social anhedonia/ withdrawal, avolition, expression of emotion); others are not (i.e., experience of emotions and self, ideational richness, and occupational functioning). The SIPS most commonly covers the past month. Items are rated on a 0 (none) to 6 (extreme) rating scale, and the anchor wording for the scale is fairly descriptive, though the anchors often conflate multiple constructs. For example, the anhedonia/withdrawal item lumps social skill, social anxiety, and minimal desire for social interaction together and does not include the concept of pleasure, which is central to anhedonia. The expression of emotion item combines blunted affect and alogia.

Interrater agreement for the SIPS negative symptom subscale is good, but unfortunately, it has not been well-validated, nor do the items sufficiently cover the negative symptom domains (Strauss et al., 2020). Furthermore, the SIPS items do not distinguish between experiential and behavioral components of negative symptoms. Extensive in-person training is required to be able to administer the SIPS, and this can be a barrier for those working in clinical settings (Mittal et al., 2021; Strauss et al., 2020). In short, the SIPS is not a good measure to assess negative symptoms for CHR groups (see also Azis et al., 2019; Strauss et al., 2020).

Another measure derived from a prospective, longitudinal study of CHR in Australia (Yung et al., 1995) is the Comprehensive Assessment of At-Risk Mental States (CAARMS; Yung et al., 2005). The CAARMS includes just three negative symptoms: alogia, avolition/apathy, and anhedonia, which are rated on three different dimensions: intensity (0–6), frequency/duration (0–6) and fluctuation of symptoms (0–2). Although interrater agreement on these items is good, the items do not fully capture the negative symptom domains, and there is just a single item for each of the three symptoms assessed (Strauss et al., 2020). Additionally, CAARMS items do not distinguish between experiential and behavioral components of symptoms. Training materials are more readily available than for the SIPS and include a manual and videos (Nelson et al., 2008). However, the videos are of actors portraying various symptoms rather than actual people who may experience them (Strauss et al., 2020). In sum, like the SIPS, the CAARMS is not an ideal measure to assess negative symptoms in CHR groups (Strauss et al., 2020).

2.2 Second Generation Measures

Following the first consensus statement recommendation (Kirkpatrick et al., 2006), two next-generation measures were developed: the Clinical Assessment Interview for Negative Symptoms (CAINS; Kring et al., 2013) and the Brief Negative Symptom Scale (BNSS; Kirkpatrick et al., 2011). Both measures assess the five consensus negative symptoms; both measures include 13 items, and both measures are recommended for use in the European Psychiatric Association guidelines (EPA; Galderisi et al., 2021). Even though they have the same number of items, the BNSS can be administered in approximately 15 minutes, whereas the CAINS can take up to 30 minutes (Blanchard et al., 2019; Lincoln et al., 2017). The CAINS likely takes longer to administer because it includes more interview probes and questions than the BNSS (though not all of these are necessary in order to make ratings).

The two teams behind development of these measures employed different strategies. The CAINS team was supported by an NIMH grant and conducted two development studies over three years with over 500 participants at four sites across the United States (Blanchard et al., 2011; Horan et al., 2011). The BNSS team sought to rapidly create a brief measure that could be deployed in studies right away. The initial development sample for the BNSS was small (Kirkpatrick et al., 2011), but subsequent studies reaffirmed the reliability and validity of the BNSS in larger samples (Strauss et al., 2012; Strauss et al., 2012). Item development for both the CAINS and BNSS was data driven and informed by the extant literature on processes and mechanisms of negative symptoms (Forbes et al., 2010). For example, distinctions between anticipatory and consummatory pleasure were built into each measure given that this distinction has proved meaningful in psychosis (e.g., Barch et al., 2017; Kring & Barch, 2014; Kring & Caponigro, 2010). Both measures assess symptoms over the past week except for anticipatory pleasure, which is assessed for the next week.

The CAINS rating scale anchors, rated on a 0 (no impairment) to 4 (severe deficit), supported by item-level analyses (Horan et al., 2011), were designed to capture both internal experience (interest, desire, motivation, emotion) and observable behaviors (social interactions, initiation, persistence, participation in recreational activities, outward expression, speech amount). Including experience and behavior in the anchors allows for a thorough assessment of the negative symptom components. A unique feature of the CAINS is that its many interview questions allow the interviewer to tailor the assessment to the individual (i.e., not all questions are applicable to all people). The inclusion of many interview questions also ensures interviewer consistency and facilitates training and dissemination. Extensive training materials (manual, training videos with people experiencing symptoms, gold standard ratings for the videos) are freely available. The CAINS has also been translated into multiple languages for use around the world.

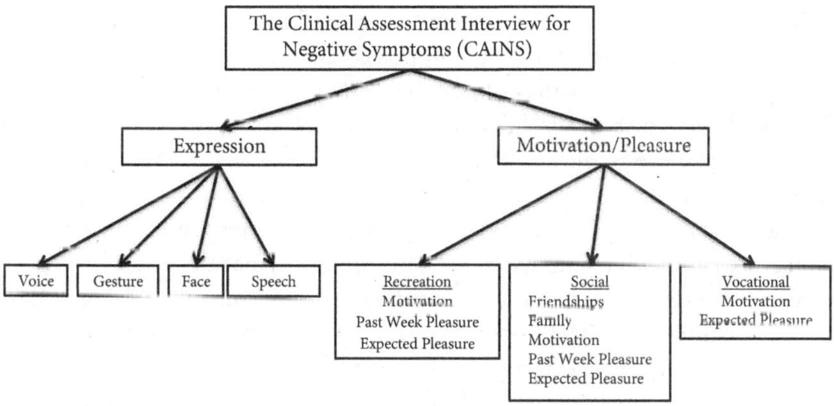

Figure 7.1 Domains covered by the Clinical Assessment Interview for Negative Symptoms (CAINS).

Another unique feature of the CAINS is that it assesses three life domains: social, work/school, and recreation (see Figure 7.1). For example, in the social domain, the CAINS covers family, friends, and romantic partners to fully assess asociality, avolition, and anhedonia. Indeed, some people with psychosis will report less interest in having close friendships compared to family (Weittenhiller et al., 2021).

The CAINS can be scored as a total score or as two subscale scores: diminished motivation and pleasure (MAP; 9 items) and diminished expression (EXP; 4 items). The CAINS has high internal consistency, test-retest reliability, interrater agreement, and strong convergent and discriminant validity (Kring et al., 2013; Blanchard et al., 2017).

The BNSS also has high internal consistency and test-retest reliability as well as strong convergent and discriminant validity. Interrater agreement was high in the pilot sample of 10 patients (Kirkpatrick et al., 2011). Training materials (manual, workbook, videos, gold standard ratings) are also readily available. The BNSS includes an item for distress (unpleasant emotions), but this is not a negative symptom. The BNSS has a two-factor structure similar to the CAINS, with EXP (5 items) and AAA (anhedonia/avolition/asociality; 7 items); the distress item does not fit on either factor (Kirkpatrick et al., 2018).

A unique and clinically useful feature of the BNSS is that it includes separate items for the experience and behavioral aspects of asociality and avolition rather than including them both in one item as the CAINS does (see Figure 7.2). This can be useful clinically to better identify the nature of a symptom. Another unique feature of the BNSS is that it includes two separate items to assess the intensity and frequency of past-week pleasure (across life domains). The CAINS only assesses frequency of past week pleasure (but separately for social, work/school, recreation).

Most of the CAINS and BNSS items are related to one another, though the anhedonia items are more distinct (Strauss & Gold, 2016). The BNSS assesses anticipatory anhedonia with just one item on the expected *intensity* of future pleasurable activities across life domains, whereas the CAINS includes three items covering the *frequency* of expected pleasurable activities separately for social, work/school, and recreational life domains. In addition, interview probes for the CAINS purposefully do not explicitly refer to responses to past-week anhedonia when asking about future pleasure given that the capacity to generate future events is part of the anticipatory pleasure construct (Kring & Elis, 2013). In contrast, the BNSS refers to responses given for past-week anhedonia by asking if a person expects to enjoy those activities in the following week.

Although both the BNSS and CAINS include two items for past-week anhedonia, the BNSS assesses past-week frequency and intensity across life domains;

whereas the CAINS assesses past-week social anhedonia frequency (days experienced) and past-week recreation anhedonia frequency (days and diversity of experiences). Past-week work/school anhedonia was removed from the final CAINS because it was not applicable to many people with psychosis who were not working (Kring et al., 2013).

There are additional differences between the two measures. The BNSS includes two items to assess alogia (amount of speech, spontaneous elaboration), whereas the CAINS includes just one item (quantity of speech) because the data from development studies indicated that two items were redundant with one another (Horan et al., 2011). Unlike the CAINS, the BNSS does not sample life domains separately. Clinically, one advantage to distinguishing among life domains as the CAINS does is the ability to pinpoint more precisely where a person may experience motivational, social, or pleasure difficulties that might be translated into treatment goals. Indeed, it is fairly common for people with psychotic disorders to provide divergent responses across life domains with, for example, a fairly severe difficulty in pleasure derived from social interactions but no difficulty in pleasure derived from recreational activities. Additionally, some people with psychosis will report difficulties with motivation in respect to work but not in respect to interacting with family.

In sum, of all the available measures, the CAINS and the BNSS stand out as excellent clinical interviews and rating scales for their congruence with the consensus negative symptom domains, strong psychometrics, ease and brevity of administration, and, in the case of the CAINS, tailored interview questions and assessment of diverse life domains. The BNSS takes less time to administer, which could be beneficial in clinical settings.

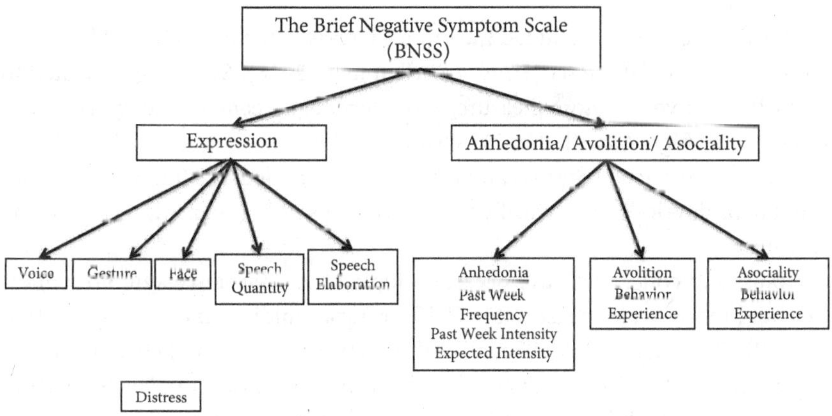

Figure 7.2 Domains covered by the Brief Negative Symptom Scale (BNSS).

These characteristics also distinguish the CAINS and BNSS as suitable tools for use in clinical practice. For example, administering one of these interviews at the beginning of treatment could provide a baseline assessment of negative symptoms that can then be reassessed at the end of treatment to gauge outcome. These measures can also be used to help in the development of treatment goals; for example, the CAINS could reveal that a client struggles less with motivation for solitary recreation but struggles more with social motivation and pleasure, a fairly common clinical presentation among people with psychotic disorders. The assessment of the expressive negative symptoms may reveal information that is less accessible to a client; that is, a client may not be aware of their inexpressiveness and the impact it might have on others.

Because these measures take 15 to 30 minutes to administer, they are not likely feasible as weekly progress monitoring measures. For that, a self-report measure (see Chapter 11 this volume) may be more practical. However, returning to a portion of the interviews weekly could be clinically helpful. For example, if a pretreatment CAINS interview reveals a challenge with anticipated pleasurable social activities, and increasing these emerges as a meaningful treatment goal, therapist and client could take five minutes to readminister this particular item on the CAINS each week to assess progress.

Turning to the development of other measures, both the CAINS and BNSS have been adapted for use in CHR populations; however, the studies were of small sample sizes (less than 30 participants). The CAINS was adapted by revising the interview questions to be more applicable to younger people, adding questions about social media and about living at home with family (Gur et al., 2015). Although the modified CAINS correlated with other measures of negative symptoms for CHR groups (e.g., SIPS), the modified CAINS did not detect a wide range of symptoms. Interrater agreement and internal consistency were not reported.

The modified BNSS included the same 13 items as the BNSS but added questions to cover social media (Strauss & Chapman, 2018). Scores were related to the SIPS negative symptom measure, and interrater agreement and internal consistency were high. As with the CAINS modification, the range of modified BNSS scores was constricted. Strauss and Chapman concluded that a new instrument ought to be developed specifically for CHR groups rather than adapting existing measures.

Strauss and colleagues have been developing a new negative-symptom interview and rating scale measure for CHR groups, building upon the adaptation of the BNSS (Pelletier-Baldelli et al., 2017; Strauss et al., 2020). Pelletier-Baldelli and colleagues (2017) introduced the Prodromal Inventory of Negative Symptoms (PINS), which included 13 items scored on a 1 (questionably present) to 6 (extreme) scale. Nine items covered motivation and pleasure (MAP); four items covered expression (EXP). The measure demonstrated good internal consistency, convergent, and discriminant validity. The authors recommended against using the measure, however, largely because it was not sufficiently sensitive to detect negative symptoms in CHR groups.

Instead, Pelletier-Baldelli and colleagues (2017) introduced and recommended the PINS-2 in the supplementary materials of their article. The PINS-2 contains 23 items rated on a 0 (absent) to 6 (extremely severe) scale. This PINS-2 is similar to the CAINS in that it distinguishes types of social relationships (family, friends, romantic partners, plus the addition of social media) and domains for anhedonia (work/school, recreation, and social). Like the BNSS, asociality and avolition have separate items for experience and behavior. The PINS-2 includes eight asociality, four avolition, four anhedonia, three transitory distress, three blunted-affect items, and one alogia item.

The PINS-2 has been subsequently renamed the Negative Symptom Inventory—Psychosis Risk (NSI-PR) and further revised (Strauss et al., 2020). Like the PINS-2, there is no published article describing the development and psychometric properties of the NSI-PR, but it has been used in a handful of published studies. The NSI-PR has 16 items, including four asociality, four avolition, three anhedonia, three blunted-affect items, and one item each for transitory distress and alogia (L. Ellman, personal communication, June 6, 2022). The NSI-PR uses a 0 (absent) to 6 (extremely severe) rating scale. A shorter revision of the NSI-PR includes 11 items (two avolition, three asociality, two anhedonia, three blunted affect, and one alogia; L. Ellman, personal communication, June 6, 2022). This shorter version uses a 0 (absent) to 5 (extremely severe) scale, removing the moderately severe anchor from the prior 0 to 6 scale, with substantial revisions to the anchors of the rating scale. Because no study has yet been published regarding the psychometric properties of this new and evolving measure, we cannot yet evaluate it and recommend it for use.

3. Other Methods for Assessing Negative Symptoms

Chapters 11 and 12 of this volume cover self-report and digital mobile health methods for evaluating negative symptoms. Here, we briefly consider two other methods: behavioral coding and machine learning. These methods are used mostly for the assessment of blunted affect (face and voice most frequently), and given the rapid changes in the field, they are evolving quickly.

3.1 Behavioral Coding

One key translation of affective science theory and methods has been in the application of coding systems for facial movement and acoustic analyses of vocal utterances. With early systems, trained human coders evaluated recordings of the face and voice according to systematic rules and procedures. Use of these methods has yielded one of the most well-replicated findings: People diagnosed with psychotic disorders are much less expressive (both facially and vocally) than people without psychotic disorder diagnoses in response to a variety of emotional situations and stimuli, such as films, foods, smells, pictures, music, and everyday life (Kring & Elis, 2013). In addition, CHR groups are less expressive than non-CHR groups (e.g., Ricard et al., 2021). Coded facial and vocal behaviors are also associated with the negative symptoms of blunted affect and alogia, or more generally, the EXP factor.

Use of these methods in clinical settings presents a challenge in that they are typically more time consuming than clinical interviews and may require specialized equipment. Nevertheless, they can provide "real-time" assessments of the behavior (and experiences) that comprise negative symptoms; they do not rely upon retrospective recall as clinical interviews and self-report measures do, and training in these methods may provide new insights for treatment professionals. Many behavioral coding systems, such as the Facial Expression Coding System (FACES; Kring & Sloan, 2007) or the Emotional Expressive Behavior Coding System (EEB; Gross & Levenson, 1993) have freely available training materials that can be used to help researchers and clinicians identify subtle yet meaningful changes in facial movement. Others, such as FACS, require a fee to obtain the system and training (Ekman & Friesen, 1978).

Over the past decade, many automated, computer-based behavioral coding systems have been developed. Some are freely available, and others are commercially available. Using automated methods does not require human coders but instead relies on algorithms to make sense of video or audio recordings. Like behavioral coding, these methods may be less feasible than clinical interviews in practice settings; further, there is work to be done improving the validity of these systems. However, these systems, and the machine learning models that are often built to use them, are increasing in availability and sophistication (Corneanu et al., 2016).

Many automated facial behavior coding systems, such as the commercial iMotions Facial Expression Analysis (https://imotions.com/biosensor/fea-facial-expression-analysis/) and Noldus Face Reader (https://www.noldus.com/facereader), or the freely available OpenFace (https://github.com/TadasBaltrusaitis/OpenFace) are based on FACS. Thus, output from these systems maps onto human-coded behavior using FACS or a system based in FACS such as EEB (e.g., Gupta et al., 2020). Unfortunately, FACS is not consistent with more recent theory and research in affective science (e.g., Barrett et al., 2019), which shows that facial displays are highly variable and context-dependent (Barrett, 2017). FACS was developed following an older emotion theory that stipulates a small set of basic emotions, but contemporary evidence does not strongly support this view. Thus, many automated facial coding systems are being designed to identify only a fraction of what the face actually does in emotional contexts.

For analysis of speech, Cohen and colleagues developed the Computerized Affect from Natural Speech (CANS; Cohen et al., 2009; Cohen et al., 2016), a program that computes pitch and intensity from speech samples, and that has been used in studies of people diagnosed with psychotic disorders. Other systems such as OpenSmile (https://www.audeering.com/research/opensmile/) and PRAAT (https://www.fon.hum.uva.nl/praat/) also provide information about pitch, intensity, pauses, and formants (i.e., acoustic signatures associated with vowel sounds) of speech. Most studies using these automated systems have focused on distinguishing between people who do and do not have a psychotic disorder or people who have predominantly positive versus negative symptoms (e.g., de Boer et al., 2021; Fu et al., 2021). Recent studies, however, show promise for linking automated coding of the voice and negative symptoms. For example, Stanislawski and colleagues (2021) used PRAAT in a small sample of people at CHR and found linkages between SIPS negative symptom ratings and pauses.

Nevertheless, the translation of these characteristics into clinical meaning remains a work in progress (Cohen et al., 2014; Cohen et al., 2016; Cohen et al., 2021; Parola et al., 2020). For example, automated ratings of facial behavior do not always align with clinical ratings of blunted affect (Cowan et al., 2022). Indeed, Cohen and colleagues (2021) use the concept of "signal resolution" to illustrate a key difference between automated and human assessment: Although automated systems can provide detailed, "high resolution" descriptions of facial movements or vocal acoustics relative to human coders' "low-resolution" ratings, it is difficult to ascertain the meaning and clinical importance of these descriptions. In short, these methods are not yet ready to be imported into clinical settings given the remaining work that needs to be done on linking their detailed output to symptoms and on improving their feasibility of use.

3.2 Machine Learning Approaches

One current wave of research activity linked to automated assessments is in the development of machine learning models for the analysis of facial and vocal expression. This method begins with a corpus of faces to "train" models on features and movements on the face, and then attempts to model the possible emotional significance of facial movements. This growing and vibrant area of investigation in psychology, engineering, and computer science is in early stages with respect to use in psychotic disorders or negative symptoms, and as such, the translation of these methods to clinical applications is currently out of reach. For example, these models do not yet comparably handle faces or voices across the spectrum of race and ethnicity, indicating more work is necessary to develop diverse corpora of training stimuli so that future models will avoid cultural bias (Hitczenko et al., 2022).

The use of mobile technology for assessing symptoms, known broadly as "digital phenotyping," is also being investigated using active (self-reports of symptoms or experiences multiple times a day) and passive (e.g., geolocation) methods. Data from these methods are then used to train machine learning algorithms to distinguish people who do and do not have a psychotic disorder (e.g., Depp et al., 2019; Narkhede et al., 2022). Efforts are also underway to use machine learning models with laboratory measures of motivation in order to develop a psychosis risk calculator that includes negative symptoms (Mittal et al., 2021). Although intriguing, additional work on the reliability and validity of these approaches is still needed.

4. Conclusions

Clinical interviews and rating scales are the most commonly used methods for assessing negative symptoms in people with psychotic disorders and those at clinical high risk. Second-generation measures including the CAINS and BNSS have excellent psychometric properties, strong validity data, and demonstrated efficacy in treatment studies. Although older rating scales are still used, the newer measures are better suited for both research and clinical settings. Both the CAINS and BNSS capture the five consensus negative symptom domains and can be scored into dimension scores: MAP covering asociality, avolition, and anhedonia; and EXP covering blunted affect and alogia. These measures assess symptoms over the past week, which reduces recall bias and also ties the assessment more closely to the development of treatment plans. The CAINS and BNSS have relative strengths and weaknesses in terms of length of time to administer, depth of interview questions, separability of life domains, and distinguishing experience from behavior. Either measure can be readily used in clinical settings given that both have training materials freely available and are intuitive interviews to conduct and rate. These measures can be used to gauge treatment effectiveness by administering them at the beginning and end of treatment. They can also be used to identify treatment goals and to provide feedback to clients about potential areas for growth.

Older behavioral coding and newer automated analysis and machine learning approaches may provide useful information in research and clinical settings, often above and beyond what clinical interviews can reveal. For example, behavioral coding of the face and voice is often done in the context of experienced emotion so that the behavior revealed is more closely tied to emotion, whereas clinical interviews may yield more dispassionate rendering of symptoms. Indeed, if a person sees many different treatment professionals, the recitation of history and symptoms can become almost rote, thus limiting the opportunity to observe expressive negative symptoms. Behavioral coding, whether automated or scored by human coders, can also yield additional information about the types of changes in the face or voice that may vary by context. These methods, however, take additional time and resources, which may not be as readily available in clinical settings. Understanding the affective science that supports the second-generation clinical interviews, including research on expression, pleasure, and motivation, can inform the assessment measure to use as well as the treatment domains to target (Aleman et al., 2017; Elis et al., 2013; Sloan & Kring, 2007).

References

Addington, J., Cadenhead, K. S., Cannon, T. D., Cornblatt, B., McGlashan, T. H., Perkins, D. O., Seidman, L. J., Tsuang, M., Walker, E. F., Woods, S. W., Heinssen, R., for the North American Prodrome Longitudinal Study [NAPLS] Group (2007). North American Prodrome Longitudinal Study: A collaborative multisite approach to prodromal schizophrenia research. *Schizophrenia Bulletin, 33*(3), 665–672.

Addington, J., Cadenhead, K. S., Cornblatt, B. A., Mathalon, D. H., McGlashan, T. H., Perkins, D. O., Seidman, L. J., Tsuang, M. T., Walker, E. F., Woods, S. W., Addington, J. A., & Cannon, T. D. (2012). North American Prodrome Longitudinal Study (NAPLS 2): Overview and recruitment. *Schizophrenia Research, 142*, 77–82.

Addington, J., Liu, L., Brummitt, K., Bearden, C. E., Cadenhead, K. S., Cornblatt, B. A., Keshavan, M., Mathalon, D. H., McGlashan, T. H., Perkins, D. O., Seidman, L. J., Stone, W., Tsuang, M. T., Walker, E. F., Woods, S. W., & Cannon, T. D. (2022). North American Prodrome Longitudinal Study (NAPLS 3): Methods and baseline description. *Schizophrenia Research*, (243)262–267.

Aleman, A., Lincoln, T. M., Bruggeman, R., Melle, I., Arends, J., Arango, C., and Knegtering, H. (2017). Treatment of negative symptoms: Where do we stand, and where do we go? *Schizophrenia Research, 186*, 55–62.

Andreasen, N. C. (1982). Negative symptoms in schizophrenia: Definition and reliability. *Archives of General Psychiatry, 39*, 784–788.

Andreasen, N. C. (1984). *The Scale for the Assessment of Negative Symptoms (SANS)*. The University of Iowa, Iowa City.

Azis, M., Strauss, G. P., Walker, E., Revelle, W., Zinbarg, R., & Mittal, V. (2019). Factor analysis of negative symptom items in the Structured Interview for Prodromal Syndromes. *Schizophrenia Bulletin, 45*(5), 1042–1050.

Barch, D. M., Gold, J. M., & Kring, A. M. (2017). Paradigms for assessing hedonic processing and motivation in humans: Relevance to understanding negative symptoms in psychopathology. *Schizophrenia Bulletin, 43*, 701–705.

Barrett, L. F. (2017). *How emotions are made: The secret life of the brain*. New York: Houghton Mifflin Harcourt.

Barrett, L. F., Adolphs, R., Marsella, S., Martinez, A. M., & Pollak, S. D. (2019). Emotional expressions reconsidered: Challenges to inferring emotion from human facial movements. *Psychological Science in the Public Interest, 20*, 1–68.

Blanchard, J. J., Bradshaw, K. R., Garcia, C. P., Nasrallah, H. A., Harvey, P. D., Casey, D., Csoboth, C. T., Hudson, J. I., Julian, L., Lentz, E., Neuchterlein, K. H., Perkins, D. O., Skale, T. G., Snowden, L. R., Tandon, R., Tek, C., Velligan, D., Vinogradov, S., & O'Gorman, C. (2017). Examining the reliability and validity of the Clinical Assessment Interview for Negative Symptoms within the Management of Schizophrenia in Clinical Practice (MOSAIC) multisite national study. *Schizophrenia Research, 185*, 137–143.

Blanchard, J. J., & Cohen, A. S. (2006). The structure of negative symptoms within schizophrenia: Implications for assessment. *Schizophrenia Bulletin, 32*, 238–245.

Blanchard, J. J., Kring, A. M., Horan, W. P., & Gur, R. (2011). Toward the next generation of negative symptom assessments: The Collaboration to Advance Negative Symptom Assessment in Schizophrenia. *Schizophrenia Bulletin, 37*, 291–299.

Blanchard, J. J., Shan, L., Andrea, A., Savage, C., Kring, A. M., & Weittenhiller, L. (2019). Negative symptoms and their assessment in schizophrenia and related disorders. In J. C. Badcock & G. Paulik (Eds.), *A clinical introduction to psychosis: Foundations for clinical psychologists* (pp. 153–175). London: Academic Press.

Cohen, A. S., Minor, K. S., Najolia, G. M., & Hong, S. L. (2009). A laboratory-based procedure for measuring emotional expression from natural speech. *Behavior Research Methods, 41*, 204–212.

Cohen, A. S., Mitchell, K. R., Docherty, N. M., & Horan, W. P. (2016). Vocal expression in schizophrenia: Less than meets the ear. *Journal of Abnormal Psychology, 125*, 299–309.

Cohen, A. S., Mitchell, K. R., & Elvevåg, B. (2014). What do we really know about blunted vocal affect and alogia? A meta-analysis of objective assessments. *Schizophrenia Research, 159*, 533–538.

Cohen, A. S., Renshaw, T. L., Mitchell, K. R., & Kim, Y. (2016). A psychometric investigation of "macroscopic" speech measures for clinical and psychological science. *Behavior Research Methods, 48*, 475–486.

Cohen, A. S., Schwartz, E., Le, T. P., Cowan, T., Kirkpatrick, B., Raugh, I. M., & Strauss, G. P. (2021). Digital phenotyping of negative symptoms: The relationship to clinician ratings. *Schizophrenia Bulletin, 47*, 44–53.

Corneanu, C. A., Simón, M. O., Cohn, J. F., & Guerrero, S. E. (2016). Survey on RGB, 3D, thermal, and multimodal approaches for facial expression recognition: History, trends, and affect-related applications. *IEEE Transactions on Pattern Analysis and Machine Intelligence, 38*(8), 1548–1568.

Cowan, T., Masucci, M. D., Gupta, T., Haase, C. M., Strauss, G. P., & Cohen, A. S. (2022). Computerized analysis of facial expressions in serious mental illness. *Schizophrenia Research, 241*, 44–51.

de Boer, J. N., Voppel, A. E., Brederoo, S. G., Schnack, H. G., Truong, K. P., Wijnen, F. N. K., & Sommer, I. E. C. (2023). Acoustic speech markers for schizophrenia-spectrum disorders: A diagnostic and symptom-recognition tool. *Psychological Medicine*, (53), 1302–1312.

Depp, C. A., Bashem, J., Moore, R. C., Holden, J. L., Mikhael, T., Swendsen, J., Harvey, P. D., & Granholm, E. L. (2019). GPS mobility as a digital biomarker of negative symptoms in schizophrenia: A case control study. *NPJ Digital Medicine, 2*(1), 1–7.

Ekman, P., & Friesen, W. V. (1978). *The Facial Action Coding System*. Palo Alto, CA: Consulting Psychological Press.

Elis, O., Caponigro, J. M., & Kring, A. M. (2013). Psychosocial treatments for negative symptoms in schizophrenia: Current practices and future directions. *Clinical Psychology Review, 33*, 914–928.

Finn, S. E. (2007). *In our clients' shoes: Theory and techniques of therapeutic assessment.* Mahwah, NJ: Erlbaum.

Forbes, C., Blanchard, J. J., Bennett, M., Horan, W. P., Kring, A. M., & Gur, R. (2010). Initial development and preliminary validation of a new negative symptom measure: The Clinical Assessment Interview for Negative Symptoms (CAINS). *Schizophrenia Research, 124*, 36–42.

Fu, J., Yang, S., He, F., He, L., Li, Y., Zhang, J., and Xiong, X. (2021). Sch-net: A deep learning architecture for automatic detection of schizophrenia. *Biomedical Engineering Online, 20*(1), 75.

Galderisi, S., Mucci, A., Dollfus, S., Nordentoft, M., Falkai, P., Kaiser, S., Giordano, G. M., Vandevelde, A., Nielsen, M. Ø., Glenthøj, L. B., Sabé, M., Pezzella, P., Bitter, I., & Gaebel, W. (2021). EPA guidance on assessment of negative symptoms in schizophrenia. *European Psychiatry, 64*(1). e23, 1–23.

Gross, J. J., & Levenson, R. W. (1993). Emotional suppression: Physiology, self-report, and expressive behavior. *Journal of Personality and Social Psychology, 64*, 970–986.

Gupta, T., Haase, C. M., Strauss, G. P., Cohen, A. S., Ricard, J. R., & Mittal, V. A. (2020). Alterations in facial expressions of emotion: Determining the promise of ultrathin slicing approaches and comparing human and automated coding methods in psychosis risk. *Emotion, 22*, 714–724.

Gur, R. E., March, M., Calkins, M. E., Weittenhiller, L., Wolf, D. H., Turetsky, B. I., & Gur, R. C. (2015). Negative symptoms in youths with psychosis spectrum features: Complementary scales in relation to neurocognitive performance and function. *Schizophrenia Research, 166*, 322–327.

Hitczenko, K., Cowan, H. R., Goldrick, M., & Mittal, V. A. (2022). Racial and ethnic biases in computational approaches to psychopathology. *Schizophrenia Bulletin, 48*(2), 285–288.

Horan, W. P., Kring, A. M., Gur, R., Reise, S., & Blanchard, J. J. (2011). Psychometric evaluation of the Clinical Assessment Interview for Negative Symptoms (CAINS) in a large outpatient schizophrenia sample. *Schizophrenia Research, 132*, 140–145.

Kaiser, S., Lyne, J., Agartz, I., Clarke, M., Mørch-Johnsen, L., & Faerden, A. (2017). Individual negative symptoms and domains—Relevance for assessment, pathomechanisms and treatment. *Schizophrenia Research, 186*, 39–45.

Kay, S. R., Fiszbein, A., & Opler, L. A. (1987). Positive and negative syndrome scale (PANSS) for schizophrenia. *Schizophrenia Bulletin, 13*, 261–271.

Kirkpatrick, B., Fenton, W. S., Carpenter, W. T., & Marder, S. R. (2006). The NIMH-MATRICS consensus statement on negative symptoms. *Schizophrenia Bulletin, 32*(2), 214–219.

Kirkpatrick, B., Strauss, G. P., Nguyen, L., Fischer, B. A., Daniel, D. G., Cienfuegos, A., & Marder, S. R. (2011). The Brief Negative Symptom Scale: Psychometric properties. *Schizophrenia Bulletin, 37*, 300–305.

Kirkpatrick, B., Saoud, J. B., Strauss, G. P., Ahmed, A. O., Tatsumi, K., Opler, M., Luthringer, R., & Davidson, M. (2018). The Brief Negative Symptom Scale (BNSS). Sensitivity to treatment effects. *Schizophrenia Research, 197*, 269–273.

Kotov, R., Jonas, K. G., Carpenter, W. T., Dretsch, M. N., Eaton, N. R., Forbes, M. K., Forbush, K. T., Hobbs, K., Reininghaus, U., Slade, T., South, S. C., Sunderland, M., Waszczuk, M. A., Widiger, T. A., Wright, A. G. C., Zald, D. H., Krueger, R. F., Watson, D., & HiTOP Utility Workgroup (2020). Validity and utility of Hierarchical Taxonomy of Psychopathology (HiTOP): I. Psychosis superspectrum. *World Psychiatry, 19*(2), 151–172.

Kotov, R., Krueger, R. F., Watson, D., Achenbach, T. M., Althoff, R. R., Bagby, R. M., Brown, T. A., Carpenter, W. T., Caspi, A., Clark, L. A., Eaton, N. R., Forbes, M. K., Forbush, K. T.,

Goldberg, D., Hasin, D., Hyman, S. E., Ivanova, M. Y., Lynam, D. R., Markon, K., . . . & Zimmerman, M. (2017). The Hierarchical Taxonomy of Psychopathology (HiTOP): A dimensional alternative to traditional nosologies. *Journal of Abnormal Psychology, 126*(4), 454–477.

Kring, A. M., & Barch, D. M. (2014). The motivation and pleasure dimension of negative symptoms: Neural substrates and behavioral outputs. *European Neuropsychopharmacology, 24*, 725–736.

Kring, A. M., & Caponigro, J. M. (2010). Emotion in schizophrenia: Where feeling meets thinking. *Current Directions in Psychological Science, 19*, 255–259.

Kring, A. M., & Elis, O. (2013). Emotion deficits in people with schizophrenia. *Annual Review of Clinical Psychology, 9*, 409–433.

Kring, A. M., Gur, R. E., Blanchard, J. J., Horan, W. P., Reise, S. P. (2013). The Clinical Assessment Interview for Negative Symptoms (CAINS): Final development and validation. *American Journal of Psychiatry, 170*, 165–172.

Kring, A. M., & Sloan, D. S. (2007). The facial expression coding system (FACES): Development, validation, and utility. *Psychological Assessment, 19*, 210–224.

Liemburg, E., Castelein, S., Stewart, R., van der Gaag, M., Aleman, A., & Knegtering, H. (2013). Two subdomains of negative symptoms in psychotic disorders: Established and confirmed in two large cohorts. *Journal of Psychiatric Research, 47*(6), 718–725.

Lincoln, T. M., Dollfus, S., & Lyne, J. (2017). Current developments and challenges in the assessment of negative symptoms. *Schizophrenia Research, 186*, 8–18.

Messinger, J. W., Trémeau, F., Antonius, D., Mendelsohn, E., Prudent, V., Stanford, A. D., & Malaspina, D. (2011). Avolition and expressive deficits capture negative symptom phenomenology: Implications for DSM-5 and schizophrenia research. *Clinical Psychology Review, 31*(1), 161–168.

Miller, T. J., McGlashan, T. H., Rosen, J. L., Cadenhead, K., Ventura, J., McFarlane, W., Perkins, D. O., Pearlson, G. D., & Woods, S. W. (2003). Prodromal assessment with the structured interview for prodromal syndromes and the scale of prodromal symptoms: Predictive validity, interrater reliability, and training to reliability. *Schizophrenia Bulletin, 29*(4), 703–715.

Mittal, V. A., Ellman, L. M., Strauss, G. P., Walker, E. F., Corlett, P. R., Schiffman, J., Woods, S. W., Powers, A. R., Silverstein, S. M., Waltz, J. A., Zinbarg, R., Chen, S., Williams, T., Kenney, J., & Gold, J. M. (2021). Computerized assessment of psychosis risk. *Journal of Psychiatry and Brain Science, 6*(3), e210011.

Mueser, K. T., Sayers, S. L., Schooler, N. R., Mance, R. M., & Haas, G. (1994). A multisite investigation of the reliability of the scale for the assessment of negative symptoms. *The American Journal of Psychiatry, 151*, 1453–1462.

Narkhede, S. M., Luther, L., Raugh, I. M., Knippenberg, A. R., Esfahlani, F. Z., Sayama, H., Cohen, A. S., Kirkpatrick, B., & Strauss, G. P. (2022). Machine learning identifies digital phenotyping measures most relevant to negative symptoms in psychotic disorders: Implications for clinical trials. *Schizophrenia Bulletin, 48*(2), 425–436.

Neale, J. M., Oltmanns, T. F., & Harvey, P. D. (1985). The need to relate cognitive deficits to specific behavioral referents of schizophrenia. *Schizophrenia Bulletin, 11*(2), 286–291.

Nelson, B., Simmons, M. B., Yung, A. R., Buckby, J. A., O'Dwyer, L., Francey, S. M., Leicester, S., Bapat, S., & McGorry, P. D. (2008). Identifying the ultra-high risk (prodromal) population: Evaluation of training workshops with mental health services. *Australian & New Zealand Journal of Psychiatry, 42*(3), 236–243.

Overall, J. E., & Gorham, D. R. (1962). The Brief Psychiatric Rating Scale. *Psychological Reports, 10*, 799–812.

Parola, A., Simonsen, A., Bliksted, V., and Fusaroli, R. (2020). Voice patterns in schizophrenia: A systematic review and Bayesian meta-analysis. *Schizophrenia Research, 216*, 24–40.

Pelletier-Baldelli, A., Strauss, G. P., Visser, K. H., & Mittal, V. A. (2017). Initial development and preliminary psychometric properties of the Prodromal Inventory of Negative Symptoms (PINS). *Schizophrenia Research, 189*, 43–49.

Peralta, V., & Cuesta, M. J. (1995). Negative symptoms in schizophrenia: A confirmatory factor analysis of competing models. *The American Journal of Psychiatry*, *152*(10), 1450–1457.
Persons, J. B. (1986). The advantages of studying psychological phenomena rather than psychiatric diagnoses. *American Psychologist*, *41*, 1252–1260.
Piskulic, D., Addington, J., Cadenhead, K. S., Cannon, T. D., Cornblatt, B. A., Heinssen, R., Perkins, D. O., Seidman, L. J., Tsuang, M. T., Walker, E. F., Woods, S. W., & McGlashan, T. H. (2012). Negative symptoms in individuals at clinical high risk of psychosis. *Psychiatry Research*, *196*, 220–224.
Rabany, L., Weiser, M., Werbeloff, N., & Levkovitz, Y. (2011). Assessment of negative symptoms and depression in schizophrenia: Revision of the SANS and how it relates to the PANSS and CDSS. *Schizophrenia Research*, *126*, 226–230.
Ricard, J. R., Gupta, T., Vargas, T., Haase, C. M., & Mittal, V. A. (2021). Genuine and non-genuine smiles in individuals meeting criteria for a clinical high-risk syndrome. *Early Intervention in Psychiatry*, *16*(8), 875–882.
Selten, J. P., Gernaat, H. B., Nolen, W. A., Wiersma, D., & van den Bosch, R. J. (1998). Experience of negative symptoms: Comparison of schizophrenic patients to patients with a depressive disorder and to normal subjects. *American Journal of Psychiatry*, *155*, 350–354.
Singh, M. M., & Kay, S. R. (1975). A comparative study of haloperidol and chlorpromazine in terms of clinical effects and therapeutic reversal with benztropine in schizophrenia: Theoretical implications for potency differences among neuroleptics. *Psychopharmacologia*, *43*, 103–110.
Sloan, D., & Kring, A. M. (2007). Measuring changes in emotion during psychotherapy: Conceptual and methodological issues. *Clinical Psychology: Science and Practice*, *14*, 307–322.
Stanislawski, E. R., Bilgrami, Z. R., Sarac, C., Garg, S., Heisig, S., Cecchi, G. A., Agurto, C., & Corcoran, C. M. (2021). Negative symptoms and speech pauses in youths at clinical high risk for psychosis. *NPJ Schizophrenia*, *7*, 3.
Strauss, G. P., and Chapman, H. C. (2018). Preliminary psychometric properties of the brief Negative Symptom Scale in youth at clinical high-risk for psychosis. *Schizophrenia Research*, *193*, 435–437.
Strauss, G. P., & Gold, J. M. (2016). A psychometric comparison of the Clinical Assessment Interview for Negative Symptoms and the Brief Negative Symptom Scale. *Schizophrenia Bulletin*, *42*(6), 1384–1394.
Strauss, G. P., Hong, L. E., Gold, J. M., Buchanan, R. W., McMahon, R. P., Keller, W. R., Fischer, B. A., Catalano, L. T., Culbreth, A. J., Carpenter, W. T., & Kirkpatrick, B. (2012). Factor structure of the Brief Negative Symptom Scale. *Schizophrenia Research*, *142*(1–3), 96–98.
Strauss, G. P., Keller, W. R., Buchanan, R. W., Gold, J. M., Fischer, B. A., McMahon, R. P., Catalano, L. T., Culbreth, A. J., Carpenter, W. T., & Kirkpatrick, B. (2012). Next-generation negative symptom assessment for clinical trials: Validation of the Brief Negative Symptom Scale. *Schizophrenia Research*, *142*(1–3), 88–92.
Strauss, G. P., Pelletier-Baldelli, A., Visser, K. F., Walker, E. F., & Mittal, V. A. (2020). A review of negative symptom assessment strategies in youth at clinical high-risk for psychosis. *Schizophrenia Research*, *222*, 104–112.
van Erp, T. G. M., Preda, A., Nguyen, D., Faziola, L., Turner, J., Bustillo, J., Belger, A., Lim, K. O., McEwan, S., Voyvodic, J., Mathalon, D. H., Ford, J., Potkin, S. G., & FBIRN. (2014). Converting positive and negative symptom scores between PANSS and SAPS/SANS. *Schizophrenia Research*, *152*(1), 289–294.
Ventura, J., Lukoff, D., Nuechterlein, K. H., Liberman, R. P., Green, M. F., & Shaner, A. (1993). Manual for the Expanded Brief Psychiatric Rating Scale. *International Journal of Methods in Psychiatric Research*, *3*, 227–243.
Walker, E. F., Davis, D. M., & Savoie, T. D. (1994). Neuromotor precursors of schizophrenia. *Schizophrenia Bulletin*, *20*, 441–451.
Walker, E. F., Grimes, K. E., Davis, D. M., & Adina, J. (1993). Childhood precursors of schizophrenia: Facial expressions of emotion. *American Journal of Psychiatry*, *150*, 1654–1660.

Weittenhiller, L., Mikhail, M., Mote, J., Campellone, T. R., & Kring, A. M. (2021). What gets in the way of social engagement in schizophrenia? *World Journal of Psychiatry*, *11*, 13–26.

Yung, A. R., McGorry, P. D., McFarlane, C. A., & Patton, G. (1995). The PACE Clinic: Development of a clinical service for young people at high risk of psychosis. *Australian Psychiatry*, *3*, 345–349.

Yung, A. R., Pan Yuen, H., McGorry, P. D., Phillips, L. J., Kelly, D., Dell'Olio, M., Francey, S. M., Cosgrave, E. M., Killackey, E., Stanford, C., Godfrey, K., & Buckby, J. (2005). Mapping the onset of psychosis: The comprehensive assessment of at-risk mental states. *Australian & New Zealand Journal of Psychiatry*, *39*(11–12), 964–971.

8

Subjective Approaches to the Assessment of Negative Symptoms

Sonia Dollfus and Camille Delouche

Clinical pearls

- Self-assessments can be used to complement observer-ratings in clinical practice.
- Self-Evaluation of Negative Symptoms (SNS) and Motivation and Pleasure Scale Self-Report (MAP-SR) are two scales that can be used for self-assessment of negative symptoms.
- These scales are easy and fast to fill in by the patients themselves and allow the practitioner to quickly identify the level of severity of negative symptoms and the kind of negative symptom from which the patients are suffering and/or are aware.

Negative symptoms are found in many patients with schizophrenia at any stage of the disorder: during the prodromal phase (Piskulic et al., 2012), the first episode of schizophrenia (Galderisi et al., 2013), or during a late stage. Multiple studies highlight that 50% to 60% of patients with schizophrenia have at least one negative symptom of moderate severity (Bobes et al., 2010). These symptoms can persist despite the improvement of positive symptoms and the antipsychotic treatment, and are responsible for poor social functioning and quality of life (Galderisi et al., 2014).

Although their frequency is high and their consequences are harmful, the load of negative symptoms is less than that of positive symptoms in the diagnostic classifications, even in the DSM-5 or ICD-11. This might be due to their tricky assessment and the fact that pharmaceutical research had been focused for a long time on positive symptoms. Moreover, negative symptoms overlap with other domains such as depression and extrapyramidal side effects of medications, which makes the identification and the definition of negative symptoms more difficult.

Sonia Dollfus and Camille Delouche, *Subjective Approaches to the Assessment of Negative Symptoms*.
In: *Psychosocial Approaches to Negative Symptoms in Psychosis*. Edited by: Tania Lincoln et al.,
Oxford University Press. © Oxford University Press (2025). DOI: 10.1093/oso/9780197676790.003.0008

To overcome this problem, the National Institute of Mental Health (NIMH) proposed in 2005 a consensus conference on the definition of negative symptom dimensions and recommended five dimensions to describe these symptoms: blunted affect, alogia, anhedonia, social withdrawal, and avolition (Kirkpatrick et al., 2006). Despite this progress, diagnosing and treating negative symptoms is still a challenge. In this context, the use of standardized and validated scales is necessary for assessing the efficacy of new treatments and for earlier detection and better evaluation of these symptoms.

Since the NIMH conference, we can classify assessment tools in two categories: the first-generation scales (developed before the conference), and the second-generation scales (developed after the conference) (Galderisi et al., 2021).

Most of the first-generation scales are based on observer ratings and aim to quantify the severity of negative symptoms (see Kring, Weittenhiller, & Cogan, Chapter 7, this volume). The most widely employed instruments are: the Scale for the Assessment of Negative Symptoms (SANS) (Andreasen, 1989), the negative sub-scale of the Positive and Negative Syndrome Scale (PANSS) (Kay et al., 1987), the "anergy" factor of the Brief Psychiatric Rating Scale (BPRS) including three items, emotional withdrawal, motor slowing and emotional blunting negative (Overall et al., 1967) and the Negative Symptom Assessment (NSA) (Axelrod et al., 1993). None of them, however, have taken into account the subjective or internal experiences of patients.

More recently, two scales based on observer ratings that meet the criteria presented at the consensus conference on the agreement of negative symptoms were devised. They are the Brief Negative Symptoms Scale (BNSS) (Kirkpatrick et al., 2011) and the Clinical Assessment Interview for Negative Symptoms (CAINS) (Blanchard et al., 2011). One advantage of both these scales, compared to the first generation scales, is to consider the patient's internal experiences. Among the 13 items of BNSS, however, only two assess internal experiences; one focuses on social withdrawal and another, avolition. Regarding CAINS, there is no specific item for subjective experiences, because internal experiences and observed behaviors are combined in the same ratings. In both scales, internal experiences are assessed with a semistructured interview and consequently, these ratings cannot be considered as self-assessments given that they are not rated by the patients themselves.

Compared to the scales based on observer ratings, self-assessments have been neglected, probably because of the idea that patients with schizophrenia are unable to report their negative symptoms accurately (Hamera et al., 1996) (Selten et al., 2000). Some authors, however, have underlined that subjective evaluation by schizophrenia patients is possible and brings an outcome measure complementary to hetero-evaluations (Fleischhacker et al., 2005; Ohata et al., 2014). Moreover, self-report scales allow the patient to self-assess their feelings and experiences related to negative symptoms. Self-evaluations provide clinical information not necessarily detected by caregivers or medical staff in a standard interview and subjective feelings on the symptoms as recognized by the patients themselves. The self-reports can be used alone or can complement the evaluations based on interviews. This is well illustrated by a network analysis that examined the interrelationship between negative symptom domains from evaluations based on self-reports and observer ratings (Wang et al., 2022). In this study concerning 204 individuals with schizophrenia assessed with the SANS, the BNSS, and the Self-Evaluation of Negative Symptoms (SNS) (Dollfus et al., 2016), self-report negative symptoms were found to be closely connected to form a cluster while the BNSS and SANS domains were intermingled together.

In the past, three scales were developed to assess subjective experiences of deficit or negative symptoms. The Subjective Deficit Syndrome Scale (SDSS) (Jaeger et al., 1990) allows reporting patient complaints. This scale, however, is not solely focused on negative symptoms, because only three items out of 19 concern negative symptoms, explaining why complaints were not found to be correlated with negative symptoms. The Subjective Experience of Deficits in Schizophrenia scale (SEDS) (Liddle & Barnes, 1988) assesses the subjective awareness of deficits on thought and mental activity and so also does not only concern negative symptoms. Indeed, only a few of the items evaluate the negative dimension, and these do not cover the five dimensions required. Moreover, the ratings are processed with a semistandardized interview, not on a self-report. The Subjective Experience of Negative Symptoms scale (SENS) (Selten et al., 1993) is an interview-based self-rating measure evaluating the subjective experiences of negative symptoms, such as awareness, causal attribution, and disruption or distress. Although this last scale was based on the latest version of the SANS (Andreasen, 1989), neither convergent nor discriminant validity was tested. Finally, these three scales cannot be considered as self-assessments and two of them were not based specifically on negative symptoms.

Recently, two self-assessment scales were designed and so supplanted the previous tools that did not meet good psychometric properties or did not cover the five negative dimensions required by the consensus conference. These scales are the Motivation and Pleasure Scale Self-Report (MAP-SR) (Llerena et al., 2013) and the Self-Evaluation of Negative Symptoms (SNS) (Dollfus et al., 2016), both specifically developed for the negative symptoms in schizophrenia.

The Motivation and Pleasure Scale Self-Report (MAP-SR) (Llerena et al., 2013) is a self-assessment developed from the CAINS Motivation and Pleasure subscale. In the first version of the measure with 18 items, poor reliability and validity of the expression items (alogia and blunted affect) were reported

(Park et al., 2012) leading to a 15-item revised version, which demonstrated good internal consistency, good discriminant validity, with small association with positive symptoms. All items are rated on a five-point Likert scale (from 0 to 4). In this 15-item version, six items tap into consummatory and anticipatory pleasures related to social, recreational, or work domains, three items tap into feelings and motivation to be around family, romantic partners, and friends, and six items concern motivation and effort to engage in activities. Engel and Lincoln developed the German version of the MAP-SR, and they also found good internal consistency, good discriminant validity as well as mostly good convergent validity (with PANSS negative subscale and Experience subscale of the CAINS) (Engel & Lincoln, 2016). A Spanish version of the MAP-SR was recently validated and demonstrated good psychometric properties, with an excellent reliability (García-Portilla et al., 2021). The MAP-SR also has been translated into Korean with good psychometric properties (Kim et al., 2016). Interestingly, Engel and Lincoln (2017) evaluated the suitability between self-rating scale and scale based on observed rating using the MAP-SR and CAINS. They found 52.9% of the healthy individuals and 46% of the patients to have relatively equal self- and observer-ratings supporting the validity of self-rating in patients with schizophrenia. Healthy subjects, however, tend to overestimate the severity while patients with schizophrenia tend to underestimate the severity of negative symptoms. However, this 15-item scale fails to cover the five negative dimensions required. Indeed, the expression items (blunted affect and alogia) were removed from the initial version because the authors considered that the patients cannot express them, and that these symptoms are based on observation of the patient. Therefore, this scale exclusively focuses on self-reported deficits in motivation and pleasure and does not take into account the emotional and alogia dimensions. The emotional dimension is important to consider because it might help to disentangle depressive and negative symptoms as pointed out elsewhere (Dollfus et al., 2016). Moreover, the MAP-SR contains many questions like "how often" and "how much," which require that patients remember and quantify what feelings or events happened in the past week, which is potentially difficult for patients with memory impairment.

Another self-report was developed in 2016 (Dollfus et al., 2016): the Self-Evaluation of Negative Symptoms (SNS). This scale was mostly devised from patients' verbatim comments collected during focus groups on negative symptoms. The SNS has 20 items with five subscales covering the five negative dimensions. Each item is scored 0, 1, or 2, wherein the patient respectively "Strongly disagrees," "Somewhat agrees," or "Strongly agrees." Thus, the total score can vary from 0 (no negative symptoms) to 40 (severe negative symptoms) and each subscore varies from 0 to 8. Each subscale contains four items and assesses one of the five domains of negative symptoms (social withdrawal, emotional range, avolition, anhedonia, and alogia) as required by the consensus conference on negative symptoms (Kirkpatrick et al., 2006). Contrarily to the MAP-SR, SNS takes into account the expression items of negative symptoms (blunted affect and alogia). Blunted affect (defined by reduced facial expression, vocal expression, and expressive gestures) is usually assessed by observed-based rating. Consequently, in order to adapt this emotional domain for a self-assessment tool, it has been replaced by the "diminished emotional range." This dimension evaluates the patients' capacity to express and feel emotions (sample item 6: *There are many happy or sad things in life but I don't feel concerned by them*). Regarding alogia, it is assessed by the patient's perception (sample item 9: *I don't have as much to talk about as most people*) and the efforts required by the patient to speak.

The first validation study of the SNS evaluated 49 patients diagnosed with schizophrenia or schizoaffective disorders (DSM-5) and found good psychometric properties (Dollfus et al., 2016). The SNS revealed good internal consistency, and good convergent validity with a strong correlation with the SANS. The study also highlighted good discriminant validity given that the SNS scores did not correlate with Parkinsonism or with Brief Psychiatric Rating Scale positive subscores. Moreover, the SNS scores did not correlate with the level of insight, assessed with the insight scale (Birchwood et al., 1994), demonstrating that patients are able to evaluate their negative symptoms independently of their level of insight into having a mental disorder. This result contradicts several publications that have stated that patients with negative symptoms cannot properly be self-assessed due to their poor insight (Saeedi et al., 2007; Sevy et al., 2004). At a symptomatic level, this result demonstrates that patients with schizophrenia are able to self-assess their negative symptoms, even if they do not attribute the symptoms to a mental health problem, such as schizophrenia. In two different studies (Dollfus et al., 2016) (Hervochon et al., 2018), it was demonstrated that patients were able to distinguish through self assessment lost or decreased emotion from a depressive mood. This also underlines the interest in taking into account the emotional feelings of the patient to allow us to distinguish negative and depressive symptoms.

A European study in 245 patients with a DSM-IV diagnosis of schizophrenia also found an association with patients' functional outcome, and the capacity to identify participants with negative symptoms that was close to the BNSS and superior to the PANSS negative subscale (Dollfus et al., 2022). Moreover, a confirmatory factor analysis investigating four models of the latent structure of SNS showed that the best model was the five-factor model. This result was reproduced in various populations, including clinically stable patients with schizophrenia (Tam et al., 2021), chronic patients with schizophrenia. (Dollfus et al, 2020), and even in healthy adolescent populations (Rodriguez-Testal et al., 2020). This construct in relation to the five consensus domains was found to be the best latent structure of SNS (Mucci et al., 2019) and was similar to that observed with the BNSS (Strauss et al., 2018).

The SNS has been employed in various countries thanks to 20 validated translations at the time of this publication, and several studies validated these foreign language versions. A Polish version was validated in 40 patients with paranoid schizophrenia demonstrating good psychometric properties (Wojciak et al., 2019). A Lithuanian study included 67 participants with paranoid schizophrenia (ICD-10) and reported good internal consistency, good convergent validity, and adequate discriminant validity (Montvidas et al., 2021b). Hajj and colleagues developed an Arabic version of the SNS. Their validation study found good reliability, as well as convergent and discriminant validities in 206 patients with schizophrenia (DSM-5) (Hajj et al., 2020). Good psychometric properties were also reported for SNS Persian and Turkish versions {Mazhari, 2021 #20232} (Polat et al., 2022). Another study employed the SNS in a population of 50 treatment-resistant and low-functioning patients with schizophrenia (Goldring et al., 2020). They showed that low-functioning patients were also able to report their subjective assessment of negative symptoms. Negative symptoms are associated with poor quality of life in patients with schizophrenia, and assessing the quality of life is crucial to understanding the subjective burden of disease. With this objective, Montvidas and colleagues showed in a population of 67 patients with schizophrenia that the SNS has the potential to predict quality of life, especially emotional well-being, vitality, and social function (Montvidas et al., 2021a).

An original study validated a Spanish version of the SNS in 4,521 adolescents (53.6% female), aged 11 to 18 (Rodriguez-Testal et al., 2020) and showed a strong relationship between SNS and depressive symptomatology, moderate with ideas of reference and low with aberrant salience. Besides the good psychometric properties displayed, this study pointed out the potential presence of negative symptoms in the general adolescent population and the interest in using self-assessments to detect negative symptoms.

Another study in a young population used the SNS to assess negative symptoms (Mallet et al., 2020). This study included 117 individuals: 58 patients and 59 healthy controls, aged 15 to 25 years. The patients were adolescents and young adults hospitalized for a first psychiatric episode, and both patients and healthy controls had no psychiatric history and no history of medication. Moreover, categorical diagnoses were updated six months after hospitalization and authors found that self-reported negative symptoms with SNS were associated with a diagnosis of psychiatric disorder at six-month follow-up (OR = 1.163, $p = .001$), whereas depressive symptoms and psychotic experiences were not. That suggests that negative symptoms can discriminate adolescents with a first psychiatric episode from healthy ones.

To determine the threshold beyond which the symptoms are considered pathological in patients with schizophrenia, a comparative study between patients with schizophrenia and healthy subjects using SNS was realized (S. Dollfus et al., 2019). In this study, 109 patients with schizophrenia and schizoaffective disorders (DSM-5) and 99 healthy controls were included and evaluated with the SNS. Receiver Operating Characteristic (ROC) curve was established to discriminate patients with schizophrenia (or schizoaffective disorders) and healthy control participants by assigning the best threshold as determined by sensitivity and specificity. The SNS appears to be an appropriate screening tool for distinguishing patients with schizophrenia and healthy controls at a threshold value of seven (<7 vs ≥7). The sensitivity and specificity were 92.7% (95% CI= 86.1–96.8]) and 85.9% (95CI=i77.4–92.1]), respectively. The results were similar after removing the patients with depressive symptoms assessed with the Calgary Depression Scale (CDS) (Addington et al., 1993; Lançon et al., 1999). Another study in an adolescent population found a higher cut-off point (13.5) on the SNS, with lower sensitivity (0.73) and specificity (0.72) probably because of the different population characterized by a high level of negative symptoms (Rodriguez-Testal et al., 2020). Indeed, the SNS scores in this study were higher than those in the French healthy-adult population (mean (SD): 10.57 (6.27) and 3.47 (3.58), respectively). According to (Mallet et al., 2020), the SNS seems to be an appropriate screening tool for distinguishing first-episode patients or patients with schizophrenia and healthy controls at a threshold value of 11. These results taken together suggest using different thresholds to identify pathological negative symptoms according the population studied. These thresholds are 7, 11, and 13 in patients with chronic schizophrenia, with a first psychotic episode or in adolescent healthy subjects, respectively

Self-assessments appear to be a powerful method to evaluate and detect negative symptoms at any stage of the disorder. This has been supported recently by the European Psychiatric Association Guidance on Assessment of Negative Symptoms (Galderisi et al., 2021), which recommends that the SNS (exploring five domains) and MAP-SR (exploring three domains) can be used for self-assessment of negative symptoms.

References

Addington, D., Addington, J., & Maticka-Tyndale, E. (1993). Assessing depression in schizophrenia: The Calgary Depression Scale. *British Journal of Psychiatry*, *163*(suppl 22), 39–44.

Andreasen, N. C. (1989). The scale for the assessment of negative symptoms (SANS): Conceptual and theoretical foundations. *British Journal of Psychiatry, 155*(suppl 7), 53–58.

Axelrod, B. N., Goldman, R. S., & Alphs, L. D. (1993). Validation of the 16-item Negative Symptom Assessment. *Journal of Psychiatric Research, 27*(3), 253–258.

Birchwood, M., Smith, J., Drury, V., Healy, J., MacMillan, F., & Slade, M. (1994). A self-report Insight Scale for psychosis: Reliability, validity and sensitivity to change. *Acta Psychitrica Scandinavica, 89*(1), 62–67.

Blanchard, J. J., Kring, A. M., Horan, W. P., & Gur, R. (2011). Toward the next generation of negative symptom assessments: The collaboration to advance negative symptom assessment in schizophrenia. *Schizophrenia Bulletin, 37*(2), 291–299.

Bobes, J., Arango, C., Garcia-Garcia, M., & Rejas, J. (2010). Prevalence of negative symptoms in outpatients with schizophrenia spectrum disorders treated with antipsychotics in routine clinical practice: Findings from the CLAMORS study. *Journal of Clinical Psychiatry, 71*(3), 280–286.

Dollfus, S., Delouche, C., Hervochon, C., Mach, C., Bourgeois, V., Rotharmel, M., . . . Morello, R. (2019). Specificity and sensitivity of the Self-Assessment of Negative Symptoms (SNS) in patients with schizophrenia. *Schizophrenia Research, 211*, 51–55.

Dollfus, S., Mach, C., & Morello, R. (2016). Self-Evaluation of Negative Symptoms: A novel tool to assess negative symptoms. *Schizophrenia Bulletin, 42*(3), 571–578.

Dollfus, S., Mucci, A., Giordano, G. M., Bitter, I., Austin, S. F., Delouche, C., . . . Galderisi, S. (2022). European validation of the Self-Evaluation of Negative Symptoms (SNS): A large multinational and multicenter study. *Front Psychiatry, 13*, 826465.

Dollfus, S. V. A., (2020). The patients' view: Self-evaluation on negative symptoms. In I. D. Bitter (Ed.), *Managing negative symptoms of schizophrenia*. Chapter 4, p 51–66. New York: Oxford University Press.

Engel, M., & Lincoln, T. M. (2016). Motivation and Pleasure Scale-Self-Report (MAP-SR): Validation of the German version of a self-report measure for screening negative symptoms in schizophrenia. *Comprehensive Psychiatry, 65*, 110–115.

Engel, M., & Lincoln, T. M. (2017). Concordance of self- and observer-rated motivation and pleasure in patients with negative symptoms and healthy controls. *Psychiatry Research, 247*, 1–5.

Fleischhacker, W. W., Rabinowitz, J., Kemmler, G., Eerdekens, M., & Mehnert, A. (2005). Perceived functioning, well-being and psychiatric symptoms in patients with stable schizophrenia treated with long-acting risperidone for 1 year. *British Journal of Psychiatry, 187*, 131–136.

Galderisi, S., Kaiser, S., Bitter, I., Nordentoft, M., Mucci, A., Sabe, M., . . . Gaebel, W. (2021). EPA guidance on assessment of negative symptoms in schizophrenia. *European Psychiatry, 64*(1), e21.

Galderisi, S., Mucci, A., Bitter, I., Libiger, J., Bucci, P., Fleischhacker, W. W., & Kahn, R. S. (2013). Persistent negative symptoms in first episode patients with schizophrenia: Results from the European First Episode Schizophrenia Trial. *European Neuropsychopharmacology, 23*(3), 196–204.

Galderisi, S., Rossi, A., Rocca, P., Bertolino, A., Mucci, A., Bucci, P., . . . Italian Network For Research on, P. (2014). The influence of illness-related variables, personal resources and context-related factors on real-life functioning of people with schizophrenia. *World Psychiatry, 13*(3), 275–287.

García-Portilla, M.P., García-Álvarez, L., de la Fuente-Tomás, L., Dal Santo, F., Velasco, A., González-Blanco, L., Zurrón-Madera, P., Fonseca-Pedrero, E., Bobes-Bascarán, M.T., Sáiz, P.A.; et al. (2021). Spanish Validation of the MAP-SR: Two Heads Better Than One for the Assessment of Negative Symptoms of Schizophrenia. *Psicothema, 33*, 473–480.

Goldring, A., Borne, S., Hefner, A., Thanju, A., Khan, A., & Lindenmayer, J. P. (2020). The psychometric properties of the Self-Evaluation of Negative Symptoms

Scale (SNS) in treatment-resistant schizophrenia (TRS). *Schizophrenia Research, 224*, 159–166.
Hajj, A., Hallit, S., Chamoun, K., Sacre, H., Obeid, S., Haddad, C., . . . Rabbaa Khabbaz, L. (2020). Validation of the Arabic version of the "self-evaluation of negative symptoms" scale (SNS). *BMC Psychiatry, 20*(1), 240.
Hamera, E. K., Schneider, J. K., Potocky, M., & Casebeer, M. A. (1996). Validity of self-administered symptom scales in clients with schizophrenia and schizoaffective disorders. *Schizophrenia. Research, 19*(2–3), 213–219.
Hervochon, C., Bourgeois, V., Rotharmel, M., Duboc, J. B., Le, G. B., Quesada, P., . . . Guillin, O. (2018). [Validation of the French version of the self-evaluation of negative symptoms (SNS)]. *Encephale, 44*(6), 512–516.
Jaeger, J., Bitter, I., Czobor, P., & Volavka, J. (1990). The measurement of subjective experience in schizophrenia: The subjective deficit syndrome scale. *Comprehensive Psychiatry, 31*(3), 216–226.
Kay, S. R., Fiszbein, A., & Opler, L. A. (1987). The Positive And Negative Syndrome Scale (PANSS) for schizophrenia. *Schizophrenia Bulletin, 13*(2), 261–275.
Kim, J. S., Jang, S. K., Park, S. C., Yi, J. S., Park, J. K., Lee, J. S., . . . Lee, S. H. (2016). Measuring negative symptoms in patients with schizophrenia: Reliability and validity of the Korean version of the Motivation and Pleasure Scale Self-Report. *Neuropsychiatric Disease and Treatment, 12*, 1167–1172.
Kirkpatrick, B., Fenton, W. S., Carpenter, W. T., Jr., & Marder, S. R. (2006). The NIMH-MATRICS consensus statement on negative symptoms. *Schizophrenia Bulletin, 32*(2), 214–219.
Kirkpatrick, B., Strauss, G., NGuyen, L., Fischer, B. A., Daniel, D. G., Cienfuegos, A., & Marder, S. R. (2011). The brief negative symptom scale: Psychometric properties. *Schizophrenia Bulletin, 37*(2), 300–305.
Lançon, C., Auquier, P., Reine, G., Toumi, M., & Addington, D. (1999). Evaluation of depression in schizophrenia: Psychometric properties of a French version of the Calgary Depression Scale. *Psychiatry Research, 89*(2), 123–132.
Liddle, P. F., & Barnes, T. R. (1988). The subjective experience of deficits in schizophrenia. *Comprehensive Psychiatry, 29*(2), 157–164.
Llerena, K., Park, S. G., McCarthy, J. M., Couture, S. M., Bennett, M. E., & Blanchard, J. J. (2013). The Motivation and Pleasure Scale-Self-Report (MAP-SR): Reliability and validity of a self-report measure of negative symptoms. *Comprehensive Psychiatry, 54*(5), 568–574.
Mallet, J., Guessoum, S. B., Tebeka, S., Le Strat, Y., & Dubertret, C. (2020). Self-evaluation of negative symptoms in adolescent and young adult first psychiatric episodes. *Progress in Neuropsychopharmacology and Biological Psychiatry, 103*, 109988.
Montvidas, J., Adomaitiene, V., Leskauskas, D., & Dollfus, S. (2021a). Health-related quality of life prediction using the Self-Evaluation of Negative Symptoms scale (SNS) in patients with schizophrenia. *Nordic Journal of Psychiatry*, 75(sup1), S21.
Montvidas, J., Adomaitiene, V., Leskauskas, D., & Dollfus, S. (2021b). Validation of the Lithuanian version of the Self-Evaluation of Negative Symptoms scale (SNS). *Nordic Journal of Psychiatry, 75*(5), 351–355.
Mucci, A., Vignapiano, A., Bitter, I., Austin, S. F., Delouche, C., Dollfus, S., . . . Galderini, S. (2019). A large European, multicenter, multinational validation study of the brief negative symptom scale. *European Neuropsychopharmacology, 29*(8), 947–959.
Ohata, H., Yotsumoto, K., Taira, M., Kochi, Y., & Hashimoto, T. (2014). Reliability and valid ity of a brief self-rated scale of health condition with acute schizophrenia. *Psychiatry and Clinical Neuroscience, 68*(1), 70–77.
Overall, J. E., Hollister, L. E., Alto, P., & Pichot, P. (1967). Major psychiatric disorders. A four-dimensional model. *Archives of General Psychiatry, 16*, 146–151.

Park, S. G., Llerena, K., McCarthy, J. M., Couture, S. M., Bennett, M. E., & Blanchard, J. J. (2012). Screening for negative symptoms: Preliminary results from the self-report version of the Clinical Assessment Interview for Negative Symptoms. *Schizophrenia Research, 135*(1–3), 139–143.

Piskulic, D., Addington, J., Cadenhead, K. S., Cannon, T. D., Cornblatt, B. A., Heinssen, R., . . . McGlashan, T. H. (2012). Negative symptoms in individuals at clinical high risk of psychosis. *Psychiatry Research, 196*(2–3), 220–224.

Polat, I., Ince Guliyev, E., Elmas, S., Karakas, S., Aydemir, O., & Ucok, A. (2022). Validation of the Turkish version of the Self-Evaluation of Negative Symptoms scale (SNS). *International Journal of Psychiatry in Clinical Practice*, 26(3):221-227.

Rodriguez-Testal, J. F., Perona-Garcelan, S., Dollfus, S., Valdes-Diaz, M., Garcia-Martinez, J., Ruiz-Veguilla, M., & Senin-Calderon, C. (2020). Spanish validation of the self-evaluation of negative symptoms scale SNS in an adolescent population. *BMC Psychiatry, 19*(1), 327.

Saeedi, H., Addington, J., & Addington, D. (2007). The association of insight with psychotic symptoms, depression, and cognition in early psychosis: A 3-year follow-up. *Schizophrenia. Research, 89*(1–3), 123–128.

Selten, J.P.; Sijben, N.E.; van den Bosch, R.J.; Omloo-Visser, J.; Warmerdam, H. (1993) The Subjective Experience of Negative Symptoms: A Self-Rating Scale. *Compr. Psychiatry, 34*, 192–197.

Selten, J. P., Wiersma, D., & Van Den Bosch, R. J. (2000). Clinical predictors of discrepancy between self-ratings and examiner ratings for negative symptoms. *Comprehensive Psychiatry, 41*(3), 191–196.

Sevy, S., Nathanson, K., Visweswaraiah, H., & Amador, X. (2004). The relationship between insight and symptoms in schizophrenia. *Comprehensive Psychiatry, 45*(1), 16–19.

Strauss, G. P., Nunez, A., Ahmed, A. O., Barchard, K. A., Granholm, E., Kirkpatrick, B., . . . Allen, D. N. (2018). The latent structure of negative symptoms in schizophrenia. *JAMA Psychiatry, 75*(12), 1271–1279.

Tam, M. H. W., Ling-Ling, W., Cheng, K. M., Wong, J. O. Y., Cheung, E. F. C., Lui, S. S. Y., & Chan, R. C. K. (2021). Latent structure of self-report negative symptoms in patients with schizophrenia: A preliminary study. *Asian Journal of Psychiatry, 61*, 102680.

Wang, L. L., Tam, M. H. W., Ho, K. K. Y., Hung, K. S. Y., Wong, J. O. Y., Lui, S. S. Y., & Chan, R. C. K. (2022). Bridge centrality network structure of negative symptoms in people with schizophrenia. *European Archives of Psychiatry and Clinical Neuroscience, 273*(3), 589–600.

Wojciak, P., Gorna, K., Domowicz, K., Jaracz, K., Szpalik, R., Michalak, M., & Rybakowski, J. (2019). Polish version of the Self-Evaluation of Negative Symptoms (SNS). *Psychiatria Polska, 53*(3), 551–559.

9

Use of Digital Technologies in the Assessment of Negative Symptoms

David Kimhy and Luz H. Ospina

Clinical pearls

- Clinical assessment of negative symptoms has typically relied on paper and pencil methods; digital technology offers clinicians a new opportunity to understand their client's experiences.
- Smart watches (such as FitBit) can help measure your client's activity levels. Activity levels are associated with negative symptoms in the literature, and may be a good objective indicator of your client's functioning and progress.
- Researchers have found that assessment using smart phones is a valid way to measure negative symptoms, therefore clinicians may want to incorporate app-based measurement into their treatment interventions.

1. Introduction

The assessment of negative symptoms has traditionally relied on clinical interviews. Specifically, a number of semi-structured interviews have been developed and employed including the Positive and Negative Syndrome Scale (PANSS; Key et al., 1987), the Scale for the Assessment of Negative Symptoms (SANS; Andreasen, 1981), the Brief Psychiatric Rating Scale (BPRS; Overall & Gorham, 1962), the Schedule for Deficit Syndrome (SDS; Kirkpatrick et al., 1989), the Brief Negative Symptoms Scale (BNSS; Kirkpatrick et al., 2011), the Negative Symptom Assessment (NSA-16; Axelrod et al., 1993), and the Clinical Assessment Interview for Negative Symptoms (CAINS; Kring et al., 2013). Such instruments typically involve clinicians rating the presence and severity of specific negative symptoms based on predefined criteria using observations of behavior during the interviews, information from informants, as well as

David Kimhy and Luz H. Ospina, *Use of Digital Technologies in the Assessment of Negative Symptoms*.
In: *Psychosocial Approaches to Negative Symptoms in Psychosis*. Edited by: Tania Lincoln et al.,
Oxford University Press. © Oxford University Press (2025). DOI: 10.1093/oso/9780197676790.003.0009

reports by patients. For example, determination of blunted affect using the PANSS is based on observation of patients' physical manifestations during the course of the interview (e.g., their affective tone and emotional responsiveness). Similarly, ratings of passive/apathetic social withdrawal are based on informants' reports (e.g., social behavior reported by primary care workers and/or family).

Yet, the employment of interview-based assessments has a number of limitations—first, conducting interviews require substantial investment of time and effort, as well as training of qualified personnel. Second, ratings by interviewers are vulnerable to subjective evaluations of behaviors that may be challenging to quantify (e.g., frequency and variability of facial expressions). Third, for symptom ratings dependent on information from informants, such informants may not always be available (e.g., patient may be estranged from their family). Finally, symptoms that are based on retrospective reports of patients are vulnerable to the influence of episodic memory difficulties and emotional states at the time of the assessment, as well as cognitive biases and reframing (Kimhy et al., 2006; Kimhy et al., 2010). This issue is particularly acute among individuals with schizophrenia given the substantial episodic memory deficits documented in this population (Leavitt & Goldberg, 2009; Gold et al., 2008). Consistent with these findings, poor memory has been found to have a detrimental impact on accuracy of recollected mood and symptoms among individuals with schizophrenia (Blum et al., 2015; Moran 2017).

Technological advances over the past decade have ushered in the promise of employing digital technologies to enhance the assessment of negative symptoms. Collection of data via digital technologies can be divided into two primary modalities: passive sensing and active digital phenotyping. Passive sensing refers to collection of data that does not require any explicit user involvement but rather relies on the built-in automated functions and operations of smartphones that are completed in the background (Trifan et al., 2019). In contrast, active digital phenotyping requires participants to explicitly provide input about their current or recent states, via either prescheduled prompts or self-initiated input (Kimhy et al., 2012; Kimhy & Vakhrusheva, 2019). Researchers have employed passive sensing, active digital phenotyping (i.e., via use of ecological momentary assessment; EMA), or both in studies of negative symptoms in schizophrenia. In the next sections, we review emerging research on the use of digital technologies to assess negative symptoms and their correlates including actigraphy, smartphones, and audio and video recordings of speech and facial expressions.

2. Assessment of Negative Symptoms Using Actigraphy

A range of commercially available actigraphy devices have been employed to study negative and other symptoms in individuals with schizophrenia, including the ActiGraph GT3X, Actiwatch, SenseWear Pro3, and Fitbit. Such motion-sensing devices are typically worn on wrist, waist, ankle, or lumbar areas over periods ranging from a day to up to a month, continuously recording movement, number of steps taken and physical activity, including during sleep, wear time, ambient light, event markers, as well as options to connect to a range of other mobile sensors for heart rate monitoring and proximity detection.

Germane to negative symptoms, a number of reports have found higher severity of overall symptoms in patients with schizophrenia was significantly correlated with lower motor activity (Wee et al., 2019; Walther et al., 2022, 2009a, 2009b; Docx et al., 2012, 2013; Shin et al., 2016; Afonso et al., 2011; Wichniak et al., 2011), although these findings are not universal (Pieters et al., 2023). These associations extend to specific negative symptoms with actigraphy-indexed lower motor activity significantly correlated with higher ratings of apathy (Kluge et al., 2018) and avolition (Docx et al., 2013). Furthermore, comparison of ratings via semistructured interview instruments of motor activity (e.g., PANSS) versus actigraphy indicated the latter was more accurate in reflecting motor activity in people with schizophrenia, suggesting actigraphy may be a more valid tool to assess motor activity in this population (Walther et al., 2009a, 2009b). Similar results were reported by Poyurovsky and colleagues (2000), who used actigraphy to assess circadian locomotor activity of patients with neuroleptic-induced akathisia and controls; the former had persistently higher daytime motor activity. Altogether, these findings suggest that for indexing ambulatory motor activity, actigraphy may offer higher accuracy compared to semi-structured interviews.

3. Assessment of Negative Symptoms Using Smartphones and Related Devices

Technological advances over the past 15 years have ushered in the broad dissemination of personal digital assistants, cell phones, and smartphones. Subsequent to the introduction of the iPhone in 2007, smartphones have become ubiquitous, with a market penetration of 91.4% of the global population (7.33 billion users; Shaikh, 2023). Ownership of smartphones among individuals with schizophrenia is similarly high, with an estimated rate of 80% to 85%

(Firth et al., 2016; Young et al., 2020; Wong et al., 2020; Naslund & Aschbrennerb, 2021), although few clinically relevant apps designed specifically for people with schizophrenia are available (Kwon et al., 2022; Firth & Torous, 2015). Given the relatively high penetration of smartphones in this population, they offer a unique technological vehicle to probe a wide range of experiences as part of ambulatory "real-world" daily functioning in both clinical and nonclinical populations.

Consistent with this state, following the initial research validation of use of mobile personal digital assistants among individuals with schizophrenia (Kimhy et al., 2006, 2010), employment of smartphones in the study of schizophrenia has increased steadily, with 50 publications listed in PubMed in 2022 (keyword search: "smartphones" + "schizophrenia"). The bulk of this research has focused on positive symptoms, mood, and social functioning, primarily among outpatients with schizophrenia, though feasibility in inpatient settings has been demonstrated (Kimhy et al., 2014a). Yet, in recent years, a burgeoning research literature focusing on use of smartphones to investigate negative symptoms and related correlates has developed.

In one example of passive sensing study design, Depp and colleagues (2019) utilized the smartphones' Global Positioning System (GPS) capabilities to track individuals with schizophrenia and healthy control comparators. The participants with schizophrenia had lower average distance traveled, lower distance traveled from home, and a higher rate of samples at-home than did the control group. The GPS-based indicators of mobility were also strongly associated with both week- and day-aggregated reports of time spent at-home as measured by concurrent EMA derived responses. Within the schizophrenia group, less distance traveled from home and overall distance traveled were significantly associated with more severe negative symptoms, in particular diminished motivation. The GPS-based metrics were unrelated to other illness-related clinical indicators including cognitive abilities, positive symptoms, or depression.

An example of combining passive sensing and active digital phenotyping has been demonstrated by Strauss and colleagues (2022) by utilizing the smartphones' accelerometry and EMA to index movement and negative symptoms. Participants (schizophrenia: n=50; healthy controls n=70) completed clinical ratings (e.g., PANSS) and then had accelerometry continuously recorded from a smartphone and smart-band for six days along with parallel EMA-based active digital phenotyping via eight brief daily surveys that collected contextual variables. These included current location ("where are you?"), activity ("what are you doing?"), and social interaction ("who are you interacting with?"). The accelerometry variables demonstrated convergent validity as indicated by significant associations with self-reports of time spent in goal-directed activities and clinical ratings of negative symptoms. The discriminant validity of the accelerometry was demonstrated by limited associations with clinical rating scale measures of positive, disorganized, and total symptoms. The authors concluded that accelerometry is a valid objective measure of negative symptoms that may complement traditional approaches to assessing the construct using clinical rating scales (Strauss et al., 2022). More recently, Lane et al., (2025) employed passive and active data from smartphones collected from cohorts of individuals with schizophrenia in the USA and India to successfully predict social functioning (e.g., social engagement) and employment.

A plurality of studies to date employing smartphones among individuals with schizophrenia have utilized the active digital phenotyping approach. For example, for negative symptoms, Moran and colleagues (2017) investigated the validity of assessing negative symptoms using EMA among individuals with schizophrenia (N=31) who completed electronic questionnaires on their smartphones four times a day over one week. Participants also completed effort-based decision-making and reinforcement learning tasks to assess the relationship between EMA and laboratory measures, which tap into negative-symptom relevant domains. The results indicated that clinician-rated and self-report measures of negative symptoms were significantly related to negative symptoms assessed via EMA. Working memory, however, moderated the relationship between EMA and retrospective measures of negative symptoms, such that there was a stronger relationship between EMA and retrospective negative-symptom measures among individuals with better working memory. The authors also found that negative symptoms assessed via EMA were related to poor performance on the effort task, whereas clinician-rated symptoms and self-reports were not. Finally, the authors reported that negative symptoms were related to poorer performance on learning reward contingencies. The findings suggest that negative symptoms can be assessed through active digital phenotyping approaches (e.g., smartphones employing EMA) and that working memory impairments frequently seen in schizophrenia may affect recall of symptoms.

In another example of the potential of utilizing smartphones in studies of negative symptoms, researchers employed machine-learning-based facial and vocal measurements acquired through automated assessments conducted remotely through smartphones (Abbas et al., 2022). Twenty individuals with schizophrenia completed two weeks of measurements of facial and vocal characteristics including facial expressivity, vocal acoustics, and speech prevalence. Results pointed to vocal markers including speech prevalence, vocal jitter, fundamental frequency, and vocal intensity as markers of negative-symptom severity.

Smartphones employing EMA have been used to examine links to a number of other negative symptom indicators including motor functioning (Abbas et al., 2021), social motivation (Mow et al., 2022), and reduced emotional experience (Jones et al., 2021), as well as other aspects of affective and social functioning (Vakhrusheva et al., 2020; Kimhy et al., 2014b), to mention a few.

The maturation of smartphone technologies along with their wide global adaptation has led to incorporation of smartphones as key tools into cognitive and behavioral interventions targeting negative symptoms in people with schizophrenia. One example demonstrating the promise of employing smartphones is a study by Granholm and coworkers (2020) that focused on outpatients with schizophrenia or schizoaffective disorder (n=31) with moderate-to-severe persistent experiential negative symptoms, as well as moderate-to-severe defeatist attitudes. The study involved a blended intervention combining weekly in-person group therapy with use of a smartphone app called CBT2go. The app extended therapy group skills, including recovery goal setting, thought challenging, scheduling of pleasurable activities and social interactions, and pleasure-savoring interventions to modify defeatist attitudes and improve experiential negative symptoms. Employing personalized statements developed in group to challenge social disinterest and defeatist attitudes in real-time, real-world environments, the app prompted and tracked each patient's goal-directed activities in the community, facilitated adherence to homework assignments involving community practice of thought-challenging skills trained in group, and prompted performance and savoring of personalized pleasurable activities and social interactions planned in group. The results indicated severity of experiential negative symptoms, as well as defeatist attitudes, declined significantly in response to the intervention, demonstrating excellent retention (87% at 18 weeks), along with large effect sizes. Specifically, ratings of motivation, anticipated pleasure, and success for completing planned activities increased significantly.

In another study (Fulford et al., 2021), an eight-week intervention employing a motivation and skills support smartphone app enhanced self-reported social functioning, particularly in female participants, although gains were not maintained at the three-month follow-up. Furthermore, increased social functioning was predicted by momentary reports of social appraisals, including perceived social competence and the extent to which social interactions were worth the effort. Altogether, the reviewed studies demonstrate the feasibility, acceptability, and promise of incorporating smartphones in studies targeting negative symptoms in schizophrenia, including in cognitive and behavioral interventions aiming to improve negative symptoms in this population.

4. Assessment of Negative Symptoms Using Audio and Video Recordings

In recent years, with the introduction of advances in artificial intelligence (AI) and machine learning, the possibility to analyze audio and video recordings to identify clinical targets has started to materialize.

Efforts to apply such analytical approaches to probe negative symptoms in schizophrenia have resulted in some exciting findings. Cohen and colleagues (2021) illustrated the potential of such technologies by conducting videotaped interviews with four patients with schizophrenia—two with high negative-symptom ratings and two with low negative-symptom ratings. Data were analyzed using a range of validated acoustic, lexical, and video analysis software indexing communication, including alogia, blunted vocal/facial expression, avolition, asociality, and anhedonia.

The authors reported a large discrepancy between clinically rated negative symptoms and ratings developed by video analysis. Following this, the researchers further examined the discrepancy using analysis on archived video interviews in 40 nonpatients recruited from the community, 78 patients with schizophrenia, and 79 "psychiatric controls" with a variety of disorders, including depression (n=19), bipolar disorder (n=21), and various personality, psychosis, mood, and trauma-related diagnoses with sufficient functional impairment to qualify for federal definitions of serious mental illness (SMI). The latter group were included to improve the transdiagnostic scope of the sample, given that negative symptoms are common in a broad range of SMI diagnoses. Overall, the individuals with schizophrenia produced fewer utterances and words overall, yet used more negative emotions and fewer filler words. Blunted affect was associated with increased pause times, fewer vocal utterances, and fewer words used. Alogia was associated with lower word count and less use of negative emotion words. In contrast, anhedonia and avolition were not significantly associated with biobehavioral features. Collectively, the biobehavioral features correlated highly with select clinical ratings, with the largest correlations observed with clinical ratings of blunted affect and behavioral measures of alogia.

In another study, Tahir and coworkers (2019) employed audio recordings to examine nonverbal speech cues, including conversational and prosody related cues, as objective measures for negative symptoms in audio recordings of 54 patients with schizophrenia and 26 healthy controls who also completed clinical assessment with NSA-16. The researchers were able to classify healthy and patient individuals using nonverbal speech features with 81.3%

accuracy. Specifically, features such as failed interrupt, overlap, mutual silence, speech pap, and response time were directly correlated with negative symptoms, and natural turns, interjections, interruptions, speaking percentage and turn duration were inversely correlated to the negative symptoms. Altogether, the results indicated that biobehavioral and communication features, indexed via objective indices extracted from video and audio recordings, are promising candidates for further development of assessment approaches for negative symptoms.

5. Summary and Future Directions

In summary, the substantial advances in digital technologies witnessed in the past 15 years have ushered in the development of novel approaches to assessing negative symptoms in people with schizophrenia. Specifically, studies employing innovative digital technologies including actigraphy, smartphones, and audio and video recordings have offered novel ways to identify the presence and severity of negative symptoms. Such technologies have a potential to revolutionize the way negative symptoms are evaluated and treated, presenting increased feasibility and convenience by offering the ability to characterize negative symptoms in patients' home environments using unobtrusive and more objective indicators. Specifically, the broad dissemination and use of telehealth services among individuals with serious mental illness (Bareis et al., 2023) allow opportunities to conduct audio and video recordings to assess negative symptoms. Additionally, the use of actigraphy and smartphones offer increased ecological validity by tracking behavior during "real world" functioning (Kimhy et al., 2012).

Although they offer great promise, future studies may need to address a number of existing challenges. First, studies to date have reported limited considerations of ethnic, racial, and cultural diversity. Future studies should aim to apply and test such technologies (e.g., audio and video recordings) among a diverse range of ethnic, racial, and cultural populations to examine similarities and potential differences. Additionally, the results, particularly from studies focusing on verbal outputs, need to be validated among non-native English speakers, as well as other languages. For assessments and treatment studies employing smartphones, future studies should examine the frequency of smartphone use and clinical benefits including negative symptoms. Additionally, novel and more sophisticated models need to be developed to track and target negative symptoms, including potential use of Just-in-Time Adaptive Interventions (Nahum-Shani et al., 2018). Finally, for both assessments and interventions targeting negative symptoms, future studies should examine better ways to integrate them into "real-world" clinical practice.

References

Abbas, A., Hansen, B. J., Koesmahargyo, V., Yadav, V., Rosenfield, P. J., Patil, O., Dockendorf, M. F., Moyer, M., Shipley, L. A., Perez-Rodriguez, M. M., & Galatzer-Levy, I. R. (2021). Facial and vocal markers of schizophrenia measured using remote smartphone assessments: Observational study. *JMIR Formative Research, 6*(1), e26276.

Abbas, A., Hansen, B. J., Koesmahargyo, V., Yadav, V., Rosenfield, P. J., Patil, O., Dockendorf, M. F., Moyer, M., Shipley, L. A., Perez-Rodriguez, M. M., & Galatzer-Levy, I. R. (2022). Facial and vocal markers of schizophrenia measured using remote smartphone assessments: Observational study. *JMIR Formative Research, 6*(1), e26276.

Afonso, P., Brissos, S., Figueira, M. L., & Paiva, T. (2011) Schizophrenia patients with predominantly positive symptoms have more disturbed sleep-wake cycles measured by actigraphy. *Psychiatry Research, 189*(1), 62–66.

Andreasen, N. C. (1981). *Scale for the assessment of negative symptoms (SANS)*. Iowa City: University of Iowa.

Axelrod, B. N., Goldman, R. S., & Alphs, L. D. (1993). Validation of the 16-item negative symptom assessment. *Journal of Psychiatric Research, 27*(3), 253–258.

Bareis, N., Tepper, M. C., Wang, R., Tang, F., Olfson, M., Dixon, L. B., Kimhy, D., Wall, M. M., Medalia, A., Finnerty, M. T., Anderson, A., & Smith, T. E. (2023). Engagement of individuals with serious mental illness in outpatient mental health services and telehealth use during the COVID-19 pandemic. *Psychiatry Research, 329*, 115497.

Blum, L. H., Vakhrusheva, J., Saperstein, A., Khan, S., Chang, R. W., Hansen, M. C., Zemon, V., & Kimhy, D. (2015). Depressed mood in individuals with schizophrenia: A comparison of retrospective and real-time measures. *Psychiatry Research, 227*(2–3), 318–323.

Cohen, A. S., Schwartz, E., Le, T. P., Cowan, T., Kirkpatrick, B., Raugh, I. M., & Strauss, G. P. (2021). Digital phenotyping of negative symptoms: The relationship to clinician ratings. *Schizophrenia Bulletin, 47*(1), 44–53.

Depp, C. A., Bashem, J., Moore, R. C., Holden, J. L., Mikhael, T., Swendsen, J., Harvey, P. D., & Granholm, E. L. (2019). GPS mobility as a digital biomarker of negative symptoms in schizophrenia: A case control study. *NPJ Digital Medicine, 2*, 108.

Docx, L., Morrens, M., Bervoets, C., Hulstijn, W., Fransen, E., De Hert, M., Baeken, C., Audenaert, K., & Sabbe, B. (2012) Parsing the components of the psychomotor syndrome in schizophrenia. *Acta Psychiatrica Scandinavica, 126*(4), 256–265.

Docx, L., Sabbe, B., Provinciael, P., Merckx, N., & Morrens, M. (2013) Quantitative psychomotor dysfunction in schizophrenia: A loss of drive, impaired movement execution or both? *Neuropsychobiology, 68*(4), 221–227.

Firth, J., & Torous, J. (2015). Smartphone apps for schizophrenia: A systematic review. *JMIR mHealth uHealth, 3*(4), e102.

Firth, J., Cotter, J., Torous, J., Bucci, S., Firth, J. A., & Yung, A. R. (2016). Mobile phone ownership and endorsement of "mHealth" among people with psychosis: A meta-analysis of cross-sectional studies. *Schizophrenia Bulletin, 42*(2), 448–455.

Fulford, D., Gard, D. E., Mueser, K. T., Mote, J., Gill, K., Leung, L., & Mow, J. (2021). Preliminary outcomes of an ecological momentary intervention for social functioning in schizophrenia: Pre-post study of the motivation and skills support app. *JMIR Mental Health, 8*(6), e27475.

Gold, J. M., Waltz, J. A., Prentice, K. J., Morris, S. E., & Heerey, E. A. (2008). Reward processing in schizophrenia: A deficit in the representation of value, *Schizophrenia Bulletin, 34*(5), 835–847.

Granholm, E., Holden, J., Dwyer, K., Mikhael, T., Link, P., & Depp, C. (2020). Mobile-assisted cognitive behavioral therapy for negative symptoms: Open single-arm trial with schizophrenia patients. *JMIR Mental Health, 7*(12), e24406.

Jones, S. E., Moore, R. C., Depp, C. A., Ackerman, R. A., Pinkham, A. E., & Harvey, P. D. (2021). Daily Ecological Momentary Assessments of happy and sad moods in people with schizophrenia and bipolar disorders: What do participants who are never sad think about their activities and abilities? *Schizophrenia Research. Cognition, 26*, 100202.

Kay, S. R., Fiszbein, A., & Opler, L. A. (1987). The positive and negative syndrome scale (PANSS) for schizophrenia. *Schizophrenia Bulletin, 13*(2), 261–276.

Kimhy, D., Delespaul, P., Corcoran, C., Ahn, H., Yale, S., & Malaspina, D. (2006). Computerized experience sampling method (ESMc): Assessing feasibility and validity among individuals with schizophrenia. *Journal of Psychiatric Research, 40*(3), 221–230.

Kimhy, D., Delespaul, P., Ahn, H., Cai, S., Shikhman, M., Lieberman, J. A., Malaspina, D., & Sloan, R. P. (2010). Concurrent measurement of "real-world" stress and arousal in individuals with psychosis: Assessing the feasibility and validity of a novel methodology. *Schizophrenia Bulletin, 36*(6), 1131–1139.

Kimhy, D., Myin-Germeys, I., Palmier-Claus, J., & Swendsen, J. (2012). Mobile assessment guide for research in schizophrenia and severe mental disorders. *Schizophrenia Bulletin, 38*(3), 386–395.

Kimhy, D., Vakhrusheva, J., Liu, Y., & Wang Y. (2014a). Use of mobile assessment technologies in inpatient psychiatric settings. *Asian Journal of Psychiatry*, 10, 90–95.

Kimhy, D., Vakhrusheva, J., Khan, S., Chang, R. W., Hansen, M. C., Ballon, J. S., Malaspina, D., & Gross, J. J. (2014b). Emotional granularity and social functioning in individuals with schizophrenia: An experience sampling study. *Journal of Psychiatric Research, 53*, 141–148.

Kimhy, D., & Vakhrusheva, J. (2019). Experience sampling in the study of psychosis. In J. Palmier-Claus, G. Haddock, & F. Varese (Eds.), *Experience sampling in mental health research* (pp. 38–52). London: Routledge.

Kirkpatrick, B., Buchanan, R. W., McKenney, P. D., Alphs, L. D., & Carpenter, W. T. (1989). The Schedule for the Deficit Syndrome: An instrument for research in schizophrenia. *Psychiatry Research, 30*(2), 119–123.

Kirkpatrick, B., Strauss, G. P., Nguyen, L., Fischer, B. A., Daniel, D. G., Cienfuegos, A., & Marder, S. R. (2011). The brief negative symptom scale: Psychometric properties. *Schizophrenia Bulletin, 37*(2), 300–305.

Kluge, A., Kirschner, M., Hager, O. M., Bischof, M., Habermeyer, B., Seifritz, E., Walther, S., & Kaiser, S. (2018). Combining actigraphy, ecological momentary assessment and neuroimaging to study apathy in patients with schizophrenia. *Schizophrenia Research, 195*, 176–182.

Kring, A. M., Gur, R. E., Blanchard, J. J., Horan, W. P., & Reise, S. P. (2013). The clinical assessment interview for negative symptoms (CAINS): Final development and validation. *American Journal of Psychiatry, 170*(2), 165–172.

Kwon, S., Firth, J., Joshi, D. & Torous, J. (2022). Accessibility and availability of smartphone apps for schizophrenia. *Schizophrenia 8*, 98.

Lane E, Gray L, Kimhy D, Jeste D, Torous J. Digital phenotyping of social functioning and employment in people with schizophrenia: Pilot data from an international sample. *Psychiatry Clin Neurosci. 2025; 79(3)*, 125–130.

Leavitt, V. M., & Goldberg, T. E. (2009). Episodic memory in schizophrenia. *Neuropsychology Review, 19*, 312–323.

Moran, E. K., Culbreth, A. J., & Barch, D. M. (2017). Ecological momentary assessment of negative symptoms in schizophrenia: Relationships to effort-based decision making and reinforcement learning. *Journal of Abnormal Psychology, 126*(1), 96–105.

Mow, J. L., Gard, D. E., Mueser, K. T., Mote, J., Gill, K., Leung, L., Kangarloo, T., & Fulford, D. (2022). Smartphone-based mobility metrics capture daily social motivation and behavior in schizophrenia. *Schizophrenia Research, 250*, 13–21.

Nahum-Shani, I., Smith, S. N., Spring, B. J., Collins, L. M., Witkiewitz, K., Tewari, A., & Murphy, S. A. (2018). Just-in-Time Adaptive Interventions (JITAIs) in mobile health: Key components and design principles for ongoing health behavior support. *Annals of Behavioral Medicine, 52*(6), 446–462.

Naslund, J., & Aschbrennerb, K. A. (2021). Technology use and interest in digital apps for mental health promotion and lifestyle intervention among young adults with serious mental illness. *Journal of Affective Disorders Reports, 6*, 100227.

Overall, J. E., & Gorham, D. R. (1962). *Brief Psychiatric Rating Scale (BPRS)* [Database record]. APA PsycTests.

Pieters, L. E., Deenik, J., de Vet, S., Delespaul, P., & van Harten, P. N. (2023). Combining actigraphy and experience sampling to assess physical activity and sleep in patients with psychosis: A feasibility study. *Frontiers in Psychiatry, 14*, 1107812.

Poyurovsky, M., Nave, R., Epstein, R., Tzischinsky, O., Schneidman, M., Barnes, T.R.E., Weizman, A. & Lavie, P. (2000). Actigraphic monitoring (actigraphy) of circadian locomotor activity in schizophrenic patients with acute neuroleptic-induced akathisia. *European Neuropsychopharmacology, 10*, 171–176.

Shaikh, M. (2023). *25 Countries with the Most Smartphone Users in the World.* Yahoo Finance. https://finance.yahoo.com/news/25-countries-most-smartphone-users-124433477.html#:~:text=According%20to%20recent%20data%2C%207.33,global%20population%20through%20mobile%20networks.&text=In%20the%20domain%20of%20operating,of%20the%20global%20smartphone%20market

Shin, S., Yeom, C. W., Shin, C., Shin, J. H., Jeong, J. H., Shin, J. U., & Lee, Y. R. (2016). Activity monitoring using a mHealth device and correlations with psychopathology in patients with chronic schizophrenia. *Psychiatry Research, 246*, 712–718.

Strauss, G. P., Raugh, I. M., Zhang, L., Luther, L., Chapman, H. C., Allen, D. N., Kirkpatrick, B., & Cohen, A. S. (2022). Validation of accelerometry as a digital phenotyping measure of negative symptoms in schizophrenia. *Schizophrenia, 8*(1), 37.

Tahir, Y., Yang, Z., Chakraborty, D., Thalmann, N., Thalmann, D., Maniam, Y., Rashid, N. A. A., Tan, B., Keong, J. L. C. & Dauwels, J. (2019). Non-verbal speech cues as objective measures for negative symptoms in patients with schizophrenia. *PLoS ONE, 14*(4), e0214314.

Trifan, A., Oliveira, M., & Oliveira, J. L. (2019). Passive sensing of health outcomes through smartphones: systematic review of current solutions and possible limitations. *JMIR mHealth and uHealth, 7*(8), e12649.

Vakhrusheva, J., Khan, S., Chang, R., Hansen, M., Ayanruoh, L., Gross, J. J., & Kimhy, D. (2020). Lexical analysis of emotional responses to "real-world" experiences in individuals with schizophrenia. *Schizophrenia Research, 216*, 272–278.

Walther, S., Vladimirova, I., Alexaki, D., Schäppi, L., Damme, K. S. F., Mittal, V. A., Shankman, S. A., & Stegmayer, K. (2022). Low physical activity is associated with two hypokinetic motor abnormalities in psychosis. *Journal of Psychiatric Research, 146*, 258–263.

Walther, S., Horn, H., Razavi, N., Koschorke, P., Muller, T. J., & Strik, W. (2009a). Quantitative motor activity differentiates schizophrenia subtypes. *Neuropsychobiology, 60*, 80–86.

Walther, S., Koschorke, P., Horn, H., & Strik, W. (2009b). Objectively measured motor activity in schizophrenia challenges the validity of expert ratings. *Psychiatric Research. 169*, 187–190.

Wee, Z. Y., Yong, S. W. L., Chew, Q. H., Guan, C., Lee, T. S., & Sim, K. (2019). Actigraphy studies and clinical and biobehavioural correlates in schizophrenia: A systematic review. *Journal of Neural Transmission, 126*(5), 531–558.

Wichniak, A., Skowerska, A., Chojnacka-Wójtowicz, J., Tafliński, T., Wierzbicka, A., Jernajczyk, W., & Jarema, M. (2011). Actigraphic monitoring of activity and rest in schizophrenic patients treated with olanzapine or risperidone. *Journal of Psychiatric Research, 45*, 1381–1386.

Wong, K. T. G., Liu, D., Balzan, R, King, D., & Galletly, C. (2020). Smartphone and internet access and utilization by people with schizophrenia in South Australia: Quantitative survey study. *JMIR Mental Health, 7*(1), e11551.

Young, A. S., Cohen, A. N., Niv, N., Nowlin-Finch, N., Oberman, R. S., Olmos-Ochoa, T. T., Goldberg, R. W. & Whelan, F. (2020). Mobile phone and smartphone use by people with serious mental illness. *Psychiatric Services, 71*(3), 280–283.

10

"Precision Therapy"

Using Functional Analysis to Guide Individualized Assessment and Intervention

Tania Lincoln

Clinical pearls

- Rather than using a one-size-fits-all approach, clinicians should select evidence-based interventions that best address a patient's symptom profile and its driving and maintaining factors.
- Functional analysis can be used to guide this type of personalized psychosocial intervention.
- Functional analysis involves a concrete description of the problematic "negative symptom" responses that characterize negative symptoms in concrete situations (e.g., staying in bed), an assessment of the situational triggers, the relevant vulnerability indicators that impact on the responses, and the rewarding or punishing consequences that precede and maintain them.
- Negative symptom triggers can be both events in the external world (e.g., a social situation) and/or internal events, such as pessimistic thoughts.
- Physical health may play an important bidirectional role in negative symptoms.

  Improving negative symptoms may involve interventions at both the micro (attention, coaching, emotional support) and macro (increases in disability benefits) levels.
- Mental health workers' responses to negative symptoms matter, workers who are overly critical may paradoxically be reinforcing negative symptoms.
- Functional analysis can inform on which psychosocial interventions may be the most impactful.

Tania Lincoln, *"Precision Therapy"*. In: *Psychosocial Approaches to Negative Symptoms in Psychosis*.
Edited by: Tania Lincoln et al., Oxford University Press. © Oxford University Press (2025).
DOI: 10.1093/oso/9780197676790.003.0010

1. Introduction

Negative symptoms are caused and maintained by numerous factors that vary between individuals. Because of this, it is unlikely that interventions that focus only on a single specific factor are going to be helpful for a large number of patients. Integrated treatment programs that combine different foci tend to show stronger effects (Granholm et al., 2014; Nguyen et al., 2016), which is probably because they are relevant to a larger group of patients. Offering a comprehensive package comprising all the different types of interventions to every patient is, however, neither feasible nor efficient. An individualized intervention derived from an assessment of the factors that can be assumed to cause and maintain symptoms in a given patient is likely to be more feasible, acceptable, and effective. To this aim, the concept of functional analysis can be used both to structure existing knowledge and to guide individualized treatment planning for negative symptoms (Lincoln et al., 2017). Here, I will briefly introduce the basic concept of functional analysis. Then, following the approach we have outlined in our previous work, I will exemplify how psychological and biological correlates of negative symptoms can be incorporated into a functional analysis framework. I will end by demonstrating the frameworks' implications for individual assessment and treatment.

Throughout the chapter, I will exemplify the approach and the usefulness of taking it using the example of Jack, a 45-year-old patient in a long-stay outpatient facility with severe symptoms in the motivational domain.

2. Introduction to the Basic Concept of Functional Analysis

Using functional analysis to guide the assessment and treatment planning of mental health problems has its origins in behavior therapy and has been around since the 1960s in different variations. A well-known version was introduced by Kanfer and Saslow (1965), which they since further elaborated. The main questions that functional analysis addresses are the circumstances in which the problematic behavior developed and the factors that are currently maintaining it. The basic idea is that the answer to these questions is most likely to be found by focusing on stimulus (S)—response (R) learning mechanisms while taking the characteristics of the person (organism = O) that contribute to the responses, the consequences of the responses (C), and the contingency (K) with which consequences are tied to the response into account. This chain is often conceptualized as a "SORKC model" as shown in Figure 10.1.[1]

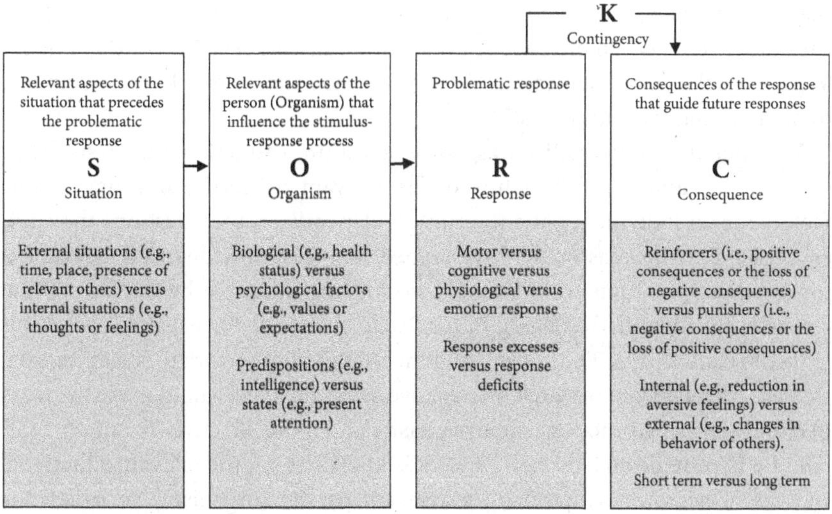

Figure 10.1 A simple version of a SORKC model.

The first generation of functional analysis models assumed a linear progression of S, R, and C. Its subsequent developments (e.g., Kanfer & Karoly, 1972) were extended to take interactions between the variables into account, assuming, for example, that previous learning history or personality can influence the way a situation is perceived and thereby change the situation. By incorporating feedback and feedforward loops, these extensions also accounted for the fact that consequences not only influence behavioral responses by reinforcing them but also by changing a persons' dispositions or states (O) or by influencing subsequent situations (S). More complex behaviors can then be described as a reaction chain in which consequences from one problematic behavior constitute situational triggers for another problematic behavior.

Functional analysis is generally used by behaviorally oriented practitioners to explain the problematic response of a *specific individual* in a *specific situation* (micro-level SORKC analysis). For Jack, a prototypical micro-level SORCK analysis might focus on the following question: Why did Jack not respond when he was asked to join the social activity group yesterday? Functional analysis is also used to take a broader view on how the problem behavior of a specific individual *developed and is being maintained over longer time-periods* (macro-level SORCK analysis, e.g., Why has Jack become more and more socially withdrawn over the last 20 years?). Micro level analysis is usually done based on letting the patient describe a typical situation in which the problem behavior occurs (e.g., Jack is sitting on his own in the corner of the common room when he is approached by a social worker asking him to join the activity group), whereas macro-level analysis tends to be based on the assessment of the patients' clinical history (e.g., When did Jack begin to withdraw and become more apathetic? What were the circumstances at that time? Which factors may have contributed to maintaining the withdrawal?).

Whether the individualized assessment within a functional analysis frame succeeds in gaining a full picture of the relevant triggering and maintaining factors for an individual patient, crucially depends on the questions the clinician asks. For this reason, we have argued that this individualized assessment for negative symptoms would benefit from being informed by the factors that research has identified as being of particular relevance for negative symptoms (Lincoln et al., 2017). Thus, if we used the SORKC framework to structure what we have learned from research on negative symptoms this would make the work of clinicians using functional analysis easier and more effective. To support this aim, I will provide an overview of what is known about the relevant situational triggers of negative symptoms, the relevant person (organism) variables, the expression of the problem behavior, and the relevant consequences of the problem behavior, that can help clinicians to ask their patients the right questions (or employ the right questionnaires or test procedures). The same assumption can be made for selecting interventions. Categorizing available interventions with a proven efficacy for negative symptoms according to which factors they address within the framework makes it easier for clinicians to select the most suitable combination of psychosocial interventions. Therefore, I will also suggest suitable evidence-based interventions for each of the factors within the framework.

3. An Overview of Core Research Findings on Negative Symptoms, Systematized to Guide Individualized Assessment

In this section, I will summarize research findings on negative symptoms relevant to the different variables of the functional analysis. The section will begin with describing the different facets of the problem behavior (R) that we are aiming to explain. I will then provide examples of research findings relevant to the S and O variable in negative symptoms, before elaborating on consequences and contingency issues. Where appropriate, macro- and micro-level perspectives will be distinguished and feedback mechanisms specified. A condensed overview of research findings that could be considered as potentially relevant to each SORCK variable is provided in Table 10.1. The selection of findings that made it into the chapter and table is largely based on an update of a previous overview (Lincoln et al., 2017) and is meant to be open to revisions and extensions as research progresses.

Table 10.1 Incorporating research findings on negative symptoms into a functional analysis framework to guide assessment

S Situation	O Organism	R Response	C Consequences
Micro level: Specific situational triggers (e.g., being approached by another person, being alone at home) or any situation preceding problem behavior. **Macro level:** Under-stimulating (e.g., institutional deprivation, poor social network, low social support) or distressing environment (e.g, trauma, social adversity, low socioeconomic status, discrimination, social undermining criticism, and stigmatization).	**Cognitive level** **Neurocognitive deficits:** e.g., impaired processing speed, attention/vigilance, working memory, verbal memory, reasoning and problem solving, verbal comprehension. **Social cognition:** e.g., impairments in theory of mind/mentalizing, impairments in discriminating facial expressions of emotion, reduced affiliative social skills	**Motor behavior level** (1) Lack of initiation or persistence in goal-directed daily activities (e.g., going to work/school, keeping up self-care, pursuing hobbies, or interactions with friends and family). (2) reduced verbal behavior, altered vocal prosody, reduced nonverbal communication (e.g., reduced smiling), reduced gesturing.	**Positive reinforcement:** Increased effort from interaction partners, attention from mental-health professionals, social, practical and financial help (e.g., disability pensions). **Negative reinforcement:** Reduction of fear, worry, or tension; short-term relief from (expected) social and affective consequences.

Continued

Table 10.1 *Continued*

S Situation	O Organism	R Response	C Consequences
	Enduring schemas about self and others: e.g., low self-esteem, reduced sense of self-efficacy, generalized low expectancy of success and pleasure, attachment insecurity. **Anticipation of pleasure and reward:** e.g., reduced anticipation of positive affect and positive outcomes (rewards). **Reward representation and decision-making:** e.g., impaired representation of value, overestimation of the costs of effort to attain rewards. **Biological level** e.g., reduced physical fitness, increased medical conditions; poorer immune functioning, side-effects of antipsychotic medication; substance abuse, genetic predispositions.	**Cognitive level** e.g., negative automatic thoughts (e.g., "I don't have what it takes to do this"; "I won't have fun," "It won't work out for me anyway"; "It's not worth trying") **Biological level** e.g., reduced muscle activity (e.g., smiling muscles).	**Punishment:** Social rejection, criticism, health-related problems. **Negative punishment:** Loss of positive responses from interaction partners, loss of social interaction, fewer pleasurable events, less experience of success.

Note: This table is a shortened and slightly modified version of Table 1 in Lincoln and colleagues (Lincoln et al., 2017).

3.1 The R-Variable—Prototypical Problem Behavior in People with Negative Symptoms

As implied in the adjective "negative," negative symptoms are characterized by an *absence or reduction* of observable *behavior (motor response in the R variable in Figure 10.1)*. As laid out in Chapter 1, negative symptoms are most commonly subdivided into a motivational and an expressive subdomain (Marder & Galderisi, 2017). The motivational subdomain of negative symptoms manifests as a lack of initiation of or persistence in goal-directed behavior, such as going out to do a valued activity or talking to people to maintain meaningful social relationships (Depp et al., 2019; Swora et al., 2022). The expressiveness subdomain manifests itself in a reduction of verbal behavior (e.g., one syllable answers) or of nonverbal behavior (e.g., reduced facial expressions or gesturing) (Lavelle et al., 2014). Although these would be categorized as behavior deficits in the SORCK model, we also witness behavior excesses in the form of increased sedentary behavior; that is, behavior that does not increase energy expenditure and includes activities such as sleeping, sitting, lying down, and screen-based entertainment (Vancampfort et al., 2017). A therapeutically relevant and well-researched aspect of the problematic *cognitive response* are automatic demotivating thoughts (Pillny et al., 2018). There has been little research on *physiological response aberrancies* in people with negative symptoms and findings in this area have been inconsistent. The research on "in-the moment" positive emotional responses in people with negative symptoms continues to be a topic of debate, and there is clear indication of reduced positive affect in daily life (Cho et al., 2017). There is also a fairly consistent indication of reduced anticipatory pleasure in schizophrenia (Visser et al., 2020; Hallford & Sharma, 2019), which has provided the basis for the major contemporary theories of negative symptoms (Chan et al., 2022). For negative emotional experiences, the evidence base is more consistent, with sufficient evidence pointing to increased levels of negative affect reported in daily life (Cho et al., 2017) and in response to emotion-inducing stimuli (Cohen & Minor, 2010).

Coming back to the example of a situation, in which Jack was approached and asked to join the activity group, his motor response could be described as "muttering 'no thanks,'" "remaining seated" and showing "no mimics or physical signs of interest or regret of not attending"; his cognitive response in terms of automatic thoughts may have been, "It won't be fun," or "It's not worth the bother." He may also be thinking, "I don't have the energy." He might also be assuming that "I don't have what it takes and will make a fool of myself," which might go along with the corresponding psychophysiological indicators of arousal, which he perceives as a brief feeling of sadness or anxiety. Finally, Jack is likely to lack a feeling of anticipatory pleasure at the thought of joining the activity group (response deficit).

3.2 The S-Variable—Relevant Situational Conditions

At the micro-level of an individual functional analysis, the S-variable can be practically any situation that precedes or triggers the problem behavior. This can be a social situation, such as Jack being invited to join the activity group. It can also be a nonsocial trigger, such as a beep from the alarm clock indicating that it is time to get up, or a thought, such as reminding oneself that one wanted to go to the gym.

To make good use of what we know from research, it is more informative to move to the macro-level, which explains individual behavior in the context of enduring external influences. In this regard, there is indication that both prolonged exposure to a depriving, under-stimulating environment (e.g., long-term institutionalization; Oshima et al., 2005), reduced social networks and support (Gayer-Anderson & Morgan, 2013), childhood neglect (Bailey et al., 2018) or to overstimulation (e.g., social adversity and stress; Catone et al., 2017; Jaya et al., 2017, 2022), are linked to negative symptoms. This is backed up by experimental research showing that even short-term social exclusion can trigger cognitive and emotional responses that are characteristic of amotivational negative symptoms (Pillny & Lincoln, 2020).

The assessment of Jacks social environment over the last decades revealed it to be understimulating. His friends from his early college years withdrew after the second and third psychotic episodes, his parents live faroff, and there seems to be little opportunity to participate in positive social interactions, interesting leisure activities, or meaningful work.

In addition to looking at external factors as triggers of the behavioral response, it is also helpful to reflect on how they impact on the O-variable, which mediates the response: For example, persistent social deprivation can have a detrimental effect on a person's cognitive abilities and cognitive functioning has been shown to improve in people with serious mental illness if they were removed from homeless shelters to group homes or independent apartments (Seidman et al., 2003). Moreover, ongoing social adversity will influence a person's view of themself or others toward the negative, such as perceiving oneself as helpless or others as bad (Jaya et al., 2017), which is likely to increase the likelihood of demotivating beliefs (e.g., "it won't be fun," "I don't have what it takes") and social withdrawal in a given situation. Also, external social risk factors are influenced by a person's prototypical responses, which adds to long-term maintenance of negative symptoms (see Chapter 2).

3.3 The O-Variable—Relevant Person-Related Factors

As can be seen in Table 10.1, much of what we know from research on negative symptoms can be conceptualized as indicators of vulnerability in the O-variable. Most findings relate to *cognitive abilities* or *predispositions.* These include neurocognitive deficits, which have been linked to reduced expressiveness in particular (Chang et al., 2014; Hartmann-Riemer et al., 2015). It also includes social cognition, such as impairments in theory of mind (or mentalizing; Brüne, 2005; Charernboon, 2020; Lincoln et al., 2011), difficulties in identifying and discriminating facial expressions of emotions (Kohler et al., 2010; Savla et al., 2013) and affiliative social skills (Blanchard et al., 2015). Moreover, enduring negative schemas about the self, such as a self-concept of not fitting in; for example, Grant & Beck's (2010) concept of "asociality beliefs" and not having the necessary abilities (defeatist performance beliefs; Rector, 2004), as well as low expectations of success and pleasure (Gard et al, 2007) can be categorized in the O-Variable. Other cognitive O variables of therapeutic relevance are general difficulties anticipating pleasure (Visser et al., 2020; Hallford & Sharma, 2019), difficulties generating, maintaining, and updating mental representations of value (Barch et al., 2014; Green et al., 2015; Hartmann et al., 2015), and cost-effort computations (Culbreth et al., 2016; Gold et al., 2013), which all help explain the reduction in goal-directed behavior observable (R variable).

Aspects to bear in mind as potentially relevant *biological* O variables include reduced physical fitness (Vancampfort et al., 2015), chronic physical illnesses (Sicras-Mainar et al., 2015), impaired functioning of the biological stress, and immune systems (Huang et al., 2020; Stogios et al., 2021), and side effects of antipsychotic medication (Galderisi et al., 2021). Moreover, genetic and epigenetic factors can be subsumed here. Physical health problems and negative symptoms might bidirectionally influence each other, in the sense that physical impairment will lead to lower activity (*motor-behavior* level of the R-variable; Gorczynski et al., 2018) and that repeated inactivity can contribute to a sedentary lifestyle, which in turn increases the risk for cardiovascular disease, weight gain, and metabolic disturbances (Vancampfort et al., 2015). Also, antipsychotics have been suggested to directly cause amotivation and subsequent impairments in goal-directed behavior by the reduction of dopaminergic transmission (Berg et al., 2022; Ikemoto et al., 2015). O variables, however, might also exert their influence via interactions with the triggering situations (S); for example, if impaired physical fitness renders an activity more strenuous and thus provides less short-term reward. In Jack's case it is reasonable to assume that the relevant O variables include both his difficulties in anticipating feelings of pleasure, biased cost-effort computations, as well as his generally low expectations of success as they are likely to be the driver of his negative automatic thoughts, such as "It won't be fun" and "It's not worth the bother." Another relevant driver may be his cardiovascular problems and obesity that lead him to think, "I don't have the energy."

3.4 The C-Variable—Consequences

The problem behavior will most likely be followed by both reinforcing (e.g., short-term increased attention, reduced negative affect) and punishing consequences (e.g., long-term loss of contacts). Given that punishers should reduce the likelihood of the problem behavior, the main focus needs to be on the positive and negative reinforcing factors that could be maintaining the problem behavior. This will have to be largely speculative, however, as—to my knowledge—there is no direct empirical research on reinforcers of negative-symptom problem behavior. In terms of *positive reinforcers*, the withdrawal and inactivity (R variable) are—at least initially—likely to increase efforts in interaction partners and, particularly, mental-health professionals to provide support and help. This may occur at the micro-level in terms of increased attention or support, or at the macro level in terms of increased practical or financial support (e.g., in form of disability pensions). In terms of *negative reinforcement*, avoidant behavior is likely to be reinforced by a reduction of fear, worry, or tension, which may be experienced as a short-term relief from the perceived or anticipated burden of effort or responsibility for one's actions along with its risk of failure. This mechanism, which is well researched in anxiety disorders, is likely to be a relevant maintaining factor in patients with negative symptoms, given their pronounced negative expectations (see O-variable section on beliefs and anticipation). The mechanism of negative reinforcement was expressed clearly by Patricia Deegan (2016) when she stated that "giving up, refusing to hope, not trying, not caring: all of these were ways to try and protect the last fragile traces of our spirit and our selfhood from undergoing another crushing" (Deegan, 2016). In line with this mechanism, some authors have suggested that negative symptoms play an adaptive role by protecting patients from further stressors and trauma (Beck et al., 2009; White et al., 2013; see also Chapter 2) and from suicidal ideation and attempts (Hawton et al., 2005).

Jack's response has a number of short and long-term consequences: For one, the decision not to get up and join the activity group produces a short-term sense of relief (i.e., reduction in arousal) because of not having to expose himself to an activity that goes along with effort and bears the risk of rejection and shame (*negative reinforcer*). Another short-term consequence is that the social worker shows signs of disapproval and rejection, "Don't be lazy" (*punisher*). In the longer term, the social worker no longer asks him to join (*negative punisher*). Another direct consequence is that Jack misses out on an opportunity to connect with his peers (*negative punisher*) that could have corrected some of his demotivating beliefs and made him feel better about himself.

Why negative symptoms are so persistent may appear somewhat puzzling in light of the numerous negative consequences and the dearth of positive ones. One reason could be that, although learning theory generally predicts punishers to reduce the likelihood of the problem behavior, punishers can also add to maintenance if they feed back into the situational or organism variables that are relevant to the problem behavior. In the case of negative symptoms, these kinds of feedback mechanisms are likely. The loss of positive reinforcement in social, achievement-, and pleasure-related domains (Gard et al., 2014, 2007) along with withdrawal of interaction partners (Lavelle et al., 2013; Riehle & Lincoln, 2018), leaves patients with reduced opportunities to improve their skills in social and cognitive domains in the O variable. This will likely impact negatively on social interactions and achievement-related successes; for example, job offers (feedback loop).

These types of feedback mechanisms from C to O also apply to Jack. The withdrawal of friends has left him with a feeling of being inept. Also, being out of work for such a long time impacts his concentration, which he worries will fail him when faced with more challenging cognitive tasks. In addition, his increased sedentary behavior has had detrimental effects on his physical health, which is making it more and more difficult for him to join physical activities.

3.5 The K-Variable—Contingencies

The persistence of negative symptoms despite their numerous negative consequences can also be explained by taking a closer look at the contingencies that describe the timing and the likelihood of the consequences. Because the reinforcing consequences (e.g., reduction of negative affect) tend to follow the problem behavior immediately and regularly, they will likely exert a stronger influence over it than the punishing ones (e.g., rejection, health-related problems) that tend to follow with a long delay and a certain irregularity. Another contingency related issue is that the strength of the effect of the consequences on future responses is determined by how meaningful the consequence is for the person involved, which is determined by a person's goals, values, and preferences. Negative symptoms are associated with having relatively more avoidance- than approach-related goals (Schlier et al., 2016). Thus, patients might value reinforcers of approach-goal-directed behavior less and learn less from them. Finally, several studies have indicated that patients with negative symptoms have difficulties learning from positive outcomes (Gold et al., 2012; Strauss et al., 2011), which may be driven by their problems in generating and *maintaining mental representations of value* mentioned above (Barch et al., 2014; Green et al., 2015; Hartmann et al., 2015). Thus, we can speculate that these patients are not learning sufficiently from situations in which they *do not show* the problem behavior.

4. Implications for Assessment

As outlined above, the functional analysis provides a helpful frame to (1) assess the relevant factors that cause and maintain negative symptoms in a *given individual* and (2) derive interventions that target the factors that cause and maintain negative symptoms in a *that individual.* Table 10.2 indicates suitable ways to assess problems in each of the variables outlined in the SORCK model (see columns 1 and 2 in Table 10.2).[2] Over and above validated assessment tools for negative symptoms, it is advisable to assess prototypical situations in collaboration with the patient. These will provide information on concrete behavioral responses (R) and can also be used to identify the situational factors (S) and the specific consequences (C). If available, ambulatory assessment devices can also provide valuable information on situational triggers of problem versus functional behavior along with its consequences and contingencies (see Chapter 9). In regard to understanding past and ongoing situational factors with relevance to the O-variable, knowledge of childhood and adolescent adversity (e.g., life-history charts) and the present living and working situation is relevant. As an assessment of all O variables goes beyond the scope of any clinician, a practical stance needs to be adopted here, focusing on those aspects deemed most relevant for a given patient: Neurocognitive deficits may be assessed by a standardized neuropsychological test-battery, such as the MATRICS, that also tests for some social-cognitive skills (Nuechterlein et al., 2008). Social-interactional and affiliate skills are best assessed by standardized interactional probes (e.g., Blanchard et al., 2015). A scale to assess a range of dysfunctional beliefs specific to negative symptoms was recently developed (Pillny et al., 2018). There are some questionnaires (e.g., the Temporal Experience of Pleasure Scale; R. C. Chan et al., 2012), which can be used to assess anticipatory pleasure. There are laboratory tests of reward anticipation and related constructs (for an overview see: R. C. K. Chan et al., 2022), but these are not suitable for standard clinical assessments. For biological O variables, a medical assessment should involve a thorough physical history and examination and elucidate the effects of antipsychotic medication and substance use on negative symptoms.

Although the assessment based on functional analysis is time consuming, the additional effort for the assessment needs to be weighed against the benefits of improving outcome for patients with severe negative symptoms. The assessment process could be facilitated if researchers developed an assessment battery for negative symptoms based on this framework. This could include a brief screening to identify domains for which more detailed assessments are necessary and standardized assessment tools for each of the potentially relevant facets.

5. Implications for Therapy

Based on the assessment, the therapist uses the functional analysis framework to develop a preliminary working model of the most relevant factors and their interactions that are driving and maintaining the problem behavior. This model is discussed with the patient and suitable interventions can be collaboratively delineated. Following the logic of the functional analysis, priority should be given to the interventions, or combinations of interventions, that are likely to change the key causing or maintaining factors. For reasons of space, I cannot detail all of the interventions. However, Table 10.2 provides an overview of therapy-relevant targets according to their focus within the functional analysis conceptualization (column 1) and of therapeutic aims (column 3). It also lists examples of (potentially) effective psychosocial interventions to address each of the various functional analysis components (column 4). Many of the interventions are described in detail in other chapters of this book. In our previous work (Lincoln et al., 2017), we have pointed out that the large variety of evidence-based interventions are an advantage when it comes to selecting suitable interventions based on individual functional analyses. However, we also identified several areas where novel interventions still need to be developed. Some of these are also specified in Table 10.2.

Interventions for the S variable could aim to reduce situations that trigger problem responses, such as environmental under-stimulation or social adversity, and increase those that are likely to trigger a healthier response. This could involve practical support (e.g., supporting a move out of the institution). Skill-based family interventions that aim at reducing the stressful emotional climate in the family (Dixon et al., 2000; see also Chapter 13) could also be considered here. However, the findings here also point to the relevance of encouraging and providing opportunities for employment and networking, which may require more interdisciplinary involvement or peer-support concepts.

Aims of *interventions addressing the O variable* could be to improve on social-cognitive skills (e.g., via trainings of affect recognition), neurocognitive skills

Table 10.2 Overview of relevant treatment targets, methods of assessment, therapeutic aims and potential, as well as existing interventions

Treatment target	Assessment[a]	Therapeutic aims	Evidence-based and potentially helpful interventions
Situation (S)			
Prototypical triggers; Persistent unfavorable conditions (e.g., social adversity, poor social support)	Ambulatory assessment devices, open interviews, questionnaires, life-history charts, informant information	Reduction of adverse situations (e.g., under-stimulation), reduction of social and environmental stressors	Family interventions (e.g., communication training, crisis management, psychoeducation) that aim to reduce psychosocial stress, providing environmental supports to prompt initiation and persistence of goal-directed behavior. Examples for this are provided in the Motivation and Enhancement Training for Negative Symptoms (MOVE; Velligan et al., 2015). Avenues for further research: providing opportunities for employment and networking.
Organism (O)			
Neurocognitive deficits	Comprehensive neuropsychological test battery (e.g., MATRICS (Nuechterlein et al., 2008)) or interview-based assessment	Improvement of attention, memory, executive functions	Cognitive skill trainings, if possible combined with motivational components see Chapter 16.
Social cognition & social interaction	Diagnostic role-plays, behavioral tests, self-report questionnaires, informant information	Improvement of affect recognition, processing of social information (e.g., theory of mind, empathy)	Training of affect recognition (e.g., Wölwer et al., 2005); Social Skills Training (Granholm et al., 2014, 2022), Social Cognition & Interaction Training (Roberts et al., 2014); Training of emotion processing (e.g., Bechi et al., 2012); Training to improve on Theory of Mind (e.g., Mazza et al., 2010)

Dysfunctional beliefs, negative self-concepts and attachment insecurity	Self-report scales, interview-based scales	Changing negative schemas about self and others	Avenues for further research: schema therapy, attachment focused interventions; Cognitive interventions (see Chapter 11);
Reward processing	Self-report scales to assess anticipatory pleasure, Laboratory tests to assess processes (Chan et al., 2022)	Anticipation of positive emotions, improving value representation and learning from positive reinforcement	Training anticipatory pleasure skills. Evidence-based examples are the training by Favrod and colleagues (see Chapter 18); or the module on anticipatory pleasure from the MOVE-program (Velligan et al., 2015); interventions that increase awareness of present positive states, such as mindfulness interventions (see Chapter 20).
	Medical assessment	Improve physical health	Treatment of medical diseases, exercise (Sabe et al., 2020) and yoga (Rao et al., 2021), decrease of substance abuse, nutrition programs (Kim et al., 2017)
Response (R)			
Negative symptoms	Self- and observer rated scales; diagnostic role-plays Informant information, observer-rated scales	Increase affiliative signals, correct dysfunctional automatic maladaptive increase active motor behavior	Behavioral activation (e.g., Jacobson et al., 2001); social skill training (see Chapter 17), trainings of affective display and nonverbal communication, such as mirror exercises (e.g., Schwartz et al., 2006; Velligan et al., 2014); cognitive interventions that challenge automatic thoughts (see Chapter 11), physical activity interventions (Sabe et al., 2020).
Consequences (C)			
Maintenance of problem behavior	Interview based assessment, ambulatory assessment, behavioral observation	Increase goal-directed, functional behavior	Avenues for research: individual schedules of reinforcement that reduce reinforcement of dysfunctional and increase reinforcement of functional behavior that can be incorporated into ward-based or family interventions (contingency management).

[a] The assessment is meant to be used flexibly. Not all factors require thorough assessment in each patient. Also, additional factors that appear relevant to a given case (e.g., presence of comorbid disorders) can be added to the individual assessment.

(e.g., via cognitive remediation), dysfunctional beliefs (e.g., via cognitive therapy), or emotion- and reward processing. For example, to address anticipatory pleasure, behavioral experiments may be helpful as a patient's expectation of achievable pleasure prior to an activity can be compared to the actual degree of achieved pleasure during the activity, such as done in the MOVE program (e.g., Velligan et al., 2015). Moreover, Favrod and colleagues (see Chapter 18) have developed an anticipatory pleasure skills training that uses a positive imagination technique to generate pleasure from anticipating activities. A novel approach would be to combine ambulatory assessment (i.e., monitoring levels of effort and pleasure in regard to momentary and upcoming events in a daily life) and ambulatory intervention (i.e., comparing anticipated effort and pleasure with the pleasure actually experienced). Another potentially helpful intervention could be to increase awareness of momentary emotional states. In support of this, mindfulness-based interventions (see Chapter 20), acceptance and commitment therapy, and loving-kindness-meditation show promising effects for negative symptoms (Liu et al., 2021), probably via increasing awareness of affective states (White et al., 2011) and positive affect (Johnson et al., 2011).

R-variable interventions primarily involve training specific behavioral skills. A prominent example is social skill training (SST) (see Chapter 17). Reports on its effectiveness, however, are mixed (Elis et al., 2013; Riehle et al., 2017; Turner et al., 2014). Its effect thus may be dependent on additional factors. One way of improving SST could be to target the specific interactional skills that are most relevant to the individual patient after a more detailed assessment. Problems are more likely to be in the realm of affiliative behavior (Blanchard et al., 2015; Brüne et al., 2008) rather than what is typically addressed in role-play based SST (i.e., assertiveness). Also, trainings that target specific affiliative behavior output, such as smiling are rare. A different approach could include bio- and other automated movement feedback (e.g., computerized feedback of video-based measures of facial expressions). Effectiveness can also be improved by combining SST with therapy for related problems, such as cognitive interventions challenging beliefs related to asociality (Granholm et al., 2014) or with cognitive training (Granholm et al., 2022).

More focus and research are needed to develop and improve on *interventions directed at C and K.* To optimize learning from consequences, the whole pattern of short- and long-term consequences of both the problem and the desired functional behavior along with their meaning and timing needs to be analyzed. Based on this analysis, individual schedules of reinforcement can be set up that involve reducing reinforcers of problem behavior, especially the immediate ones, as far as possible and increasing immediate reinforcers of functional behavior (e.g., verbal praise, allowances, tokens that can be exchanged for individually meaningful reinforcers). For reasons of transparency and also to assure that reinforcers are meaningful for the patient, the patient needs to be involved in setting up the reinforcement plan and should also be encouraged to self-reinforce. Outside of an institution, family members, who are among the likeliest to be able to provide meaningful reinforcers could be involved in reinforcement schedules. These should take into account that short-term and immediate consequences have the strongest effect on learning new behavior whereas intermittent consequences are more relevant to maintaining behavior. Well-thought contingency schedules can have an effect as stand-alone interventions, but they can also boost the effectiveness of any of the interventions introduced above by frequent and intense reinforcement of goal-directed behavior. The necessity of goal-setting and reinforcement of goal directed behavior has already been recognized and is included in some of the existing approaches (Grant et al., 2012; Medalia & Saperstein, 2011; Velligan et al., 2015). However, with the exception of the Behavioral Activation approach, to my knowledge, no approach so far works with individualized schedules of reinforcement and personally meaningful rewards to improve on negative symptoms.

For Jack, a main treatment goal would be to increase participation in common daily—in particular social and physical—activities. Interventions on the S-, O-, and C-variables may be particularly beneficial for Jack, given that his inactivity appears to be influenced by situational characteristics, problems in anticipation of pleasure, and defeatist performance and asociality beliefs, and maintained by the behavioral consequences.

The defeatist performance and asociality beliefs can be addressed with CBT techniques (see Chapter 11). These could be supplemented with behavioral experiments and diary techniques that could help Jack make more positive predictions about participating in daily activities. To address behavioral consequences (C variable), the staff in the supervised housing could be encouraged to avoid open displays of disappointment and criticism and sensitized to not reduce interpersonal efforts when Jack does not respond to their offers. Rather they could reward small steps in the direction of goal directed behavior within an individual contingency management plan (shaping) and support Jack in making his living environment more stimulating (S-variable).

To further improve treatment efficacy, clinicians can attempt to take the feedback loops between different variables into account.

For example, if Jack is encouraged to take more exercise to improve health-related factors (O) this will likely also increase the likelihood of social encounters (S). If Jack increases his social network (S), his environment is likely to become more stimulating, which may prompt him towards more active behavior (R, e.g., responding to a text message). Also, using positive reinforcers (C), such as specific positive feedback (e.g., "I really liked the way you showed the younger boy how to throw the ball, Jack"), could not only reinforce the target behavior (R), but also help correct Jack's belief of being socially inept (O).

Following the logic of functional analysis, we would not necessarily expect a single evidence-based intervention to show an effect on negative symptoms for a randomly selected sample of patients with negative symptoms. An important criterion for an intervention, however, is that it is successful in improving the factor it addresses. Thus, interventions challenging dysfunctional performance beliefs should demonstrate that they can improve these beliefs in patients with these types of beliefs, affect-recognition programs should improve affect recognition in those with a deficit in this domain, and so on. Assuming that each of the interventions fulfills this criterion and that the clinician gets a reasonable understanding of the triggering and maintaining factors for an individual patient, a selection of the suitable interventions should theoretically lead to much stronger effects than a single intervention or a one-size-fits all program.

Notes

1 The *contingencies (K)* describe the timing and the likelihood of a specific consequence that follows a particular behavior. Consequences that occur regularly after a behavior improve the learning of a new behavior, while sporadically occurring consequences lead to a higher maintenance of the response. Additionally, immediate consequences tend to be more relevant to learning than delayed ones.

2 This table is a shortened and slightly modified version of Table 2 in Lincoln and colleagues (Lincoln et al., 2017).

References

Bailey, T., Alvarez-Jimenez, M., Garcia-Sanchez, A. M., Hulbert, C., Barlow, E., & Bendall, S. (2018). Childhood trauma is associated with severity of hallucinations and delusions in psychotic disorders: A systematic review and meta-analysis. *Schizophrenia Bulletin, 44*(5), 1111–1122.

Barch, D. M., Treadway, M. T., & Schoen, N. (2014). Effort, anhedonia, and function in schizophrenia: Reduced effort allocation predicts amotivation and functional impairment. *Journal of Abnormal Psychology, 123*(2), 387–397.

Beck, A. T., Rector, N. A., Stolar, N., & Grant, P. M. (2009). A cognitive conceptualization of negative symptoms. In A. T. Beck, N. A. Rector, N. Stolar, & P. M. Grant (Hrsg.), *Schizophrenia. Cognitive theory research and therapy* (pp. 142-159). Guilford Press.

Berg, M., Rief, W., & Lincoln, T. (2022). Going the extra mile? The influence of Amisulpride on effort-based decisions. *Schizophrenia Research, 240*, 113–115.

Blanchard, J. J., Park, S. G., Catalano, L. T., & Bennett, M. E. (2015). Social affiliation and negative symptoms in schizophrenia: Examining the role of behavioral skills and subjective responding. *Schizophrenia Research, 196*(4), 282–288.

Brüne, M. (2005). "Theory of Mind" in schizophrenia: A review of the literature. *Schizophrenia Bulletin, 31*, 21–42.

Brüne, M., Sonntag, C., Abdel-Hamid, M., Lehmkämper, C., Juckel, G., & Troisi, A. (2008). Nonverbal behavior during standardized interviews in patients with schizophrenia spectrum disorders. *The Journal of Nervous and Mental Disease, 196*(4), 282–288.

Catone, G., Marotta, R., Pisano, S., Lennox, B., Carotenuto, M., Gritti, A., Pascotto, A., & Broome, M. R. (2017). Psychotic-like experiences in help-seeking adolescents: Dimensional exploration and association with different forms of bullying victimization—A developmental social psychiatry perspective. *International Journal of Social Psychiatry, 63*(8), 752–762.

Chan, R. C. K., Wang, L., & Lui, S. S. Y. (2022). Theories and models of negative symptoms in schizophrenia and clinical implications. *Nature Reviews Psychology, 1*(8), 454–467.

Chan, R. C., Shi, Y. F., Lai, M. K., Wang, Y. N., Wang, Y., & Kring, A. M. (2012). The Temporal Experience of Pleasure Scale (TEPS): Exploration and confirmation of factor structure in a healthy Chinese sample. *PLoS One, 7*(4), e35352.

Chang, W. C., Hui, C. L. M., Chan, S. K. W., Lee, E. H. M., Wong, G. H. Y., & Chen, E. Y. H. (2014). Relationship between diminished expression and cognitive impairment in first-episode schizophrenia: A prospective three-year follow-up study. *Schizophrenia Research, 152*(1), 146–151.

Charernboon, T. (2020). Different subdomains of negative symptoms in clinically stable patients with schizophrenia: Determining the nature of their relationships with emotion recognition, theory of mind and neurocognition. *Cogent Psychology, 7*(1), 1849892.

Cho, H., Gonzalez, R., Lavaysse, L. M., Pence, S., Fulford, D., & Gard, D. E. (2017). Do people with schizophrenia experience more negative emotion and less positive emotion in their daily lives? A meta-analysis of experience sampling studies. *Schizophrenia Research, 183*, 49–55.

Cohen, A. S., & Minor, K. S. (2010). Emotional experience in patients with schizophrenia revisited: Meta-analysis of laboratory studies. *Schizophrenia Bulletin, 36*(1), 143–150.

Culbreth, A., Westbrook, A., & Barch, D. M. (2016). Negative symptoms are associated with an increased subjective cost of cognitive effort. *Journal of Abnormal Psychology, 125*(4), 528–536.

Deegan, P. (2016, October 5). *Letter of hope*. http://recoverydevon.co.uk/wp-content/uploads/2016/05/Pat-Deegan-letter-of-hope.pdf.

Depp, C. A., Bashem, J., Moore, R. C., Holden, J. L., Mikhael, T., Swendsen, J., Harvey, P. D., & Granholm, E. L. (2019). GPS mobility as a digital biomarker of negative symptoms in schizophrenia: A case control study. *Npj Digital Medicine, 2*(1), 1–7.

Dixon, L., Adams, C., & Lucksted, A. (2000). Update on family psychoeducation for schizophrenia. *Schizophrenia Bulletin, 26*(1), 5–20.

Elis, O., Caponigro, J. M., & Kring, A. M. (2013). Psychosocial treatments for negative symptoms in schizophrenia: Current practices and future directions. *Clinical Psychology Review, 33*(8), 914–928.

Favrod, J., Giuliani, F., Ernst, F., & Bonsack, C. (2010). Anticipatory pleasure skills training: A new intervention to reduce anhedonia in schizophrenia. *Perspectives in Psychiatric Care, 46*(3), 171–181.

Galderisi, S., Kaiser, S., Bitter, I., Nordentoft, M., Mucci, A., Sabé, M., Giordano, G. M., Nielsen, M. Ø., Glenthøj, L. B., Pezzella, P., Falkai, P., Dollfus, S., & Gaebel, W. (2021). EPA guidance on treatment of negative symptoms in schizophrenia. *European Psychiatry, 64*(1):e21.

Gard, D. E., Kring, A. M., Gard, M. G., Horan, W. P., & Green, M. F. (2007). Anhedonia in schizophrenia: Distinctions between anticipatory and consummatory pleasure. *Schizophrenia Research, 93*, 253–260.

Gard, D. E., Sanchez, A. H., Cooper, K., Fisher, M., Garrett, C., & Vinogradov, S. (2014). Do people with schizophrenia have difficulty anticipating pleasure, engaging in effortful behavior, or both? *Journal of Abnormal Psychology, 123*(4), 771–782.

Gayer-Anderson, C., & Morgan, C. (2013). Social networks, support and early psychosis: A systematic review. *Epidemiology and Psychiatric Sciences, 22*(2), 131–146.

Gold, J. M., Strauss, G. P., Waltz, J. A., Robinson, B. M., Brown, J. K., & Frank, M. J. (2013). Negative symptoms of schizophrenia are associated with abnormal effort-cost computations. *Biological Psychiatry, 74*(2), 130–136.

Gold, J. M., Waltz, J. A., Matveeva, T. M., Kasanova, Z., Strauss, G. P., Herbener, E. S., Collins, A. G. E., & Frank, M. J. (2012). Negative symptoms and the failure to represent the expected reward value of actions: Behavioral and computational modeling evidence. *Archives of General Psychiatry, 69*(2), 129–138.

Gorczynski, P., Vancampfort, D., & Patel, H. (2018). Evaluating correlations between physical activity, psychological mediators of physical activity, and negative symptoms in individuals living with psychosis and diabetes. *Psychiatric Rehabilitation Journal, 41*(2), 153–156.

Granholm, E., Holden, J., Link, P. C., & McQuaid, J. R. (2014). Randomized clinical trial of cognitive behavioral social skills training for schizophrenia: Improvement in functioning and experiential negative symptoms. *Journal of Consulting and Clinical Psychology, 82*(6), 1173–1185.

Granholm, E., Twamley, E. W., Mahmood, Z., Keller, A. V., Lykins, H. C., Parrish, E. M., Thomas, M. L., Perivoliotis, D., & Holden, J. L. (2022). Integrated cognitive-behavioral social skills training and compensatory cognitive training for negative symptoms of psychosis: Effects in a pilot randomized controlled trial. *Schizophrenia Bulletin, 48*(2), 359–370.

Grant, P. M., & Beck, A. T. (2010). Asocial beliefs as predictors of asocial behavior in schizophrenia. *Psychiatry Research, 177*(1-2), 65–70.

Grant, P. M., Huh, G. A., Perivoliotis, D., Stolar, N. M., & Beck, A. T. (2012). Randomized trial to evaluate the efficacy of cognitive therapy for low-functioning patients with schizophrenia. *Archives of General Psychiatry, 69*(2), 121–127.

Green, M. F., Horan, W. P., Barch, D. M., & Gold, J. M. (2015). Effort-based decision making: A novel approach for assessing motivation in schizophrenia. *Schizophrenia Bulletin, 41*(5), 1035–1044.

Hallford, D. J., & Sharma, M. K. (2019). Anticipatory pleasure for future experiences in schizophrenia spectrum disorders and major depression: A systematic review and meta-analysis. *The British Journal of Clinical Psychology, 58*(4), 357–383.

Hartmann, M., Kluge, A., Kalis, A., Mojzisch, A., Tobler, P. N., & Kaiser, S. (2015). Apathy in schizophrenia as a deficit in the generation of options for action. *Journal of Abnormal Psychology, 124*(2), 309–318.

Hartmann-Riemer, M. N., Hager, O. M., Kirschner, M., Bischof, M., Kluge, A., Seifritz, E., & Kaiser, S. (2015). The association of neurocognitive impairment with diminished expression and apathy in schizophrenia. *Schizophrenia Research, 169*(1), 427–432.

Hawton, K., Sutton, L., Haw, C., Sinclair, J., & Deeks, J. J. (2005). Schizophrenia and suicide: Systematic review of risk factors. *The British Journal of Psychiatry, 187*, 9–20.

Huang, W.-C., Liu, W.-S., Chen, T., Chen, W.-H., & Huang, W.-L. (2020). Parasympathetic activity as a potential biomarker of negative symptoms in patients with schizophrenia. *Asia-Pacific Psychiatry, 12*(3), e12392.

Ikemoto, S., Yang, C., & Tan, A. (2015). Basal ganglia circuit loops, dopamine and motivation: A review and enquiry. *Behavioural Brain Research, 290*, 17–31.

Jacobson, N. S., Martell, C. R., & Dimidjian, S. (2001). Behavioral activation treatment for depression: Returning to contextual roots. *Clinical Psychology: Science and Practice, 8*(3), 255–270.

Jaya, E. S., Ascone, L., & Lincoln, T. M. (2017). Social adversity and psychosis: The mediating role of cognitive vulnerability. *Schizophrenia Bulletin, 43*(3), 557–565.

Jaya, E. S., Pillny, M., Lincoln, T. M., & Riehle, M. (2022). Does social defeat cause negative symptoms? A prospective study in a multi-national community sample. *Comprehensive Psychiatry, 113*, 152289.

Kanfer, F. H., & Karoly, P. (1972). Self-control: A behavioristic excursion into the lion's den. *Behavior Therapy, 3*(3), 398–416.

Kanfer, F. H., & Saslow, G. (1965). Behavioral analysis: An alternative to diagnostic classification. *Archives of General Psychiatry, 12*(6), 529–538.

Kim, E. J., Lim, S. Y., Lee, H. J., Lee, J.-Y., Choi, S., Kim, S.-Y., Kim, J.-M., Shin, I.-S., Yoon, J.-S., Yang, S. J., & Kim, S.-W. (2017). Low dietary intake of n-3 fatty acids, niacin, folate, and vitamin C in Korean patients with schizophrenia and the development of dietary guidelines for schizophrenia. *Nutrition Research, 45*, 10–18.

Kohler, C. G., Walker, J. B., Martin, E. A., Healey, K. M., & Moberg, P. J. (2010). Facial emotion perception in schizophrenia: A meta-analytic review. *Schizophrenia Bulletin, 36*(5), 1009–1019.

Lavelle, M., Healey, P. G. T., & McCabe, R. (2013). Is nonverbal communication disrupted in interactions involving patients with schizophrenia? *Schizophrenia Bulletin, 39*(5), 1150–1158.

Lavelle, M., Healey, P. G. T., & McCabe, R. (2014). Nonverbal behavior during face-to-face social interaction in schizophrenia: A review. *The Journal of Nervous and Mental Disease, 202*(1), 47–54.

Lincoln, T. M., Mehl, S., Kesting, M.-L., & Rief, W. (2011). Negative symptoms and social cognition. Detecting suitable targets for psychological interventions. *Schizophrenia Bulletin, 37*, S23–S32.

Lincoln, T. M., Riehle, M., Pillny, M., Helbig-Lang, S., Fladung, A.-K., Hartmann-Riemer, M., & Kaiser, S. (2017). Using functional analysis as a framework to guide individualized treatment for negative symptoms. *Frontiers in Psychology, 8*. Dec 5;8:2108. doi: 10.3389/fpsyg.2017.02108.

Liu, Y.-C., Li, I.-L., & Hsiao, F.-H. (2021). Effectiveness of mindfulness-based intervention on psychotic symptoms for patients with schizophrenia: A meta-analysis of randomized controlled trials. *Journal of Advanced Nursing, 77*(6), 2565–2580.

Marder, S. R., & Galderisi, S. (2017). The current conceptualization of negative symptoms in schizophrenia. *World Psychiatry, 16*(1), 14–24.

Mazza, M., Lucci, G., Pacitti, F., Pino, M. C., Mariano, M., Casacchia, M., & Roncone, R. (2010). Could schizophrenic subjects improve their social cognition abilities only with observation and imitation of social situations? *Neuropsychological Rehabilitation, 20*(5), 675–703.

Medalia, A., & Saperstein, A. (2011). The role of motivation for treatment success. *Schizophrenia Bulletin, 37*(suppl 2), S122–S128.

Nguyen, A., Frobert, L., McCluskey, I., Golay, P., Bonsack, C., & Favrod, J. (2016). Development of the positive emotions program for schizophrenia: An intervention to improve pleasure and motivation in schizophrenia. *Frontiers in Psychiatry, 7* (FEB), 1–9.

Nuechterlein, K. H., Green, M. F., Kern, R. S., Baade, L. E., Barch, D. M., Cohen, J. D., Essock, S., Fenton, W. S., Frese, F. J., Gold, J. M., Goldberg, T., Heaton, R. K., Keefe, R. S. E., Kraemer, H., Mesholam-Gately, R., Seidman, L. J., Stover, E., Weinberger, D. R., Young, A. S., . . . Marder, S. R. (2008). The MATRICS consensus cognitive battery, part 1: Test selection, reliability, and validity. *American Journal of Psychiatry, 165*(2), 203–213.

Oshima, I., Mino, Y., & Inomata, Y. (2005). Effects of environmental deprivation on negative symptoms of schizophrenia: A nationwide survey in Japan's psychiatric hospitals. *Psychiatry Research, 136*(2–3), 163–171.

Pillny, M., Krkovic, K., & Lincoln, T. M. (2018). Development of the Demotivating Beliefs Inventory and test of the Cognitive Triad of Amotivation. *Cognitive Therapy and Research, 42*(6), 867–877.

Pillny, M., & Lincoln, T. M. (2020). The demotivating effect of social exclusion: An experimental test of a psychosocial model on the development of negative symptoms in psychosis. *Schizophrenia Research, 215*, 330–336.

Rao, N. P., Ramachandran, P., Jacob, A., Joseph, A., Thonse, U., Nagendra, B., Chako, D. M., Shiri, S., Hassan, H., Sreenivas, V., Maran, S., Durgam, D., Nandakumar, K., Varambally, S., & Gangadhar, B. N. (2021). Add on yoga treatment for negative symptoms of schizophrenia: A multi-centric, randomized controlled trial. *Schizophrenia Research, 231*, 90–97.

Rector, N. A. (2004). Dysfunctional attitudes and symptom expression in schizophrenia: Differential associations with paranoid delusions and negative symptoms. *Journal of Cognitive Psychotherapy, 18*(2), 163–173.

Riehle, M., & Lincoln, T. M. (2018). Investigating the social costs of schizophrenia: Facial expressions in dyadic interactions of people with and without schizophrenia. *Journal of Abnormal Psychology, 127*(2), 202–215.

Riehle, M., Straková, A., & Lincoln, T. M. (2024). Emotional experience of people with schizophrenia and people at risk for psychosis: A meta-analysis. *JAMA Psychiatry, 81*(1), 57–66.

Riehle, M., Pillny, M., & Lincoln, T. M. (2017). Are the negative symptoms of schizophrenia treatable at all? A systematic review on efficacy studies for targeted psychological interventions for negative symptoms. *Verhaltenstherapie, 27*(3), 199–208.

Sabe, M., Kaiser, S., & Sentissi, O. (2020). Physical exercise for negative symptoms of schizophrenia: Systematic review of randomized controlled trials and meta-analysis. *General Hospital Psychiatry, 62*, 13–20.

Savla, G. N., Vella, L., Armstrong, C. C., Penn, D. L., & Twamley, E. W. (2013). Deficits in domains of social cognition in schizophrenia: A meta-analysis of the empirical evidence. *Schizophrenia Bulletin, 39*(5), 979–992.

Schlier, B., Engel, M., Fladung, A. K., Fritzsche, A., & Lincoln, T. M. (2016). The relevance of goal-orientation for motivation in high versus low proneness to negative symptoms. Manuscript submitted for publication. *Journal of Behavioral Therapy and Experimental Psychiatry, 55*, 113–120.

Schwartz, B. L., Mastropaolo, J., Rosse, R. B., Mathis, G., & Deutsch, S. I. (2006). Imitation of facial expressions in schizophrenia. *Psychiatry Research, 145*(2–3), 87–94.

Seidman, L. J., Schutt, R. K., Caplan, B., Tolomiczenko, G. S., Turner, W. M., & Goldfinger, S. M. (2003). The effect of housing interventions on neuropsychological functioning among homeless persons with mental illness. *Psychiatric Services, 54*(6), 905–908.

Sicras-Mainar, A., Maurino, J., Ruiz-Beato, E., & Navarro-Artieda, R. (2015). Prevalence of metabolic syndrome according to the presence of negative symptoms in patients with schizophrenia. *Neuropsychiatric Disease and Treatment, 11*, 51–57.

Stogios, N., Gdanski, A., Gerretsen, P., Chintoh, A. F., Graff-Guerrero, A., Rajji, T. K., Remington, G., Hahn, M. K., & Agarwal, S. M. (2021). Autonomic nervous system dysfunction in schizophrenia: Impact on cognitive and metabolic health. *Npj Schizophrenia, 7*(1), 1–10.

Strauss, G. P., Frank, M. J., Waltz, J. A., Kasanova, Z., Herbener, E. S., & Gold, J. M. (2011). Deficits in positive reinforcement learning and uncertainty-driven exploration are associated with distinct aspects of negative symptoms in schizophrenia. *Biological Psychiatry, 69*(5), 424–431.

Swora, E., Boberska, M., Kulis, E., Knoll, N., Keller, J., & Luszczynska, A. (2022). Physical activity, positive and negative symptoms of psychosis, and general psychopathology among people with psychotic disorders: A meta-analysis. *Journal of Clinical Medicine, 11*(10), 2719.

Turner, D. T., van der Gaag, M., Karyotaki, E., & Cuijpers, P. (2014). Psychological interventions for psychosis: A meta-analysis of comparative outcome studies. *American Journal of Psychiatry, 171*(5), 523–538.

Vancampfort, D., Firth, J., Schuch, F. B., Rosenbaum, S., Mugisha, J., Hallgren, M., Probst, M., Ward, P. B., Gaughran, F., De Hert, M., Carvalho, A. F., & Stubbs, B. (2017). Sedentary behavior and physical activity levels in people with schizophrenia, bipolar disorder and major depressive disorder: A global systematic review and meta-analysis. *World Psychiatry: Official Journal of the World Psychiatric Association (WPA), 16*(3), 308–315.

Vancampfort, D., Rosenbaum, S., Probst, M., Soundy, A., Mitchell, A. J., De Hert, M., & Stubbs, B. (2015). Promotion of cardiorespiratory fitness in schizophrenia: A clinical overview and meta-analysis. *Acta Psychiatrica Scandinavica, 132*(2), 131–143.

Velligan, D., Maples, N., Roberts, D. L., & Medellin, E. M. (2014). Integrated psychosocial treatment for negative symptoms. *American Journal of Psychiatric Rehabilitation, 17*(1), 1–19.

Velligan, D., Roberts, D., Mintz, J., Maples, N., Li, X., Medellin, E., & Brown, M. (2015). A randomized pilot study of MOtiVation and Enhancement (MOVE) training for negative symptoms in schizophrenia. *Schizophrenia Research, 165*(2–3), 175–180.

Visser, K. F., Chapman, H. C., Ruiz, I., Raugh, I. M., & Strauss, G. P. (2020). A meta-analysis of self-reported anticipatory and consummatory pleasure in the schizophrenia-spectrum. *Journal of Psychiatric Research, 121*, 68–81.

White, R., Laithwaite, H., & Gilbert, P. (2013). Negative symptoms in schizophrenia. The role of social defeat. In A. I. Gumley, A. Gillham, K. Taylor, & M. Schwannauer (Hrsg.), *Psychosis and emotion: The role of emotions in understanding psychosis*, therapy and recovery (pp. 177–190). Routledge.

PART III

PSYCHOSOCIAL AND BEHAVIORAL INTERVENTIONS

11

Cognitive Behavioral Treatment for Negative Symptoms

Mark van der Gaag

Clinical pearls

- Cognitive behavioral therapy (CBT) has been adapted specifically to treat negative symptoms.

Behavioral activation is always a part of effective CBT for negative symptoms.

- Defeatist Performance Beliefs (i.e., thoughts that one will not be good at something) are one type of maladaptive cognition that is addressed in CBT for negative symptoms.

Poor Anticipatory Pleasure (i.e., difficulty being able to imagine having a good time or experiencing pleasure at a future event) is one factor that maintains negative symptoms, which can be addressed with CBT for negative symptoms.

- Difficulties with emotional expression can be addressed through using social skills training as a component of CBT for negative symptoms.

An individualized functional analysis is necessary to target specific dysfunctional beliefs that are driving negative symptoms.

1. Introduction

This chapter is about Cognitive Behavioral Therapy for negative symptoms (CBTn). As the components of negative symptoms are heterogenous, different accents in CBTn have been present over the decades. At the same time, research on the structure and composition of negative symptoms, and research

Mark van der Gaag, *Cognitive Behavioral Treatment for Negative Symptoms*. In: *Psychosocial Approaches to Negative Symptoms in Psychosis*. Edited by: Tania Lincoln et al., Oxford University Press. © Oxford University Press (2025). DOI: 10.1093/oso/9780197676790.003.0011 into cognitive mediators and moderators, has changed CBTn from a generic approach to a more targeted approach. Negative symptoms can be divided into two groups of symptoms: expressive deficits reflecting loss of initiative and behavioral responsiveness; and social amotivation reflecting withdrawal and avoidance. Expressive deficits may improve from behavioral interventions aimed to help clients participate in more social activities and improve communication through social skills training. Social amotivation is associated with problems in anticipatory pleasure, and may be treated with interventions that target a lack of accuracy in anticipating pleasurable events, a low expectancy of cognitive capacity, and a high expectancy of low social performance. Social amotivation overlaps with demoralization and social defeat. Demoralization means experiencing hopelessness and helplessness, social incompetence, and less perceived social support. For people experiencing demoralization, connectedness between past and future is broken, and earlier failures are re-experienced (Wellen, 2010). Social defeat is induced by repeated exposure to an aggressive and dominant person who subdues the victim to submission and inactivity. Beliefs about social defeat are also prospectively strongly associated with negative symptoms (Jaya et al., 2022; Clay et al., 2021).

2. Strategies in Cognitive Behavioral Therapy for Negative Symptoms

A recent meta-analysis with negative symptoms as a primary outcome (Riehle et al., 2020), plus open studies (Staring et al., 2013; Granholm et al., 2020; Penadés et al., 2006) showed that different therapeutic strategies have been used in the treatment of negative symptoms using CBT. Most CBTn studies focus on expressive deficits (with behavioral activation and social skills training) and social activation (with focus on self-defeatist attitudes, negative self-esteem, and enhancing anticipatory pleasure) at the same time. We will illustrate the various protocols and packages.

The expressive deficits approach overlaps with behavior therapy for depression, in activating the patient to engage in pleasurable activities, teach skills to participate in group activities, and reinforce all activities. The approach focused on social amotivation is different and more recent. Originally it was assumed that patients with anhedonia experienced less pleasure and expressed less pleasure. Research shows, however, that patients with negative symptoms experience normal levels of pleasure when they participate in pleasurable events. Gard and colleagues found evidence for an anticipatory but not so much for a consummatory pleasure deficit in schizophrenia. This means that they did not experience pleasure looking forward to pleasurable events in the future. This lack of anticipatory pleasure was related to clinical ratings of anhedonia and functional outcomes (Gard et al., 2007; Chan et al., 2010a).

3. CBTn and Behavioral Activation

All but one CBTn protocol have used behavioral activation as a core of the intervention (Bailer et al., 2001) (Klingberg et al., 2011; Grant et al., 2012; Staring et al., 2013; Velligan et al., 2015; Choi et al., 2016; Pos et al., 2019). The behavioral activation procedures in the different protocols vary from individual to group formats, and in the number of sessions and focus. The study by Grant and colleagues pursues social recovery and is described in a separate chapter. See Table 11.1 for the different mechanisms targeted in various CBTn protocols.

Behavioral activation was originally developed for the treatment of depression. The primary target is to activate the patient to engage in activities that are pleasurable. The experienced pleasure is antagonistic to depressed mood and the patient will repeatedly engage in pleasurable activities because of positive reinforcement. The patient is educated about the vicious circle of inactivity that results in depressed mood, which will lead to further inactivity. The procedures are that the patient will monitor all his activities during the week and the things that really matter for the patient are transferred into goals and activities. The meaningful and pleasurable activities are then scheduled and performed. Mastery is reinforced and eventual barriers are addressed with problem-solving. See Box 11.1 for a condensed narrative of behavioral activation. In depression therapy this is the best documented and effective intervention (Cuijpers et al., 2007; Kanter et al., 2010).

There is also a more cognitive form of behavioral activation used in Cognitive Behavioral Social Skills Training (CBSST). Patients received 24 weekly two-hour group therapy sessions. In the manual, social skills training components include symptom management, communication role play, and problem-solving modules. The cognitive interventions target beliefs about psychotic symptoms and negative attributions, as well as self-efficacy beliefs that interfered with functioning behaviors. Symptoms are a relatively minor focus and are only addressed in the context of education about warning signs and communication role-plays with providers about medications and by modifying beliefs about hallucinations that interfere with functional goals. The training was tested in older schizophrenia patients and found effective for skills and community functioning, but not for positive and negative symptoms (Granholm et al., 2007). When integrated with compensatory cognitive training there was a small effect on negative symptoms and verbal learning (Granholm et al., 2022).

Table 11.1 Intervention Targets in Cognitive Behavioral Therapies Aimed at Negative Symptom Reduction

Study	Individual case formulation	Interventions					Study design						Results
		Behavioral Activation	Skills training	CBT for NS	CBT for DPB	CBT for Anticipatory pleasure	N	Design	Therapy Format	Number of Sessions	Therapy Duration	Control condition	Significant effects on
Bailer, 2001	X	X	X	X			39	Cross-over	Indiv	24	12 weeks	TAU	NS
Klingberg, 2011	X	X		X			198	RCT	Indiv	20	9 months	CR	—
Choi, 2016	Goals	X	X	X			47	RCT	Group	10	n.a.	TAU	NS
Grant, 2012	Recov Goal	X	X	X	X		60	RCT	Indiv	weekly	18 months	TAU	Avolition Apathy
Granholm, 2020	Daily Action plan	X		X	X		31	Open	Group blended	12	12 weeks	—	DPB
Granholm, 2022	Course	X	X	X mCBT	X mCBT		55	RCT	Group	25 twice weekly	12.5 weeks	SC	NS Verbal learning
Staring, 2013	X	X	X	X	X	X	34	Open	Indiv	20	6 months	—	NS DPB
Velligan, 2015		X	X	X	X	X	92	RCT	Indiv		9 months	TAU	NS
Pos, 2019	X	X	X	X	X	X	99	RCT	8 Group 6 Indiv	14	3 months	TAU	NS GAF
Favrod, 2019	Course				X	X	80	RCT	Group	8		TAU	Apathy + Anhedonia

Note. CBT = Cognitive Behavioral Therapy; mCBT = mobile-assisted Cognitive Behavioral Therapy; TAU = Treatment as usual; CR = cognitive remediation; SC = supportive contact; NS = negative symptoms; DPB—Defeatist Performance Beliefs; RCT = randomized controlled study; NS = negative symptom.

Box 11.1 A Condensed Narrative of Behavioral Activation

T: Great that you monitored all your activities last week and rated them on pleasure and on satisfaction.
P: Yeah, it took discipline to fill in the form each day, but I succeeded.
T: You did very well, and I see you have been watching television every day without much pleasure and no satisfaction. We have been talking about how low activity or passive entertainment may enhance depressed mood and foster further inactivity and withdrawal. I guess we have to reduce these moments. Do you agree?
P: Yeah, I do not really like television with all its commercials over and over, but I have no energy to get involved in other activities.
T: Here on Tuesday, you wrote that you liked playing guitar for an hour. You rated pleasure and satisfaction very high.
P: I liked to pick up that dusty guitar, and I found out I still can play it.
T: Great, how about playing the guitar twice a week, next week, for an hour each time?
P: I could try that.
T: OK, what time in the week would be an opportunity?
P: I think after lunch at 1 p.m.
T: Good, what days will you plan in your diary?
P: Let's see. I think Tuesday and Friday are good moments.
T: OK, put that in your diary and next week we will come back and look at this homework assignment.
P: OK.
T: Did you run into any obstacles last week?
P: Sunday I really felt like a loser.
T: What happened that caused you to think you were a loser?

4. CBTn and Defeatist Attitudes

Defeatist performance beliefs, or negative thoughts about one's ability to successfully perform goal-directed behavior, may inhibit the initiation of behavior and engagement. These defeatist thoughts include, "If I fail partly, it is as bad as being a complete failure," "If you cannot do something well, there is little point in doing it at all," and "If I fail at work, I'm a failure as a person" (Beck et al., 2009).

Defeatist performance beliefs mediated between cognitive impairment and both negative symptoms and functioning. These effects were independent of depression and positive symptom levels (Grant & Beck, 2009) and defeatist performance beliefs was introduced as a new psychotherapeutic target. Defeatist performance beliefs also mediated the effects of treatment on negative symptoms and social functioning in the CBSST study, while asocial beliefs mediated only negative symptoms (Granholm et al., 2018). However, in a prospective study from baseline to posttreatment, reduction of amotivation was associated with improvement of functioning, whereas reduction of defeatist performance beliefs was unrelated to improvements in functioning or amotivation (Pillny & Lincoln, 2016). Although results are not all in line with one another, the association between defeatist performance beliefs and negative symptoms is confirmed in meta-analysis. There is shared variance between defeatist performance beliefs and negative symptoms and between defeatist performance beliefs and functional outcomes, but the effect sizes of these relationships fall in the small range with $r = -0.27$ (Campellone et al., 2016).

Defeatist performance beliefs were targeted explicitly in seven studies (See Table 11.1). Three studies did not measure the effects on defeatist performance attitudes (Grant et al., 2012; Velligan et al., 2015; Favrod et al., 2019). Two open studies showed an effect on defeatist performance beliefs (Staring et al., 2013; Granholm et al., 2020), but this was not replicated in two randomized controlled studies (Pos et al., 2019; Granholm et al., 2022). This is disappointing, and more studies are necessary to develop enough statistical power to detect small-to-moderate effects in meta-analysis.

5. CBTn and Anticipatory Pleasure

Anhedonia consists of the inability to experience pleasure. Only recently has it become clear that pleasure is still experienced, but anhedonic patients seem to be unable to anticipate pleasure and stop seeking pleasure. Beliefs about pleasure had no significant mediation effect between social anhedonia and prediction of pleasant events, but were shown to influence the subjective prediction of pleasant events completely through emotional experience. These findings suggest that beliefs about pleasure and emotional experience may be considered promising factors for interventions in individuals with anhedonia (Hu et al., 2018). The Temporal Experience of Pleasure Scale (TEPS) measures consummatory pleasure and anticipatory pleasure. The distinction between reward anticipation and consumption is demonstrated in several studies using the TEPS (Gard et al., 2007) (Favrod et al., 2009; Chan et al., 2010b), but these results could not be replicated for anticipatory pleasure in another study (Strauss et al., 2011). Yet, the idea is innovative and has been put to the test in trials. Enhancing anticipatory pleasure is targeted by an open study and another three randomized studies (see Table 11.1). The study protocol PEPS targeted at enhancing anticipatory pleasure is described in a separate chapter (see Chapter 18); (Favrod et al., 2019).

The treatment manual of Staring and colleagues (Staring et al., 2013) is based on the work of Grant and colleagues (Grant et al., 2012; Perivoliotis & Cather, 2009), but adapted to focus on anticipatory pleasure. Specifically, the treatment targets: (1) Negative expectancies about cognitive abilities, such as memory, concentration, and energy levels; (2) Negative expectancies about agency, performance, and social skills; and (3) Negative expectancies about the ability to enjoy and experience positive emotions. These expectancies seem to result in a negative self-image, self-stigmatization, and expectation of social exclusion, all of which result in avoidance behaviors such as withdrawal, less emotional expression, inactivity, defeatist attitudes, and thought and emotion suppression.

The treatment manual starts with a structured interview in order to develop an individual case formulation based on the model. Individual goals are assessed, and psychoeducation about neurocognitive impairments and dysfunctional attitudes is provided. General activity scheduling and registrations of performed activities are applied, and significant others are informed about the treatment rationale. When the first treatment goal has been chosen, the case formulation provides insight into possible obstacles toward achieving that goal. Dysfunctional beliefs and avoidance behaviors that stand in the way of the goal then constitute the targets of CBT-techniques, such as cognitive restructuring and roleplay. Behavioral experiments and other cognitive methods take place within the treatment sessions as much as possible. In a study of the protocol, 21 patients were recruited for up to 20 sessions (mean was 17.5 session). The results of this open, unblinded trial included large within-group effect sizes of 1.26 on PANSS negative symptoms and 0.95 of dysfunctional beliefs, and dysfunctional beliefs partially mediated the effect on negative symptoms. A condensed narrative of this approach is presented in Box 11.2.

Box 11.2 A Condensed Narrative Version of Exploring Anticipatory Estimations and Actually Experienced Rating of a Social Birthday Event

T: Let us look at events in the coming week.

P: My mother has her birthday, but I am considering not paying her a visit on that day.

Continued

Continued

T: Why not? Wouldn't your mom be pleased to see you wish her a happy birthday?

P: Yeah, but I think I am not capable of doing so.

T: What are your doubts?

P: I am afraid that I cannot tolerate all the people around me talking and asking questions and laughing. I also think I have nothing to talk about that will interest my family members. I will not enjoy the event.

T: OK, let's see. How much time do you think you can stand being in a room with many people?

P: Maybe 20 minutes.

T: How much time could you talk with someone before the conversation will stop?

P: Five minutes?

T: How much joy do you think you will experience on a scale of 1 to 10?

P: I guess 3!

T: Maybe you are right, but maybe you are much more capable than you think you are. Can we agree that you will visit your mom for her birthday and make a note when you leave, how much time you spent there, how your social conversations went, how much time you spent conversing, and finally your joy on a scale of 1 to 10?

P: OK, I will go and see.

One week later ... T: How was your mother's birthday party?

P: Actually, it was nice. I stayed at the party for three hours, talked with my mom, my sister, and her husband most of the time, and I enjoyed it with a score of 7.5.

T: Nice to hear you enjoyed it so much! How come it went better than you anticipated?

P: I don't know. I just tired much later than I anticipated. We had a nice conversation about past holidays that I have pleasant memories of. I enjoyed it much more than I thought I would.

T: Good to hear! I think this is one key feature we have to pay more attention to. You tend to underestimate your capacity to be social: It takes much more time than you think before you find it exhausting. You also underestimated your social skills. Your family liked to talk with you, didn't they?

P: Yes, they were all happy that I was there and were interested in my well-being. We shared a bunch of happy memories from the past.

T: Wonderful experience! You anticipated a score of 3 enjoyment, but experienced a 7.5. That's great, you can still enjoy birthday parties.

A randomized study included the steps from the Staring protocol in a slightly adapted way to fit in eight group sessions and six individual sessions (Pos et al., 2019). In the group, goals are set by participants and obstacles to those goals, in the form of dysfunctional beliefs, are identified. The focus of the sessions is on challenging anticipated obstacles using standardized interventions such as cognitive restructuring worksheets, role-plays, and on-site behavioral experiments. Additionally, individual therapy sessions focus on the continuation of social activation and achievement of personal goals through a personalized focus on the person's main dysfunctional beliefs and associated behaviors, as well as methods of countering these obstacles to accomplish their goals. The treatment manual provides material for psychoeducation and interventions that can be used if needed (e.g., cognitive techniques used to investigate dysfunctional beliefs and behavior, such as Socratic dialogue, behavioral and cognitive experiments; dimensional evaluation of negative or stereotype self-image; cognitive imagery techniques of the steps needed to achieve the set goal; and behavioral techniques such as activity scheduling and exposure to feared situations).

Some 99 first-episode psychosis patients were randomized and 25 patients dropped out. Intention-to-treat analysis showed a small effect on negative symptoms (d = −0.29), but this did not stand at 6-months follow-up. Both groups improved strongly as is often the case in studies with first-episode patients (Pos et al., 2019).

Velligan and colleagues tested the package MOtiVation and Enhancement (MOVE) (Velligan et al., 2015). Although defeatist performance beliefs and anticipatory pleasure were targeted in this diverse treatment package, they were not measured and evaluated in this study, and results are only evaluated for negative symptoms.

6. Evidence Base of Meta-Analytic Effects of CBTn

A meta-analysis including studies until 2006 showed a moderate effect-size of CBT (Hedges' g = 0.44) on negative symptoms (Wykes et al., 2008). But most studies were targeted primarily at positive-symptom reduction. A more recent meta-analysis of CBT showed no statistically significant effects on negative symptoms, regardless of whether the reduction of negative symptoms was a secondary or primary aim of the study (Velthorst et al., 2015). A later meta-analysis reported five more studies, but also removed 15 studies that were included by Velthorst and colleagues, and showed a significant small effect size of 0.34 on negative symptoms (Lutgens et al., 2017). A problem with these contradictory meta-analyses is that some studies had patients with low levels of negative symptoms at baseline, and the most recent meta-analysis selected only studies with patients with clinical levels of negative symptoms (Riehle et al., 2020). The effect-size was moderate (g = 0.46), but in RCTs, it was reduced to 0.24. So, evidence of the effectiveness of CBT on negative symptoms is still weak and dependent on study selection in different meta-analyses.

7. Discussion

The findings in research in CBTn are mixed. Behavioral activation is part of almost all CBTn protocols and is effective in all studies that compared CBTn with treatment as usual. The largest study that had an active control condition of cognitive remediation showed no differential effect. Both conditions strongly improved. So, activating patients is probably what accounts for the effects shown in meta-analyses of CBT.

Defeatist performance beliefs are associated to negative symptoms, but findings in open unblinded studies could not be replicated in two single-blind randomized controlled trials. More research is needed in CBT studies that solely target defeatist performance beliefs, before this should become a part of CBTn packages directed at negative symptoms and mediators of negative symptoms.

Targeting beliefs in anticipatory pleasure has only been researched with tailor-made outcome measurement on expectations of cognitive, social, and hedonic functioning in one small open study, while the RCT was probably too short to evoke statistically significant effects, and it did not evaluate the anticipatory pleasure as was done in the open trial.

Each of the CBTn packages show improvement in negative symptoms, and most of these effects stem from the use of behavioral activation. The effect-size is small to moderate and further improvement is necessary. Defeatist performance beliefs and anticipatory beliefs on competence and pleasure are promising cognitive approaches, but at this moment, evidence is still lacking. Although CBTn showed small-to-moderate effect sizes in meta-analyses with a limited number of studies, there is much room for improvement.

CBTn may be more indicated in patients with persistent and moderate-to-severe negative symptoms. To be effective on negative symptoms, negative symptoms must contribute to the suffering of the patient. The effects may also be more visible in patients with persistent symptoms given that the symptom levels in the control group will be more stable. A majority of 58% of first-episode patients have full symptomatic remission after their first treatment with antipsychotic medication (Lally et al., 2017), so control groups will also improve.

Although the research on defeatist performance beliefs and anticipatory pleasure has not provided convincing results, it is clear that a set of demotivating beliefs prevents patients with negative symptoms from looking forward to social activities and thus, provides a possible psychological explanation for the social withdrawal of patients with negative symptoms. This is potentially bidirectional, as social exclusion contributes to reduced motivation, anticipatory anhedonia, and demotivating beliefs (Pillny & Lincoln, 2020), as well as negative symptoms in general (Jaya et al., 2022). CBTn must further develop its cognitive interventions targeting beliefs that prevent recovery. A recently developed measure is the Demotivating Beliefs Inventory with three factor scores on self-defeating beliefs, social indifference beliefs, and low-expectancy-of-pleasure beliefs (Pillny et al., 2018). This is a broad measure of demotivating beliefs and may be helpful to better evaluate differential effects of interventions and to help conceptualize the numerous symptomatic, behavioral, and cognitive components of negative symptoms.

There is a big challenge to develop more effective interventions for negative symptoms. Research started with generic CBT interventions and procedures, with an unspecified basket of heterogenic symptoms as treatment targets. This is like hunting with a shot of hail at a flock of birds. Some will be hit, but then the shot may miss too many birds to be "statistically significant." As the structure of negative symptoms is now more refined, interventions should be tested on specific domains. These might be two (expressive deficits and social amotivation) or five (anhedonia, asociality, avolition, blunted affect, and alogia; see Chapter 1). For the different outcome domains, different interventions may be necessary. Another road to improved effectiveness is not targeting the behavioral symptoms, but targeting moderating and mediating beliefs such as defeatist performance beliefs, anticipatory pleasure, low self-esteem, and so on. The chapter on Functional Analysis does elaborate on this issue (see Chapter 10). A comprehensive model with mediators, obstacles, and intervention options is emerging, but it is far from complete. Further research is needed and must be done in a very systematic way as was done in the development of the Feeling Safe program by identifying mediators of paranoia and consolidators of paranoia and by developing interventions specifically focused on these perpetuating factors (Freeman, 2011). This approach was first described as the interventionist-causal model approach (Kendler & Campbell, 2009). The model defines causation in terms of intervention effects. The association between defeatist beliefs and negative symptoms is causal if only an intervention that reduces defeatist beliefs is also reducing negative symptoms. Interventionism allows variables of many different types—psychological, economic, and biological, for example—to be used together in stating the causes of a disorder in a multilevel model. In this way a single, clear empirical framework for the evaluation of all causal claims of relevance to treatment of negative symptoms is developed. Only then will an improved protocol starting from a personalized case formulation and a personalized treatment plan with known effectiveness become available.

References

Bailer, J., Takats, I., & Westermeier, C. (2001). Die Wirksamkeit individualisierter Kognitiver Verhaltenstherapie bei schizophrener Negativsymptomatik und socialer Behinderung [Efficacy of individualized cognitive-behavioral therapy for schizophrenic patients with negative symptoms and social disabilities: a controlled trial]. *Zeitschrift für Klinische Psychologie und Psychotherapie, 30*(4), 268–278.

Beck, A. T., Rector, N. A., Stolar, N., & Grant, P. (2009). *Schizophrenia: Cognitive theory, Research, and Therapy*. The Guilford Press.

Campellone, T. R., Sanchez, A. H., & Kring, A. M. (2016). Defeatist Performance Beliefs, Negative Symptoms, and Functional Outcome in Schizophrenia: A Meta-analytic Review. *Schizophrenia Bulletin, 42*(6), 1343–1352.

Chan, C. L., Ngai, E. K., Leung, P. K., & Wong, S. (2010a). Effect of the adapted Virtual Reality cognitive training program among Chinese older adults with chronic schizophrenia: a pilot study. *Int J Geriatr Psychiatry, 25*(6), 643–649.

Chan, R. C. K., Wang, Y., Huang, J., Shi, Y., Wang, Y., Hong, X., Ma, Z., Li, Z., Lai, M. K., & Kring, A. M. (2010b). Anticipatory and consummatory components of the experience of pleasure in schizophrenia: cross-cultural validation and extension. *Psychiatry Research, 175*(1-2), 181–183.

Choi, K. H., Jaekal, E., & Lee, G. Y. (2016). Motivational and Behavioral Activation as an Adjunct to Psychiatric Rehabilitation for Mild to Moderate Negative Symptoms in Individuals with Schizophrenia: A Proof-of-Concept Pilot Study. *Front Psychol, 7*, 1759.

Clay, K. B., Raugh, I. M., Bartolomeo, L. A., & Strauss, G. P. (2021). Defeatist performance beliefs in individuals at clinical high-risk for psychosis and outpatients with chronic schizophrenia. *Early Intervention in Psychiatry, 15*(4), 865–873.

Cuijpers, P., van Straten, A., & Warmerdam, L. (2007). Behavioral activation treatments of depression: a meta-analysis. *Clinical Psychology Review, 27*(3), 318–326.

Favrod, J., Ernst, F., Giuliani, F., & Bonsack, C. (2009). [Validation of the Temporal Experience of Pleasure Scale (TEPS) in a French-speaking environment]. *Encephale, 35*(3), 241–248.

Favrod, J., Nguyen, A., Chaix, J., Pellet, J., Frobert, L., Fankhauser, C., Ismailaj, A., Brana, A., Tamic, G., Suter, C., Rexhaj, S., Golay, P., & Bonsack, C. (2019). Improving Pleasure and Motivation in Schizophrenia: A Randomized Controlled Clinical Trial. *Psychotherapy and Psychosomatics, 88*(2), 84–95.

Freeman, D. (2011). Improving cognitive treatments for delusions. *Schizophrenia Research, 132*(2–3), 135–139.

Gard, D. E., Kring, A. M., Gard, M. G., Horan, W. P., & Green, M. F. (2007). Anhedonia in schizophrenia: distinctions between anticipatory and consummatory pleasure. *Schizophrenia Research, 93*(1–3), 253–260.

Granholm, E., Holden, J., Dwyer, K., Mikhael, T., Link, P., & Depp, C. (2020). Mobile-Assisted Cognitive Behavioral Therapy for Negative Symptoms: Open Single-Arm Trial With Schizophrenia Patients. *JMIR Mental Health, 7*(12), e24406.

Granholm, E., Twamley, E. W., Mahmood, Z., Keller, A. V., Lykins, H. C., Parrish, E. M., Thomas, M. L., Perivoliotis, D., & Holden, J. L. (2022). Integrated Cognitive-Behavioral Social Skills Training and Compensatory Cognitive Training for Negative Symptoms of

Psychosis: Effects in a Pilot Randomized Controlled Trial. *Schizophrenia Bulletin, 48*(2), 359–370.

Granholm, E., Holden, J., & Worley, M. (2018). Improvement in Negative Symptoms and Functioning in Cognitive-Behavioral Social Skills Training for Schizophrenia: Mediation by Defeatist Performance Attitudes and Asocial Beliefs. *Schizophrenia Bulletin, 44*(3), 653–661.

Granholm, E., McQuaid, J. R., McClure, F. S., Link, P. C., Perivoliotis, D., Gottlieb, J. D., Patterson, T. L., & Jeste, D. V. (2007). Randomized controlled trial of cognitive behavioral social skills training for older people with schizophrenia: 12-month follow-up. *Journal of Clinica Psychiatry, 68*(5), 730–737.

Grant, P. M., & Beck, A. T. (2009). Defeatist beliefs as a mediator of cognitive impairment, negative symptoms, and functioning in schizophrenia. *Schizophrenia Bulletin, 35*(4), 798–806.

Grant, P. M., Huh, G. A., Perivoliotis, D., Stolar, N. M., & Beck, A. T. (2012). Randomized Trial to Evaluate the Efficacy of Cognitive Therapy for Low-Functioning Patients with Schizophrenia. *Archives of General Psychiatry, 69*(2), 121–127.

Hu, H. X., Chu, M. Y., Yang, Y., Wang, L. L., Zhang, R. T., Lui, S. S. Y., Cheung, E. F. C., & Chan, R. C. K. (2018). Mediation effect of beliefs about pleasure and emotional experience between social anhedonia and prediction of pleasant events. *Psychiatry Research, 264*, 39–45.

Jaya, E. S., Pillny, M., Lincoln, T. M., & Riehle, M. (2022). Does social defeat cause negative symptoms? A prospective study in a multi-national community sample. *Comprehensive Psychiatry, 113*, 152289.

Kanter, J. W., Manos, R. C., Bowe, W. M., Baruch, D. E., Busch, A. M., & Rusch, L. C. (2010). What is behavioral activation? A review of the empirical literature. *Clinical Psychology Review, 30*(6), 608–620.

Kendler, K. S., & Campbell, J. (2009). Interventionist causal models in psychiatry: repositioning the mind–body problem. *Psychological Medicine, 39*(6), 881–887.

Klingberg, S., Wölwer, W., Engel, C., Wittorf, A., Herrlich, J., Meisner, C., Buchkremer, G., & Wiedemann, G. (2011). Negative Symptoms of Schizophrenia as Primary Target of Cognitive Behavioral Therapy: Results of the Randomized Clinical TONES Study. *Schizophrenia Bulletin, 37 Suppl 2*, S98–S110.

Lally, J., Ajnakina, O., Stubbs, B., Cullinane, M., Murphy, K. C., Gaughran, F., & Murray, R. M. (2017). Remission and recovery from first-episode psychosis in adults: Systematic review and meta-analysis of long-term outcome studies. *British Journal of Psychiatry, 211*, 350–358.

Lutgens, D., Gariepy, G., & Malla, A. (2017). Psychological and psychosocial interventions for negative symptoms in psychosis: systematic review and meta-analysis. *British Journal of Psychiatry, 210*(5), 324–332.

Penadés, R., Catalán, R., Salamero, M., Boget, T., Puig, O., Guarch, J., & Gastó, C. (2006). Cognitive remediation therapy for outpatients with chronic schizophrenia: A controlled and randomized study. *Schizophrenia Research, 87*(1–3), 323–331.

Perivoliotis, D., & Cather, C. (2009). Cognitive behavioral therapy of negative symptoms. *J Clin Psychol, 65*(8), 815–830.

Pillny, M., & Lincoln, T. M. (2020). The demotivating effect of social exclusion: An experimental test of a psychosocial model on the development of negative symptoms in psychosis. *Schizophrenia Research, 215*, 330–336.

Pillny, M., Krkovic, K., & Lincoln, T. M. (2018). Development of the Demotivating Beliefs Inventory and Test of the Cognitive Triad of Amotivation. *Cognitive Therapy and Research, 42*(6), 867–877.

Pillny, M., & Lincoln, T. M. (2016). Predictors of improved functioning in patients with psychosis: The role of amotivation and defeatist performance beliefs. *Psychiatry Research, 244*, 117–122.

Pos, K., Franke, N., Smit, F., Wijnen, B. F. M., Staring, A. B. P., Van der Gaag, M., Meijer, C., de Haan, L., Velthorst, E., & Schirmbeck, F. (2019). Cognitive behavioral therapy for social activation in recent-onset psychosis: Randomized controlled trial. *Journal of Consulting and Clinical Psychology, 87*(2), 151–160.

Riehle, M., Böhl, M. C., Pillny, M., & Lincoln, T. M. (2020). Efficacy of Psychological Treatments for Patients With Schizophrenia and Relevant Negative Symptoms: A Meta-Analysis. *Clinical Psychology in Europe, 2*(3), e2899.

Staring, A. B. P., Ter Huurne, M.-A. B., & van der Gaag, M. (2013). Cognitive Behavioral Therapy for negative symptoms (CBT-n) in psychotic disorders: A pilot study. *Journal of Behavior Therapy and Experimental Psychiatry, 44*(3), 300–306.

Strauss, G. P., Wilbur, R. C., Warren, K. R., August, S. M., & Gold, J. M. (2011). Anticipatory vs. consummatory pleasure: what is the nature of hedonic deficits in schizophrenia? *Psychiatry Research, 187*(1–2), 36–41.

Velligan, D. I., Roberts, D., Mintz, J., Maples, N., Li, X., Medellin, E., & Brown, M. (2015). A randomized pilot study of MOtiVation and Enhancement (MOVE) Training for negative symptoms in schizophrenia. *Schizophrenia Research, 165*, 175–180.

Velthorst, E., Koeter, M., van der Gaag, M., Nieman, D. H., Fett, A.-K. J., Smit, F., Staring, A. B. P., Meijer, C., & de Haan, L. (2015). Adapted cognitive-behavioural therapy required for targeting negative symptoms in schizophrenia: Meta-analysis and meta-regression. *Psychological Medicine, 45*, 453–465.

Wellen, M. (2010). Differentiation between demoralization, grief, and anhedonic depression. *Current Psychiatry Reports, 12*(3), 229–233.

Wykes, T., Steel, C., Everitt, B., & Tarrier, N. (2008). Cognitive behavior therapy for schizophrenia: effect sizes, clinical models, and methodological rigor. *Schizophrenia Bulletin, 34*(3), 523–537.

12

Recovery-Oriented Cognitive Therapy for Negative Symptoms

Ellen Inverso and Paul Grant

Clinical pearls

- *Develop a formulation for challenges and for empowerment.* For challenges, consider the question: "Why might it be . . . ?" —Perhaps the person believes other people don't care, or maybe they have negative expectations for future experiences. For empowerment, ask: "What's the person doing when they are at their best, even if it's been a while?" and evaluate why the activity brings out their best self—it could be competence, connection, or energy, for example.
- *To start—be brief, be active.* Lead with action to create brief, frequent, predictable attempts at connection—and to reduce emphasis on verbal communication. This increases the likelihood of success by lowering interpersonal pressure and demand on cognitive resources. Each success is an opportunity to gradually increase the amount and type of activity and to strengthen beliefs about energy, connection, social competence, and vulnerability.
- *Focus on the future.* With greater access to energy, connection, and trust, pivot to aspirations. Developing and enriching meaningful future targets galvanizes motivation and drive to focus positive action to grow and sustain their desired life. Negative expectations can be neutralized. Hope and possibility become more accessible and can lead to richer action that opens a wellspring of energy, resilience in the face of stress, and increased meaningful social interaction and contribution—further strengthening beliefs about social competence and value.
- *Make meaning through guided discovery.* Every time an individual experiences energy and connection, showcases a skill or area of knowledge, or has success, it is an opportunity to draw conclusions about what it means about them, about themselves in relation to others, and what it

Ellen Inverso and Paul Grant, *Recovery-Oriented Cognitive Therapy for Negative Symptoms*. In: *Psychosocial Approaches to Negative Symptoms in Psychosis*. Edited by: Tania Lincoln et al., Oxford University Press.
 DOI: 10.1093/oso/9780197676790.003.0012

might mean about future possibilities. Guided discovery is a powerful and flexible intervention that helps the person discover their inner power and develop it. They can develop resilience beliefs that contribute to sustaining the life of their choosing in the community.

1. Introduction

Marked by reductions in the very activities that promote wellness—physical movement, valued connection with others, contributing to something larger than oneself, empowerment relative to stress (Lieberman et al., 2020 Mittal et al., 2021)—negative symptoms are promising targets for treatment. Individuals experiencing negative symptoms are likely to experience more frequent, longer hospitalizations, with a greater likelihood of rehospitalization (Patel et al., 2015). Making a positive impact on negative symptoms would appear to improve social determents of health, raise quality of life, and facilitate participation in one's chosen community (Harding, 2019; Murthy, 2020; World Health Organization, 2021).

Therein is a paradox—the factors that make negative symptoms appealing treatment targets also make them very challenging to address clinically. Individuals experiencing negative symptoms frequently do not seek "help." They may not readily engage—or see any value—in treatment (Kreyenbuhl et al., 2009). If they do engage, they may stop. Researchers have shown that negative symptoms include comfort with inactivity (Kirkpatrick et al., 2011) and predict considerable difficulty getting immediate or lasting benefits from rewarding experiences (Strauss et al. 2014; Abram et al., 2022).

We need a framework that conceptualizes the inherent challenges of negative symptoms (e.g., limited access to motivation and energy, low expectations for success) and includes practical procedures that can be ultimately sustained by the person. This understanding should drive strategies and active procedures that meet the person where they are, being able to capture their attention, reveal the value of continuing together, and establish trust (Dixon et al., 2016). The approach should involve creating and making the most of success experiences, generalizing to other desired activities (Grant et al., 2018). Ultimately the person pursues a vision of their desired life, strengthening their best self. Recovery-Oriented Cognitive Therapy (CT-R) is expressly designed to achieve all of this; it addresses negative symptoms in the broader context of wellness and personal flourishing (Beck et al., 2021).

2. History and Theoretical Background

CT-R began as an attempt to address negative symptoms for individuals given a serious mental health condition diagnosis. While the psychiatric literature at the time placed the cause of negative symptoms in static neurological deficiencies (e.g., enlarged ventricles) or neurocognitive deficits (Andersen, 1984; Crow, 1980; Heinrichs & Zakzanis, 1998), one of us (Grant) and Aaron Beck posited the existence of psychological factors more proximal to the observed reductions in action and expressivity. Grant and Beck conducted interviews with providers, family members, and individuals with lived experience. Explaining why they no longer tried activities previously preferred (say, basketball, fishing, or chess), the individuals said, "I can't do that anymore," "I am broken now," "I am no good." Labeling these statements *defeatist beliefs*, Grant and Beck (2009) conducted a research study linking them to negative symptoms and reduced psychosocial functioning, findings that have been confirmed by meta-analysis (Campellone et al., 2016), experimental studies (Reddy et al., 2018), and experience sampling studies (Raugh et al., 2019). The interviews revealed a second set of beliefs, *asocial beliefs*—"I prefer to be by myself," "I am fine alone,"—that research studies confirmed predicted reduced social activity (Grant & Beck, 2010; Thomas et al., 2017). With defeatist and asocial beliefs as core targets, Beck and Grant developed the first version of CT-R, validated in a clinical trial (Grant et al., 2012; Grant et al., 2017).

Since then, CT-R has been extended to all areas of care—long-term, forensic, and acute inpatient; residential programs, community teams, and the Veterans Administration—as well as a variety of settings, from community agencies to municipal and state systems of care. CT-R guides treatment and fits within the scope of practice of social workers, psychologists, psychiatrists, psychiatric rehabilitation specialists, recreational/occupational therapists, nursing staff, drug and alcohol counselors, and peer specialists (Grant, 2019).

The framework that guides CT-R practice has three components: theory of modes, the cognitive model, and narrowing of attentional focus (Grant, et al., submitted). Beck's theory of modes (1996) and the cognitive model (1963) fit together to provide a framework for understanding how people can get stuck and how they thrive. Negative symptoms are more prevalent when a person is in a *disconnected mode*; that is, they have difficulty accessing motivation and energy, which is driven by their expectation to fail in purpose-giving, pleasurable, or social activities. The *adaptive mode*, by contrast, manifests the person's best self within activities that stimulate positive beliefs about self, others, and the future. The attentional narrowing mechanism (Gable et al., 2015; Hicks et al., 2015) explains how a person remains in the disconnected mode for prolonged periods, and how information that might counter negative beliefs or provide opportunity for action is screened out. Attention also explains the rapid switch from the disconnected to adaptive mode, as a stimulus such as a song widens the scope of attention, creating an often-dramatic switch in affect, cognition, and behavior (Beck et al., 2021).

Following an individualized formulation, CT-R enables providers to access each person's adaptive mode, energize it through appealing activity, develop it by eliciting and enriching aspirations for the future, actualize it through daily activity that achieves the valued meanings, and strengthen it through guided discovery that makes meanings and resilience (Beck et al., 2021).

3 Practical Procedure

Charlie's alarm rings—7:30am—when he used to get up for school. He rolls over, turns it off. Getting up, putting on clothes laying on the floor, he goes downstairs. Mom invites him to join her for coffee and a walk with the dog. He quietly declines, sitting on the porch, spending the day there. When his family has dinner, they bring him some. It gets dark. Charlie goes upstairs; gets into bed. Concerned about Charlie's ever-growing withdrawal and isolation, his family urges him to see a therapist. To quiet them, Charlie agrees, with little intention to participate.

3.1 CT-R Formulation and Recovery Map

Conceptualizing is the start of CT-R. Why might Charlie—or anyone—get up in the morning but sit isolated and quiet all day long? Why might it be that opportunities for togetherness or fun are declined? Defeatist and asocial beliefs give us a starting place. Might Charlie have no sense of purpose and think, "What's the point?" Does he expect to inevitably fail? Perhaps he believes he is unlike others and, therefore, is better off staying to himself, avoiding rejection. Maybe he feels that no one understands him, that he can't share meaningful experiences. He could perceive that answering "no" is the only control he has.

Composed initially of hypotheses, a case formulation for Charlie can then be fit into a "Recovery Map," a one-page document that captures the intentionality of CT-R, guiding the intervention, with the intent of revision as one proceeds. When creating a Recovery Map, it is important to gather information directly from the individual, family members or loved ones, past providers, medical records, current providers from varied disciplines, and/or through observations of the individual. Elicit responses from the individual as much as possible,

Recovery Map	
ACCESSING & ENERGIZING THE ADAPTIVE MODE	
Interests/Ways to Engage:	**Beliefs Activated while in Adaptive Mode:**
ASPIRATIONS	
Goals:	**Meaning of Accomplishing Identified Goal:**
CHALLENGES	
Current Behaviors/Challenges:	**Beliefs Underlying Challenges:**
POSITIVE ACTION & EMPOWERMENT	
Current Strategies and Interventions:	**Belief/Aspiration/Meaning/Challenge Targeted:**

Figure 12.1 Blank Recovery Map.

recognizing that this may not happen immediately, due to the need to build up trust. Recovery Maps are not meant for use as handouts during sessions.

The flow of the CT-R process is mirrored in the sections of the Recovery Map: Accessing and Energizing the Adaptive Mode, Developing the Adaptive Mode (Aspirations), and Actualizing the Adaptive Mode (Challenges and Positive Action). Figure 12.1. shows a blank Recovery Map.

For Charlie, we mostly know his challenges at the start of therapy. Figure 12.2. depicts Charlie's Recovery Map *Challenges* row.

CHALLENGES	
Current Behaviors/Challenges: Reduced access to energy and motivation Isolation and withdrawal from family, social situations, and past interests	**Beliefs Underlying Challenges:** *Guesses:* I can't enjoy things the way I used to, it won't be worth it I have to wait until I have more energy to do things What's the point of trying things, I won't be successful

Figure 12.2 Charlie's Recovery Map—Challenges.

3.2 Accessing and Energizing the Adaptive Mode

Accessing a person's adaptive mode is foundational in CT-R. Most early therapeutic attention focuses on it, especially for individuals impacted by negative symptoms. Consistent with theory and research in reward processing (Strauss et al., 2017), the approach is fundamentally experiential; you access the adaptive mode by locating activities to do together that increase energy, focus, and initiative—operationalizing the recovery markers of connection and trust. Predictable shared activity makes CT-R appealing, enjoyable, and worth continuing. Overarching strategies in this phase include:

- Increasing energy—this strengthens beliefs that the person can do it themselves.
- Creating brief, frequent, predictable opportunities for connection—this gives the person control.
- Observing the benefit of positive action—this enhances beliefs that doing activities is worthwhile and should be done more often.
- Specific interventions:
- Engage in pleasurable activity together: playing games, going for walks, creating art, listening to music, watching videos of events—any activity that may be related to the individual's current or past interests.
- Seek expertise: person pulls from their knowledge, interests, and experience (e.g., cars, comic book characters, plants).

One impact of negative symptoms is a decrease in verbal communication. Therefore, making observations and using cultural cues are ways to locate potential adaptive modes. Does the person sport a specific team's clothing? When others need help, do they try to assist? Such observations can help you learn more (e.g., the sports teams they like, values related to helping others in need). A rule of thumb: determine what was popular in the broader culture—such as sporting events, political events, or popular music and movies—during the time prior to the onset of the person's challenges. You might try watching a video together from this period. Another tack is cultural knowledge, such as family recipes or traditions. You can seek the individual's expertise: "I'm so glad you're here, I was looking to try the new Indian restaurant in town but don't know what to order—what do you recommend I try?"

Charlie is not forthcoming about his interests. He doesn't talk much, in general, typically saying, "I don't know," when asked about preferred activities. You can ask his family, "What is Charlie like and what is he doing when he's at his best—even if it's been a long time since he's done those things?" They share high school debate club and a youth group. You then ask what might have been energizing and motivating about those activities. They explain Charlie advocates for others and enjoys being a part of a bigger community that shares values. The promising path to connection appears to be helping people; so you could start by offering Charlie the opportunity to help you. You can ask him to help you pick between two group therapy activities or two inspirational quotes—what will most impact group members.

Choice-based questions about helping *other* people accomplishes several aims: (1) It provides clients with the opportunity to help while reducing pressure, the need for energy, and cognitive resources; (2) it allows for connection through possible values and meanings of previously enjoyed activities; and (3) it utilizes brief attempts at connection that will ultimately offer the chance to provide positive feedback and invite future opportunities to help and connect.

In subsequent sessions, you can give Charlie positive feedback—letting him know that others liked the activity he selected, that the inspirational quote brightened someone's day. At this point, you can ask whether he would like to do more of this. When he agrees, you float the idea that he is a helpful person, "You are making sure I do a better job in group with the inspirational quotes you recommend—seems you're quite helpful, would you agree?" Charlie smirks and looks down. Together, you can develop a between-session action plan with him: finding more inspirational sayings that might benefit others.

Helping others gets Charlie into his adaptive mode. By asking Charlie if he'd mind helping again, you shift to the second stage in CT-R—*energizing* the adaptive mode. Helping you can allow Charlie to springboard to finding opportunities to aid others, activating his adaptive mode more frequently and predictably. Positive action of this sort has a feedforward effect: It increases energy to do (or simply consider!) more positive action; more positive action increases how often the person experiences connection, demonstrates skill and capability, and accesses positive beliefs about self, others, and future. Continuing to energize the adaptive mode counters negative beliefs—such as believing you are incapable of meaningful connection, that others don't care, or that nothing is worthwhile. Quite the contrary, as we see with Charlie, things are more meaningful with others, risks are worth taking, and success is possible.

At this point, you want to determine what positive beliefs might be activated when accessing the adaptive mode. Ask, "What's the best part about doing this together?" If that is too abstract, you can adjust the question and float possibilities: "What's the best part about doing this together? *I wonder if it's that you feel energized doing it or maybe that it's something you feel knowledgeable about? Maybe something else?*"

After a couple helping instances, you can ask Charlie, "You've been helping me for a few weeks now, I'm wondering what the *best part* about it is? Is it being creative with ideas, or helping others?" He says group members appreciate that someone cares about them. This confirms an important piece of the formulation: Charlie values caring for others. Then, we can float the possibility he might care for even more people—for example, his parents. He talks about possibly watering the family garden or playing with the dog in the yard. A gradual progression moves positive action out of session and into the broader world of Charlie's life, with a high likelihood of success. His ideas are now added action plans.

Especially in these earlier phases of treatment, it is important to be specific about how session activity will expand into daily life. You can, for example, create a positive action schedule together. This can look like a calendar or a list or can be made creatively using technology or art (e.g., cell phone prompts, memes, posters) to visually represent the plans. Decide together how to remember the action plans, how to keep track of follow-through, and how to involve family and friends. The purpose is having a way for the person to succeed and notice the benefits of continued positive action. Figure 12.3. contains Charlie's Recovery Map up to this point.

ACCESSING & ENERGIZING THE ADAPTIVE MODE	
Interests/Ways to Engage:	**Beliefs Activated while in Adaptive Mode:**
Past: part of debate club in high school; attended youth group Currently helping identify enjoyable activities for others; giving opinions on inspirational quotes, phrases, and lyrics Possible: dogs, gardening	Caring for others *Ideas from family:* Advocating and caring for others, helpful Connection, belonging, being a part of a spiritual community *Additional Guesses:* Being part of a team, sense of purpose and worth

Figure 12.3 Charlie's Recovery Map—Accessing and energizing.

3.3 Developing the Adaptive Mode

Accessing and energizing the adaptive mode establishes connection through activity. The person comes to see you as a partner, interested in what they are interested in, a sounding board for discussing possible action. For the person experiencing negative symptoms, your work thus far has leveraged the environmental variation in the experience of low energy and difficulty accessing motivation (Mote et al., 2018; Strauss, 2021). This success together breeds trust and creates energy, allowing you an opportunity to project the person's future and consider highly desired, long-term, life targets or *aspirations.* As you move on to developing the adaptive mode, the locus of control moves inward, and operationalizes the wellness target of hope.

In this phase, you will want to *identify* the right aspirations, *enrich* each target, and *elicit* the meaning of achieving them—all prior to helping the person to plan aspiration-related action.

Identifying. The most straightforward way to locate an aspiration is to ask, "If everything was how you wanted it to be, what would you be doing or getting?" However, if a person has difficulty answering an open-ended question about their most desirable future there are other approaches to elicit aspirations, enabling you to meet the person where they are:

- Generalize from an activity that taps into their motivation. For example, if you are cooking a dish from the person's culture together, you can say, "I know we both enjoy doing this together. Is this something you can see yourself doing more of in the future?" If the answer is "yes," you can explore what this would look like; "Are there other things related to cooking that you would want to be doing?" In this way, exciting activities can lead to aspirations.
- Generalize from your observations of their valued action. You can say, "I notice you help a lot on the unit. It seems that helping people is important to you. Do I have that right? Is this something you want to do more of?" Noticing the person's values can allow you to springboard to future targets.
- Get specific. "If you were not here right now on a Tuesday afternoon, what would you be doing or getting?"

With Charlie, we can start with the observation that helping people is a core value for him. You can ask, "It seems that caring for people is very important to you. Do I have that right? What are ways you can see yourself helping people in the future?" Charlie responds that he has always dreamed that he would be good at making play structures for kids. He explains that the jungle gym at his youth group wasn't safe, and sometimes people would get hurt. His affect brightens considerably when he describes being part of making a safer, more fun play space.

Enriching. Aspirations tap into the wellsprings of motivation, which makes them central for working with people who experience negative symptoms. We can get the most from aspirations by enriching them. This involves imagery, which, as cognitive and sports psychology have shown, is a dependable way to elicit positive emotions, energy, and hope for success (Simonsmeier et al., 2021).

You can ask the person to paint you a picture, using as many sensory modalities as you can, "I want to see it how you see it." "What would the best day be? What would you be doing?" As the person enriches their aspiration, start to notice the affective change that comes over them. You can say, "I can't help but notice you smile a little as we talk about this. Did you notice that? If it feels this good just to imagine it, how do you think you will feel when you do it?"

Meaning. Aspirations are ambitious targets, and a person may feel discouraged at being a long way off from becoming a healthcare worker, being a beauty technician, or starting up a business. The meaning of the aspiration can buffer against the person becoming demoralized. Indeed, the meaning is the key to the person's desired life, as they can experience it daily. The cardinal question to elicit the meaning of an aspiration is, "what would be the best part about that?" Answers to this question will tend to hit values related to others and to personal capability (e.g., "I'd be a good person." "Others would appreciate me." "I'd be someone." "Serving others.").

When asked about his aspirations, Charlie pictures himself at his former youth center. First, he sees the dilapidated state of the play set, then sees his hands as he helps install the new jungle gym, then he sees himself smiling and "high fiving" kids as they safely use the slide. This last image creates a big shift in emotion. You can call his attention to this. When you ask him how he feels, he says, "I feel hopeful. I can do that." When asked what the best part would be and how he would see himself, Charlie says, "I would be caring for people for real. The kid's lives would be better than mine was. I would be a part of that."

As you work on aspirations, summarize frequently. This highlights your curiosity and interest, making the experience that much richer, as well as ensuring you are getting it right. The person feels heard, because they are the expert in what they want in life. If you are fortunate enough that the person identifies multiple aspirations and meanings, it's best to focus on them one at a time. This will protect against a diffusion of the motivation, energy, and hope that each aspiration contains.

While working on aspirations, be mindful of the strong pull of the negative beliefs and be ready to return to accessing the adaptive mode. At the beginning of treatment, the cognitive schemas that contain these beliefs are highly accessible

ASPIRATIONS	
Goals: Build safe play structures for playgrounds, kids Help others	**Meaning of Accomplishing Identified Goal:** Caring for others Helpful Contributing, productive, and valuable member of my community

Figure 12.4 Charlie's Recovery Map—Aspirations.

to the person and may have kept the person safe for a long time. Your early CT-R work is critical for enhancing the accessibility of the person's positive self-image. However, pursuing aspirations increases the risk of experiencing "failure" and "rejection," and you should expect the occasional return to the disconnected mode. You will know this is happening if the person's affect shifts, and they seem down, less responsive, and warm. Or, they make statements such as, "never mind, this is too far out of reach," or "I can never get what I want." Noticing this shift, you can return to the proven activities that experientially create connection, capability, or that relate to the meaning or values underlying the person's aspirations. You can empathize with their fear, concern, and vulnerability, while still expressing their values: "I hear you clearly that sometimes it feels too hard, or even impossible, to do the things that matter to you. But I also know that feeling productive and like you're contributing to your community are so important to you. If we can find a way to bring some of those meanings into your day-to-day right now as we work toward those big targets, would it be worth us at least trying?"

With this new information filled in, Figure 12.4. contains the *Aspirations* section of Charlie's Recovery Map.

3.4 Actualizing the Adaptive Mode

Meaningful positive action is the antithesis of negative symptoms. Aspirations provide motivation, express personal values, embody the person's desired life, and, thus, are terrific guides to self-sustainable positive action. Actualizing the adaptive mode involves steps leading toward achieving the aspiration and actions that meet the meaning of the aspiration. During this phase, resiliency will be a focus, as the person encounters life's stressors and develops their own empowerment in pursuit of a desired life.

When you actualize the adaptive mode, you will want to do a *recovery check* at each encounter. For example, you can ask Charlie, "We've been working together toward your aspiration of being part of a construction team, which you said would be a way to feel like an important contributor to your community and that you'd be able to really help people. Have I got that right? Is that what we should continue working on, or is there anything that has changed since we last talked?" This recovery check achieves several objectives:

- It guarantees that you are working collaboratively on the person's desired aspirations, putting them in the driver's seat as much as possible.
- It creates a bridge between meetings rooted in what is most important to the person, ensuring consistency.
- It increases access to the adaptive mode—bringing energy, momentum, and positive emotion to the session from the outset—making your work together maximally efficient.
- It provides an opportunity to detect and better understand doubts and negative beliefs that can crop up, such as when the person no longer expresses interest in steps toward an aspiration

Creating the steps toward achieving an aspiration can be a fun exercise that enhances the person's sense of hope and possibility that they can successfully do it. Start by considering the steps *anyone* might need to take. You can also consider more personalized steps that pertain to this person's aspiration. These steps can come out in any order. You can arrange the sequence after generating them. For Charlie, there might be actions he is currently taking that get him closer to his aspiration. He's getting up each day—which for some individuals with negative symptoms is a huge step in and of itself.

Given all this, are there other things he can do to push the momentum forward? Charlie sets a plan to research volunteer groups in the community. A next step would be for him to attend an informational meeting or participate in a time-limited volunteer initiative. We can plot these steps out with Charlie diagrammatically, putting each in the order he would do them, creating a stairway to his aspiration.

Because Charlie's desire to help build playground structures is a target that takes considerable planning, organization, and time, we can also consider ways to experience valuable meanings, such as caring, more often to maintain motivation. He's been helping with the garden and walking the family dog, and he's helping come up with group activities and aspirational phrases. Can he further expand these caring actions outside of family and therapy?

Noticing success in aspiration-focused positive action is crucial to the continued building of momentum. Every time a person takes a step—or a partial step—draw attention to how this gets them closer to their aspirations.

While taking steps the person is likely to confront the challenges—things not working out, people not responding favorably—that contributed to their negative symptoms. For Charlie, he researches organizations that help kids and submits an application online, but learns that the company is not taking new volunteers. Another organization has an educational requirement he does not meet. These outcomes are deflating for Charlie. You ask what he makes of all this. Charlie says, "What's the point? I won't ever qualify," and "This is probably for everyone else, not for me." Over the next few days, he ignores the garden and struggles to get up in the morning. This is a natural set back, life is full of them, and you can help Charlie see his own resiliency and ability to overcome and persevere. You can, during the next session, have him help you with a task and then begin searching for other ways that he can show care; for example, making birthday cards for kids who are in the hospital.

Figure 12.5 contains the updated version of Charlie's Recovery Map, with confirmed negative beliefs that contribute to the challenges, and strategies and interventions for positive action.

3.5 Strengthening the Adaptive Mode

The core of CT-R is interests-and-aspiration-focused positive action coupled with meaning-making through guided discovery. Early in treatment, the negative beliefs of the disconnected mode are dominant (see Figure 12.6.), inhibiting action, energy, and motivation. The positive experiences of accessing and energizing the adaptive mode switch on positive beliefs; actively pursuing aspirations creates opportunity to experience one's desired self. Asking the right questions can help the person get the most out of each instance of positive action, drawing attention to strengths, strengthening positive beliefs, cultivating resilience, and helping the person sustain change long-term. The formulation in the Recovery Map is your guide for what to ask.

For Charlie, your understanding identifies several target beliefs—being caring, helpful, capable, as well as it being worthwhile to take risks—which run counter to the negative beliefs—defeatist beliefs and incapability—that underly his negative symptoms. In addition to strengthening these positive beliefs, you can also help empower Charlie when things do not work out, helping him to push through. As Charlie re-engages in meaningful positive action, you can further strengthen resilience beliefs, "What does it say about you that you kept trying, even after you hit a few roadblocks?" and "What does it mean about someone who bounces back from stress and finds solutions to the challenges?"

Guided discovery questions can be either closed- or open-ended, based on your formulation. Closed-ended questions are most helpful when the person is more tentative or seems in the moment to have reduced cognitive resources.

Recovery Map	
ACCESSING & ENERGIZING THE ADAPTIVE MODE	
Interests/Ways to Engage: Past: part of debate club in high school; attended youth group Currently helping identify enjoyable activities for others; giving opinions on inspirational quotes, phrases, and lyrics Possible: dogs, gardening	**Beliefs Activated while in Adaptive Mode:** Caring for others *Ideas from family:* Advocating and caring for others, helpful Connection, belonging, being a part of a spiritual community *Additional Guesses:* Being part of a team, sense of purpose and worth
ASPIRATIONS	
Goals: Build safe play structures for playgrounds, kids Help others	**Meaning of Accomplishing Identified Goal:** Caring for others Helpful Contributing, productive, and valuable member of my community
CHALLENGES	
Current Behaviors/Challenges: Reduced access to energy and motivation Isolation and withdrawal from family, social situations, and past interests	**Beliefs Underlying Challenges:** "What's the point? I won't ever qualify." "This is probably for everyone else, not for me." *Additional Guesses:* I can't enjoy things the way I used to, it won't be worth it I have to wait until I have more energy to do things What's the point of trying things, I won't be successful
POSITIVE ACTION & EMPOWERMENT	
Current Strategies and Interventions:	**Belief/Aspiration/Meaning/Challenge Targeted:**
1. Identify pathways and increase access to the adaptive mode through interventions that provide maximal opportunity for control a. Seek advice on group activities b. Get opinion on affirmations and inspirational quotes to be shared with others	1. Increase energy, connection, sense of control; reduce defeatist beliefs
2. Energize adaptive mode to increase frequency of caring actions a. Create positive action schedule together to plan future activity (e.g., helping at home) b. Gradually increase activities and notice benefits each session	2. Increase frequency and predictability of connection, action toward values of helping, and control; strengthen beliefs about capability
3. Develop and enrich aspirations a. Use current successes in helping to identify other desires and values b. Create a vivid recovery image that represents the aspiration	3. Increase motivation, hope, and continued energy toward sustained action; strengthen beliefs about capability, purpose, and worth
4. Identify opportunities to help others in the broader community a. Research volunteer opportunities	4. Increase connection and belonging, sustain positive action, reduce beliefs about not being like others, reduce defeatist beliefs

Figure 12.5 Charlie's full Recovery Map.

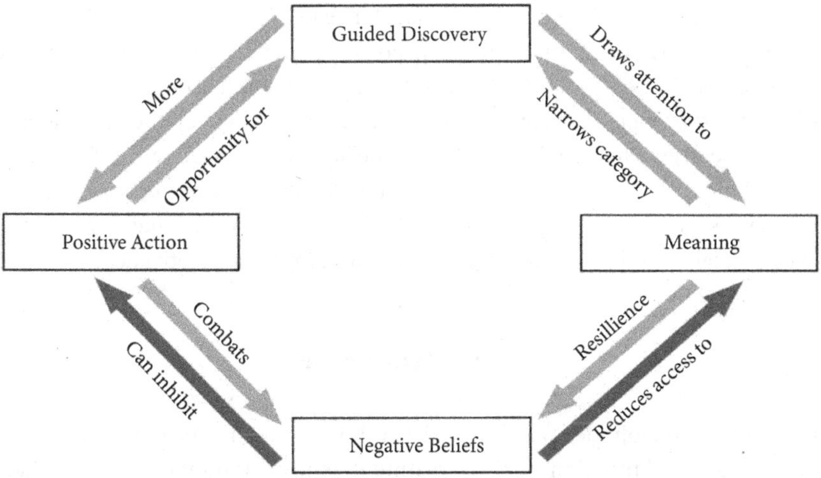

Figure 12.6 Guided discovery—CT-R pathways to change.

Open-ended questions to ask after positive experiences could include:

- "What does it mean about you that you did this?"
- "What does it say about you that you took a chance and came through in the end?"
- Equivalent closed-ended questions float possible conclusions or observations:
- "I couldn't help but notice you seem to have more energy as we were doing this, did you notice that? Seems the more we do that we enjoy the more energized we get, would you agree?"
- "You mentioned you didn't think this would go very well, but we took a chance—did it go better or worse than you expected? I wonder if sometimes it's worth taking a risk, because sometimes it works out. What do you think about that?"

3.6 CT-R Applicability and Considerations

By design, CT-R is flexible. CT-R can be adapted in session length and overall treatment duration (e.g., abbreviated to meet short-term institutional requirements, or extended over a longer period)—the principal rule being that shorter duration requirements should prioritize identifying and enriching aspirations as early as possible in treatment. Also, people often present in treatment with multiple areas of concern. Because CT-R uses the cognitive model, which is used to understand myriad challenges including medical illnesses (Winterowed et al.,

2003; Daniels, 2015; Bae et al., 2021), substance use (Leise & Beck, 2022), positive symptoms (hallucinations and delusions; Beck et al., 2019), and aggressive behavior (Beck, 1999), the CT-R formulation can be built around co-occurring issues. Interventions that have been found to be effective for these challenges can also be used when applicable during the actualizing stage of CT-R therapy, at which point challenges are addressed in the context of a person's aspirations. Further research on the application of CT-R to these or other challenges would be beneficial to understanding nuances and determining effectiveness.

4. Evidence Base

In a randomized, blinded, clinical trial, CT-R was shown to be more effective at improving global functioning than treatment-as-usual (Grant et al., 2012). Participants in the clinical trial were individuals given diagnoses of schizophrenia or schizoaffective disorder who presented at assessment with elevated negative symptoms on the Scales for the Assessment of Negative Symptoms (SANS; Andreasen, 1989). The majority of participants were ethnic minorities from socially and economically disadvantaged areas across a major city. Compared to Standard Treatment (ST), individuals who also received CT-R had better overall functioning as determined by the Global Assessment Scale (GAS; Endicott et al., 1976; $d = 0.56$). Gains included pursuing employment, increased number of social relationships, educational involvement, and other improvements. Participants receiving CT-R also had marked reductions in negative symptoms (avolition-apathy) as determined by the SANS ($d = -0.66$). And, although not the principal target of the trial, individuals who received CT-R had significant reductions in positive symptoms as determined by the Scales for the Assessment of Positive Symptoms (SAPS; Andreasen, 1984; $d = -0.46$). The gains made by individuals receiving CT-R were sustained over a follow-up period when no therapy was delivered (GAS $d = 0.53$; SANS $d = -0.60$; SAPS $d = -1.36$), and even individuals who had been given their diagnosis decades prior to enrolling in the study showed benefit (Grant et al., 2017). Additionally, preliminary evidence emerged that an increase in positive beliefs correlates with an increase in community functioning over the two years of trial participation (Grant & Best, 2019).

In the time since the trial, clinical efforts have been made to reduce the length of time it takes individuals, especially those who have been involved in highly restrictive levels of care for many years, to make gains in the pursuit of their desired lives. These include prioritizing engagement in meaningful aspiration-driven interventions earlier in the process and using more creative approaches to accessing the adaptive mode based on needs identified in the cognitive formulation. Future clinical trials will use these innovations to assess any possible differences in effectiveness from the earlier rendition of the therapy.

5. Outlook and Future Directions

CT-R theory and practice have developed robustly in recent years. The psychological model of understanding that underlies CT-R has been demonstrated across the globe (Campellone et al., 2016). Research on a short-course of CT-R conducted in Mexico City, Mexico (Morales-Vigil, 2014) demonstrated large effect sizes in improvements in functioning (DSM-IV, 1994; GAF psychosocial functioning scale $d = 2.49$), negative symptoms, and self-efficacy (Total PANSS Kay et al., 1987) $d = 1.39$; SANS $d = 1.49$; Cognitive Symptoms $d = 0.97$; Excitability $d = 1.12$). Even still, it will be greatly beneficial for additional studies and clinical trials on CT-R to be conducted by researchers who can expand the reach geographically, socioeconomically, and culturally.

One continued need is better measures of positive beliefs and the adaptive mode, which contribute to the basic science. This could also assist with identifying treatment mechanisms, showing how (the ways and trajectory) people improve, and allowing for the possibility of enhancing the mechanism of positive change. Better outcome measures are also needed to align with the social determents of health, such as measures related to personal empowerment and possible cognitive mediators of those determinants (Pekonen et al., 2020). An early measure of this sort is a modified version of the Beck Self Esteem Scale (developed for Grant et al., 2018). These measures can then be used in clinical trials, which move beyond symptom reduction to measure recovery and thriving as primary outcomes, utilizing positive beliefs as mediating variables.

Future program evaluation studies could test the cost-effectiveness of the CT-R approach, its ability to reduce hospitalization, increase days in the community, lower jail days, and so on. Formalized versions of CT-R family therapy can be developed and tested utilizing a family-to-family paradigm. Importantly, the core competencies of peer specialists (SAMHSA, 2022) align quite well with CT-R. Current pilot projects show the feasibility of CT-R driven peer work (Grant, 2019). A project that meets Lisa Dixon and colleagues' (2016) call for innovative treatment approaches utilizing peer specialists is currently underway in collaboration with New Jersey's Department of Health, Mental Health and Addiction Services, funded by the National Association for State Mental Health Program Directors, to train peer specialists in CT-R. The project aims to determine CT-R feasibility with peers, peer attitudes toward using CT-R, and recovery outcomes for individuals receiving CT-R from peers. Future projects could determine the impact of peers using CT-R on outcomes, determining if these improve lives and produce cost savings.

References

Abram, S. V., Weittenhiller, L. P., Bertrand, C. E., McQuaid, J. R., Mathalon, D. H., Ford, J. M., & Fryer, S. L. (2022). Psychological dimensions relevant to motivation and pleasure in schizophrenia. *Frontiers in Behavioral Neuroscience, 23*(16), 827260.

Andreasen, N. C. (1984). *The broken brain: The biological revolution in psychiatry.* New York: Harper & Row.

Andreasen, N. C. (1984). *The Scale for the Assessment of Positive Symptoms (SAPS).* Iowa City: The University of Iowa.

Andreasen, N. C. (1989). Scale for the Assessment of Negative Symptoms (SANS). *The British Journal of Psychiatry, 155*(Suppl 7), 53–58.

Bae, J. Y., Sung, H. K., Kwon, N. Y., Go, H. Y., Kim, T. J., Shin, S. M., & Lee, S. (2021). Cognitive Behavioral Therapy for migraine headache: A systematic review and meta-analysis. *Medicina (Kaunas, Lithuania), 58*(1), 44.

Baumeister, R. F., & Leary, M. R. (1995). The need to belong: Desire for interpersonal attachments as a fundamental human motivation. *Psychological Bulletin, 117*(3), 497–529.

Beck, A. T. (1963). Thinking and depression: I. Idiosyncratic content and cognitive distortions. *Archives of General Psychiatry, 9*(4), 324–333.

Beck, A. T. (1996). Beyond belief: A theory of modes, personality, and psychopathology. In P. M. Salkovskis (Ed.), *Frontiers of cognitive therapy* (pp. 1–25). New York: Guilford Press.

Beck, A. T. (1999). *Prisoners of hate: The cognitive basis of anger, hostility, and violence.* New York: Harper.

Beck, A. T. (2019a). My journey through psychopathology, beginning and ending with schizophrenia. *Psychiatric Services, 70*(11), 1061–1063.

Beck, A. T. (2019b). A 60-year evolution of cognitive theory and therapy. *Perspectives on Psychological Science, 14*(1), 16–20.

Beck, A. T., Finkel, M., & Beck, J. S. (2021). The theory of modes: Applications to schizophrenia and other psychological conditions. *Cognitive Therapy and Research, 45*, 391–400.

Beck, A. T., Grant, P., Inverso, E., Brinen, A. P., & Perivoliotis, D. (2021). *Recovery-oriented cognitive therapy for serious mental health conditions.* New York: Guilford Publications.

Beck, A. T., Himelstein, R., & Grant, P. M. (2019). In and out of schizophrenia: Activation and deactivation of the negative and positive schemas. *Schizophrenia Research, 203*, 55–61.

Beck, A. T., Himelstein, R., Bredemeier, K., Silverstein, S. M., & Grant, P. (2018). What accounts for poor functioning in people with schizophrenia: A re-evaluation of the contributions of neurocognitive v. attitudinal and motivational factors. *Psychological Medicine, 48*(16), 2776–2785.

Beck, A. T., Rector, N. R., Stolar, N. M., & Grant, P. M. (2009). *Schizophrenia: Cognitive theory, research and therapy.* New York: Guilford Press.

Blanchard, J. J., & Cohen, A. S. (2006). The structure of negative symptoms within schizophrenia: Implications for assessment. *Schizophrenia Bulletin, 32*(2), 238–245.

Callard, A. (2018). *Aspiration: The agency of becoming.* New York: Oxford University Press.

Campellone, T. R., Sanchez, A. H., & Kring, A. M. (2016). Defeatist performance beliefs, negative symptoms, and functional outcome in schizophrenia: A meta-analytic review. *Schizophrenia Bulletin, 42*(6), 1343–1352.

Cohen, A. N., Hamilton, A. B., Saks, E. R., Glover, D. L., Glynn, S. M., Brekke, J. S., & Marder, S. R. (2017). How occupationally high-achieving individuals with a diagnosis of schizophrenia manage their symptoms. *Psychiatric Services, 68*(4), 324–329.

Crow T. J. (1980). Molecular pathology of schizophrenia: More than one disease process? *British Medical Journal, 280*(6207), 66–68.

Daniels S. (2015). Cognitive Behavior Therapy for patients with cancer. *Journal of The Advanced Practitioner in Oncology, 6*(1), 54–56.

Diagnostic and statistical manual of mental disorders: DSM-IV. (1994). Washington, DC: American Psychiatric Association.

Dixon, L. B., Holoshitz, Y., & Nossel, I. (2016). Treatment engagement of individuals experiencing mental illness: Review and update. *World Psychiatry, 15*(1), 13–20.

Endicott, J., Spitzer, R. L., Fleiss, J. L., & Cohen, J. (1976). The Global Assessment Scale: A procedure for measuring overall severity of psychiatric disturbance. *Archives of General Psychiatry, 33*(6), 766–771.

Fuligni, A. J. (2019). The need to contribute during adolescence. *Perspectives in Psychological Science, 14*(3), 331–343.

Gable, P. A., Poole, B. D., & Harmon-Jones, E. (2015). Anger perceptually and conceptually narrows cognitive scope. *Journal of Personality and Social Psychology, 109*(1), 163.

Galderisi, S., Mucci, A., Buchanan, R. W., & Arango, C. (2018). Negative symptoms of schizophrenia: New developments and unanswered research questions. *Lancet Psychiatry, 5*(8), 664–677.

Grant, P. M. (2019). *Recovery-oriented cognitive therapy: A Theory-driven, evidence-based, transformative practice to promote flourishing for individuals with serious mental health conditions that is applicable across mental health systems.* Alexandria, VA: National Association of State Mental Health Program Directors.

Grant, P. M., & Beck, A. T. (2009). Defeatist beliefs as a mediator of cognitive impairment, negative symptoms, and functioning in schizophrenia. *Schizophrenia Bulletin, 35*(4), 798–806.

Grant, P. M., & Beck, A. T. (2010). Asocial beliefs as predictors of asocial behavior in schizophrenia. *Psychiatry Research, 177*(1–2), 65–70.

Grant, P. M., Lewis-Hatheway, F., Luther, L., Lustig, N., Best, M., Feldman, J., & Beck, A. T. (Submitted). Keys to their kingdom: preliminary evidence to support the role of positive beliefs in recovery-oriented cognitive therapy for negative symptoms and community participation. *Schizophrenia Bulletin.*

Grant, P. M. & Best, M. (2019). It is Always Sunny in Philadelphia: The Adaptive Mode and Positive Beliefs as a New Paradigm for Understanding Recovery and Empowerment for Individuals with Serious Mental Health Challenges. *International CBT (Cognitive Behavioral Therapy) for Psychosis Annual Meeting*, Philadelphia, PA.

Grant, P. M., Bredemeier, K., & Beck, A. T. (2017). Six-month follow-up of recovery-oriented cognitive therapy for low-functioning individuals with schizophrenia. *Psychiatric Services, 68*(10), 997–1002.

Grant, P. M., Huh, G. A., Perivoliotis, D., Stolar, N. M., & Beck, A. T. (2012). Randomized trial to evaluate the efficacy of cognitive therapy for low-functioning patients with schizophrenia. *Archives of General Psychiatry, 69*(2), 121–127.

Grant, P. M., Perivoliotis, D., Luther, L., Bredemeier, K., & Beck, A. T. (2018). Rapid improvement in beliefs, mood, and performance following an experimental success experience in an analogue test of recovery-oriented cognitive therapy. *Psychological Medicine, 48*(2), 261–268.

Harding, K. (2019). *The Rabbit Effect: Live longer, happier, and healthier with the groundbreaking science of kindness.* New York: Atria Books.

Heinrichs, R. W., & Zakzanis, K. K. (1998). Neurocognitive deficit in schizophrenia: A quantitative review of the evidence. *Neuropsychology, 12*(3), 426–445.

Hicks, J. A., Fields, S., Davis, W. E., & Gable, P. A. (2015). Heavy drinking, impulsivity and attentional narrowing following alcohol cue exposure. *Psychopharmacology, 232*(15), 2773–2779.

Kay, S. R., Fiszbein, A., & Opler, L. A. (1987). The Positive and Negative Syndrome Scale (PANSS) for schizophrenia. *Schizophrenia Bulletin, 13*(2), 261–276.

Kirkpatrick, B., Strauss, G. P., Nguyen, L., Fischer, B. A., Daniel, D. G., Cienfuegos, A., & Marder, S. R. (2011). The brief negative symptom scale: psychometric properties. *Schizophrenia Bulletin, 37*(2), 300–305.

Koh, A. W. L., Lee, S. C., & Lim, S. W. H. (2018). The learning benefits of teaching: A retrieval practice hypothesis. *Applied Cognitive Psychology, 32*, 401–410.

Kreyenbuhl, J., Nossel, I. R., & Dixon, L. B. (2009). Disengagement from mental health treatment among individuals with schizophrenia and strategies for facilitating connections to care: A review of the literature. *Schizophrenia Bulletin, 35*(4), 696–703.

Lee, E. E., Liu, J., Tu, X., Palmer, B. W., Eyler, L. T., & Jeste, D. V. (2018). A widening longevity gap between people with schizophrenia and general population: A literature review and call for action. *Schizophrenia Research, 196*, 9–13.

Leise, B. S., & Beck, A. T. (2022). *Cognitive therapy of addictive disorders*. New York: Guilford Press.

Lieberman, J. A., Stroup, T. S., Perkins, D. O., & Dixon, L. B. (Eds.). (2020). *The American Psychiatric Association Publishing Textbook of Schizophrenia* (2nd ed.). Washington, DC: American Psychiatric.

Mittal, V. A., Bernard, J. A., Strauss, G. P., & Walther, S. (2021). New insights into sedentary behavior highlight the need to revisit the way we see motor symptoms in psychosis. *Schizophrenia Bulletin, 47*(4), 877–879.

Morales-Vigil, T. (2014, May 3–7). Self-efficacy and recovery-oriented cognitive-behavioral therapy in patients with paranoid schizophrenia (part 1) [Poster session]. American Psychiatric Association Annual Meeting 2014, New York, NY, United States.

Mote, J., Grant, P. M., & Silverstein, S. M. (2018). Treatment implications of situational variability in cognitive and negative symptoms of schizophrenia. *Psychiatric Services, 69(10)*, 1065–1097.

Murthy, V. H. (2020). *Together: The healing power of human connection in a sometimes lonely world*. New York: Harper Collins.

Patel, R., Jayatilleke, N., Broadbent, M., Chang, C.-K., Foskett, N., Gorrell, G., . . . Stewart, R. (2015). Negative symptoms in schizophrenia: A study in a large clinical sample of patients using a novel automated method. *BMJ Open, 5*(9), e007619.

Pekonen, A., Eloranta, S., Stolt, M., Virolainen, P., & Leino-Kilpi, H. (2020). Measuring patient empowerment—A systematic review. *Patient Education and Counseling, 103*(4), 777–787.

Raugh, I. M., Chapman, H. C., Bartolomeo, L. A., Gonzalez, C., & Strauss, G. P. (2019). A comprehensive review of psychophysiological applications for ecological momentary assessment in psychiatric populations. *Psychological Assessment, 31*(3), 304–317.

Reddy, L. F., Horan, W. P., Barch, D. M., Buchanan, R. W., Gold, J. M., Marder, S. R., Wynn, J. K., Young, J., & Green, M. F. (2018). Understanding the association between negative symptoms and performance on effort-based decision-making tasks: The importance of defeatist performance beliefs. *Schizophrenia Bulletin, 44*(6), 1217–1226.

Saha, S., Chant, D., & McGrath, J. (2007). A systematic review of mortality in schizophrenia: Is the differential mortality gap worsening over time? *Archives of General Psychiatry, 64*(10), 1123–1131.

Substance Abuse Mental Health Services Administration. (2022). Core Competencies for Peer Workers. https://www.samhsa.gov/brss-tacs/recovery-support-tools/peers/core-competencies-peer-workers.

Simonsmeier, B. A., Andronie, M., Buecker, S., & Frank, C. (2021). The effects of imagery interventions in sports: A meta-analysis. *International Review of Sport and Exercise Psychology, 14*(1), 186–207.

Strauss G. P. (2021). A bioecosystem theory of negative symptoms in schizophrenia. *Frontiers in Psychiatry, 12*, 655471.

Strauss, G. P., Frost, K. H., Lee, B. G., & Gold, J. M. (2017). The positivity offset theory of anhedonia in schizophrenia. *Clinical Psychological Science: A Journal of The Association For Psychological Science, 5*(2), 226–238.

Strauss, G. P., Waltz, J. A., & Gold, J. M. (2014). A review of reward processing and motivational impairment in schizophrenia. *Schizophrenia Bulletin, 40*(Suppl_2), S107–S116.

Thomas, E. C., Luther, L., Zullo, L., Beck, A. T., & Grant, P. M. (2017). From neurocognition to community participation in serious mental illness: The intermediary role of dysfunctional attitudes and motivation. *Psychological Medicine, 47*(5), 822–836.

Winterowed, C., Beck, A. T., & Gruener, D. (2003). *Cognitive Therapy with Chronic Pain Patients*. New York: Springer Publishing Company.

World Health Organization. (2021). *Guidance on community mental health services: Promoting person-centered and rights-based approaches*. Geneva: World Health Organization. (Guidance and technical packages on community mental health services: promoting person-centered and rights-based approaches). Licence: CC BY-NC-SA 3.0 IGO.

13

Working with Families and Multidisciplinary Teams to Improve Expressivity and Motivation

Hilary Mairs

Clinical pearls

- More recent approaches that embed family-based interventions into all aspects of mental health care appear to offer the most promise in reducing negative symptoms, particularly in the early stages of psychosis.
- Models of psychoeducation require refinement to allow for appraisals of reduced activity and expression that do not always focus on medical explanations.
- Although not yet supported by high quality evidence, team-based formulation may be a helpful way of increasing and maintaining team members own levels of motivation to support the recovery of people with reduced volition and expressivity.

1. Family Based Interventions: Background and Theory

The origins of family-based approaches for psychosis can be traced back to findings that service users discharged from residential settings to family homes marked by high levels of expressed emotion were more likely to relapse than those discharged to other community settings and low expressed emotion environments (Barrowclough & Tarrier, 1997). High expressed emotion is characterized by: generalized hostile comments about the service user; repeated critical comments about aspects of their behaviors that imply resentment or irritation and/or emotional over-involvement; exaggerated emotional responses; and/or intrusive, self-sacrificing behaviors (Kuipers et al., 2002). The early pioneers of family-based approaches developed several interventions that have consistently

Hilary Mairs, *Working with Families and Multidisciplinary Teams to Improve Expressivity and Motivation*.
In: *Psychosocial Approaches to Negative Symptoms in Psychosis*. Edited by: Tania Lincoln et al.,
Oxford University Press. © Oxford University Press (2025). DOI: 10.1093/oso/9780197676790.003.0013

been found to reduce rates of high expressed emotion within family environments and further, decrease rates of service user relapse and rehospitalization (Pharoah et al., 2010). Data also suggests that family interventions improve relationships within the family (Pharoah et al., 2010) and improve caregiver well-being (Claxton et al., 2017). The success of family-based interventions in reducing rates of relapse and enhancing carer well-being has prompted their inclusion in treatment guidelines in various countries; for example, The Polish Psychiatric Association (Samochowiec et al., 2021) specifically recommend family psychotherapy as a treatment for negative symptoms. The National Institute for Health and Care Excellence (NICE) (2014) in the United Kingdom recommends family intervention for the more general management of psychosis. The guidance specifies that family interventions should include the person with psychosis and be a minimum of 10 sessions delivered over three to twelve months. Additionally, the family preference for a single or multifamily intervention can be considered, with a focus on a specific supportive, educational, or treatment function. These functions, based on the individual needs of the family, often include:

- Sharing information about psychosis to dispel any misconceptions held by family members and to develop a shared understanding of any problem/s.
- Developing effective communication skills within the family, including active listening, expressing both pleasant and difficult feelings, and making requests.
- Exploring early warning signs and providing the family with relapse prevention skills to inform the construction of a "staying well" plan for the service user.
- Helping families develop problem-solving skills.
- Goal setting to increase service user independence/engagement in activities away from the family home (Division of Clinical Psychology, 2021).

Individual family interventions are usually held in the family home. One or two therapists meet regularly with the family, setting a collaborative agenda for each session, and work together to develop and reach family goals at an appropriate pace. Multifamily groups are, alternatively, held in healthcare or community settings and follow a more prescribed agenda with several families attending the group sessions. Inclusion of the service user, in both single and multifamily group interventions, is usually preferred, though some interventions delay this, until a couple of sessions with relatives, either individually or collectively have been completed.

Study reports do not always detail personnel facilitating the intervention; for example, Cai, Zhu, Zhang, Wang, and Zhang (2015) detail only that the intervention was facilitated by psychiatric health professionals. However, Bradley and colleagues (2006) report that their single and multiple family group interventions were facilitated by several members of the multidisciplinary team including psychiatrists, psychologists, social workers, and occupational therapists.

2. Family-Based Interventions: Evidence Base

As noted above, the most robust evidence for family intervention relates to its impact on reducing rates of relapse and rehospitalization (NICE, 2014). The first trial to target negative symptoms as a primary outcome measure was reported Dyck and colleagues (2000). Sixty-three outpatients and their families were randomly allocated to a multiple family group psychoeducation treatment or a treatment as usual control group. A significant effect on negative symptoms, as measured by the Modified Scale for the Assessment of Negative Symptoms (MSANS; Andreasen, 1984) was reported at 12 months post-baseline assessment for those allocated to the active intervention. When the team explored the impact on the five negative symptom domains measured by the MSANS, significant effects were observed for avolition, flattening affect, alogia, and asociality, Mechanisms of action were hypothesized to be the enhanced social environment afforded by attendance at the groups and the opportunity to enhance social skills for the service user, and/or the clear communication and problem-solving skills acquired by family members.

A recent and widely cited systematic review and meta-analysis of psychological and psychosocial interventions for negative symptoms (Lutgens et al., 2017) included the Dyck et al. (2000) study along with the following five other studies of family interventions, which had included negative symptom as an outcome measure. Buchkremer, Klinsberg, Hollie, Schulze Monking and Hornung (1997) assessed a psychoeducational psychotherapy for schizophrenic patients and their key relative, Calvo and colleagues (2014) evaluated an intervention for patients with early onset psychosis and their families. Wang, Zhou, Yu, Qui, and Wang (2013) assessed a psychosocial rehabilitation training package including family intervention, Cai and colleagues (2015) evaluated a comprehensive family therapy approach, while Bradley and colleagues (2006) explored a multifamily group treatment for both English- and Vietnamese-speaking families living with schizophrenia. The meta-analysis of these six studies found no effect for family intervention on negative symptoms either individually or as a group of negative symptoms, regardless of the control or comparison group at the end of treatment. In addition, neither of the two studies measuring outcomes at follow up

(Buchkremer et al., 1997 or Cai et al., 2015) reported a significant effect on either expressivity or motivation.

Importantly, although metanalytic studies of individual family interventions or multifamily groups did not demonstrate an impact on negative symptoms in the meta-analysis, it is notable that several recent longitudinal evaluations of specialized early intervention or first episode for psychosis treatment services, which include family-based interventions aligned to NICE recommendations outlined above, do show a reduction in negative symptoms. For example, Pelizza and colleagues (2022) have reported a statistically significant reduction in negative symptoms over the two-year follow up of service users accessing a first episode for psychosis service in Italy, offering an intensive coordinated multidisciplinary team-based treatment approach for service users between 12 and 35 years of age. The approach included a combination of a specific pharmacological treatment and multicomponent psychosocial intervention; the latter comprising individual cognitive behavioral psychotherapy and family psychoeducation underpinned by assertive case management. The case management, provided by members of the multidisciplinary team, was based on an integrated biopsychosocial approach and focused on preventing long-term disability and promoting early recovery. Case managers would meet with service users twice a month for 60 minutes for the first year and once a month for the second year. Lutgens and colleagues (2018) also report a significant improvement in negative symptoms over the first two years of early intervention in Canada in a cohort of 178 first-episode service users. As in the Pelizza (2022) study, the service provided assertive case management, low-dose antipsychotic medication, as well as a range of psychological and psychosocial interventions, including individually targeted cognitive behavioral therapy and a number of different family-based approaches including psychoeducation, multifamily interventions, and family support groups.

Lutgens and colleagues (2018) acknowledge the limitations inherent in their study design, given the absence of a control group, but do point to other studies, which have found when early intervention focuses only on antipsychotic medication, negative symptom remission is limited (Pelayo-Teran et al., 2014) as is the case when regular treatment (i.e., medication with no specific psychological or family treatment offered) is compared with specialist early intervention services (Harvey et al., 2007). A further query is whether this positive outcome observed is because of the intensive nature of the intervention (indeed, Pelizza et al., 2022, found that the more intensive case management predicted reduction in negative symptoms) or because it is offered in the early stages of psychosis, before the negative symptoms have become "solidified" (Lutgens et al., 2018).

3. Addressing the Limitations of Traditional Psychoeducation Approaches

Another reason for these mixed findings may relate to the approach taken to family psychoeducation in some studies (Mairs, 2017). Some commentators have noted the limitations of "educating" families about psychosis because of the endorsement of an entirely biomedical perspective (Division of Clinical Psychology, 2021). There is evidence that the critical comments that mark high expressed emotion are often related to the behaviors associated with negative symptoms. Barrowclough (2001) has observed that "the major proportion of burdensome behaviors [for carers] seems to come from negative symptoms" (p. 3). Kuipers and colleagues (2002) concur, reporting that up to 70% of critical comments are about limited expressivity and motivation. Accounts suggest that carer critical comments are fueled by emotions such as anger and irritation mediated by appraisals that limited activity levels and reduced expression were intentional on the part of the service user (Barrowclough & Tarrier, 1997). To address this, psychoeducation was used to modify such appraisals, offering an alternative explanation that inactivity was a key part of an illness (i.e., schizophrenia). Treatment manuals gave unambiguous messages that "negative symptoms are caused by an illness and are not under the patient's control" (Kuipers et al., 2002, p. 28). Although this reattribution may have reduced the expression of critical comments, it also led to lowered expectations about their relative's abilities, resulting in some family members taking on additional duties to support and care for the service user (Provensher & Mueser, 1997), in effect, becoming more emotionally overinvolved. So, while one marker of high expressed emotion (critical comments) is reduced, another one (emotional overinvolvement) is intensified. In light of this it has been suggested that rather than focusing on a rather simplistic, dichotomous illness/personality attribution, therapists working with families may be better placed to offer a number of different causal explanations for reduced expression and activity, individualized to each service user (Mairs, 2017). For example, other explanations that can be offered to families include the concept that the behaviors associated with "negative symptoms" are an understandable response to the shock and trauma that comes with a first episode of psychosis. Kingdon and Turkington (2005) have suggested that it can be helpful to understand reduced expressivity and motivation as a period of recuperation in much the same way as there is an expectation that people spend time in convalescence after a period of physical illness or major surgery. Thus, normalizing negative symptoms may be an important component of psychoeducation for family members.

Family members of people with negative symptoms often struggle to see their family member as "trying" to improve. Therefore, it can also be helpful to share information that service users *also* find negative symptoms frustrating and often make unsuccessful attempts to increase their participation in a range of activities. For example, Mueser, Valentine, and Agresta (1997) found that people with negative symptoms actively try to socialize and engage in activities (such as attend a day program, exercise, leave the house). This information may be surprising for families, and in turn, may ease their own levels frustration (Mairs, 2017).

A further limitation of traditional psychoeducation approaches are the messages conveyed about the effectiveness of antipsychotic medication. Although the prescription of antipsychotic medication can be effective in reducing the distress associated with positive symptoms of psychosis (hearing voices other people cannot hear and unusual, distressing beliefs) the effects on negative symptoms are not judged large enough to be clinically meaningful (Fusar-Poli et al., 2015). At the same time, there is data to suggest that medication may make negative symptoms worse (Lewander, 1994). Some of the earliest descriptions of the effects of chlorpromazine (the first antipsychotic medication) record a service-user being "motionless," "silent for most of the time," responding "after a delay, slowly in an indifferent monotone" expressing themselves "with few words and quickly becoming mute" (Delay & Deniker, 1952, pp. 503–504). More recently, a team of researchers in Spain set out to explore the effects of a single dose of two different antipsychotic medications on people with no previous history of mental health problems or psychosis. In a double-blind trial, Artaloytia and colleagues (2006) randomly assigned participants to one of three groups, to receive either a single dose of haloperidol (a first-generation antipsychotic medication), risperidone (a second-generation antipsychotic medication), or a placebo. When standardized measures of negative symptoms were completed, those taking the first- or second-generation antipsychotic medication were much more likely to be rated as displaying negative symptoms than those who had been given the placebo. Hence, a single dose of an antipsychotic medication could induce the behaviors associated with "negative symptoms" in people with no history of mental health problems.

Service users themselves have also observed how the prescription of antipsychotic medication has decreased their drive to engage in meaningful activities. (See Chapter 5, this volume.) Some 13% of the people interviewed by Selten, Sijben, Van Den Bosch, Omloo-Visner, & Warmerdam (1993) attributed low levels of expression and activity to the psychotropic medications they were prescribed. One participant in a more recent study described the sedating effects of medication leading to a reduction in expressivity and motivation

(Gee et al., 2018). Another participant in the same study linked their limited activity levels with the rapid weight gain they experienced as a side-effect of their antipsychotic medications (Foley & Morley, 2011), stating that "when I was lighter, I was more active and doing loads of things" (Gee et al., 2018, p. 776). Therefore, helping families understand the trade-off between ameliorating hallucinations and delusions and potentially exacerbating negative symptoms and/or inducing the weight gain that might also have an adverse impact on motivation, will require a high level of skill on the part of the team members working with the family.

4. Team Based Approaches: Background and Theory

As noted above, integrated approaches, which include case management facilitated by a member of the multidisciplinary team may contribute to enhanced negative symptom outcomes. Multidisciplinary teams (MDT) have been described as the "backbone of treatment delivery" (Bucci et al., 2019, p. 43) for people with complex mental health needs, such as psychosis, and they may constitute the only social networks where service users are estranged from their families. MDTs typically include a range of professionals including cognitive behavioral therapists, clinical psychologists, healthcare support workers, mental health nurses, occupational therapists, psychiatrists, peer specialists, and social workers, who work together with the service user to identify the targets of treatment, as well as assist in the management of acute episodes (Department of Health, 1999). The quality of relationship between team members and the service user has been found to be a moderating factor in recovery (Berry et al., 2012) and can be adversely affected when marked negative symptoms are present (Browne et al., 2019). Specifically, research has indicated that members of an MDT may at times hold defeatist and pessimistic beliefs that reduced expressivity and motivation are not amenable to treatment, and further, that there are significant barriers to engaging people with severe levels of negative symptoms in therapeutic relationships and psychosocial treatment approaches (Mairs et al., 2012). Notably there is evidence that regular meetings with individual members of the MDT and adopting an empathic and nondirective approach to discussing neutral topics such as current affairs, has been found sufficient in and of itself in reducing negative symptoms, although gains are not maintained once the meetings are withdrawn (Sensky et al., 2000).

This chapter goes on to explore the extant literature regarding multidisciplinary team-based approaches for enhancing expressivity and avolition and helping multidisciplinary team members maintain their own levels of motivation when working with service users with reduced expressivity and avolition.

5. Team-Based Approaches: Background and Theory

Given that some multidisciplinary teams, particularly in long-term or residential settings, will assume the role of family, the family-based interventions discussed above may hold some utility for MDTs, too. Indeed, sharing up-to-date information with teams may be helpful to counteract some of the negative assumptions that some members of the MDT may hold, including: (1) the belief that people with reduced expression and activity have chosen to become inactive and lack motivation to change; (2) that it is not possible to treat negative symptoms; and (3) that negative symptoms do not constitute a priority for intervention because they are not associated with the same critical risks as other symptom dimensions (Mairs et al., 2012). Browne and colleagues (2019) call for a focus on training and supervision of multidisciplinary team members to emphasize the positive alliance so critical to a successful outcome of psychological and psychosocial treatments for people with psychosis; particularly where teams are working with people with marked negative symptoms and may hold the views identified above. Another approach that is recommended when service users are treated by a number of people, such as in an MDT, is the use of team formulation (Hartley, 2021; Division of Clinical Psychology, 2011). Formulation is a process of developing an understanding of what is happening for a service user, and why, to inform the development of a treatment plan (Hartley, 2021). It is a fluid and dynamic process, drawing on psychological theories to develop a shared working hypothesis about the development and maintenance of a service user's problems and the optimal treatment strategies to help a service user work toward their individual goals. It is most usually undertaken as part of individual therapies, such as cognitive-behavioral approaches (e.g., see Chapter 10, this volume), and is often seen as an alternative or adjunct to psychiatric diagnosis (Johnstone, 2014). When implemented within MDT settings, Hartley (2022) has proposed that team formulation can help meet service user needs by ensuring an effective and holistic care plan. It can also help increase team members' confidence in the potential success of the treatment intervention and ensure a more consistent approach among MDT members. Hartley (2022) further suggests the potential functions of team formulation include:

- Organizing information to develop a shared understanding of a service user's problems.

- Increasing collaboration and consistency within the MDT and between team members and the service user.
- Facilitating team member reflection of their own responses and relationships with each service user and helping them think differently about the service users they work with.
- Engendering compassionate understanding of service users' challenges.
- Developing team cohesion to support working with service users perceived to be particularly challenging or complex.
- Drawing on expertise of all team members.
- Addressing burnout and raising staff morale.
- Communicating positive messages to the team about hope for positive change/recovery.

Geach, Moghaddam, and de Boos (2018) suggest a number of approaches to team formulation have been documented in the literature. For example, Christofides, Johnstone, and Musa (2011) described how the clinical psychologists they interviewed used informal strategies; such as formulation-based thinking to offer proposals about various ways of working in team meetings, case presentations, and staff training and supervision events. More formal descriptions of team formulation, mainly facilitated by psychologists and psychiatrists have also been documented (Johnstone & Dallos, 2014). The key components of a structured team formulation have been distilled in the recently published Team Formulation Quality Scale (TFQS) developed by Bucci and colleagues (2019). They propose team formulation sessions align to the structure observed in cognitive behavioral therapy treatment sessions and progress through the following process: Sessions begin with a description of the service user, identifying key problems and needs, as well as an account of their strengths, resources, goals, and values. Early experiences and significant life events are then considered to contribute to an understanding of the service user's beliefs about themselves, the world, other people, their coping styles, and interpersonal relationships. Teams are encouraged to share their own feelings and responses to working with the service user as well as consider any relevant social and cultural aspects (such as race, gender, physical health, and so on).

Team formulations usually draw on a core model, often a cognitive behavioral one, while others use a more integrated approach (Berry & Hartwell, 2023). Simple templates have been used to guide the development of the formulation and to help embed the shared formulation within the team. The team would consider how a service user's problems are often strategies to cope with stress and distress, given the beliefs they have developed about themselves and other people with respect to early, often traumatic, experiences. Discussion of the factors maintaining the problem/s may then prompt team members to think of different ways of interacting with the service user to help them manage the problem more effectively, and develop action or support plans. Support plans are usually parsimonious interventions that can be implemented by the wider team including those without extensive training in psychological therapies. Berry and colleagues (2015) provide an example of a support plan, which includes using a positive log, where members of the team schedule regular meetings with a service user to create a record of their positive achievements as part of a process to counteract defeatist beliefs and negative automatic thoughts (for both the service user and members of the MDT).

Hartley (2022) highlights the relative contribution that members of the multidisciplinary team may make to the formulation process. For example, she suggests that healthcare support workers may know about the interests and hobbies that motivate a service user, whereas their nurse may know more about their history and any difficult (past or present) family relationships. Likewise, the occupational therapist may offer critical insights into the service user's goals and values, while the psychologist may have completed several assessments, which can inform the development of a team formulation. Other team members may contribute to the discussion by sharing their own thoughts and feelings when engaging with individual service users.

6. Team-Based Approaches: Evidence Base

There are few published evaluations for multidisciplinary team training targeting negative symptoms specifically, and as mentioned previously, these evaluations may be limited due to factors such as how psychoeducation is framed (i.e., a potential overreliance on biomedical perspectives on negative symptoms). McLeod and colleagues (2002) evaluated a three-day training for multidisciplinary team members including nurses, psychologists, psychiatrists, occupational therapists, social workers, and case managers, observing a shift to more positive attitudes and enhanced empathy. This training, however, was more specific to positive symptoms such as hearing voices and unusual, suspicious beliefs. In contrast, Endley and Berry (2011) did focus on negative symptoms (among other challenging aspects of psychosis) in their shorter training program. They reported a positive increase in the degree of effort staff thought service users made to cope with their mental health problems. Although arguably more amenable to controlled evaluation that the more complex family-based interventions discussed above, neither study included a control or comparison group. It is also important to note that in attempting to target high expressed emotion, Endley and Berry sought to help MDT members reattribute reduced expressivity and motivation to illness (as in the early family psychoeducation criticized earlier in the chapter) though they did also suggest that such behaviors may be linked to the difficult environments service users were living in. They conclude that the team formulation approaches outlined above may hold more utility than formal educational approaches.

Team formulation has been subject to further empirical scrutiny although only one randomized controlled trial has been published to date. Berry and colleagues (2015) evaluated the effects of a ward-based team formulation intervention compared to treatment as usual. The wards randomly assigned to the intervention participated in weekly one hour team formulation sessions over a period of six months. The model underpinning the formulation was a cognitive behavioral one, and the sessions were facilitated by an experienced clinical psychologist. At six-month follow-up staff confidence and understanding of service user problems increased, service users felt less criticized by staff, reported better interpersonal relationships on the unit, and an improved ward atmosphere. There were, however, no significant improvements in negative symptoms or indeed any other illness dimensions measured as secondary outcomes. The authors concede that any future studies would need to plan follow-up outcome measurement more rigorously; because so many participants were lost to follow up (although those discharged were arguably less symptomatic). Berry and colleagues (2015) suggest a larger study with more robust plans for follow up; that is, beyond discharge for symptom measurement, is warranted. A follow-up qualitative study seeking to identify specific mechanism of effect suggests that the enhanced understanding of service users generated in the team formulation discussions may have reduced the number of critical comments made by team members; in line with the literature discussed earlier, re: family-based interventions and expressed emotion (Berry et al., 2017).

Clearly evidence to support team formulation is in its infancy and not yet of a high quality (Geach et al., 2018) and evidence focused on negative symptoms is particularly limited. Future investigation, however, may lend itself more easily to controlled evaluations (Berry et al., 2017) than the multifaceted family-based interventions described earlier in the chapter.

7. Conclusion

This chapter outlined team-based interventions to support families to cope with reduced expressivity and motivation, as well as help professional members of the MDT maintain their own levels of motivation while working with marked negative symptoms. Limitations in the evidence base for these approaches have been identified and future directions for research highlighted. Given the critical role relationships and family relatives and MDT members play in supporting service users increase their activity levels, further attention is clearly warranted.

References

Andreasen, N. C. (1984). Modified scale for the assessment of negative symptoms. *Bethesda, MD: US Department of Health and Human Services.*

Artaloytia, J. F., Arango, C., Lahti, A., Sanz, J., Pascual, A. Cubero, P., & Paloma, T. (2006). Negative signs and symptoms secondary to anti-psychotics: A double blind randomised controlled trial of a single dose placebo, haloperidol and risperidone in healthy volunteers. *American Journal of Psychiatry, 163*(3), 488–493.

Barrowclough, C., & Tarrier, N. (1997). *Families of schizophrenic patients: Cognitive behavioural interventions.* Cheltenham: Stanley Thornes.

Barrowclough, C. Haddock, G., Lowens, I., Connor, A., Pidliswyj, J., & Tracey, N. (2001). Staff expressed emotion and causal attributions on a low security unit: An exploratory study. *Schizophrenia Bulletin, 27*(3), 517–526.

Berry, K., Gregg, L., Sa, D. V., Haddock, G., & Barrowclough, C. (2012). Staff-patient relationships and outcomes in schizophrenia: The role of staff attributions. *Behaviour Therapy and Research, 50*(3) 201–214.

Berry, K., Haddock, G., Kellett, S., Roberts, C., Drake, R., & Barrowclough, C. (2015). Feasibility of ward-based psychological intervention to improve staff and patient relationships in psychiatric rehabilitation settings. *British Journal of Clinical Psychology*, 55, 236–252.

Berry, K. Haddock, G. Kellett, S. Awenat, Y., Szpak, K., & Barrowclough, C. (2017). Understanding outcomes in a randomized controlled trial of a ward-based intervention on psychiatric inpatient wards: A qualitative analysis of staff and patient experiences. *Journal of Clinical Psychology, 73*(10), 1211–1225.

Berry, K., & Hartwell, R. (2023). Using CBT interpersonal case formulation on mental health inpatient wards. *Journal of Clinical Psychology. 79*(6), 1551–1561.

Bradley, G. M., Couchman, G. M., Perlesz, A., Nguyen, A. T., Singh, B., & Reiss, C. (2006). Multiple family group treatment for English and Vietnamese-speaking families living with schizophrenia. *Psychiatric Services, 57*, 521–530.

Browne, J. Nagendra, A., Kurtz, M., Berry, K. & Penn, D. L. (2019). The relationship between the therapeutic alliance and client variables in individual treatment for schizophrenia spectrum disorders and early psychosis: Narrative review. *Clinical Psychology Review, 71*, 51–62.

Bucci, S., Hartley, S., Knott, J. Raphael, J., & Berry, K. (2019). The Team Formulation Quality Rating Scale (TFQS): Development and evaluation. *Journal of Mental Health, 30*(1) 43–50.

Buchkremer, G., Klinsberg, S., Hollie, R., Schulze Monking, H., & Hornung, W. P. (1997). Psychoeducational psychotherapy for schizophrenic patients and their key relative or care givers: Results of a 2 year follow up. *Acta Psychiatrica Scandinavica, 96*, 483–491.

Cai, J., Zhu, Y., Zhang, W., Wany, Y. & Zhang, C. (2015). Comprehensive family therapy: An effective approach for cognitive rehabilitation in schizophrenia. *Neuropsychiatric Disease & Treatment, 11*, 1247–1253.

Claxton, C. M., Onwumere, J., & Fornells-Ambrojo, M. (2017) Do family interventions improve outcomes in early psychosis? A systematic review and meta-analysis. *Frontiers in Psychiatry, 8*, 371.

Calvo, A., Moreno, M., Ruiz-Sancho, A., Rapado-Castro, M., Moreno, C., & Sanchez-Gutierrez, T. (2014). Intervention for adolescents with early onset psychosis and their families: A randomised controlled trial. *Journal of American Academic Child and Adolescent Psychiatry, 53*, 688–696.

Christofides, S., Johnstone, L., & Musa, M. (2011). 'Chipping in' Clinical psychologist descriptions of their use of formulation in multidisciplinary working. *Psychology and Psychotherapy: Theory, Research and Practice, 85*(4), 424–435.

Delay, J. Deniker, P. (1952). 38 cas de psychoses traits par la cure prolongée et al. *C R Cong Med Alien Neuro France, 50*(38), 503–513.

Department of Health. (1999). A National Service Framework for Mental Health. Available from https://www.gov.uk/government/publications/quality-standards-for-mental-health-services.

Division of Clinical Psychology. (2011). Good Practice Guidelines on the use of psychological formulation. Available from https://www.sisdca.it/public/pdf/DCP-Guidelines-for-Formulation-2011.pdf.

Division of Clinical Psychology. (2021). Family Interventions in Psychosis: Guidelines for psychologist and practitioners supporting families and social networks. Available from https://www.bps.org.uk/sites/www.bps.org.uk/files/Policy/Policy%20-%20Files/Family%20interventions%20in%20psychosis.pdf.

Dyck, D. G., Short, R.A., Hendryx, M.S., Norell, D., Myers, M., Patterson, T., McDonnell, M.G., Voss, W.D., & McFarlane, W. R. (2000). Management of negative symptoms among patients with schizophrenia attending multi-family groups. *Psychiatric Services, 51*(4), 513–519.

Endley, L., & Berry, K. (2011). Increasing staff awareness of expressed emotion: An evaluation of a staff training session. *Journal of Psychiatric and Mental Health Nursing, 18*(3), 277–280.

Foley, K. L. & Morley, K. I. (2011). Systematic review of cardio-metabolic outcomes of the first treated episode of psychosis. *Archives of General Psychiatry, 68*(6), 609–616.

Fusar-Poli, P., Papanastasiou, E., Stahl, D., Rocchetti, M., Carpenter, W., Shergill, S., & McGuire, P. (2015). Treatments of negative symptoms in schizophrenia. A meta-analysis of 168 randomised placebo-controlled trials. *Schizophrenia Bulletin, 41*(4), 892–899.

Geach, N., Moghaddam, N. G., & de Boos, D. (2018). A systematic review of team formulation in clinical psychology practice: Definition, implementation and outcome. *Psychology and Psychotherapy: Theory, Research and Practice, 91*(2), 186–215.

Gee, B., Hodgekins, J., Lavis, J., Notley, C., Birchwood, M., & Everard, L. (2018). Lived experiences of negative symptoms in first episode psychosis: A qualitative secondary analysis. *Early Intervention in Psychiatry, 13*, 773–779.

Hartley, S. (2021) Using team formulation in mental health practice. *Mental Health Practice, 24*(1).

Harvey, P. O. Lepage, M., & Malla, A. (2007). Benefits of enriched interventions compared with standard care for patients with recent onset psychosis: A meta-analytic approach. *The Canadian Journal of Psychiatry, 52*(7), 464–472.

Johnstone, L. (2014). Using formulation in teams. In I. Johnstone & R. Dallis (Eds.). *Formulation in psychology and psychotherapy: Making sense of people's problems* (pp. 236–262). Hove: Routledge.

Kingdon, D., & Turkington, D. (2005). *Cognitive therapy for schizophrenia*. New York: The Guildford Press.

Kuipers, L., Leff, J., & Lam, D. (2002). *Family work for schizophrenia: A practical guide*. London: Royal College of Psychiatrist Publications.

Lewander, T. (1994) Neuroleptics and the neuroleptic induced deficit syndrome. *Acta Psychiatrica Scandinavia, 89*, 8–13.

Lutgens, D., Gariepy, G., & Malla, A. (2017). Psychological and psychosocial interventions for negative symptoms in psychosis: Systematic review and meta-analysis. *British Journal of Psychiatry, 210*, 324–332.

Lutgens, D., Joober, R., Iyer, S., Lepage, M. Norman, R., Schmitz, N., Mustafa, S., Abadi, S., & Malla, A. (2018). Progress of negative symptoms over the initial 5 years of a first episode of psychosis. *Psychological Medicine, 49*, 66–74.

Mairs, H., Lovell, K., & Keeley, P. (2012). Clinician views of referring people with negative symptoms to outcome research: A questionnaire survey. *International Journal of Mental Health Nursing, 21*(2), 138–144.

Mairs, H. (2017). *Revisiting negative symptoms: Working with reduced expression and activity in psychosis*. London: Palgrave Macmillan Education.

McLeod, H. J., Deane, F. P., & Hogbin, B. (2002). Changing staff attitudes and empathy for working with people with psychosis. *Behavioural and Cognitive Psychotherapy, 30*(4), 459–470.

Mueser, K., Valentine, D. P., & Agresta, J. (1997). Coping with negative symptoms of schizophrenia: Patient and family perspectives. *Schizophrenia Bulletin, 23*(2), 329–339.

National Institute for Health and Care Excellence (NICE). (2014). Psychosis and schizophrenia in adults: Prevention and management. Clinical Guideline CG178. Available from https://www.nice.org.uk/guidance/cg178/resources/psychosis-and-schizophrenia-in-adults-prevention-and-management-pdf-35109758952133.

Pelayo-Teran, J., Diaz, F. J., Perez-Iglesias, R., Suarez-Pinilla, P., Tabares-Seisdedos, R., & de Leon, J. (2014). Trajectories of symptom dimensions in short term response to antipsychotic medication in patients with a first episode psychosis. *Psychological Medicine, 44*(1), 37–50.

Pelizza, L., Maestri, D., Leuci, E., Quattrone, E. Azzali, S., Paulillo, G.,& Pellegrini, P. (2022). Association between case management and longitudinal decrease in negative symptoms in patients with first episode psychosis: A 2-year follow up. *Early Intervention in Psychiatry, 16*(11), 1185–1191.

Pharoah, F., Mari, J., Rathbone, J., & Wong, W. (2010). Family intervention for schizophrenia. *The Cochrane Database of Systematic Reviews* (12) CD000088.

Provencher, H. L., & Mueser, K. T. (1997). Positive and negative symptoms behaviours and caregiver burden in relatives of people with schizophrenia. *Schizophrenia Research, 26*(1), 71–80.

Samochowiec, J., Szulc, A., Bienkowski, P., Dudek, D., Galecki, P., Heitzman, J., Wojnar, M., & Wichniak, A. (2021). Polish Psychiatric Association working group consensus statement on non-pharmacological methods in the treatment of negative symptoms. *Psychiatrica Polska, 55*(4), 719–742.

Selten, J. P., Sijben, N. E., Van den Bosch, R. J., Omloo-Visner, J., & Warmerdam, H. (1993). Subjective experiences of negative symptoms: A self-rating scale. *Comprehensive Psychiatry, 34*(3), 192–197.

Sensky, T., Turkington, D., Kingdon, D. Scott, J., Siddle, R, O'Carroll, M., & Barnes, R. T. E. (2000). A randomised controlled trial of cognitive behavioural therapy for persistent symptoms in schizophrenia resistant to medication. *Archives of General Psychiatry, 57*(2), 165–172.

Wang, L., Zhou, J., Yu, X., Qui, J., & Wang, B. (2013). Psychosocial rehabilitation training in the treatment of schizophrenia outpatients: A randomized psychosocial rehabilitation and monomedication controlled study. *Pakistan Journal of Medical Sciences. 29*, 597–600.

14

Science, Theory & Practice: The Benefits of Physical Exercise on Negative Symptoms

Luz H. Ospina, Amanda Lister, and David Kimhy

Clinical pearls

- Negative symptoms are connected to sedentary activity (e.g., sitting and reclining), therefore, increasing physical activity can help decrease negative symptoms.
- Clinicians should assess baseline levels of physical activity in their patients, using measures such as The Simple Physical Activity Questionnaire SIMPAQ (Rosebaum & Ward, 2016).
- No specific aerobic activity has been demonstrated to lead to more improvements in negative symptoms than others (e.g., running/jogging, yoga, walking, and dancing).
- No confirmed clinical protocols exist for exercise for negative symptoms, so a useful guideline clinicians can use is the European Society of Cardiology recommendations for schizophrenia, which include: moderate-to-vigorous intensity of physical activity during at least half an hour most days of the week, with intensity defined as 60% to 75% of the individual's maximum heart rate.

1. Introduction

Schizophrenia is characterized by the presentation of negative symptoms, which have long been considered a core component of the diagnosis (Kraepelin, 1919). Kraepelin (1919) conceptualized negative symptoms as a loss or deficit of common functions, "a weakened volition leading to subsequent emotional dullness

Luz H. Ospina, Amanda Lister, and David Kimhy, *Science, Theory & Practice: The Benefits of Physical Exercise on Negative Symptoms*. In: *Psychosocial Approaches to Negative Symptoms in Psychosis*. Edited by: Tania Lincoln et al., Oxford University Press. © Oxford University Press (2025). DOI: 10.1093/oso/9780197676790.003.0014 and loss of drive for vocation." Subsequent research has identified two distinct domains of negative symptoms: diminished motivation (including avolition, asociality, and anhedonia), and reduced expressivity (such as blunted affect and alogia) (Horan et al., 2011; Kirkpatrick et al., 2006). Extensive evidence suggests negative symptoms are significant predictors of a range of clinical outcomes including social and vocational functioning, well-being, and quality of life, as well as disability (Milev et al., 2005; Rabinowitz et al., 2012). Specifically, motivational symptoms have been found to play a significant role in predicting general functioning (Foussias & Remington, 2010; Strauss et al., 2013). Available pharmacological and psychosocial interventions have demonstrated minimal-to-moderate benefits on improving negative symptoms in psychotic disorders (Elis et al., 2013; Fusar-Poli et al., 2015). Therefore, there remains an unmet therapeutic need for the development of novel treatment interventions targeting negative symptoms in schizophrenia spectrum disorders.

Notably, negative symptoms have been linked to sedentary behaviors (Nyboe et al., 2016; Vancampfort et al., 2017), with individuals diagnosed with psychosis spending between 8 and 13 waking hours per day engaged in sedentary activities (e.g., sitting, reclining; Stubbs et al., 2016). Relatedly, individuals with schizophrenia display significantly poorer aerobic fitness (Kimhy et al., 2014), as well as higher cardiovascular disease, increased risk of metabolic syndrome (e.g., high BMI, high blood pressure and blood sugar; Leucht et al., 2007; Sicras-Mainar et al., 2015), and increased mortality rate (Walker et al. 2015). Given the strong link between negative symptoms and sedentary behaviors in schizophrenia spectrum disorders, recent research has focused on implementing physical exercise interventions and examining its effect on physical fitness, clinical symptoms, cognition, and functional outcome in this clinical group. Therefore, in this chapter, we will review the literature on the various exercise interventions employed among individuals with schizophrenia spectrum disorders; detail the potential benefits of high- and low-intensity physical activity for negative symptoms and underlying neurobiological pathophysiology; and discuss practical recommendations for the employment of physical exercise interventions in people with psychotic disorders.

2. Physical Exercise Interventions in Psychosis—Characteristics, Feasibility, and General Mental Health Benefits

Physical exercise is traditionally defined as planned, structured, and repetitive physical movement with the purpose of improvement or maintenance of one or more components of physical fitness, such as cardiorespiratory fitness, body composition, muscle strength, physical endurance, and flexibility

(Caspersen et al., 1985; Garber et al., 2011). Research into the benefits of physical exercise as a therapeutic treatment for individuals with psychosis has increased substantially over the past decade, given its purported benefits on numerous clinical and functional domains including physical fitness, clinical symptoms, cognition, and functional outcome (Firth et al., 2015).

A number of exercise modalities have been investigated including aerobic exercise, resistance training, and mind–body exercises. Aerobic exercise (AE), or cardiorespiratory fitness training, can be defined as training that is intended to improve the efficiency and capacity of aerobic, energy-producing systems and is effective in improving cardiorespiratory endurance. AE consists of moderate-to-vigorous activity or combination of activities that utilize large muscle groups, can be continuously maintained, and is rhythmical in nature (e.g., walking, running, cycling, dancing, rowing, swimming; Garber et al., 2011). A recent systematic review and meta-analysis of 20 studies (N = 659 participants) of moderate-to-vigorous AE interventions among individuals with schizophrenia (Firth et al., 2015) included AE programs where duration ranged between 8 to 24 weeks, two to five sessions per week, with 25 to 120 minutes of exercise duration per session. Results revealed the most significant improvements in mental health in individuals with psychosis in response to AE exercises (e.g., cycling, running, sports training), but only if these exercises were administered at a high enough dose (greater than 90 minutes per week). Relatedly, recent preliminary evidence suggests that in-session exercise intensity is also related to cognitive benefits in a dose-response manner (Kimhy et al., 2016) and improve cardiovascular health (Armstrong et al., 2016). Reported feasibility indices demonstrated a total attrition rate of 22%, with within-group attrition rates for solitary exercisers almost double compared to group exercisers (43% vs. 22%), and adherence rates for group exercisers being higher compared to solitary exercisers (78.8% vs. 55%) (Firth et al., 2015). Supervised AE sessions also yielded higher adherence (77%), compared to unsupervised AE sessions (30%) (Firth et al., 2015). Overall results for these systematic reviews suggest that AE is feasible and confers potential improvement on various mental and physical health outcomes in schizophrenia, with the greatest benefits elicited by AE programs of sufficient intensity and duration, specifically moderate-to vigorous exercise for at least 90 minutes per week (Morgan et al., 2013; Perraton et al., 2010).

Another frequently administered exercise intervention in individuals with psychosis disorders is strength training (ST), defined as repeated exercises intended to increase an individual's ability to exert or resist force by typically using weights, weight machines, or elastic bands/cords (Garber et al., 2011). Muscle strength is inversely associated with mortality risk and metabolic syndrome (Jurca et al., 2005; Rantanen et al., 2000), and preliminary evidence has linked ST with improved mood and anxiety symptoms in clinical populations

(Cassilhas et al., 2010). A recent systematic review found six studies utilizing ST (N = 187), with two examining the isolated impact of ST in individuals with schizophrenia (Keller-Varady et al., 2018). Of these, one eight-week intervention using leg presses did not improve clinical symptoms or quality of life measures. Another RCT using machine-based ST for large muscle groups reported enhanced strength and overall psychopathology reduction, but no effects on depressive symptoms or quality of life.

The other studies used ST (e.g., leg and arm presses, extensions, curls, abdominal crunches, squats) in conjunction with AE exercise (e.g., treadmill walking and running) with duration and dosage ranging from 8 to 24 weeks, two to three sessions per week, and with 25 to 90 minutes session durations. Results for combined ST-AE studies have been mixed—one study that compared isolated ST with ST-AE combined found comparable enhancements in physical and mental outcomes for both types of training, with ST demonstrating greater reductions in negative symptoms compared to ST-AE combined (Silva et al., 2015). However, two other studies that included isolated ST reported inconsistent results. Adherence rates were between 80% and 90%, with attendance rate of approximately 70%, suggesting feasibility for ST-AE interventions. However, future studies assessing the impact of isolated ST should include systematically designed RCTs with accurate nomenclature for specific exercises, along with details of intervention schedule and dosage.

Other sports training has also been used as a promising physical activity intervention in individuals diagnosed with psychosis spectrum disorders. Sports training traditionally includes physical activities and skills with an element of competition, combined with a set of rules that participants are expected to follow in order to ensure pursuance of fair competition (Khan et al., 2012). A recent systematic review by Soundy et al. (2015) examined 10 studies (5 clinical trials, 2 qualitative and 3 case studies; N = 185) employing soccer, basketball, horse riding, indoor climbing, canoeing, hiking, and running as focus of interventions. The programs duration ranged from 5 days to 24 months, with frequency and intensity ranging one to five sessions per week, and 20 minutes to 10 hours duration per session. Results indicated some improvements in physical health, including reduction in weight and BMI, as well as improvement in psychiatric symptoms. Specifically, the interventions resulted in a reduction of 2.4 to 7.4 points on the total score of the Positive and Negative Syndrome Scale (PANSS). Only two of ten studies reported adherence metrics, with 82% of participants completing running training and an average of six out of eight to twelve individuals completing a hiking/rock climbing program. Although this review suggests some benefits of sports training on various clinical outcomes, limitations include the modest sample size of the studies; heterogeneity of outcome measures; inclusion of various type of sports training hindering the generalizability of the findings; and lack of consideration of potential negative psychological effects due to competition.

Finally, mind-body exercise (MBE) programs have also been employed with individuals with psychosis spectrum disorders. MBE integrates slow, low-impact, and low-intensity physical movements (e.g., stretching and relaxation of skeletal muscles), sometimes combined with an inner mental focus (e.g., meditation, mindfulness), including yoga, tai-chi, and qi-gong (La Forge, 2016). Mind-body techniques act largely through their down-regulating effects on the autonomic nervous system and hypothalamic-pituitary-adrenal (HPA) axis, and thereby are hypothesized to reduce anxiety and stress (Mayer & Saper, 2000). One early systematic review investigating the use of yoga RCTs in psychosis found three studies (N = 125), two studies conducted in India compared a yoga program to an AE comparison group, while the third U.S. study compared yoga to a wait-list control condition (Vancampfort et al., 2012). In the first two studies, the yoga interventions included loosening exercises (sitting, prone, and supine positions), breathing exercises and relaxation, while the third study integrated a number of yoga movements such as warm-ups (gentle movements of various muscle groups and joint rotations), postures including standing, balancing, and twisting movements, as well as forward and backward bends and relaxation techniques. All three studies demonstrated lower clinical scores (PANSS) and improved quality of life scores compared to their comparison groups. None of the studies, however, reported attrition and attendance rates, thereby limiting the recommendation of dose-response relationships for subsequent applications. A more recent systematic review of the effects of tai-chi in Chinese schizophrenia patients examined six RCTS (N = 483), with comparison groups including routine care, health education, waitlist, and AE (Zheng et al., 2016). Duration and dosage ranged from 12 to 24 weeks, with one to seven sessions per week and 30 to 60 minutes session duration. Results overwhelmingly indicated improvement of negative symptoms compared to the control condition, with no significant change in positive symptoms. Reported adherence rates were high (80%–100%), suggesting high feasibility. Similar to yoga studies, however, there were limited data to provide type- and dose-response effects, with various studies employing distinct tai-chi styles.

Finally, a recent meta-analysis including all types of MBE (yoga or tai-chi) found 13 suitable studies, with six conducted in India, three in China, two in Japan, one in Turkey and one in the United States (N = 1,159; 11 RCTs, one non-randomized CT, and one quasi-experimental study; Wei et al., 2020). Control groups were treatment-as-usual, and reported duration and dosage ranged from six weeks to six months, one to seven sessions per week, with 20 to 120 minutes duration. Results showed better clinical outcomes at study's end, with beneficial effects on positive, negative, and depressive symptoms. Interestingly, session length was associated with negative symptom scores. However, the MBE were administered as an adjunctive treatment with preexisting treatment, making it difficult to determine whether the beneficial results are due to MBEs only, or the combination of MBE and psychiatric treatment. Also, feasibility metrics were not reported, so exercise adherence remains unclear. Overall, these studies indicate some clinical improvement after completing MBE; however, future research must investigate the intensity, frequency, and duration of these interventions in order to make a reliable recommendation for use in people with psychosis.

3. The Impact of Physical Exercise on Negative Symptoms

Given substantial evidence for beneficial effects of physical exercise on negative symptoms in psychosis, various meta-analytic reviews have recently been conducted to rigorously summarize and quantify these effects.

3.1 Effects of Moderate-to-Vigorous Aerobic Exercise on Negative Symptoms in Psychosis

Recent meta-analytic reviews by Sabe and colleagues (2020) and Vogel and colleagues (2019) have examined RCTs investigating the effects of physical exercise on negative symptoms, contrasting the findings between moderate-to-vigorous versus none-to-low AE. Subsequent to these publications, a number of recent RCTs have also focused on the impact of physical exercise on negative symptoms. The moderate-to-vigorous AE programs included one or more of the following types of exercises: walking, jogging, cycling, jump rope, rowing, cross-trainer, dancing, boxing, circuit training, and completing exercise videos. Dosage and frequency ranged from 30 to 120 minutes per session, from twice to six times per week, and exercise program length ranged from four weeks to eight months. All studies met physical recommendations of at least 90 minutes of weekly moderate-to-vigorous physical exercise. Altogether, 13 of the 19 studies (N = 820) demonstrated significant reductions in negative symptoms in participants diagnosed with schizophrenia or related disorders, with three studies showing reductions at trend level. Of these 13 studies, however, five studies demonstrated improvement not only in the intervention group but also the control group, which included a passive control such as treatment as usual (TAU; four studies), or an active control such as ST (one study) (see Table 14.1).

Overall, the findings suggest beneficial effects of moderate-to-vigorous AE on negative symptoms of psychosis spectrum disorders. Both meta-analytic

Table 14.1 RCTs Assessing Effects of Moderate-to-Vigorous Aerobic Exercise on Negative Symptoms in Psychosis

	Sample Characteristics				Exercise Intervention		Results
	Aerobic Exercise (n)	Control (n)	Mean Age (years)	Pop	Activity	Duration & Frequency	Negative Symptom Change
Garcia-Garces et al. 2021	86	ST (29), Mixed (29)	42.9	SZ	AE: brisk walking; ST: resistance band; Mixed: both AE/ST exercises	60 minutes, 3 times per week for 16 weeks	PANSS; Symptom reduction for all groups; no group*time interaction
Khonsari et al. 2021	20	TAU (20)	35	SZ	AE: Cycling, jump rope, jogging	30 minutes, 3 times per week for 8 weeks	PANSS; Symptom reduction for both groups, with greater reduction for AE group
Kern et al. 2020	35	Yoga (18)	56	SZ	AE: Brisk walking, including uphill	40 minutes, 3 times per week for 12 weeks	BPRS; No difference in symptom change between or within groups
Senormanci et al. 2021	20	TAU (19)	41.8	SZ	AE: Jogging, resistance band, Pilates ball	60 minutes, 2 times per week for 12 weeks	SANS; Symptom reduction for both groups; no group*time interaction

Continued

Table 14.1 *Continued*

	Sample Characteristics				Exercise Intervention		Results
	Aerobic Exercise (n)	Control (n)	Mean Age (years)	Pop	Activity	Duration & Frequency	Negative Symptom Change
Shimada et al. 2019	16	TAU (15)	–	SZ, Schizo-affective	AE: Treadmill, stationary bicycle, exercise videos	60 minutes, 2 times (1 alone, 1 group) per week for 12 weeks	PANSS; Symptom reduction for both groups, with greater reduction for AE group
Wang et al. 2018	24	Stretching and Toning (22)	38.5	SZ	AE: ?; Stretching: flexibility, toning and balance exercises	40 minutes, 3 times per week for 12 weeks	PANSS: Symptom reduction for AE; no change for stretching group
Curcic et al. 2017	40	TAU (40)	40.9	SZ	AE: Walking, jogging	45 minutes, 4 times per week for 12 weeks	PANSS; Symptom reduction for both groups; no group*time interaction
Bhatia et al. (2017)	90	Yoga (104), TAU (91)	35.2	SZ	AE: walking, jogging, cardio	60 minutes, 6 times per week for 3 weeks	SANS; No difference in symptom change between or within groups
Su et al. 2016	22	Stretching and Toning (22)	37.2	SZ, Schizo-affective	AE: ?; Stretching: flexibility, toning and balance exercises	40 minutes, 4–5 times per week for 12 weeks	PANSS: No difference in symptoms between groups

Ho et al. 2016	51	Tai-chi (51), waitlist (49)	54	SZ	AE: walking, stretching, stepping, weights; Tai-chi: Wu style	45–60 minutes, 3 times per week for 12 weeks	PANSS: Symptom Reduction for AE, symptom worsening for tai-chi and waitlist
Svatkova et al. 2015	40 (16 SZ; 24 HC)	OT (17 SZ); life as usual (24 HC)	29.2	SZ; HC	AE: Bicycling, rowing, cross trainer, treadmill, weights	60 minutes, 2 times per week for 6 months	PANSS: Trend reduction for AE only; no group*time interaction
Silva et al. 2015	9	ST (12); TAU (13)	33.3	SZ	AE: walking and cycling ST: arm & leg press, curls, traction, extensions, abdominal crunch; AE+ST: same ST exercises with running and walking	60 minutes, 2 times per week for 20 weeks	PANSS; group*time interaction, with symptom reduction for the ST group, compared to AE and TAU
Lin et al. 2015	31	Yoga (38), waitlist (33)	24.6	Psychosis spectrum disorders	AE: Walking and cycling Yoga: Integrative (poses, breathing, meditation)	60 minutes, 3 times per week for 12 weeks	PANSS; Symptoms improved in yoga group only
Kaltsatou et al. 2015	16	TAU (15)	59.9	SZ	AE: Greek traditional dancing	60 minutes, 3 times per week for 8 months	PANSS: Trend reduction for AE only

Continued

Table 14.1 *Continued*

	Sample Characteristics				Exercise Intervention		Results
	Aerobic Exercise (n)	Control (n)	Mean Age (years)	Pop	Activity	Duration & Frequency	Negative Symptom Change
Oertel-Knöchel et al. 2014	16 (8 SZ, 8 MDD)	Mental Relaxation (11 SZ, 6 MDD); waiting (10 SZ, 8 MDD)	39.7	SZ; MDD	AE: boxing, circuit training; Mental relaxation: breathing, mental imagery	75 minutes, 3 times per week for 4 weeks	PANSS; Symptom reduction for AE and mental relaxation groups, compared to waitlist
Scheewe et al. 2013a	31	OT (32)	29.7	Psychosis spectrum disorders	AE: Cardio (?), muscle strength exercises	60 minutes, 1–2 times per week for 6 months	PANSS; Trend symptom reduction for AE only
Takahashi et al. 2012	13	TAU (10)	41.7	SZ	AE: Walking, jogging, muscle-stretching, basketball	60-120 minutes, 6 times per week for 12 weeks	PANSS; No difference in symptom change between or within groups
Pajonk et al. 2010	8	TAU (8); HC (8)	35	SZ; HC	AE: Cycling	30 minutes, 3 times per week for 12 weeks	PANSS: Trend reduction for AE, and worsening for TAU
Acil et al. 2008	15	TAU (15)	32.4	SZ	AE:?	40 minutes, 3 times per week for 10 weeks	SANS; Symptom reduction for AE; no change for TAU group

Abbreviations: TAU: Treatment as Usual; SZ: Schizophrenia; AE: Aerobic Exercise; ST: Strength Training; SANS: Scale for the Assessment of Negative Symptoms; PANSS: Positive and Negative Syndrome Scale; HC: Healthy controls; OT: Occupational Therapy; MDD: Major Depressive Disorder.

reviews (Sabe et al., 2020; Vogel et al. 2019) reported small to moderate, yet clinically relevant effect sizes relating to the beneficial effects of AE programs on negative symptoms. Interestingly, subgroup analyses comparing the effects between moderate-to-vigorous and none-to-low AE programs yielded inconsistent results, with one review demonstrating greater alleviation of negative symptoms in response to moderate-to-vigorous versus none-to-low AE program administration (Sabe et al., 2020), while the other review suggested greater reduction in negative systems after administration of MBE compared to AE interventions (Vogel et al., 2019). These discrepant results may be accounted for by the type of control group used. Specifically, studies utilizing passive control groups (e.g., TAU, waitlist) were more likely to find improvements in negative symptoms after administration of the AE intervention, while studies with null results tended to include more active control (e.g., yoga) conditions. Second, a smaller sample (five studies) of eligible none-to-low AE RCTs were included in the meta-analysis by Sabe et al. (2020), thereby potentially amplifying the positive effect of moderate-to-vigorous AE on negative symptoms in psychosis. Indeed, the meta-analysis by Vogel and colleagues (2019) included 12 eligible none-to-low AE studies, thereby explaining their results of greater benefits of none-to-low AE, compared to moderate-to-vigorous AE, on negative symptoms. Third, there was high heterogeneity in the kinds of AE programs used; therefore, it remains unclear which types of AE bestow the greatest effects on negative symptoms; as such, no recommendations of specific exercise types can be made for future therapeutic use. Finally, while studies classified physical exercise interventions as moderate-to-vigorous or none-to-low AE, very few studies included objective measures (e.g., heart rate, VO_2 max) assessing the participant's actual metabolic intensity during exercise completion. Individuals with schizophrenia are less likely to engage in exercise and less likely to reach a sufficient intensity level of practice (Pearsall et al., 2014). Previous studies have typically indexed intervention fidelity via number of exercise sessions attended. Our group, however, has criticized the lack of indices of in-session training fidelity (e.g., exercising at target intensity; Kimhy et al., 2015; Kimhy et al., 2016; Vakhrusheva et al., 2016; Ospina et al., 2019a; Ospina et al., 2019b). Thus, monitoring and characterizing autonomic intensity during RCTs examining AE interventions is critical for both predicting the effects of exercise on negative symptoms, as well as comparing findings from discrepant studies. Relatedly, a recent report by our group has demonstrated that increased aerobic fitness via AE improved social functioning (Kimhy et al., 2021), a close correlate of negative symptoms. Employing a single-blind, randomized clinical trial design, 33 individuals with schizophrenia were randomized to receive 12 weeks of TAU (n = 17) or TAU + AE (n = 16) utilizing active-play video games (Xbox

360 Kinect) and traditional AE equipment. Participants completed an evaluation of aerobic fitness (VO_2max) as well as self-, informant-, and clinician-reported social functioning measures at baseline and after 12 weeks. Twenty-six participants completed the study (79%; TAU = 13; AE = 13). At follow-up, the AE participants improved their VO2max by 18.0% versus −0.5% in the controls (group∗time interaction, $F_{1,24}=12.88$; $p=.002$). Hierarchical stepwise regression analyses indicated improvements in VO_2max significantly predicted enhancement in social functioning as indexed by self-, informant-, and clinician-reported measures, predicting 47%, 33%, and 25% of the variance, respectively (controlling for baseline demographics, medications, mood symptoms, and social networks). These results indicate that VO_2max enhancement leads to improvements in social functioning in people with schizophrenia. Furthermore, low VO_2max represents a modifiable risk factor of social functioning in people with schizophrenia, for which AE training offers a safe, non-stigmatizing, and nearly side-effect-free intervention (Kimhy et al., 2021).

Notably, recent investigations have extended the inquiry of the potential benefit of exercise on negative symptoms to individuals at clinical high risk for psychosis (see Chapter 21)—a recent pilot RCT examined the clinical benefits of AE in 32 individuals at clinical high risk for psychosis randomized to AE (n = 17) or waitlist (no exercise; n = 15) conditions (Damme et al., 2022). The exercising group showed improved aerobic fitness, increased cognitive performance, and a decrease in positive symptoms compared with the waitlist group. Additionally, the exercise group showed stable hippocampal volumes, with waitlist individuals displaying a 3.57% decreased hippocampal subfield volume. The intervention did not reduce negative symptoms as expected. The severity of negative symptoms was, however, relatively low, suggesting a potential "floor-effect." Relatedly, within the context of the COVID-19 pandemic, it has been suggested that AE interventions may have a protective mental health benefit for children and adolescents (Mittal et al., 2020).

3.2 Effects of Mind-Body and Low Aerobic Exercises on Negative Symptoms in Psychosis

Recent systematic reviews by Sabe and colleagues (2019) and Vogel and colleagues (2019), along with subsequent publications, reported on 25 RCTs evaluating the effects of various types of none-to-low AE programs, including ST and MBE, on negative symptoms in psychosis spectrum disorders. Sixteen of the 25 studies (N = 1212) demonstrated significant reductions in negative symptoms in participants diagnosed with schizophrenia or related disorders. None-to-low AE programs included one or more of the following types of exercises: walking,

ST (e.g., arm & leg press, curls, traction, extensions, abdominal crunch, resistance bands, Pilates ball), stretching and flexibility exercises, tai-chi, yoga, and dance. Dosage and frequency ranged from 40 to 90 minutes per session, from two to seven times per week, and program length ranging from three weeks to one year. Of these 16 studies, however, seven studies demonstrated improvement not only in the intervention group but also the control group, which included a passive control such as TAU (three studies) and waitlist (four studies), or an active control such as none-to-light AE (three studies), moderate-to-vigorous AE (four studies) and daycare (one study) (see Table 14.2).

Overall, these findings suggest that none-to-low AE programs, particularly yoga, confer beneficial effects on negative symptoms in people diagnosed with schizophrenia spectrum disorders. All meta-analytic reviews (Sabe et al., 2019; Sabe et al., 2020; Vogel et al., 2019) reported small-to-moderate effect sizes relating to the beneficial effects of none-to-low AE programs (e.g., MBE) on negative symptoms. Regarding subgroup analyses comparing the effects between moderate-to-vigorous AE and none-to-low AE programs, results were inconsistent, with one review suggesting greater reduction in negative systems after administration of MBE compared to moderate-to-vigorous AE interventions (Vogel et al., 2019), with the other demonstrating greater alleviation of negative symptoms in response to moderate-to-vigorous AE, versus none-to-low AE program administration (Sabe et al., 2020). As previously discussed, various explanations may address these inconsistencies. The type of control arm used (active vs. passive) is an important consideration when developing these RCTs, because including an active control may differentially effect results compared to using a passive control. Also, a larger sample of eligible none-to-low AE RCTs were included in the meta-analysis by Vogel and colleagues (2019) (16 of 22 total studies), compared to a much smaller sample of non-AE RCT studies indicated in Sabe and colleagues (2020) (five of 17 total studies), which potentially may have heightened the positive effect of none-to-low AE on negative symptoms in psychosis due to increased power. Furthermore, high heterogeneity among the none-to-low AE programs used obfuscates their specific effects on negative symptoms; future research must standardize the types of none-to-low AE programs used, or at the least fully describe the type of physical exercises implemented. Finally, the distinction between none-to-low and moderate-to-vigorous AE interventions cannot be made unless an objective measure of autonomic activity (e.g., heart rate, VO_2max) is incorporated to be used within exercise sessions. While most none-to low AE studies showed improvements in negative symptoms, this effect may have been due to actual significant increases in cardiovascular activity reaching 64% to 76% of participants' age-predicted maximal heart rate, which classifies such physical exercise as moderate-to-vigorous (American College of Sports Medicine, 2013). Again, monitoring metabolic

Table 14.2 RCTs Assessing Effects of None-to-Low Aerobic Exercise on Negative Symptoms in Psychosis

	Sample Characteristics				Exercise Intervention		Results
	Non-Aerobic Exercise (n)	Control (n)	Mean Age (years)	Pop	Activity	Duration & Frequency	Negative Symptom Change
Kurebayashi et al. 2021	Light AE (5)	TAU (17)	55	SZ	Light AE: Tai-chi, light aerobics	1 hour, 2 times per week for 8 weeks	PANSS; No difference in symptom change between or within groups
Garcia-Garces et al. 2021	ST (29)	AE (86), Mixed (29)	42.9	SZ	AE: brisk walking; ST: resistance band; Mixed: both AE/ST exercises	60 minutes, 3 times per week for 16 weeks	PANSS; Decrease in symptoms within all groups; no group*time interaction
Kern et al. 2020	Yoga (18)	AE (35)	56	SZ	Yoga: Sitting, supine and prone postures, breathing exercises; AE: Brisk walking, including uphill	40 minutes, 3 times per week for 12 weeks	BPRS; No difference in symptom change between or within groups
Senormanci et al. 2021	ST (20)	TAU (19)	41.8	SZ	ST: Jogging, resistance band, Pilates ball	60 minutes, 2 times per week for 12 weeks	SANS; Decrease in symptoms for both groups
Wang et al. 2018	Stretching and Toning (22)	AE (24)	38.5	SZ	AE: ?; Stretching: flexibility, toning and balance exercises	40 minutes, 3 times per week for 12 weeks	PANSS: Symptom reduction for AE; no change for stretching group

Bhatia et al. (2017)	Yoga (104)	AE (90), TAU (91)	35.2	SZ	Yoga: Sitting, supine and prone postures, breathing exercises; AE: walking, jogging, cardio	60 minutes, 6 times per week for 3 weeks	SANS; No difference in symptom change between or within groups
Ikai et al. 2017	Chair yoga (28)	TAU (28)	55.3	SZ (49), mood disorder (3), dementia (2), alcohol dependence (2)	Yoga: breathing, coordination, modified postural exercises seated in chair	20 minutes, twice per week for 12 weeks	PANSS; No difference in symptom change between or within groups
Kang et al. 2016	Tai-chi with social-skills training (118)	TAU (126)	45.9	SZ	Tai-chi: Wu style;	45 minutes tai chi+45 minutes social-skills training, twice per month for 12 months	PANSS; group*time interaction, where symptoms improved for the Tai-chi group, compared to TAU
Su et al. 2016	Stretching and Toning (22)	AE (22)	37.2	SZ, Schizo-affective	Stretching: flexibility, toning and balance exercises; AE:?	40 minutes, 4–5 times per week for 12 weeks	PANSS: No difference in symptoms between groups
Ho et al. 2016	Tai-chi (51)	AE (51), waitlist (49)	54	SZ	Tai-chi: Wu style (22 simple physical movements); AE: walking, stretching, stepping, weights;	45–60 minutes, 3 times per week for 12 weeks	PANSS: Symptom reduction for AE, symptom worsening for tai-chi and waitlist

Continued

Table 14.2 *Continued*

	Sample Characteristics				Exercise Intervention		Results
	Non-Aerobic Exercise (n)	Control (n)	Mean Age (years)	Pop	Activity	Duration & Frequency	Negative Symptom Change
Loh et al. 2016	Light AE (52)	TAU (52)	50	SZ	Light AE: Walking	30–50 minutes, 3 times per week for 12 weeks	PANSS: Symptom reduction for light AE; no change for TAU
Isuru et al. 2015	Dance, yoga (33)	TAU (40)	40.4	SZ	Dance/yoga: Body posture, breathing exercises	6 hours per session, 8 total sessions over a 3-week period	PANSS; Decrease in symptoms for both groups; no group*time interaction
Silva et al. 2015	ST (12)	AE (9); TAU (13)	33.3	SZ	ST: arm & leg press, curls, traction, extensions, abdominal crunch; AE+ST: same ST exercises with running and walking	60 minutes, 2 times per week for 20 weeks	PANSS; group*time interaction, with symptom reduction for the ST group, compared to AE and TAU
Lin et al. 2015	Yoga (38)	AE (31), waitlist (33)	24.6	Psychotic spectrum disorders	Yoga: Sitting, supine and prone postures, breathing exercises; AE: walking and cycling	60 minutes, 3 times per week for 12 weeks	PANSS; Symptoms reduction in yoga group only

Paikkatt et al. 2015	Yoga (15)	TAU (15)	20 years and older	SZ	Yoga: Sitting, supine and prone postures, breathing exercises	90 minutes, 7 times per week (except holidays) for 4 weeks	PANSS; Symptom reduction for yoga; no change for TAU
Ikai et al. 2014	Yoga (25)	Waitlist (25)	50.9	Psychotic spectrum disorders	Yoga hatha: Sitting, supine and prone postures, breathing exercises	60 minutes, once per week for 8 weeks	PANSS: No difference in symptom change between groups
Ikai et al. 2013	Yoga (25)	Daycare program (24)	53.1	Psychotic spectrum disorders	Yoga: Sitting, supine and prone postures, breathing exercises	60 minutes, once per week for 8 weeks	SANS; Symptoms reduction in yoga group only
Jayaram et al. 2013	Yoga (15)	Waitlist (28)	28.9	SZ	Yoga: Sitting, supine and prone postures, breathing exercises	4 weeks (dosage & frequency: ?)	SANS; Decrease in symptoms for both groups
Manjunath et al. 2013	Yoga (35)	Light AE (25)	31.4	SZ	Yoga: Sitting, supine and prone postures, breathing exercises; AE: Walking, jogging, sitting and standing movements	60 minutes, daily for 2 weeks (supervised), additional 4 weeks (un-supervised)	PANSS; Decrease in symptoms for both groups, no group*time interaction

Continued

Table 14.2 *Continued*

	Sample Characteristics				Exercise Intervention		Results
	Non-Aerobic Exercise (n)	Control (n)	Mean Age (years)	Pop	Activity	Duration & Frequency	Negative Symptom Change
Ho et al. 2012	Tai-chi (15)	Waitlist (15)	53	SZ	Tai-chi: Wu style	60 minutes, twice a week for 6 weeks	SANS; No difference in symptom change between or within groups
Varambally et al. 2012	Yoga (46)	Light AE (36), Waitlist (37)	32.3	SZ	Yoga: Sitting, supine and prone postures, breathing exercises; AE: Walking, jogging, sitting and standing movements	45 minutes per session, 25 sessions in 4 weeks	PANSS: Symptom reduction for yoga; no change for other 2 groups
Visceglia et al. 2011	Yoga (10)	Waitlist (8)	42.8	SZ	Yoga: postures, breathing and relaxation exercises	45 minutes, 2 times per week for 8 weeks	PANSS; Symptom reduction for yoga; no change for waitlist

Behere et al. 2011	Yoga (27)	Light AE (17), Wait list (22)	31.7		Yoga: Sitting, supine and prone postures, breathing exercises; AE: Walking, jogging, sitting and standing movements	60 minutes, ? times per week for 4 weeks	PANSS; Symptom reduction for yoga; no change for other 2 groups
Duraiswamy et al. 2007	Yoga (21)	Light AE (20)	31.9	SZ	Yoga: Sitting, supine and prone postures, breathing exercises; Light AE: Walking, jogging, sitting and standing movements	60 minutes per day, 5 days a week for 3 weeks	PANSS; Symptom reduction for both groups, with greater reduction for yoga group
Beebe et al. 2005	Light AE (4)	TAU (6)	52	SZ	Light AE: Treadmill running	30 minutes, 3 times per week for 16 weeks	PANSS; No difference in symptom change between or within groups

Abbreviations: TAU: Treatment as Usual; SZ: Schizophrenia; AE: Aerobic Exercise; ST: Strength Training; SANS: Scale for the Assessment of Negative Symptoms; PANSS: Positive and Negative Syndrome Scale. HC: Healthy controls; OT: Occupational Therapy; MDD: Major Depressive Disorder.

parameters during exercise training is crucial in determining the actual training intensity level reached, which aids in correctly classifying the type of exercise completed and tracking participants' metabolic improvement.

4. Underlying Neurobiological Mechanisms Linking Physical Exercise and Negative Symptoms

A number of neurobiological models have been developed to account for the various benefits of physical exercise on mental health in psychosis spectrum disorders, including improvement of negative symptoms (Maurus et al., 2019). One hypothesis posits that physical exercise leads to upregulation of neurotrophins, particularly brain-derived neurotrophic factor (BDNF), a neural growth factor that is significantly expressed in the hippocampal region and is associated with facilitating neurogenesis, synaptic plasticity, learning and memory (Gomez-Pinilla et al., 2008). In individuals with schizophrenia spectrum disorders, one meta-analysis including 16 studies (N = 1114 patients) demonstrated reduced blood BDNF levels in drug-naive and medicated male and female patients (Green et al. 2011). Neurodevelopmental models propose that reduced BDNF may partly underlie the core signs and symptoms of the disorder; indeed, some studies have shown a significant relationship between levels of BDNF and negative symptomatology (Binford et al., 2018; Niitsu et al., 2011). Therefore, increased release of BDNF, as a result of physical activity may lead to reductions in many of the clinical symptoms (e.g., negative symptoms), as well as neurocognitive deficits (Kimhy et al., 2015; Vakhrusheva et al., 2016) characteristic of psychosis spectrum disorders, via increased neuronal growth and survival. For example, one review by Vakhrusheva and colleagues (2016) assessing the impact of physical exercise on BDNF, which included four RCTs (N = 154), with three studies using AE (Kim et al., 2014; Kimhy et al., 2015; Kuo et al., 2013) and one study (Silva et al., 2015) using an ST program, demonstrated increased BDNF levels only after completion of a moderate-to-vigorous AE program. Furthermore, higher BDNF levels were associated with improved aerobic fitness in this population. This suggests that increased upregulation of BDNF in schizophrenia patients is most likely to occur after implementation of a moderate-to-vigorous AE program, compared to a none-to-low AE program, highlighting the importance of participants observing and meeting sufficient frequency, duration, and in-session intensity metrics to determine the specific level of dose-response needed in order to generate structural and neurochemical changes. Also, few if any studies have directly assessed the potential mediating effect of changes in BDNF levels on the relationship between changes in aerobic fitness and negative symptoms; future research is necessary to elucidate the relative effect of

BDNF and other potential neurotrophins (e.g., insulin growth factor-1; Silva et al., 2015) on potential clinical symptom improvement in response to physical exercise.

Physical exercise has also been shown to reduce peripheral inflammation—while acute exercise leads to rapid increases in peripheral inflammatory markers called cytokines, regular exercise ultimately downregulates systemic inflammation (Berk et al., 2013). Inflammatory dysregulation is apparent in people with schizophrenia, with results showing increased brain inflammatory markers and systemic, low-grade inflammation in this population (Potvin et al., 2008; Trépanier et al., 2016). Systemic inflammation in this population has been associated with impaired synaptic processes, and has been associated with impaired neurocognition (Kogan et al., 2020), social cognition (Ospina et al., 2021), and clinical deficits such as greater negative symptoms (Goldsmith & Rapaport, 2020). Therefore, reducing inflammation in this population via physical exercise may lead to benefits in many key areas in cognitive and functional outcomes. In schizophrenia, one recent study has demonstrated significant decreases in inflammatory biomarkers such as interleukin-6 (IL-6) and interferon-γ after completion of a combined moderate-to-vigorous AE and ST program (Lavratti et al., 2017). Another study showed decreases in C-reactive protein (CRP) after eight weeks of an ST program in schizophrenia patients; however, the difference between the exercise and the TAU group was not significant (Heggelund et al., 2011). Finally, one other study failed to find any change in inflammatory biomarkers, including IL-6, CRP, and tumor necrosis factor-α (TNF-α) after a 10-week lifestyle intervention, which included psychosocial treatment, behavior therapy, and moderate-to-vigorous AE (Kuo et al., 2013). These results suggest potential benefits of physical exercise on inflammatory levels, although it remains unclear how changes in inflammation directly relate to changes in negative symptoms. Also, circulating peripheral cytokines are confounded by a variety of factors that are common in schizophrenia and further contribute to its clinical profile, including smoking, sleep difficulties, and obesity; further research must account for these variables in order to disentangle the effects of elevated inflammation on clinical symptoms in these individuals.

Physical exercise has been demonstrated to enact changes in brain anatomical structures, such as the hippocampus, via neurogenesis and neural plasticity (Van Praag, 2008). Specific to psychosis disorders, one review which included three RCTs (N = 141) (Malchow et al., 2016; Pajonk et al., 2010; Scheewe et al., 2013b) assessing the effects of AE programs on brain structure and function, reported increases in hippocampal volume in participants only if the AE program was administered with sufficient dosage and frequency (i.e., minimum of 90 minutes of moderate-to-vigorous AE) (Vakhrusheva et al., 2016). This brain region is particularly relevant given that patients with psychosis have been observed to have smaller hippocampal volumes (Steen et al., 2006), as well as abnormalities in the hippocampal neurons (Reif et al., 2006) compared to nonclinical populations. Furthermore, one recent neuroimaging study demonstrates a significant negative association between hippocampal volume and negative symptoms in 36 patients with adolescent-onset schizophrenia (Duan et al., 2021). Despite these promising results, however, one recent meta-analysis by Firth and colleagues (2018b), including 14 eligible studies (N = 737), found no significant effect of AE on changes in total hippocampal volume. Once compared to the control condition, however, AE appeared to significantly increase *left* hippocampal volume; post-hoc analyses revealed that this increase was driven by AE's effect of maintaining left hippocampal volume (vs. reduction in right hippocampal volume) in the active participants, compared to controls. Additional changes in brain structures after exercise implementation include increases in white matter integrity, demonstrated in healthy (Voss et al., 2013) and older adults (Burdette et al., 2010). White matter integrity abnormalities have been reported in individuals with psychosis spectrum disorders, particularly in frontal and temporal cortices as demonstrated in diffusion tensor imaging (DTI) studies (Fitzsimmons et al., 2013). One exercise intervention study conducted in 33 schizophrenia patients (Svatkova et al., 2015) using a six-month combined AE and ST program showed increased white matter integrity in brain regions related to motor functioning (e.g., corpus collosum, corticospinal tract) in individuals who completed the exercise program, while the life-as-usual group showed decreased fiber integrity.

In summary, these studies suggest that physical exercise, particularly moderate-to-vigorous AE, is able to produce neurochemical, neuroanatomical, and neuronal integrity changes in individuals with psychosis. Further research with larger samples is necessary, however, to assess the direct and indirect effects of neurochemical and neuroanatomical effects on negative symptoms in response to physical exercise in individuals with schizophrenia spectrum disorders.

5. Application and Usage of Physical Exercise Interventions Among Individuals with Psychosis

Early studies focusing on physical activity interventions in psychosis spectrum disorders generally demonstrated beneficial effects on multiple outcomes such as physical, clinical, and mental performance. Not all studies, however, demonstrated improved effects of physical activity, which is likely due to factors such as lack of clear duration and frequency measures, variability in types of administered physical activity training programs, lack of an

RCT design, and absence of objective physiological measures to confirm training intensity has been met. One of the first systematic reviews to investigate recommendation metrics using clinical practice guidelines for AE fitness interventions in schizophrenia (Vancampfort et al., 2011) revealed that only four out of 12 articles reviewed included advice on specific program variables such as duration and frequency of exercise, with only one study meeting the full requirements of frequency, intensity, time, and type principles of exercise prescription (De Hert et al., 2009).

Given the paucity of studies in schizophrenia incorporating interventions within clinical practice guidelines, recommendations specifically for targeting negative symptoms in patients with psychosis are not available. However, recommendations made by the European Society of Cardiology (Timmis et al., 2020) remain applicable in this population to decrease the incidence of cardiometabolic complications, which includes moderate-to-vigorous intensity of physical activity during at least half an hour most days of the week, *with intensity defined as 60% to 75% of the individual's maximum heart rate* (Graham et al., 2007). Overall, their review stresses the absolute need for considering duration, frequency, and feasibility variables when executing and reporting exercise studies in schizophrenia spectrum disorders in order to inform subsequent studies and clinical recommendations.

Ensuing research since Vancampfort and colleagues (2011) review has increasingly included feasibility parameters such as duration, frequency, and time. For example, Firth and colleagues (2015) review of physical exercise interventions suggests *the most benefits resulting from exercise programs comprised of at least 90 minutes per week of any moderate-to-vigorous exercise*. Also, exercise programs in general demonstrate good feasibility, with 72% average attendance of sessions, and a drop-out rate of 32.5%, suggesting that exercise is a safe and well-tolerated therapy in individuals with psychosis. Other factors must be considered, however, in terms of potential barriers to completion of exercise therapy in this population, as suggested by a review including 12 studies (N = 6,431) (Firth et al., 2016; Yung and Firth, 2017). Clinical status, such as elevated negative symptoms, may lead to poor motivation to complete exercise; relatedly, anxiety about exercising in public and/or with others may prohibit completion of exercise therapy. Also, comorbid health issues such as obesity may hinder mobility, while tiredness and low energy linked to the sedative effects of antipsychotic medication may also play a role in preventing adequate exercise. Social barriers such as lack of support or lack of a training partner may also impede exercise training. Finally, structural barriers such as transportation availability to exercise facilities and the individual's socioeconomic status must also be considered when prescribing exercise as a therapy. Alternatively, the study authors also assessed facilitating factors for exercise in individuals with severe mental illness, suggesting a desire to lose weight, improve mood, and reduce stress as the most common motivators in these individuals.

Taking into consideration facilitating factors and barriers, exercise therapy for people with psychotic illnesses should be developed to improve physical and cardiorespiratory fitness, preferably receiving supervision or assistance in overcoming psychological and social barriers to achieving their physical fitness goals; these situations may likelier prove more motivating for patients, resulting in higher exercise adherence. One potential model that has demonstrated some success in people with first-episode psychosis includes *the addition of a physical therapist as part of regular clinical care along with availability of on-site gym facilities* (Curtis et al., 2016). Additionally, providing supervised gym classes to people with psychosis in their community has also shown promise in increasing exercise engagement (Firth et al., 2018a); in contrast, unsupervised exercise sessions, even within the context of clinical assistance and access to facilities, have been found to be less effective for increasing physical activity (Archie et al., 2003).

Finally, one recent meta-review investigating the effects of physical activity on serious mental illness (SMI) (Stubbs et al., 2018) found similar results within people with schizophrenia. Their review included eight RCTs (N = 659), which demonstrated *a reduction of total psychiatric symptoms when interventions used at least 90 minutes of moderate-to-vigorous physical activity per week*. Ten studies (N = 285) focusing on cognition discovered that the greatest cognitive improvements were found *when interventions were delivered by exercise professionals* (e.g., physiotherapists, exercise scientists). Given their findings, Stubbs and colleagues (2018) proposed a series of practical, clinical recommendations for incorporating physical exercise as an adjuvant for treatment in people with schizophrenia:

1. Engagement in moderate-to-vigorous AE 150 minutes per week at a frequency of two to three sessions per week. There is limited data for ST programs, and more research is necessary to adequately compare the specific benefits of various forms of physical activity to each other.
2. Baseline levels of physical activity should be screened, given significantly low physical activity levels evidenced in this population. For example, the SIMPAQ (Rosebaum & Ward, 2016) screens physical activity and sedentary behavior in people with SMI. Depending on screener results, increasing physical activity may be advised.
3. Additionally, individuals with schizophrenia and related disorders contemplating physical exercise may benefit from consulting with a physician prior to initiating any exercise activities.

4. As mentioned above, more research is needed to develop specific recommendations for implementing exercise interventions in the treatment of schizophrenia spectrum disorders. Based on the available literature, however, a few additional recommendations are as follows: Physical activity screener results can be used to guide and tailor physical activity interventions as an adjunct to treatment for individuals with schizophrenia spectrum disorders. Based on the screener results, for example, it may be necessary to start an individual at lower intensity exercise if this individual mainly engages in sedentary behavior and gradually increase exercise intensity as this person's fitness level increases.
5. Given that the addition of a physical therapist/supervised exercise appears to increase adherence rates (Curtis et al., 2016; Firth et al., 2018a), it is recommended that an exercise professional (e.g., physical therapist, physical trainer) be present to guide the exercise sessions for individuals with schizophrenia spectrum disorders.

In summary, exercise has been reliably shown to improve physical and mental health in people with schizophrenia spectrum disorders. Ideally, exercise should be used in addition to other treatments including pharmacological and psychosocial therapies. Importantly, exercise participation must be viewed as integral to therapy, in an effort to enhance patient motivation. Sufficient resources are necessary to ensure that patients receive appropriate supervision and ongoing psychological and social support in order to receive an adequate dose of exercise. Notably, a physical therapist should be included as part of the clinical team and considered as essential to the patient's therapeutic care.

References

Acil, A. A., Dogan, S., & Dogan, O. (2008). The effects of physical exercises to mental state and quality of life in patients with schizophrenia. *Journal of Psychiatric and Mental Health Nursing*, *15*(10), 808–815.

American College of Sports Medicine. (2013). *ACSM's Guidelines for Exercise Testing and Prescription*. Lippincott Williams & Wilkins.

Archie, Suzanne, et al. (2003). Pilot study: Access to fitness facility and exercise levels in olanzapine treated patients. *The Canadian Journal of Psychiatry* *48*(9), 628–632.

Armstrong HF, Bartels MN, Paslavski O, Cain D, Shoval HA, Ballon JS, Khan S, Sloan RP, & Kimhy D (2016). The impact of aerobic exercise training on cardiopulmonary functioning in individuals with schizophrenia. *Schizophrenia Research*, *173*(1–2), 116–117.

Beebe, L. H., Tian, L., Morris, N., Goodwin, A., Allen, S. S., & Kuldau, J. (2005). Effects of exercise on mental and physical health parameters of persons with schizophrenia. *Issues in Mental Health Nursing*, *26*(6), 661–676.

Behere, R. V., Arasappa, R., Jagannathan, A., Varambally, S., Venkatasubramanian, G., Thirthalli, J., Subbakrishna, D. K., Nagendra, H. R., & Gangadhar, B. N. (2011). Effect of yoga therapy on facial emotion recognition deficits, symptoms and functioning in patients with schizophrenia. *Acta Psychiatrica Scandinavica*, *123*(2), 147–153.

Berk, M., Williams, L. J., Jacka, F. N., O'Neil, A., Pasco, J. A., Moylan, S., Allen, N. B., Stuart, A. L., Hayley, A. C., Byrne, M. L., & Maes, M. (2013). So depression is an inflammatory disease, but where does the inflammation come from? *BMC Medicine, 11*(1), 1–16.

Bhatia, T., Mazumdar, S., Wood, J., He, F., Gur, R. E., Gur, R. C., Nimgaonkar, V. L., & Deshpande, S. N. (2017). A randomised controlled trial of adjunctive yoga and adjunctive physical exercise training for cognitive dysfunction in schizophrenia. *Acta Neuropsychiatrica, 29*(2), 102–114.

Binford, S. S., Hubbard, E. M., Flowers, E., Miller, B. L., & Leutwyler, H. (2018). Serum BDNF is positively associated with negative symptoms in older adults with schizophrenia. *Biological Research for Nursing, 20*(1), 63–69.

Burdette, J. H., Laurienti, P. J., Espeland, M. A., Morgan, A. R., Telesford, Q., Vechlekar, C. D., Hayasaka, S., Jennings, J. M., Katula, J. A., Kraft, R. A. & Rejeski, W. J. (2010). Using network science to evaluate exercise-associated brain changes in older adults. *Frontiers in Aging Neuroscience, 2*, 23.

Caspersen, C. J., Powell, K. E., & Christenson, G. M. (1985). Physical activity, exercise, and physical fitness: Definitions and distinctions for health-related research. *Public Health Reports, 100*(2), 126.

Cassilhas, R. C., Antunes, H. K. M., Tufik, S., & De Mello, M. T. (2010). Mood, anxiety, and serum IGF-1 in elderly men given 24 weeks of high resistance exercise. *Perceptual and Motor Skills, 110*(1), 265–276.

Curcic, D., Stojmenovic, T., Djukic-Dejanovic, S., Dikic, N., Vesic-Vukasinovic, M., Radivojevic, N., Andjelkovic, M., Borovcanin, M. & Djokic, G. (2017). Positive impact of prescribed physical activity on symptoms of schizophrenia: Randomized clinical trial. *Psychiatria Danubina, 29*(4), 459–465.

Curtis, J., Watkins, A., Rosenbaum, S., Teasdale, S., Kalucy, M., Samaras, K., & Ward, P. B. (2016). Evaluating an individualized lifestyle and life skills intervention to prevent antipsychotic-induced weight gain in first-episode psychosis. *Early Intervention in Psychiatry, 10*(3), 267–276.

Damme, K. S., Gupta, T., Ristanovic, I., Kimhy, D., Bryan, A. D., & Mittal, V. A. (2022). Exercise intervention in individuals at clinical high risk for psychosis: Benefits to fitness, symptoms, hippocampal volumes, and functional connectivity. *Schizophrenia Bulletin, 48*(6), 1394–1405.

De Hert, M., Dekker, J. M., Wood, D., Kahl, K. G., Holt, R. I. G., & Möller, H. J. (2009). Cardiovascular disease and diabetes in people with severe mental illness: Position statement from the European Psychiatric Association (EPA), supported by the European Association for the Study of Diabetes (EASD) and the European Society of Cardiology (ESC). *European Psychiatry, 24*(6), 412–424.

Duan, X., He, C., Ou, J., Wang, R., Xiao, J., Li, L., Wu, R., Zhang, Y., Zhao, J., & Chen, H. (2021). Reduced hippocampal volume and its relationship with verbal memory and negative symptoms in treatment-naive first-episode adolescent-onset schizophrenia. *Schizophrenia Bulletin, 47*(1), 64–74.

Duraiswamy, G., Thirthalli, J., Nagendra, H. R., & Gangadhar, B. N. (2007). Yoga therapy as an add-on treatment in the management of patients with schizophrenia–a randomized controlled trial. *Acta Psychiatrica Scandinavica, 16*(3), 226–232.

Elis, O., Caponigro, J. M., & Kring, A. M. (2013). Psychosocial treatments for negative symptoms in schizophrenia: Current practices and future directions. *Clinical Psychology Review, 33*(8), 914–928.

Firth, J., Carney, R., Elliott, R., French, P., Parker, S., McIntyre, R., McPhee, J., & Yung, A. R. (2018a). Exercise as an intervention for first-episode psychosis: A feasibility study. *Early Intervention in Psychiatry, 12*(3), 307–315.

Firth, J., Stubbs, B., Vancampfort, D., Schuch, F., Lagopoulos, J., Rosenbaum, S., & Ward, P. B. (2018b). Effect of aerobic exercise on hippocampal volume in humans: A systematic review and meta-analysis. *Neuroimage, 166*, 230–238.

Firth, J., Rosenbaum, S., Stubbs, B., Gorczynski, P., Yung, A. R., & Vancampfort, D. (2016). Motivating factors and barriers towards exercise in severe mental illness: A systematic review and meta-analysis. *Psychological Medicine, 46*(14), 2869–2881.

Firth, J., Cotter, J., Elliott, R., French, P., & Yung, A. R. (2015). A systematic review and meta-analysis of exercise interventions in schizophrenia patients. *Psychological Medicine, 45*(7), 1343–1361.

Fitzsimmons, J., Kubicki, M., & Shenton, M. E. (2013). Review of functional and anatomical brain connectivity findings in schizophrenia. *Current Opinion in Psychiatry, 26*(2), 172–187.

Foussias, G., & Remington, G. (2010). Negative symptoms in schizophrenia: Avolition and Occam's razor. *Schizophrenia Bulletin, 36*(2), 359–369.

Fusar-Poli, P., Papanastasiou, E., Stahl, D., Rocchetti, M., Carpenter, W., Shergill, S., & McGuire, P. (2015). Treatments of negative symptoms in schizophrenia: Meta-analysis of 168 randomized placebo-controlled trials. *Schizophrenia Bulletin, 41*(4), 892–899.

Garber, C. E., Blissmer, B., Deschenes, M. R., Franklin, B. A., Lamonte, M. J., Lee, I. M., Niemen, D. C., & Swain, D. P. (2011). American College of Sports Medicine position stand. Quantity and quality of exercise for developing and maintaining cardiorespiratory, musculoskeletal, and neuromotor fitness in apparently healthy adults: Guidance for prescribing exercise. *Medicine and Science in Sports and Exercise, 43*(7), 1334 1359.

Goldsmith, D. R., & Rapaport, M. H. (2020). Inflammation and negative symptoms of schizophrenia: Implications for reward processing and motivational deficits. *Frontiers in Psychiatry, 11*, 46.

Gomez-Pinilla, F., Vaynman, S., & Ying, Z. (2008). Brain-derived neurotrophic factor functions as a metabotrophin to mediate the effects of exercise on cognition. *European Journal of Neuroscience, 28*(11), 2278–2287.

Graham, I., Atar, D., Borch-Johnsen, K., Boysen, G., Burell, G., Cifkova, R., Dallongeville, J., Backer, G. D., Ebrahim, S., Gjelsvik, B., Herrmann-Lingen, C., Hoes, A., Humphries, S., Knapton, M., Perk, J., Priori, S. G., Pyorala, K., Reiner, Z., Ruilope, L., Sans-Menendez, S., Zampelas, A. (2007). European guidelines on cardiovascular disease prevention in clinical practice: Executive summary: Fourth Joint Task Force of the European Society of Cardiology and Other Societies on Cardiovascular Disease Prevention in Clinical Practice (Constituted by representatives of nine societies and by invited experts). *European Heart Journal, 28*(19), 2375–2414.

Green, M. J., Matheson, S. L., Shepherd, A., Weickert, C. S., & Carr, V. J. (2011). Brain-derived neurotrophic factor levels in schizophrenia: A systematic review with meta-analysis. *Molecular Psychiatry, 16*(9), 960–972.

Heggelund, J., Nilsberg, G. E., Hoff, J., Morken, G., & Helgerud, J. (2011). Effects of high aerobic intensity training in patients with schizophrenia A controlled trial. *Nordic Journal of Psychiatry, 65*(4), 269–275.

Ho, R. T., Fong, T. C., Wan, A. H., Au-Yeung, F. S., Wong, C. P., Ng, W. Y., Cheung, I., Lo, P., Ng, S. M., Chan, C. & Chen, E. Y. (2016). A randomized controlled trial on the psychophysiological effects of physical exercise and Tai-chi in patients with chronic schizophrenia. *Schizophrenia Research, 171*(1–3), 42–49.

Ho, R. T., Au Yeung, F. S., Lo, P. H., Law, K. Y., Wong, K. O., Cheung, I. K., & Ng, S. M. (2012). Tai-chi for residential patients with schizophrenia on movement coordination, negative symptoms, and functioning: A pilot randomized controlled trial. *Evidence-Based Complementary and Alternative Medicine, 2012*, 923925.

Horan, W. P., Kring, A. M., Gur, R. E., Reise, S. P., & Blanchard, J. J. (2011). Development and psychometric validation of the Clinical Assessment Interview for Negative Symptoms (CAINS). *Schizophrenia Research, 132*(2–3), 140–145.

Ikai, S., Uchida, H., Mizuno, Y., Tani, H., Nagaoka, M., Tsunoda, K., Mimura, M., & Suzuki, T. (2017). Effects of chair yoga therapy on physical fitness in patients with psychiatric disorders: A 12-week single-blind randomized controlled trial. *Journal of Psychiatric Research, 94*, 194–201.

Ikai, S., Suzuki, T., Uchida, H., Saruta, J., Tsukinoki, K., Fujii, Y., & Mimura, M., (2014). Effects of weekly one-hour Hatha yoga therapy on resilience and stress levels in patients with schizophrenia-spectrum disorders: An eight-week randomized controlled trial. *The Journal of Alternative and Complementary Medicine, 20*(11), 823–830.

Ikai, S., Uchida, H., Suzuki, T., Tsunoda, K., Mimura, M., & Fujii, Y. (2013). Effects of yoga therapy on postural stability in patients with schizophrenia-spectrum disorders: A single-blind randomized controlled trial. *Journal of Psychiatric Research, 47*(11), 1744–1750.

Isuru, L. L. A., Dahanayake, D. M. A., de Alwis, A., Weerasinghe, A., Hewage, S. N., Ranasinghe, C. K. (2015). Impact of dance, drama, yoga and music therapy workshops on symptom reduction in patients with schizophrenia: A randomized controlled study. *South Asian Journal of Psychiatry, 3*(2), 1–7.

Jayaram, N., Varambally, S., Behere, R. V., Venkatasubramanian, G., Arasappa, R., Christopher, R., & Gangadhar, B. N. (2013). Effect of yoga therapy on plasma oxytocin and facial emotion recognition deficits in patients of schizophrenia. *Indian Journal of Psychiatry, 55*(Suppl 3), S409.

Jurca, R. A. D. I. M., Lamonte, M. J., Barlow, C. E., Kampert, J. B., Church, T. S., & Blair, S. N. (2005). Association of muscular strength with incidence of metabolic syndrome in men. *Medicine and Science in Sports and Exercise, 37*(11), 1849.

Kaltsatou, A., Kouidi, E., Fountoulakis, K., Sipka, C., Theochari, V., Kandylis, D., & Deligiannis, A. (2015). Effects of exercise training with traditional dancing on functional capacity and quality of life in patients with schizophrenia: A randomized controlled study. *Clinical Rehabilitation, 29*(9), 882–891.

Kang, R., Wu, Y., Li, Z., Jiang, J., Gao, Q., Yu, Y., Gao, K., Yan, Y., & He, Y. (2016). Effect of community-based social skills training and tai-chi exercise on outcomes in patients with chronic schizophrenia: A randomized, one-year study. *Psychopathology, 49*(5), 345–355.

Keller-Varady, K., Varady, P. A., Roeh, A., Schmitt, A., Falkai, P., Hasan, A., & Malchow, B. (2018). A systematic review of trials investigating strength training in schizophrenia spectrum disorders. *Schizophrenia Research, 192*, 64–68.

Kern, R. S., Reddy, L. F., Cohen, A. N., Young, A. S., & Green, M. F. (2020). Effects of aerobic exercise on cardiorespiratory fitness and social functioning in veterans 40 to 65 years old with schizophrenia. *Psychiatry Research, 291*, 113258.

Khan, K. M., Thompson, A. M., Blair, S. N., Sallis, J. F., Powell, K. E., Bull, F. C., & Bauman, A. E. (2012). Sport and exercise as contributors to the health of nations. *The Lancet, 380*(9836), 59–64.

Khonsari, N. M., Badrfam, R., Mohammdi, M. R., Rastad, H., Etemadi, F., Vafaei, Z., & Zandifar, A. (2021). Effect of aerobic exercise as adjunct therapy on the improvement of negative symptoms and cognitive impairment in patients with schizophrenia: A randomized, case-control clinical trial. *Journal of Psychosocial Nursing and Mental Health Services, 60*(5), 38–43.

Kim, H. J., Song, B. K., So, B., Lee, O., Song, W., & Kim, Y. (2014). Increase of circulating BDNF levels and its relation to improvement of physical fitness following 12 weeks of combined exercise in chronic patients with schizophrenia: A pilot study. *Psychiatry Research, 220*(3), 792–796.

Kimhy D, Tay C, Vakhrusheva J, Beck-Felts K, Ospina LH, Ifrah C, Parvaz M, Gross JJ, & Bartels MN. (2021). Enhancement of aerobic fitness improves social functioning in individuals with schizophrenia. *European Archives of Psychiatry and Clinical Neuroscience, 271*(2), 367–376.

Kimhy D, Lauriola V, Bartels MN, Armstrong HF, Vakhrusheva J, Ballon JS, & Sloan RP. (2016). Aerobic exercise for cognitive deficits in schizophrenia—The impact of frequency, duration, and fidelity with target training intensity. *Schizophrenia Research 172*(1–3), 213–215.

Kimhy, D., Vakhrusheva, J., Bartels, M. N., Armstrong, H. F., Ballon, J. S., Khan, S., Chang, R. W., Hansen, M. C., Ayanruoh, L., Lister, A., Castrén, E., Smith, E. E. & Sloan, R. P. (2015). The impact of aerobic exercise on brain-derived neurotrophic factor and neurocognition in individuals with schizophrenia: A single-blind, randomized clinical trial. *Schizophrenia Bulletin, 41*(4), 859–868.

Kimhy D, Vakhrusheva J, Bartels MN, Armstrong HF, Ballon JS, Khan S, Chang RW, Hansen MC, Ayanruoh L, Smith EE, & Sloan RP (2014). Aerobic fitness and body mass index in individuals with schizophrenia: Implications for neurocognition and daily functioning. *Psychiatry Research, 220*(3), 784–791.

Kirkpatrick, B., Fenton, W. S., Carpenter, W. T., & Marder, S. R. (2006). The NIMH-MATRICS consensus statement on negative symptoms. *Schizophrenia Bulletin, 32*(2), 214–219.

Kogan, S., Ospina, L. H., Mittal, V. A., & Kimhy, D. (2020). The impact of inflammation on neurocognition and risk for psychosis: A critical review. *European Archives of Psychiatry and Clinical Neuroscience, 270*(7), 793–802.

Kraepelin, E. (1919). *Dementia praecox and paraphrenia*. Livingstone.

Kuo, F. C., Lee, C. H., Hsieh, C. H., Kuo, P., Chen, Y. C., & Hung, Y. J. (2013). Lifestyle modification and behavior therapy effectively reduce body weight and increase serum level of brain-derived neurotrophic factor in obese non-diabetic patients with schizophrenia. *Psychiatry Research, 209*(2), 150–154.

Kurebayashi, Y., Mori, K., & Otaki, J. (2021). Effects of mild-intensity physical exercise on neurocognition in inpatients with schizophrenia: A pilot randomized controlled trial. *Perspectives in Psychiatric Care, 58*(3), 1037–1047.

La Forge, R. (2016). Mind-body (mindful) exercise in practice. *ACSM's Health & Fitness Journal, 20*(4), 6–8.

Lavratti, C., Dorneles, G., Pochmann, D., Peres, A., Bard, A., de Lima Schipper, L., Lago, P. D., Wagner, L. C. & Elsner, V. R. (2017). Exercise-induced modulation of histone H4 acetylation status and cytokines levels in patients with schizophrenia. *Physiology & Behavior, 168*, 84–90.

Leucht, S., Burkard, T., Henderson, J., Maj, M., & Sartorius, N. (2007). Physical illness and schizophrenia: A review of the literature. *Acta Psychiatrica Scandinavica, 116*(5), 317–333.

Lin, J., Chan, S. K., Lee, E. H., Chang, W. C., Tse, M., Su, W. W., Sham, P., Hui, C., Joe, G., Chan, C., Khong, P. L., So, K. F., Honer, W. G., & Chen, E. Y. (2015). Aerobic exercise and yoga improve neurocognitive function in women with early psychosis. *NPJ Schizophrenia, 1*(1), 1–7.

Loh, S. Y., Abdullah, A., Bakar, A. K. A., Thambu, M., & Jaafar, N. R. N. (2016). Structured walking and chronic institutionalized schizophrenia inmates: A pilot RCT study on quality of life. *Global Journal of Health Science, 8*(1), 238.

Malchow, B., Keeser, D., Keller, K., Hasan, A., Rauchmann, B. S., Kimura, H., Schneider-Axmann, T., Dechent, P., Gruber, O., Ertl-Wagner, B., Honer, W. G., Hillmer-Vogel, U., Schmitt, A., Wobrock, T., Niklas, A., & Falkai, P. (2016). Effects of endurance training on brain structures in chronic schizophrenia patients and healthy controls. *Schizophrenia Research, 173*(3), 182–191.

Manjunath, R. B., Varambally, S., Thirthalli, J., Basavaraddi, I. V., & Gangadhar, B. N. (2013). Efficacy of yoga as an add-on treatment for in-patients with functional psychotic disorder. *Indian Journal of Psychiatry, 55*(Suppl 3), S374.

Maurus, I., Hasan, A., Röh, A., Takahashi, S., Rauchmann, B., Keeser, D., Malchow, B., Schmitt, A., & Falkai, P. (2019). Neurobiological effects of aerobic exercise, with a focus on patients with schizophrenia. *European Archives of Psychiatry and Clinical Neuroscience, 269*(5), 499–515.

Mayer, E. A., & Saper, C. B. (Eds.). (2000). *The biological basis for mind body interactions.* Elsevier.

Milev, P., Ho, B. C., Arndt, S., & Andreasen, N. C. (2005). Predictive values of neurocognition and negative symptoms on functional outcome in schizophrenia: A longitudinal first-episode study with 7-year follow-up. *American Journal of Psychiatry, 162*(3), 495–506.

Mittal VA, Firth J, & Kimhy D. (2020). Combating the dangers of sedentary activity on child and adolescent mental health during the time of COVID-19. *Journal of the American Academy of Child and Adolescent Psychiatry, 59*(11), 1197–1198.

Morgan, W. P., & Goldston, S. E. (2013). *Exercise and mental health.* Taylor & Francis.

Niitsu, T., Shirayama, Y., Matsuzawa, D., Hasegawa, T., Kanahara, N., Hashimoto, T., Shiraishi, T., Shiina, A., Fukami, G., Fujisaki, M., Watanabe, M., Nakazato, M., Asano, M., Kimura, S., Hashimoto, K., & Iyo, M. (2011). Associations of serum brain-derived neurotrophic factor with cognitive impairments and negative symptoms in schizophrenia. *Progress in Neuro-Psychopharmacology and Biological Psychiatry, 35*(8), 1836–1840.

Nyboe, L., Moeller, M. K., Vestergaard, C. H., Lund, H., & Videbech, P. (2016). Physical activity and anomalous bodily experiences in patients with first-episode schizophrenia. *Nordic Journal of Psychiatry, 70*(7), 514–520.

Oertel-Knöchel, V., Mehler, P., Thiel, C., Steinbrecher, K., Malchow, B., Tesky, V., Ademmer, K., Prvulovic, D., Banzer, W., Zopf, Y., Schmitt, A., & Hänsel, F. (2014). Effects of aerobic exercise on cognitive performance and individual psychopathology in depressive and schizophrenia patients. *European Archives of Psychiatry and Clinical Neuroscience, 264*(7), 589–604.

Ospina, L. H., Beck-Felts, K., Ifrah, C., Shagalow, S., Lister, A., Russo, S. J., Gross, J. J., & Kimhy, D. (2021). Relationships among inflammation, social cognition, and social functioning in schizophrenia. *Schizophrenia Research*, 248, 366-367.

Ospina, L. H., Wall, M., Jarskog, L. F., Ballon, J. S., McEvoy, J., Bartels, M. N., Buchsbaum, R., Sloan, R. P., Stroup, T. S., & Kimhy, D. (2019a). Improving cognition via exercise (ICE): Study protocol for a multi-site, parallel-group, single-blind, randomized clinical trial examining the efficacy of aerobic exercise to improve neurocognition, daily functioning, and biomarkers of cognitive change in individuals with schizophrenia. *Journal of Psychiatry and Brain Science*, 4:e190020. doi: 10.20900/jpbs.20190020. Epub 2019 Dec 30. PMID: 31938726; PMCID: PMC6958554.

Ospina L. H., Ballon J. B., & Kimhy D. (2019b). *Role of aerobic exercise in the treatment of early psychosis in intervening early in psychosis: A team approach.* American Psychiatric Publishing.

Paikkatt, B., Singh, A. R., Singh, P. K., Jahan, M., & Ranjan, J. K. (2015). Efficacy of yoga therapy for the management of psychopathology of patients having chronic schizophrenia. *Indian Journal of Psychiatry, 57*(4), 355.

Pajonk, F. G., Wobrock, T., Gruber, O., Scherk, H., Berner, D., Kaizl, I., Kierer, A., Müller, S., Oest, M., Meyer, T., Backens, M., Schneider-Axmann, T., Thornton, A. E., Honer, W. G., & Falkai, P. (2010). Hippocampal plasticity in response to exercise in schizophrenia. *Archives of General Psychiatry, 67*(2), 133–143.

Pearsall, R., Smith, D. J., Pelosi, A., & Geddes, J. (2014). Exercise therapy in adults with serious mental illness: A systematic review and meta-analysis. *BMC psychiatry, 14*(1), 1–17.

Perraton, L. G., Kumar, S., & Machotka, Z. (2010). Exercise parameters in the treatment of clinical depression: A systematic review of randomized controlled trials. *Journal of Evaluation in Clinical Practice, 16*(3), 597–604.

Potvin, S., Stip, E., Sepehry, A. A., Gendron, A., Bah, R., & Kouassi, E. (2008). Inflammatory cytokine alterations in schizophrenia: A systematic quantitative review. *Biological Psychiatry, 63*(8), 801–808.

Rabinowitz, J., Levine, S. Z., Garibaldi, G., Bugarski-Kirola, D., Berardo, C. G., & Kapur, S. (2012). Negative symptoms have greater impact on functioning than positive symptoms in schizophrenia: Analysis of CATIE data. *Schizophrenia Research, 137*(1–3), 147–150.

Rantanen, T., Harris, T., Leveille, S. G., Visser, M., Foley, D., Masaki, K., & Guralnik, J. M. (2000). Muscle strength and body mass index as long-term predictors of mortality in initially healthy men. *The Journals of Gerontology Series A: Biological Sciences and Medical Sciences*, *55*(3), M168–M173.

Reif, A., Fritzen, S., Finger, M., Strobel, A., Lauer, M., Schmitt, A., & Lesch, K. P. (2006). Neural stem cell proliferation is decreased in schizophrenia, but not in depression. *Molecular Psychiatry*, *11*(5), 514–522.

Rosenbaum, S., & Ward, P. B. (2016). The simple physical activity questionnaire. *The Lancet Psychiatry*, *3*(1), e1.

Sabe, M., Sentissi, O., & Kaiser, S. (2019). Meditation-based mind-body therapies for negative symptoms of schizophrenia: Systematic review of randomized controlled trials and meta-analysis. *Schizophrenia research*, *212*, 15–25.

Sabe, M., Kaiser, S., & Sentissi, O. (2020). Physical exercise for negative symptoms of schizophrenia: Systematic review of randomized controlled trials and meta-analysis. *General Hospital Psychiatry*, *62*, 13–20.

Scheewe, T. W., Backx, F. J. G., Takken, T., Jörg, F., Van Strater, A. C. P., Kroes, A. 1., Kahn, R. S., & Cahn, W. (2013a). Exercise therapy improves mental and physical health in schizophrenia: A randomised controlled trial. *Acta Psychiatrica Scandinavica*, *127*(6), 464–473.

Scheewe, T. W., van Haren, N. E., Sarkisyan, G., Schnack, H. G., Brouwer, R. M., de Glint, M., Hulshoff Pol, H. E., Backx, F., Kahn, R. S., & Cahn, W. (2013b). Exercise therapy, cardiorespiratory fitness and their effect on brain volumes: A randomised controlled trial in patients with schizophrenia and healthy controls. *European Neuropsychopharmacology*, *23*(7), 675–685.

Şenormancı, G., Korkmaz, N., Şenormancı, Ö., Uğur, S., Topsaç, M., & Gültekin, O. (2021). Effects of exercise on resilience, insight and functionality in patients with chronic schizophrenia in a psychiatric nursing home setting: A randomized controlled trial. *Issues in Mental Health Nursing*, *42*(7), 690–698.

Shimada, T., Ito, S., Makabe, A., Yamanushi, A., Takenaka, A., & Kobayashi, M. (2019). Aerobic exercise and cognitive functioning in schizophrenia: A pilot randomized controlled trial. *Psychiatry Research*, *282*, 112638.

Sicras-Mainar, A., Maurino, J., Ruiz-Beato, E., & Navarro-Artieda, R. (2015). Prevalence of metabolic syndrome according to the presence of negative symptoms in patients with schizophrenia. *Neuropsychiatric Disease and Treatment*, *11*, 51.

Silva, A. E., B., Cassilhas, R. C., Attux, C., Cordeiro, Q., Gadelha, A. L., Telles, B. A., Bressan, R. A., Ferreira, F. N., Rodstein, P. H., Daltio, C. S., Tufik, S., & Mello, M. T. D. (2015). A 20 week program of resistance or concurrent exercise improves symptoms of schizophrenia: Results of a blind, randomized controlled trial. *Brazilian Journal of Psychiatry*, *37*, 271–279.

Soundy, A., Roskell, C., Stubbs, B., Probst, M., & Vancampfort, D. (2015). Investigating the benefits of sport participation for individuals with schizophrenia: A systematic review. *Psychiatria Danubina*, *27*(1), 0–13.

Steen, R. G., Mull, C., Mcclure, R., Hamer, R. M., & Lieberman, J. A. (2006). Brain volume in first-episode schizophrenia: Systematic review and meta-analysis of magnetic resonance imaging studies. *The British Journal of Psychiatry*, *188*(6), 510–518.

Strauss, G. P., Horan, W. P., Kirkpatrick, B., Fischer, B. A., Keller, W. R., Miski, P., Buchanan, R. W., Green, M. F., & Carpenter Jr, W. T. (2013). Deconstructing negative symptoms of schizophrenia: Avolition-apathy and diminished expression clusters predict clinical presentation and functional outcome. *Journal of Psychiatric Research*, *47*(6), 783–790.

Stubbs, B., Vancampfort, D., Hallgren, M., Firth, J., Veronese, N., Solmi, M., Brand, S., Cordes, J., Malchow, B., Gerber, M., Schmitt, A., Correll, C. U., De Hert, M., Gaughran, F., Schneider, F., Kinnafick, F., Falkai, P., Möller, H., & Kahl, K. G. (2018). EPA guidance on physical activity as a treatment for severe mental illness: A meta-review of the evidence and Position Statement from the European Psychiatric Association (EPA), supported by the International Organization of Physical Therapists in Mental Health (IOPTMH). *European Psychiatry, 54,* 124–144.

Stubbs, B., Williams, J., Gaughran, F., & Craig, T. (2016). How sedentary are people with psychosis? A systematic review and meta-analysis. *Schizophrenia Research, 171*(1–3), 103–109.

Su, C. Y., Wang, P. W., Lin, Y. J., Tang, T. C., Liu, M. F., & Chen, M. D. (2016). The effects of aerobic exercise on cognition in schizophrenia: A 3-month follow-up study. *Psychiatry Research, 244,* 394–402.

Svatkova, A., Mandl, R. C., Scheewe, T. W., Cahn, W., Kahn, R. S., & Hulshoff Pol, H. E. (2015). Physical exercise keeps the brain connected: Biking increases white matter integrity in patients with schizophrenia and healthy controls. *Schizophrenia Bulletin, 41*(4), 869–878.

Takahashi, H., Sassa, T., Shibuya, T., Kato, M., Koeda, M., Murai, T., Matsuura, M., Asai, K., Suhara, T., & Okubo, Y. (2012). Effects of sports participation on psychiatric symptoms and brain activations during sports observation in schizophrenia. *Translational Psychiatry, 2*(3), e96–e96.

Timmis, A., Townsend, N., Gale, C. P., Torbica, A., Lettino, M., Petersen, S. E., Mossiaos, E. A., Maggioni, A. P., Kazakiewicz, D., May, H. T., De Smedt, D., Flather, M., Zuhlke, L., Beltrame, J. F., Huculeci, R., Tavazzi, L., Hindricks, G., Bax, J., Casadei, B., Achenbach, S. ... Vardas, P. (2020). European Society of Cardiology: Cardiovascular disease statistics 2019. *European Heart Journal, 41*(1), 12–85.

Trépanier, M. O., Hopperton, K. E., Mizrahi, R., Mechawar, N., & Bazinet, R. P. (2016). Postmortem evidence of cerebral inflammation in schizophrenia: A systematic review. *Molecular Psychiatry, 21*(8), 1009–1026.

Vakhrusheva, J., Marino, B., Stroup, T. S., & Kimhy, D. (2016). Aerobic exercise in people with schizophrenia: Neural and neurocognitive benefits. *Current Behavioral Neuroscience Reports, 3*(2), 165–175.

Van Praag, H. (2008). Neurogenesis and exercise: Past and future directions. *Neuromolecular Medicine, 10*(2), 128–140.

Vancampfort, D., Firth, J., Schuch, F. B., Rosenbaum, S., Mugisha, J., Hallgren, M., Probst, M., Ward, P. B., Gaughran, F., De Hert, M., Carvalho, A. F., & Stubbs, B. (2017). Sedentary behavior and physical activity levels in people with schizophrenia, bipolar disorder and major depressive disorder: A global systematic review and meta-analysis. *World Psychiatry, 16*(3), 308–315.

Vancampfort, D., Vansteelandt, K., Scheewe, T., Probst, M., Knapen, J., De Herdt, A., & De Hert, M. (2012). Yoga in schizophrenia: A systematic review of randomised controlled trials. *Acta Psychiatrica Scandinavica, 126*(1), 12–20.

Vancampfort, D., Sweers, K., Probst, M., Mitchell, A. J., Knapen, J., & De Hert, M. (2011). Quality assessment of physical activity recommendations within clinical practice guidelines for the prevention and treatment of cardio-metabolic risk factors in people with schizophrenia. *Community Mental Health Journal, 47*(6), 703–710.

Varambally, S., Gangadhar, B. N., Thirthalli, J., Jagannathan, A., Kumar, S., Venkatasubramanian, G., Muralidhar, D., Subbakrishna, D. K., & Nagendra, H. R. (2012). Therapeutic efficacy of add-on yogasana intervention in stabilized outpatient schizophrenia: Randomized controlled comparison with exercise and waitlist. *Indian Journal of Psychiatry, 54*(3), 227.

Visceglia, E., & Lewis, S. (2011). Yoga therapy as an adjunctive treatment for schizophrenia: A randomized, controlled pilot study. *The Journal of Alternative and Complementary Medicine, 17*(7), 601–607.

Vogel, J. S., van der Gaag, M., Slofstra, C., Knegtering, H., Bruins, J., & Castelein, S. (2019). The effect of mind-body and aerobic exercise on negative symptoms in schizophrenia: A meta-analysis. *Psychiatry Research, 279,* 295–305.

Voss, M. W., Heo, S., Prakash, R. S., Erickson, K. I., Alves, H., Chaddock, L., Szabo, A. N., Mailey, E. L., Wójcicki, T. R., White, S. M., Gothe, N., McAuley, E., Sutton, B. P., & Kramer, A. F. (2013). The influence of aerobic fitness on cerebral white matter integrity and cognitive function in older adults: Results of a one-year exercise intervention. *Human Brain Mapping, 34*(11), 2972–2985.

Walker, E. R., McGee, R. E., & Druss, B. G. (2015). Mortality in mental disorders and global disease burden implications: A systematic review and meta-analysis. *JAMA Psychiatry, 72*(4), 334–341.

Wang, P. W., Lin, H. C., Su, C. Y., Chen, M. D., Lin, K. C., Ko, C. H., & Yen, C. F. (2018). Effect of aerobic exercise on improving symptoms of individuals with schizophrenia: A single blinded randomized control study. *Frontiers in Psychiatry, 9*, 167.

Wei, G. X., Yang, L., Imm, K., Loprinzi, P. D., Smith, L., Zhang, X., & Yu, Q. (2020). Effects of mind-body exercises on schizophrenia: A systematic review with meta-analysis. *Frontiers in Psychiatry, 819.*

Yung, A. R., & Firth, J. (2017). How should physical exercise be used in schizophrenia treatment? *Expert Review of Neurotherapeutics, 17*(3), 213–214.

Zheng, W., Li, Q., Lin, J., Xiang, Y., Guo, T., Chen, Q., Cai, D., & Xiang, Y. (2016). Tai chi for schizophrenia: A systematic review. *Shanghai Archives of Psychiatry, 28*(4), 185–194.

15
Use of Digital and Mobile Technologies in the Treatment of Negative Symptoms

Lauren Luther, Ruth L. Firmin, and Benjamin Buck

Clinical pearls

- Harnessing digital technologies to target negative symptoms outside of the clinic and in daily life presents a promising approach for treating negative symptoms.
- These approaches can also help bolster clinic-based care by supporting the translation of techniques learned in the clinic into daily life as well as provide real-time personalized treatment as negative symptom exacerbations may occur in daily life.
- Studies have shown that delivering interventions via mobile phones either through text-messages or smartphone apps is feasible and acceptable to those with schizophrenia and can successfully improve negative symptoms.
- Current mobile health interventions target negative symptoms using elements of Cognitive Behavioral Therapy and Behavioral Activation, while others have a more explicit focus on targeting components of reward processing (e.g., reward learning and value representation) and anticipatory pleasure (e.g., emotion maintenance) to improve negative symptoms.
- Although widespread implementation and testing of these interventions in community-based clinics are still ongoing, the field of mHealth is poised to make critical progress in treating and improving some of the most functionally disabling symptoms—negative symptoms—in schizophrenia.

1. Overview and Benefits of Digital Health Interventions

Digital interventions have been increasingly deployed in mental health treatment. These interventions generally utilize mobile phones, wireless technologies (e.g., tablets, activity tracking devices), or computers but have also recently

Lauren Luther, et al., *Use of Digital and Mobile Technologies in the Treatment of Negative Symptoms*.
In: *Psychosocial Approaches to Negative Symptoms in Psychosis*. Edited by: Tania Lincoln et al.,
Oxford University Press. DOI: 10.1093/oso/9780197676790.003.0015

expanded to using virtual or gaming technology. Mobile health (mHealth), the category of digital health interventions using mobile devices (Kay et al., 2011), has received the largest interest in recent years. This is in part because mHealth may offer unique benefits by gathering assessments or providing support in a person's daily environment in real-time. Indeed, mHealth technologies offer unique opportunities for remote monitoring via active (i.e., ecological momentary assessment (EMA; Shiffman et al., 2008) and passive (i.e., geolocation sensing, accelerometry) technologies. In turn, mobile devices can provide remotely delivered intervention content to prompt and support adaptive behaviors (Tal & Torous, 2017). Digital and mobile interventions have been found to be clinically useful for a wide range of mental and physical health outcomes, including schizophrenia, anxiety, depression, weight loss, diabetes, and smoking (Doyle-Delgado & Chamberlain, 2020; Firth et al., 2018; Firth & Torous, 2015; Patel et al., 2021; Rehman et al., 2017; Tokgöz et al., 2021).

Digital and mobile interventions are particularly well-suited to address some limitations of clinic-based care, including limited access and service availability. Indeed, among those with schizophrenia, use of in-person care is often limited, with many never receiving or engaging in treatment (Kreyenbuhl et al., 2009). Further, many who do receive care obtain it in community mental health centers, which are often unable to meet service demands (Mojtabai et al., 2009). mHealth interventions could help to reduce this service gap and lessen some of the barriers common to clinic-based care, including transportation, scheduling conflicts, and long clinic wait-lists, thereby potentially making treatment more accessible for a wider range of people. Indeed, mHealth interventions have been shown to reduce in-person service needs and treatment costs among those with schizophrenia (Ben-Zeev et al., 2019, 2021). Further, mHealth interventions have the tools to augment and support clinic-based care by supporting adherence to self-guided intervention components in daily life when they are most needed (Buck et al., 2020). Similarly, they can also provide continuity of care when in-person services may be unavailable (e.g., during the global pandemics and/or shelter in-place requirements). Thus, mHealth interventions may not only help to overcome some of the limitations of clinic-based care but also expand and provide services to a group who may need it most.

Research has shown digital interventions are becoming increasingly feasible among those with schizophrenia. Much like the general population, the rate of phone ownership continues to increase among those with schizophrenia-spectrum disorders. Recent studies have shown that between 84% to 91% of people diagnosed with schizophrenia own a mobile phone (Firth et al., 2016; Luther et al., 2022; Young et al., 2020), with as many as 68% owning a smartphone (Gay et al., 2016). Computer access is also as high as 70% (Lal et al., 2015), while fewer have tablet access (16%–38%)

(Gay et al., 2016; Lal et al., 2015). Importantly, as many as 81% report interest in receiving mental health services on their phones (Firth et al., 2016).

1.1 Potential Utility and Advantages of mHealth Interventions

Given the opportunities of mHealth and the rise in mobile device ownership, a growing number of researchers have sought to develop mobile interventions for people with schizophrenia-spectrum disorders. Early mHealth interventions often focused on sending text-message reminders or providing phone calls to support medication management or problem solving (Beebe et al., 2014; Montes et al., 2012) or involved using technologies to track and identify changes in clinical targets such as suicidality, mood, or activity that would then trigger messages with intervention content or send messages to alert clinical teams of the changes (Granholm et al., 2012; Spaniel et al., 2008). More recently, researchers have developed more comprehensive mHealth and digital interventions that involve symptom assessments, interactive messaging between users/peers, and on-demand and just-in-time adaptive intervention (JITAI) content to target outcomes such as relapse prevention or social functioning (Alvarez-Jimenez et al., 2019; Ben-Zeev et al., 2013). Other recent efforts have expanded the use of mHealth technologies to enhance therapeutic alliance and shared decision-making with treating clinicians (Vitger et al., 2019, 2022; Stefancic et al., 2022).

Few of these interventions, however, have been specifically created to target negative symptoms. Therefore, there is an underutilized potential of mHealth interventions to address negative symptoms. First, mHealth interventions could potentially help to cue, sequence, and reinforce goal-directed behavior and pleasurable activity engagement in real-time and real-place. Traditionally, targeting negative symptoms has been limited to clinic visits where goals and barriers are discussed prior to implementation. mHealth interventions, however, reach individuals in the exact context and time in which they are working toward goals or facing barriers. Second, integrating assessments and treatment in daily life could allow for highly individualized or so-called JITAIs. Such interventions could adjust in moments when a person may face greater symptom intensity or increases in underlying mechanisms (e.g., defeatist performance beliefs; Grant & Beck, 2009). Providing temporally specific in-the-moment assessment and intervention may be particularly useful given the commonly observed episodic memory difficulties experienced by people with schizophrenia (Leavitt & Goldberg, 2009) that may make it more challenging to retrospectively recall the exact time and context of experiences and/or when symptoms were elevated as well as remember techniques to reduce symptoms. JITAI mobile interventions can also help to translate therapeutic principles learned in the clinic into daily life by guiding and supporting implementation of strategies to combat negative symptoms in real-world environments. Thus, these interventions may provide a step forward in the direction of personalized and high-precision negative symptom care.

1.2 Extant Negative Symptom mHealth and Digital Interventions

Although mHealth and digital health have clear potential applications to negative symptoms, only a handful of interventions exist expressly for this purpose. Specifically, we identified only four digital negative symptom inventions, including: (1) Mobile-Assisted Cognitive Behavioral Therapy (CBT) for negative symptoms (mCBTn; Granholm et al., 2020); (2) Mobile Enhancement of Motivation in Schizophrenia (MEMS; Luther et al., 2020); (3) Motivation and Skills Support (MASS; Fulford et al., 2020, 2021); and (4) Personalized Real-Time Intervention for Motivational Enhancement (PRIME; Schlosser et al., 2016, 2018). These interventions will now be discussed in detail and are reviewed in Table 15.1. We included only interventions that have been explicitly created to target negative symptoms and are delivered primarily in a digital format.

1.3 Delivery Modality

All four identified interventions are delivered via mobile phones. MEMS is entirely delivered via text-messages, making it available to those without smartphones or reliable data plans. At the same time, however, the SMS modality requires more human support and involves fewer multimedia or interactive intervention components. Further, as smartphone ownership rates increase among people with schizophrenia, the advantage of greater accessibility for SMS interventions may become less notable.

Three app-based interventions were created by research teams. MASS was developed via the Ethica Data web platform, CBT2go (the application that mCBTn is delivered on) was developed in web-based program Mobile Online Behavioral Intervention Technology (MOBIT), and PRIME was developed in conjunction with IDEO, a global design and innovation firm. PRIME and mCBTn were created solely for the iPhone operating system, while MASS was created for Android. To deliver the interventions, studies either relied on participants using their own devices or provided a smartphone when participants did not own one.

Table 15.1 Overview of Negative Symptom Digital Interventions

Intervention name	Description of intervention	Duration	Intervention type	Treatment target	Evidence base
Mobile-Assisted CBT for negative symptoms (mCBTn; Granholm et al., 2020)	CBT2go app prompts creating daily action plan (goal step, social interaction, pleasurable activity, or homework assignment, or take day off). Motivation, pleasure, and success rated before and after action plan; discrepancies discussed at in-person group. When relevant, app suggests behavioral experiments and pleasure savoring activities and offers on-demand short and long-term steps for recovery goals. Cognitive Skills module of CBSST delivered concurrently in weekly in-person group.	24-weeks	Ecological Momentary Intervention (EMI) blended with weekly in-person group therapy	Mechanisms: Defeatist attitudes. Primary Clinical Outcome: MAP negative symptoms (CAINS-MAP)	Open single-arm trial (n = 31 with persistent negative symptoms and defeatist beliefs). Acceptability/Feasibility: high retention (87%); lower response rate (19.2–22%) to action plan prompts. Efficacy: Defeatist attitudes and interviewer-rated experiential negative symptoms significantly declined (medium to large effects).

Continued

Table 15.1 *Continued*

Intervention name	Description of intervention	Duration	Intervention type	Treatment target	Evidence base
Mobile Enhancement of Motivation in Schizophrenia (MEMS; Luther et al., 2020)	Each weekday, 3 sets of personalized, interactive texts sent to support daily progress toward larger recovery goal. Texts involve inquiry and assessments about daily goal effort, encouragement and reinforcement supporting effort expenditure and adaptive effort-cost computations, and messages connecting effort expenditure to rewards.	8-weeks	EMI	Mechanisms: effort-cost computations and reduced future reward-value representation maintenance. Primary Clinical Outcome: Avolition (CAINS)	Pilot RCT (n = 56 SZ with ≥ moderate avolition). Feasibility: High retention (92.6%) and response rate (86.1%). Efficacy: MEMS led to significantly greater improvements in interviewer-rated motivation and goal attainment versus control group who set goals at baseline; no significant group differences in targeted mechanisms.

Motivation and Skills Support (MASS; Fulford et al., 2020, 2021)	Twice every day, app delivers push notification prompts for EMA surveys about motivation and anticipated progress for daily social goal. App incorporates elements of CBT and social skills training via daily goal selected toward overall social goal, messages with custom feedback in response to reported low motivation, and on-demand videos of social skills that align with daily goal step.	8-weeks	EMI	Mechanisms: social motivation (desire, quantity of interactions, interaction appraisal. Primary Clinical Outcomes: Social functioning (QLS-IR), Negative symptoms (CAINS-MAP)	Two-site, open pilot study (n = 31 SZ). Acceptability/Feasibility: high retention (83.8%); Acceptable response rate (42.5%). Efficacy: Significant pre-post increase in social functioning and some mechanisms (e.g., interaction appraisals) but not negative symptoms or social desire mechanisms; mechanism of number of EMA-reported interactions decreased.

Continued

Table 15.1 *Continued*

Intervention name	Description of intervention	Duration	Intervention type	Treatment target	Evidence base
Personalized Real-Time Intervention for Motivational Enhancement (PRIME; Schlosser et al., 2016, 2018)	Largely on-demand app targeting work toward a long-term goal with the support of virtual community of SZ peers and masters-level CBT motivational coaches. Participants select daily challenge and share accomplishments with community and coach. Coach available for direct messaging and goal support; participants can directly message each other.	12-weeks	On-demand; Peer and clinical support	Mechanisms: Reward learning, anticipated pleasure, effort expenditure. Primary Clinical Outcomes: Avolition (MAP-SR; PANSS)	Waitlist RCT (n = 43 early onset SZ). Acceptability/Feasibility: High retention (88.4%) and post-PRIME satisfaction ratings. Weekly average of 1.5 challenges completed and 4 days of app engagement. Variability in initiation of messages to coaches and peers. Efficacy: PRIME showed significantly greater increases in anticipated pleasure, effort expenditure to increase likelihood of future interactions, and trend in reward learning from positive outcomes versus waitlist. Trend improvements in self-reported MAP-SR negative symptoms; no change in interviewer-rated overall negative symptoms.

Note. CAINS = Clinical Assessment Interview for Negative Symptoms (Kring et al., 2013); CBTSST = Cognitive Behavioral Social Skills Training; CBT = Cognitive Behavioral Therapy; MAP = motivation and pleasure; MAP-SR = Motivation and Pleasure-Self-Report (Llerena et al., 2013); PANSS = Positive and Negative Syndrome Scale (Kay et al., 1987); QLS-IR = Heinrichs Quality of Life Scale-Interpersonal Relations; RCT = randomized controlled trial; SZ = schizophrenia.

2. Intervention Designs

2.1 Development

Two of these interventions, PRIME and MASS, identify user-centered design principles in articles describing their app development (Fulford et al., 2020; Schlosser et al., 2016). PRIME and MASS conducted interviews and focus groups with key stakeholders (e.g., people with schizophrenia, providers) to identify intervention needs. Follow up input on usability and acceptability of an app prototype was also gathered. User-centered design principles may help reduce engagement or usability issues (McCurdie et al., 2012), which may be particularly relevant in the context of cognitive impairments and limited technology literacy that can be found among some with schizophrenia (Rotondi et al.,2017).

2.2 Length

Intervention lengths were 8-weeks, 12-weeks, or 24-weeks. This is significantly briefer than many in-person negative symptom interventions (e.g., 9–18 months (Granholm et al., 2014; Grant et al., 2012). Treatment effects may be hastened by the fact that these mHealth interventions often involve daily engagement. The essential dose of these interventions to facilitate negative symptom change is less clear, but preliminary work with mCBTn suggested that a minimum of 12 weeks was needed to achieve a medium-effect-size improvement in negative symptoms.

2.3 Training and Additional Contact

A training session precedes each intervention to ensure participants are comfortable with basic phone and/or app functions. Once the intervention begins, interactions outside of the main mobile delivered intervention content vary. Participants in MASS receive approximately once weekly phone call checks-ins to address technical issues or other questions. mCBTn participants attend weekly 90-minute in-person sessions where they complete the Cognitive Skills module of Cognitive-Behavioral Social Skills Training (CBTSST) (Granholm et al., 2016). In this session, participant goals and personalized statements are programmed into the app to challenge defeatist beliefs or low expectations of success or pleasure. For PRIME, no other explicit interaction was described outside of the coaching or peer messages that were part of the mobile application. Finally, for MEMS, participants are only contacted outside of the text-messages if participants do not respond to text-messages for three consecutive days or to schedule follow-up assessments.

2.4 Intervention Design

Three interventions, mCBTn, MASS, and MEMS, use Ecological Momentary Assessment, blending EMA with intervention content delivered in participants' daily lives. A benefit of this approach is EMA can help to identify fluctuations in treatment targets or clinical outcomes, allowing for personalized real-time interventions. All three of the app-based interventions (mCBTn, MASS, and PRIME) also provide on-demand content, such as recovery goal information or message boards to interact with peers or coaches.

Importantly, all interventions use elements of JITAIs, attempting to provide the right type and amount of support at the right time, while eliminating support provision that is not beneficial (Nahum-Shani et al., 2018). Three of the interventions state clear decision rules that are used to guide when and what type of intervention should be delivered. In mCBTn, MASS, and MEMS, participants are queried via EMA questions about motivation, effort, and anticipated success and/or pleasure prior to working on a daily behavioral plan (e.g., goal step, pleasurable or social activity). Participant responses are used to systematically tailor interventions. Specifically, high/adaptive ratings are generally positively reinforced, while lower ratings are met with validating or normalizing statements, encouraging or challenging statements to enhance motivation, and/or feedback using evidence from prior ratings to challenge current lower ratings. These logic-based decision rules provide targeted, tailored interventions based on participants' current in-the-moment needs. At times, this involves providing no intervention (e.g., when the participant ignores the prompt).

Interventions range from user-initiated to daily pre-set prompts/messages that can trigger intervention content depending on participants' responses. Three interventions, mCBTn, MASS, and MEMS, have daily prompts or questions sent via text-messages or push notifications; responses to these can trigger intervention content. Most PRIME content is user-initiated, but PRIME coaches also send brief, personalized messages with resources or interventions to address goal barriers or clinical concerns "most days" a week. MASS delivers EMA questions and associated interventions twice a day each day of the week using semirandom administrations (2.5 hour blocks), while mCBTn delivers a morning action plan and prompts participants to choose an activity for the day (e.g., goal step, pleasurable activity, homework assignment); additional content varies based on selection (e.g., pleasure-savoring experiences, reminder to use homework sheets). MEMS delivers three sets of daily text-messages each weekday, with each sent at a participant-identified time within two-hour time blocks.

Harnessing the ability to deliver individualized intervention content right when participants need it is a critical tool for mHealth interventions for negative symptoms. Questions remain about ideal timing and frequency of intervention content delivery as well as methods for updating/modifying interventions based on changing patient needs or preferences. Personalized prediction modeling or machine learning could help to ascertain when and what type of interventions might be most effective.

3. Evidence-Base for Negative Symptom mHealth Interventions

3.1 Acceptability

In three studies (MASS, MEMS, and PRIME), users were asked about intervention acceptability via qualitative interviews or quantitative likert-scale questions. Mean acceptability ratings were high for PRIME (mean 8.21 out of a possible score of 10), while participants reported moderate enjoyment and helpfulness (mean of 3.1–3.5 on 1–5 scale) and limited difficulty (mean 1.1 and 1.6 on 1–5 scale) using the MASS program. For MEMS, most (96%) reported that the intervention was easy to use and all reported satisfaction with the text-messages. However, a few (12%–16%) participants endorsed difficulties understanding MEMS text-messages and/or typing their responses. In general, these results suggest that users found these interventions to be acceptable.

3.2 Feasibility

All studies assessed intervention feasibility via retention and engagement. All studies had high retention during the course of the trials (i.e., over 73%). Specifically, 74% completed the 12-week PRIME intervention, 83.8% completed the eight-week MASS, 92.6% completed the eight-week MEMS, and 28 (90%), 27 (87%), and 25 (81%) of participants completed 12-, 18-, and 24 weeks of mCBTn, respectively. These are consistent with other mHealth interventions in schizophrenia (Firth & Torous, 2015; Granholm et al., 2012) but are particularly noteworthy given targeted recruitment of individuals with elevated negative symptoms for mCBTn and MEMS.

Engagement was variable across studies. mCBTn found a 22% and then 19.2% response rate to their daily action plan prompt at 12 and 24 weeks, respectively, indicating approximate weekly engagement. MASS participants averaged a 42.5% response rate to push notifications and 13.5 video views (range: 0–422), and MEMS participants averaged an 86.1% (SD = 16.7%) response rate to text-message prompts. Finally, in PRIME, participants accessed the app over four days per week, completed an average 1.5 challenges a week, had an average of 128.8 coaching interactions over 12-weeks, and reached out to peers one tenth as frequently as coaches. PRIME authors noted that engagement peaked the first month, dropped, but leveled over months two and three. Thus, studies with greater personalized messaging (MEMS, PRIME) had greater engagement. There was notable variability, however, in levels of engagement across the four interventions, which may be due to the focus and different methods of assessing engagement. All studies concluded that the tested interventions were feasible. It is notable, however, that other schizophrenia mHealth interventions have found higher engagement rates (Ben-Zeev et al., 2014; Firth & Torous, 2015; Granholm et al., 2012). At the same time, little is known about the level and frequency of engagement needed to yield negative symptom changes.

3.3 Safety

Only the mCBTn study assessed safety through reporting the number of adverse events, reporting one hospitalization that was not directly related to the intervention. Safety procedures, however, have been described in more detail in relapse prevention mHealth interventions in schizophrenia (Spaniel et al., 2008). Continuing to publish procedures for clinical emergencies will be important for addressing potential adverse events (Gumley et al., 2022) and supporting clinicians during mHealth implementation (Berry et al., 2017).

3.4 Design of Trials

The impact of these interventions on clinical outcomes was assessed using pre-post single arm designs, a small RCT with a mostly treatment as usual control condition, or a waitlist-controlled trial. Samples were small, ranging from 31 to 56. The MASS and PRIME studies had follow-up periods of three months to see if treatment effects remained. Two (mCBTn and MEMS) of the four studies required participants to have impairments in their primary negative symptom clinical outcome. Consistent with NIH's experimental therapeutic program and focus on mechanisms of change, Granholm and colleagues (2020) utilized the strictest inclusion criteria, requiring reductions in the primary clinical outcome and treatment mechanism (defeatist attitudes). Beyond these largely preliminary efficacy trials, there is a need for additional evidence supporting the effectiveness of these mHealth interventions for negative symptoms in real-world clinical settings.

4. Theoretical or Intervention Framework Guiding the Interventions

Evidence examining mechanisms of negative symptoms is largely derived from laboratory studies, and it is unclear whether these mechanisms similarly contribute or are the most critical to target to decrease negative symptoms in real-time real-place. For example, self-report scales often completed in laboratory settings suggest that anticipatory but not consummatory pleasure is impaired in schizophrenia (Fortunati et al., 2015; Mote et al., 2014); however, EMA studies in real-time and real-place have not consistently supported this and have found that anticipatory pleasure in daily life may be intact in schizophrenia (Gard et al., 2014; Luther et al., 2023). This may suggest that mechanisms contributing to negative symptoms vary across activities or environments. Thus, additional work using EMA or passive sensing (e.g., GPS mobile phone tracking) is needed to help identify what might be the most essential mechanisms to target to improve negative symptoms in daily life.

Each negative symptom mHealth intervention reviewed was guided by specific theoretical and empirical work. Studies ranged from targeting two key mechanisms to several; as a result, it is challenging to disentangle what the critical elements or the primary mechanisms of change are in these interventions. Work involving optimizing intervention components (Campbell et al., 2007) and careful testing of mechanisms in cross-over designs may help to reveal the most critical intervention ingredients.

First, consistent with evidence that modified forms of CBT effectively improve negative symptoms (Granholm et al., 2018; Grant et al., 2012), all four used CBT elements (e.g., goal monitoring, behavioral experiments, examining and testing appraisals of effort, motivation, competence, defeatist performance beliefs). Three studies (MASS, MEMS, and PRIME) also incorporated findings from the reward processing literature in schizophrenia and targeted presumed impairments in effort-cost computations (e.g., integrating information about rewards and effort to guide behavior), value representation (e.g., generating, updating, or maintaining the value of rewards to guide decision-making), and reward learning. This involved inquiry and assessments about effort, social encouragement and positive reinforcement supporting effort expenditure and adaptive effort-cost computations, linking effort expenditure to rewards, and reminders about the value of an action. Although initial evidence suggested that these reward processing domains were impaired in schizophrenia and linked with negative symptoms, more recent work has been mixed (Green et al., 2015; Luther et al., 2018). Researchers have suggested several reasons for this, including limited temporal resolution of clinical ratings scales (Cohen et al., 2021); e.g., measuring symptoms across time and contexts).

Relatedly, three interventions (mCBTn, MASS, PRIME) explicitly targeted anticipatory pleasure mechanisms (e.g., emotion maintenance). This domain was targeted by reminding participants of prior positive or successful experiences when working toward a similar goal, validating and encouraging statements, highlighting discrepancies between expectations around pleasure and actual enjoyment, pleasure-savoring activities (e.g., taking a selfie, journaling), and sharing positive experiences or successes with peers or coaches also using the app. This intervention target is based on the temporal experience of pleasure model in schizophrenia (Gard et al., 2007), which is based on evidence showing that those with schizophrenia have a dissociation between "wanting" and "liking." In seminal work by Gard and colleagues (2007), people with schizophrenia showed intact in-the-moment or consummatory pleasure but reductions in anticipatory pleasure compared to controls; this anticipatory pleasure deficit is posited to lead to difficulties translating hedonic responses into motivated behavior. Follow-up work has failed to consistently find an anticipatory pleasure reduction in schizophrenia (Visser et al., 2020). However, a review by Frost and Strauss (2016) suggests that some components of anticipatory pleasure (e.g., prospection, associative learning between reward predictive cues and outcomes) may be more consistently impaired, while other elements have more inconsistent evidence (e.g., anticipatory affect and affective forecasting). Thus, it may be that certain, but not all, components of anticipatory pleasure are impaired and therefore important to differentiate with respect to targets for intervention. Finally, PRIME coaches also used mindfulness, behavioral activation, and psychoeducation, and two studies (mCBTn, MASS) that were also interested in social functioning as an additional primary outcome targeted social skills training via encouraging social interactions, assessing social appraisals, and providing videos demonstrating social skills.

5. Impact on Mechanisms and Primary Negative Symptom Outcomes

All four interventions targeted experiential negative symptoms, with three (MASS, MEMS, PRIME) primarily targeting avolition. None expressly targeted expressive negative symptoms (e.g., blunted affect or alogia). Two interventions, MASS and PRIME, did not lead to significant improvements on negative symptom clinical-rating scales; however, PRIME led to trend improvements in self-reported motivation and pleasure, while MASS was not associated with improvements in EMA reports of desire and motivation but was linked with improvements in another primary target: social functioning. Both mCBTn and MEMS yielded improvements in clinician-rated negative symptoms, but MEMS did not produce significant improvements in self-reported motivation and pleasure compared to the control condition. These negative symptom effects were observed at 12 weeks and remained at 24 weeks in mCBTn. Both of the mCBTn and MEMS studies included negative symptom impairments as an inclusion criterion; it is possible this design feature made it more likely that clinical improvements could be detected.

Three studies, mCBTn, MASS, PRIME, saw changes in some or all of their primary mechanisms of change. PRIME led to greater improvements than the waitlist condition in an experimental task measuring their primary mechanisms of anticipated pleasure and effort expenditure for social interventions with positive outcomes; they also observed a trend-level ($p = .07$) improvement in learning from positive outcomes. Those in mCBTn demonstrated significant pre-post improvements in their main mechanism of self-reported defeatist beliefs. MASS participants showed significant pre-post improvement in some but not all of their primary mechanisms, while one additional mechanism decreased; social motivation appraisals (e.g., social desire or motivation measured via EMA) did not significantly increase over the trial, while a composite EMA social interaction appraisal variable (e.g., how likable they were in an interaction) did significantly improve in the intervention period. However, the number of EMA reported social interactions decreased across the intervention, which may be partially related to missing EMA surveys. On the other hand, those in MEMS did not show greater improvements than a control condition in the putative mechanisms of effort-cost computations or value representation measured via experimental tasks. In MEMS, however, a higher text-message response rate was associated with greater improvements in effort-cost computations. Thus, mCBTn led to significant improvements in both the primary clinical negative symptom outcome and targeted mechanism; PRIME led to improvements in most of the targeted mechanisms and trend improvements in self-reported negative symptoms; MASS led to some increases (but also one decrease) in mechanisms and no change in negative symptoms (but change in another primary target of social functioning); while MEMS led to change in the primary negative symptom outcome and targeted mechanism in only those with higher engagement. Future studies may benefit from greater congruence or resolution (e.g., in the moment vs. across one week in rating scales) between targeted mechanisms, the measurement of that target, as well as their clinical outcome (e.g., negative symptoms in daily life). Alternatively, it may be that longer trials are needed for some of the identified mechanisms of change to lead to outcomes in clinical variables. Although mCBTn provides the most convincing evidence, this evidence was limited by a smaller sample and pre-post design; however, a current larger scale randomized trial is underway. Indeed, for consumers, clinicians, and researchers to have greater confidence in these interventions, more rigorous well-powered efficacy or effectiveness trials of these interventions are needed.

6. Future Directions

6.1 Delivery modalities

Notably missing from the negative symptom digital health intervention literature are web-based (i.e., nonmobile) interventions or virtual reality interventions. Several groups have developed web-based platforms to provide interventions such as CBT for psychosis (Gottlieb et al., 2013) or to deliver more comprehensive interventions that integrate elements of social media environments, peer support, and tailored interventions to target social functioning and recovery in early psychosis (Ludwig et al., 2021). For example, Alvarez-Jimenez and colleagues developed HORYZONS (Alvarez-Jimenez et al., 2021), an 18-month comprehensive internet-based intervention for first-episode psychosis that integrates: (1) peer-to-peer social networking; (2) individually tailored psychosocial interventions targeting social functioning, vocational recovery, and release prevention; (3) peer support and moderation; and (4) expert clinician and vocational support. Initial work indicated that these web-based interventions were acceptable and possibly effective in people with schizophrenia, suggesting that this platform may also be a useful modality to deliver interventions specific to negative symptoms. Similarly, virtual reality platforms have shown promise for enhancing social skills and reducing positive symptoms (Monaghesh et al., 2022) in schizophrenia. This approach could be leveraged to allow for carefully controlled environments where behavioral experiments to test defeatist thinking linked to negative symptoms could be deployed or where participants could gain and practice techniques in contexts where negative symptoms may be elevated (e.g., work or performance-based contexts (Luther et al., 2023).

One important future direction for mHealth negative symptom interventions is to better harness mobile technologies to provide even more personalized JITAIs. Indeed, our current mHealth interventions deliver content largely after prompts that are initiated on behalf of the intervention. Many of these prompts are delivered only a handful of times a day, likely missing critical movements when negative symptoms might be elevated. EMA also relies on participant report, which could be vulnerable to low participant engagement or demand characteristics. One possibility that could address these limitations involves the use of passive sensors available on smartphones (e.g., accelerometers, GPS). For example, CrossCheck (Ben-Zeev et al., 2017), a multimodal smartphone data collection system, has been used in a number of trials to identify factors associated with relapse (Buck, Scherer, et al., 2019), symptom exacerbation (Wang et al., 2017), and persecutory ideation (Buck, Hallgren, et al., 2019). Recent work has found that geolocation and accelerometry are valid real-world negative symptoms markers (Raugh et al., 2020; Strauss et al., 2022). These tools could be incorporated into future negative symptom mHealth interventions in a number of ways. For example, these passive tools could identify periods of low activity or environments where negative symptoms may often increase; when identified, intervention content to address low goal-directed activity could be automatically sent. Carefully designed interventions that harness both active (i.e., EMA) and passive assessments to identify when participants might most need an intervention could provide potentially more effective interventions during critical windows of time when interventions may be most needed.

6.2 Novel Mechanisms

In addition to clarifying the most critical mechanisms underlying negative symptoms in daily life (e.g., do laboratory-based mechanisms translate to daily life?), future work could also harness mHealth to target other components contributing to negative symptoms. For example, a growing literature has identified that poor emotion awareness and low emotion granularity may be an important contributor to psychiatric symptoms and poor social functioning in schizophrenia (see Kimhy et al., 2012, 2014, 2016, and 2020). Similarly, emerging work has suggested that environmental or contextual factors may influence the emergence and maintenance of negative symptoms, with studies showing that contexts such as locations, social partners, and activities have a dynamic influence on negative symptoms in schizophrenia and youth at clinical-high risk for psychosis (Luther et al., 2023; Luther et al., 2023).

6.3 Implementation

As noted by others (Lattie et al., 2020; Mohr et al., 2018), few studies have moved beyond feasibility and small RCTs to examine real-world effectiveness and implementation of mHealth and digital approaches. Although some larger scale effectiveness trials in community mental health centers have recently been completed (Gumley et al., 2022) or are underway, the majority of mHealth work in schizophrenia has focused on feasibility and acceptability. This feasibility and acceptability work has limited utility and impact without additional work examining real-world implementation in larger samples. At the same time, structural and policy issues also impede clinical implementation. For example, to support integration into clinical care, consistent policies addressing financial/insurance reimbursement for delivering mobile applications (Powell et al., 2019) and models for training and integration into clinical workflows are needed. Although studies have begun to involve key stakeholders when designing applications for specific symptoms (Ben-Zeev et al., 2013; Fulford et al., 2020; Schlosser et al., 2016), it will be important to also leverage the perspectives of patients, clinicians, and other stakeholders while developing plans for large-scale intervention delivery. Some models of training clinicians in mHealth-augmented care are in development (Rodriguez-Villa et al., 2020). Online training approaches for clinicians to deliver mobile interventions that can be accessed on-demand much like those developed for the in-person negative symptom Positive Emotion Program for Schizophrenia (see Chapter 18, this volume; Nguyen et al., 2022) may enhance feasibility of larger scale training for community-based clinicians. Developing mHealth delivery platforms that can be easily personalized, updated, and used across or within existing electronic medical records or treatment delivery platforms may also support implementation. Further, as additional effectiveness evidence from ongoing large-scale trials is published, this information could be incorporated into client psychoeducation to increase client familiarity and potentially enhance engagement. Increasing support for evaluating the efficacy of mainstream digital health technologies through such resources as the APP Advisor from the American Psychiatric Association may also help to promote implementation.

6.4 Ethical Considerations for Mobile Interventions

Ethical and safety issues are also paramount in digital mental health. Although many others have described the potential pitfalls and ethical concerns of mHealth (Chivilgina et al., 2021; Karcher & Presser, 2018), we here highlight key considerations for future work in this area. First, confidentiality and privacy are key areas of concern. Messaging on mobile devices has important security limitations (e.g., could be accessed by others). It is important to clearly outline the purpose of the intervention and to ensure there is mutual agreement about the treatment and client's expectations (Torous & Roberts, 2017). Next, the limits of confidentiality should also be clearly discussed during the informed consent process, along with the inevitable collection of personally identifiable information. Methods for enhancing confidentiality (e.g., passwords, encryption services) should also be encouraged and discussed with clients. Other important components of informed consent include discussions around how the digital intervention integrates with current care, safety procedures, and limits around clinician availability (e.g., after-hours services). Finally, given that technology is constantly evolving, it is also important for those creating and using the apps to stay aware of how technological updates may impact issues around confidentiality, privacy, and intervention delivery.

7. Conclusions

Digital health remains a promising approach to improving negative symptoms in schizophrenia-spectrum disorders. These tools appear feasible and acceptable, enhance access to care, reduce in-person treatment costs, and provide real-time personalized treatment in a person's daily life. Despite these benefits, however, the field faces several barriers limiting uptake and utility of mHealth and other digital interventions. First, there are issues around identifying the critical mechanisms of negative symptoms and how and when they are most effectively targeted in daily life. Moving toward JITAIs for negative symptoms that combine both active and passive assessments to provide real-time interventions at the precise time when symptom exacerbations may occur could provide more precise, personalized, and effective interventions. Second, although more large-scale, well-powered studies of mHealth approaches are currently underway, the field needs to continue to move beyond feasibility and acceptability studies toward efficacy and effectiveness trials in order to adequately guide clinicians and clients in the benefits and limits of these tools. Relatedly, in line with some approaches (e.g., Berry et al., 2020), eventual implementation of these approaches needs to involve key stakeholders to design interventions consistent with user-centered design principles, to address implementation barriers, and to manage ethical pitfalls effectively. Notwithstanding these issues, the field of mHealth is poised to make critical progress in treating and improving some of the most functionally disabling symptoms—negative symptoms—in schizophrenia.

References

Alvarez-Jimenez, M., Bendall, S., Koval, P., Rice, S., Cagliarini, D., Valentine, L., D'Alfonso, S., Miles, C., Russon, P., Penn, D. L., Phillips, J., Lederman, R., Wadley, G., Killackey, E., Santesteban-Echarri, O., Mihalopoulos, C., Herrman, H., Gonzalez-Blanch, C., Gilbertson, T., ... Gleeson, J. F. (2019). HORYZONS trial: protocol for a randomised controlled trial of a moderated online social therapy to maintain treatment effects from first-episode psychosis services. *BMJ Open*, *9*(2), e024104.

Alvarez-Jimenez, M., Koval, P., Schmaal, L., Bendall, S., O'Sullivan, S., Cagliarini, D., D'Alfonso, S., Rice, S., Valentine, L., Penn, D. L., Miles, C., Russon, P., Phillips, J., McEnery, C., Lederman, R., Killackey, E., Mihalopoulos, C., Gonzalez-Blanch, C., Gilbertson, T., ... Gleeson, J. F. M. (2021). The Horyzons project: a randomized controlled trial of a novel online social therapy to maintain treatment effects from specialist first-episode psychosis services. *World Psychiatry: Official Journal of the World Psychiatric Association (WPA)*, *20*(2), 233–243.

Beebe, L., Smith, K. D., & Phillips, C. (2014). A comparison of telephone and texting interventions for persons with schizophrenia spectrum disorders. *Issues in Mental Health Nursing*, *35*(5), 323–329.

Ben-Zeev, D., Brian, R., Wang, R., Wang, W., Campbell, A. T., Aung, M. S. H., Merrill, M., Tseng, V. W. S., Choudhury, T., Hauser, M., Kane, J. M., & Scherer, E. A. (2017). CrossCheck: Integrating self-report, behavioral sensing, and smartphone use to identify digital indicators of psychotic relapse. *Psychiatric Rehabilitation Journal*, *40*(3), 266–275.

Ben-Zeev, D., Buck, B., Hallgren, K., & Drake, R. E. (2019). Effect of Mobile Health on In-person Service Use Among People With Serious Mental Illness. *Psychiatric Services*, *70*(6), 507–510.

Ben-Zeev, D., Kaiser, S. M., Brenner, C. J., Begale, M., Duffecy, J., & Mohr, D. C. (2013). Development and usability testing of FOCUS: a smartphone system for self-management of schizophrenia. *Psychiatric Rehabilitation Journal*, *36*(4), 289–296.

Ben-Zeev, D., Kaiser, S. M., & Krzos, I. (2014). Remote "hovering" with individuals with psychotic disorders and substance use: feasibility, engagement, and therapeutic alliance with a text-messaging mobile interventionist. *Journal of Dual Diagnosis*, *10*(4), 197–203.

Ben-Zeev, D., Razzano, L. A., Pashka, N. J., & Levin, C. E. (2021). Cost of mHealth Versus Clinic-Based Care for Serious Mental Illness: Same Effects, Half the Price Tag. *Psychiatric Services*, *72*(4), 448–451.

Berry, N., Bucci, S., & Lobban, F. (2017). Use of the Internet and Mobile Phones for Self-Management of Severe Mental Health Problems: Qualitative Study of Staff Views. *JMIR Mental Health*, *4*(4), e52.

Berry, N., Machin, M., Ainsworth, J., Berry, K., Edge, D., Haddock, G., Lewis, S., Morris, R., & Bucci, S. (2020). Developing a Theory-Informed Smartphone App for Early Psychosis: Learning Points From a Multidisciplinary Collaboration. *Frontiers in Psychiatry*, *11*, 602861.

Buck, B., Chander, A., & Ben-Zeev, D. (2020). Clinical and demographic predictors of engagement in mobile health vs. clinic-based interventions for serious mental illness. *Journal of Behavioral and Cognitive Therapy*, *30*(1), 3–11.

Buck, B., Hallgren, K. A., Scherer, E., Brian, R., Wang, R., Wang, W., Campbell, A., Choudhury, T., Hauser, M., Kane, J. M., & Ben-Zeev, D. (2019). Capturing behavioral indicators of persecutory ideation using mobile technology. *Journal of Psychiatric Research*, *116*, 112–117.

Buck, B., Scherer, E., Brian, R., Wang, R., Wang, W., Campbell, A., Choudhury, T., Hauser, M., Kane, J. M., & Ben-Zeev, D. (2019). Relationships between smartphone social behavior and relapse in schizophrenia: A preliminary report. *Schizophrenia Research*, *208*, 167–172.

Campbell, N. C., Murray, E., Darbyshire, J., Emery, J., Farmer, A., Griffiths, F., Guthrie, B., Lester, H., Wilson, P., & Kinmonth, A. L. (2007). Designing and evaluating complex interventions to improve health care. *BMJ (Clinical Research Ed.)*, *334*(7591), 455–459.

Chivilgina, O., Elger, B. S., & Jotterand, F. (2021). Digital technologies for schizophrenia management: A descriptive review. *Science and Engineering Ethics*, *27*(2), 25.

Cohen, A. S., Schwartz, E., Le, T. P., Cowan, T., Kirkpatrick, B., Raugh, I. M., & Strauss, G. P. (2021). Digital phenotyping of negative symptoms: the relationship to clinician ratings. *Schizophrenia Bulletin*, *47*(1), 44–53.

Doyle-Delgado, K., & Chamberlain, J. J. (2020). Use of Diabetes-Related Applications and Digital Health Tools by People With Diabetes and Their Health Care Providers. *Clinical Diabetes: A Publication of the American Diabetes Association, 38*(5), 449–461.

Firth, J., Cotter, J., Torous, J., Bucci, S., Firth, J. A., & Yung, A. R. (2016). Mobile Phone Ownership and Endorsement of "mHealth" Among People With Psychosis: A Meta-analysis of Cross-sectional Studies. *Schizophrenia Bulletin, 42*(2), 448–455.

Firth, J., Torous, J., Carney, R., Newby, J., Cosco, T. D., Christensen, H., & Sarris, J. (2018). Digital technologies in the treatment of anxiety: recent innovations and future directions. *Current Psychiatry Reports, 20*(6), 44.

Firth, J., & Torous, J. (2015). Smartphone apps for schizophrenia: A systematic review. *JMIR MHealth and UHealth, 3*(4), e102.

Fortunati, R., Ossola, P., Camerlengo, A., Bettini, E., De Panfilis, C., Tonna, M., Maggini, C., & Marchesi, C. (2015). Anhedonia in schizophrenia: The role of subjective experiences. *Comprehensive Psychiatry, 62*, 152–160.

Frost, K. H., & Strauss, G. P. (2016). A review of anticipatory pleasure in schizophrenia. *Current Behavioral Neuroscience Reports, 3*(3), 232–247.

Fulford, D., Gard, D. E., Mueser, K. T., Mote, J., Gill, K., Leung, L., & Mow, J. (2021). Preliminary Outcomes of an Ecological Momentary Intervention for Social Functioning in Schizophrenia: Pre-Post Study of the Motivation and Skills Support App. *JMIR Mental Health, 8*(6), e27475.

Fulford, D., Mote, J., Gard, D. E., Mueser, K. T., Gill, K., Leung, L., & Dillaway, K. (2020). Development of the Motivation and Skills Support (MASS) social goal attainment smartphone app for (and with) people with schizophrenia. *Journal of Behavioral and Cognitive Therapy, 30*(1), 23–32.

Gard, D. E., Kring, A. M., Gard, M. G., Horan, W. P., & Green, M. F. (2007). Anhedonia in schizophrenia: distinctions between anticipatory and consummatory pleasure. *Schizophrenia Research, 93*(1-3), 253–260.

Gard, D. E., Sanchez, A. H., Cooper, K., Fisher, M., Garrett, C., & Vinogradov, S. (2014). Do people with schizophrenia have difficulty anticipating pleasure, engaging in effortful behavior, or both? *Journal of Abnormal Psychology, 123*(4), 771–782.

Gay, K., Torous, J., Joseph, A., Pandya, A., & Duckworth, K. (2016). Digital Technology Use Among Individuals with Schizophrenia: Results of an Online Survey. *JMIR Mental Health, 3*(2), e15.

Gottlieb, J. D., Romeo, K. H., Penn, D. L., Mueser, K. T., & Chiko, B. P. (2013). Web-based cognitive-behavioral therapy for auditory hallucinations in persons with psychosis: a pilot study. *Schizophrenia Research, 145*(1-3), 82–87.

Granholm, E., Ben-Zeev, D., Link, P. C., Bradshaw, K. R., & Holden, J. L. (2012). Mobile Assessment and Treatment for Schizophrenia (MATS): a pilot trial of an interactive text-messaging intervention for medication adherence, socialization, and auditory hallucinations. *Schizophrenia Bulletin, 38*(3), 414–425.

Granholm, E., Holden, J., Dwyer, K., Mikhael, T., Link, P., & Depp, C. (2020). Mobile-Assisted Cognitive Behavioral Therapy for Negative Symptoms: Open Single-Arm Trial With Schizophrenia Patients. *JMIR Mental Health, 7*(12), e24406.

Granholm, E., Holden, J., Link, P. C., & McQuaid, J. R. (2014). Randomized clinical trial of cognitive behavioral social skills training for schizophrenia: improvement in functioning and experiential negative symptoms. *Journal of Consulting and Clinical Psychology, 82*(6), 1173–1185.

Granholm, E., Holden, J., & Worley, M. (2018). Improvement in Negative Symptoms and Functioning in Cognitive-Behavioral Social Skills Training for Schizophrenia: Mediation by Defeatist Performance Attitudes and Asocial Beliefs. *Schizophrenia Bulletin, 44*(3), 653–661.

Granholm, E. L., McQuaid, J. R., & Holden, J. L. (2016). *Cognitive-behavioral social skills training for schizophrenia: A practical treatment guide.* Guilford Publications.

Grant, P. M., & Beck, A. T. (2009). Defeatist beliefs as a mediator of cognitive impairment, negative symptoms, and functioning in schizophrenia. *Schizophrenia Bulletin*, *35*(4), 798–806.

Grant, P. M., Huh, G. A., Perivoliotis, D., Stolar, N. M., & Beck, A. T. (2012). Randomized trial to evaluate the efficacy of cognitive therapy for low-functioning patients with schizophrenia. *Archives of General Psychiatry*, *69*(2), 121–127.

Green, M. F., Horan, W. P., Barch, D. M., & Gold, J. M. (2015). Effort-Based Decision Making: A Novel Approach for Assessing Motivation in Schizophrenia. *Schizophrenia Bulletin*, *41*(5), 1035–1044.

Gumley, A. I., Bradstreet, S., Ainsworth, J., Allan, S., Alvarez-Jimenez, M., Aucott, L., Birchwood, M., Briggs, A., Bucci, S., Cotton, S. M., Engel, L., French, P., Lederman, R., Lewis, S., Machin, M., MacLennan, G., McLeod, H., McMeekin, N., Mihalopoulos, C., ... Gleeson, J. (2022). The EMPOWER blended digital intervention for relapse prevention in schizophrenia: a feasibility cluster randomised controlled trial in Scotland and Australia. *The Lancet Psychiatry*, *9*(6), 477–486.

Karcher, N. R., & Presser, N. R. (2018). Ethical and legal issues addressing the use of mobile health (mhealth) as an adjunct to psychotherapy. *Ethics & Behavior*, *28*(1), 1–22.

Kay, M., Santos, J., & Takane, M. (2011). mHealth: New horizons for health through mobile technologies. *World Health Organization*, *64*(7), 66–71.

Kay, S. R., Fiszbein, A., & Opler, L. A. (1987). The positive and negative syndrome scale (PANSS) for schizophrenia. *Schizophrenia Bulletin*, *13*(2), 261–276.

Kimhy, D., Gill, K. E., Brucato, G., Vakhrusheva, J., Arndt, L., Gross, J. J., & Girgis, R. R. (2016). The impact of emotion awareness and regulation on social functioning in individuals at clinical high risk for psychosis. *Psychological Medicine*, *46*(14), 2907–2918.

Kimhy, D., Lister, A., Liu, Y., Vakhrusheva, J., Delespaul, P., Malaspina, D., Ospina, L.H., Mittal, V.A., Gross, J.J, & Wang, Y. (2020). The impact of emotion awareness and regulation on psychotic symptoms during daily functioning. *npj Schizophrenia*, *6*(1), 7.

Kimhy, D., Vakhrusheva, J., Jobson-Ahmed, L., Tarrier, N., Malaspina, D., & Gross, J. J. (2012). Emotion awareness and regulation in individuals with schizophrenia: Implications for social functioning. *Psychiatry Research*, *200*(2–3), 193–201.

Kimhy, D., Vakhrusheva, J., Khan, S., Chang, R. W., Hansen, M. C., Ballon, J. S., ... & Gross, J. J. (2014). Emotional granularity and social functioning in individuals with schizophrenia: an experience sampling study. *Journal of Psychiatric Research*, *53*, 141–148.

Kreyenbuhl, J., Nossel, I. R., & Dixon, L. B. (2009). Disengagement from mental health treatment among individuals with schizophrenia and strategies for facilitating connections to care: a review of the literature. *Schizophrenia Bulletin*, *35*(4), 696–703.

Kring, A. M., Gur, R. E., Blanchard, J. J., Horan, W. P., & Reise, S. P. (2013). The Clinical Assessment Interview for Negative Symptoms (CAINS): final development and validation. *The American Journal of Psychiatry*, *170*(2), 165–172.

Lal, S., Dell'Elce, J., & Malla, A. K. (2015). Technology access and use among young adults with a first episode of psychosis. *Psychiatric Services*, *66*(7), 764–765.

Lattie, E. G., Nicholas, J., Knapp, A. A., Skerl, J. J., Kaiser, S. M., & Mohr, D. C. (2020). Opportunities for and Tensions Surrounding the Use of Technology-Enabled Mental Health Services in Community Mental Health Care. *Administration and Policy in Mental Health*, *47*(1), 138–149.

Leavitt, V.M., Goldberg, T.E. (2009) Episodic Memory in Schizophrenia. *Neuropsychology Review*, *19*, 312–323.

Llerena, K., Park, S. G., McCarthy, J. M., Couture, S. M., Bennett, M. E., & Blanchard, J. J. (2013). The Motivation and Pleasure Scale-Self-Report (MAP-SR): reliability and validity of a self-report measure of negative symptoms. *Comprehensive Psychiatry*, *54*(5), 568–574.

Ludwig, K. A., Browne, J. W., Nagendra, A., Gleeson, J. F., D'Alfonso, S., Penn, D. L., & Alvarez-Jimenez, M. (2021). Horyzons USA: A moderated online social intervention for first episode psychosis. *Early Intervention in Psychiatry, 15*(2), 335–343.

Luther, L., Buck, B. E., Fischer, M. A., Johnson-Kwochka, A. V., Coffin, G., & Salyers, M. P. (2022). Examining Potential Barriers to mHealth Implementation and Engagement in Schizophrenia: Phone Ownership and Symptom Severity. *Journal of Technology in Behavioral Science, 7*(1), 13–22.

Luther, L., Firmin, R. L., Lysaker, P. H., Minor, K. S., & Salyers, M. P. (2018). A meta-analytic review of self-reported, clinician-rated, and performance-based motivation measures in schizophrenia: Are we measuring the same "stuff"? *Clinical Psychology Review, 61*, 24–37.

Luther, L., Fischer, M. W., Johnson-Kwochka, A. V., Minor, K. S., Holden, R., Lapish, C. L., McCormick, B. & Salyers, M. P. (2020). Mobile enhancement of motivation in schizophrenia: A pilot randomized controlled trial of a personalized text message intervention for motivation deficits. *Journal of Consulting and Clinical Psychology, 88*(10), 923–936.

Luther, L., Raugh, I.M., Collins, D.E., Berglund, A., Knippenberg, A.R., Mittal, V.A., Walker, E.F. and Strauss, G.P., (2023). Environmental context predicts state fluctuations in negative symptoms in youth at clinical high risk for psychosis. *Psychological Medicine, 53*(16), 7609–7618.

Luther, L., Raugh, I. M., Collins, D. E., Knippenberg, A. R., & Strauss, G. P. (2023). Negative symptoms in schizophrenia differ across environmental contexts in daily life. *Journal of Psychiatric Research, 161*, 10–18.

McCurdie, T., Taneva, S., Casselman, M., Yeung, M., McDaniel, C., Ho, W., & Cafazzo, J. (2012). mHealth consumer apps: the case for user-centered design. *Biomedical Instrumentation & Technology/Association for the Advancement of Medical Instrumentation, Suppl*, 49–56.

Mohr, D. C., Riper, H., & Schueller, S. M. (2018). A Solution-Focused Research Approach to Achieve an Implementable Revolution in Digital Mental Health. *JAMA Psychiatry, 75*(2), 113–114.

Mojtabai, R., Fochtmann, L., Chang, S.-W., Kotov, R., Craig, T. J., & Bromet, E. (2009). Unmet need for mental health care in schizophrenia: an overview of literature and new data from a first-admission study. *Schizophrenia Bulletin, 35*(4), 679–695.

Monaghesh, E., Samad-Soltani, T., & Farhang, S. (2022). Virtual reality-based interventions for patients with paranoia: A systematic review. *Psychiatry Research, 307*, 114338.

Montes, J. M., Medina, E., Gomez-Beneyto, M., & Maurino, J. (2012). A short message service (SMS)-based strategy for enhancing adherence to antipsychotic medication in schizophrenia. *Psychiatry Research, 200*(2-3), 89–95.

Mote, J., Minzenberg, M. J., Carter, C. S., & Kring, A. M. (2014). Deficits in anticipatory but not consummatory pleasure in people with recent-onset schizophrenia spectrum disorders. *Schizophrenia Research, 159*(1), 76–79.

Nahum-Shani, I., Smith, S. N., Spring, B. J., Collins, L. M., Witkiewitz, K., Tewari, A., & Murphy, S. A. (2018). Just-in-Time Adaptive Interventions (JITAIs) in Mobile Health: Key Components and Design Principles for Ongoing Health Behavior Support. *Annals of Behavioral Medicine, 52*(6), 446–462.

Nguyen, A., Frobert, L., Kollbrunner, A., & Favrod, J. (2022). An evaluation of an online training platform for teaching positive emotions for people with schizophrenia. *Frontiers in Psychiatry, 13*, 798019.

Patel, M. L., Wakayama, L. N., & Bennett, G. G. (2021). Self-Monitoring via Digital Health in Weight Loss Interventions: A Systematic Review Among Adults with Overweight or Obesity. *Obesity, 29*(3), 478–499.

Powell, A. C., Bowman, M. B., & Harbin, H. T. (2019). Reimbursement of apps for mental health: current practices and potential pathways. *JMIR Ment Health, 6*(8): e41724.

Raugh, I. M., James, S. H., Gonzalez, C. M., Chapman, H. C., Cohen, A. S., Kirkpatrick, B., & Strauss, G. P. (2020). Geolocation as a digital phenotyping measure of negative symptoms and functional outcome. *Schizophrenia Bulletin*, *46*(6), 1596–1607.

Rehman, H., Kamal, A. K., Sayani, S., Morris, P. B., Merchant, A. T., & Virani, S. S. (2017). Using mobile health (mhealth) technology in the management of diabetes mellitus, physical inactivity, and smoking. *Current Atherosclerosis Reports*, *19*(4), 16.

Rodriguez-Villa, E., Rauseo-Ricupero, N., Camacho, E., Wisniewski, H., Keshavan, M., & Torous, J. (2020). The digital clinic: Implementing technology and augmenting care for mental health. *General Hospital Psychiatry*, *66*, 59–66.

Rotondi, A. J., Spring, M. R., Hanusa, B. H., Eack, S. M., & Haas, G. L. (2017). Designing eHealth Applications to Reduce Cognitive Effort for Persons With Severe Mental Illness: Page Complexity, Navigation Simplicity, and Comprehensibility. *JMIR Human Factors*, *4*(1), e1.

Schlosser, D., Campellone, T., Kim, D., Truong, B., Vergani, S., Ward, C., & Vinogradov, S. (2016). Feasibility of PRIME: A Cognitive Neuroscience-Informed Mobile App Intervention to Enhance Motivated Behavior and Improve Quality of Life in Recent Onset Schizophrenia. *JMIR Research Protocols*, *5*(2), e77.

Schlosser, D. A., Campellone, T. R., Truong, B., Etter, K., Vergani, S., Komaiko, K., & Vinogradov, S. (2018). Efficacy of PRIME, a mobile app intervention designed to improve motivation in young people with schizophrenia. *Schizophrenia Bulletin*, *44*(5), 1010–1020.

Shiffman, S., Stone, A. A., & Hufford, M. R. (2008). Ecological momentary assessment. *Annual Review of Clinical Psychology*, *4*, 1–32.

Spaniel, F., Vohlídka, P., Hrdlicka, J., Kozený, J., Novák, T., Motlová, L., Cermák, J., Bednaník, J., Novák, D., & Höschl, C. (2008). ITAREPS: information technology aided relapse prevention programme in schizophrenia. *Schizophrenia Research*, *98*(1-3), 312–317.

Stefancic, A., Rogers, R. T., Styke, S., Xu, X., Buchsbaum, R., Nossel, I., Cabassa, L.J., Stroup, T.S., & Kimhy, D. (2022). Development of the First Episode Digital Monitoring mHealth Intervention for People with Early Psychosis: Qualitative Interview Study With Clinicians. *JMIR Mental Health*, *9*(11), e41482.

Strauss, G. P., Raugh, I. M., Zhang, L., Luther, L., Chapman, H. C., Allen, D. N., Kirkpatrick, B., & Cohen, A. S. (2022). Validation of accelerometry as a digital phenotyping measure of negative symptoms in schizophrenia. *Schizophrenia*, *8*(1), 37.

Tal, A., & Torous, J. (2017). The digital mental health revolution: Opportunities and risks. *Psychiatric Rehabilitation Journal*, *40*(3), 263–265.

Tokgöz, P., Hrynyschyn, R., Hafner, J., Schönfeld, S., & Dockweiler, C. (2021). Digital health interventions in prevention, relapse, and therapy of mild and moderate depression: scoping review. *JMIR Mental Health*, *8*(4), e26268.

Torous, J., & Roberts, L. W. (2017). The ethical use of mobile health technology in clinical psychiatry. *The Journal of Nervous and Mental Disease*, *205*(1), 4–8.

Visser, K. F., Chapman, H. C., Ruiz, I., Raugh, I. M., & Strauss, G. P. (2020). A meta-analysis of self-reported anticipatory and consummatory pleasure in the schizophrenia-spectrum. *Journal of Psychiatric Research*, *121*, 68–81.

Vitger, T., Austin, S. F., Petersen, L., Tønder, E. S., Nordentoft, M., & Korsbek, L. (2019). The Momentum trial: the efficacy of using a smartphone application to promote patient activation and support shared decision making in people with a diagnosis of schizophrenia in outpatient treatment settings: a randomized controlled single-blind trial. *BMC psychiatry*, *19*(1), 1–11.

Vitger, T., Hjorthøj, C., Austin, S. F., Petersen, L., Tønder, E. S., Nordentoft, M., & Korsbek, L. (2022). A Smartphone App to Promote Patient Activation and Support Shared Decision-making in People with a Diagnosis of Schizophrenia in Outpatient Treatment Settings (Momentum Trial): Randomized Controlled Assessor-Blinded Trial. *Journal of Medical Internet Research*, *24*(10), e40292.

Wang, R., Scherer, E. A., Walsh, M., Wang, W., Aung, M. S. H., Ben-Zeev, D., Brian, R., Campbell, A. T., Choudhury, T., Hauser, M., & Kane, J. (2017). Predicting Symptom Trajectories of Schizophrenia using Mobile Sensing. *Proceedings of the ACM on Interactive, Mobile, Wearable and Ubiquitous Technologies*, *1*(3), 1–24.

Young, A. S., Cohen, A. N., Niv, N., Nowlin-Finch, N., Oberman, R. S., Olmos-Ochoa, T. T., Goldberg, R. W., & Whelan, F. (2020). Mobile phone and smartphone use by people with serious mental illness. *Psychiatric Services*, *71*(3), 280–283.

16

Motivation and Cognitive Enhancement Therapies for Negative Symptoms

Alice Saperstein, Lauren Gonzales, and Alice Medalia

Clinical pearls

- Current evidence-based treatments for negative symptoms in schizophrenia target motivation and cognitive functioning to promote recovery and quality of life.
- Motivation and cognition can improve in response to behavioral interventions.
- Psychosocial interventions for negative symptoms can foster motivation by promoting an individual's sense of agency, perceived self-competency, and expectations for success.
- Additional consideration is needed regarding sociocultural influences on these factors and how they may determine individual outcomes.

1. Introduction

Amotivation and cognitive deficits are two prominent features of schizophrenia symptomatology that each have significant implications for social and functional outcomes across phases of illness. Motivation, the internal state that directs, initiates, and sustains goal-directed behavior, is frequently diminished in people with schizophrenia (Kirkpatrick et al., 2006). Amotivation (avolition) is recognized as one of the five principal negative symptom domains by the National Institute of Mental Health's Measurement and Treatment Research to Improve Cognition in Schizophrenia (NIMH-MATRICS; Kirkpatrick et al., 2006) Consensus Development Conference on Negative Symptoms, and has increasingly been appreciated as an important target for therapeutic intervention. Therapeutic initiatives are facilitated by research indicating that motivation is not a static entity in schizophrenia, but rather, a dynamic process that is malleable (Choi & Medalia, 2010; Medalia & Saperstein, 2011). Since recovery-oriented therapies

Alice Saperstein, Lauren Gonzales and Alice Medalia, *Motivation and Cognitive Enhancement Therapies for Negative Symptoms*. In: *Psychosocial Approaches to Negative Symptoms in Psychosis*. Edited by: Tania Lincoln et al., Oxford University Press. © Oxford University Press (2025). DOI: 10.1093/oso/9780197676790.003.0016 strive to promote independence, attention has increasingly focused on methods to enhance autonomous volition and intrinsic motivation for goal-directed behavior.

Schizophrenia, from prodrome to end of life, is also associated with cognitive deficits which, unless addressed, can have a deleterious impact on functioning. For example, the cognitive abilities to pay attention, sustain focus, and quickly and accurately process information directly impact how well one is able to perform at work, communicate effectively, and function independently in the community. These and additional cognitive abilities, such as remembering verbal information and reasoning, impact the acquisition of social, vocational, educational, and independent living skills critical for community integration (Bowie & Harvey, 2006; Green et al., 2004). Further, working memory is needed to hold goal properties of tasks and representations of reward in mind while performing goal-directed behaviors. Executive skills are needed to plan, sequence, and execute actions to initiate and sustain behaviors aligned with functional recovery goals. Cognition interacts with attitudes and beliefs about one's competency and one's expectancies for a successful outcome to impact motivation and pursuit of valued activities.

This chapter reviews the evidence base for behavioral treatments that address deficits in motivation and cognition, and the impact of these interventions on negative symptoms, everyday functioning, and quality of life for people with a diagnosis of schizophrenia. Several specific approaches are described, each with a unique perspective on how motivation and cognition may be targeted to promote recovery.

2. Cognitive Remediation

Cognitive Remediation (CR) is an evidence-based, recovery-oriented behavioral intervention, which aims to durably improve cognitive processes with the ultimate goal of enhancing daily functioning. It differs from Cognitive Behavioral Therapy, which focuses on the content and form of thoughts and beliefs, in that CR targets the processes that underlie thinking including the abilities to take in and process information quickly, sustain focus, remember, plan, sequence, and execute actions. Psychiatric rehabilitation provides the framework for CR through the aims of decreasing disability, promoting adaptation, and thereby improving psychosocial functioning. CR is increasingly being paired with vocational training, supported education, social skills and independent living skills training, thereby providing a broader rehabilitation context for symptom and functional improvement.

CR is predicated on the capacity for learning, mediated by neuroplasticity, the process by which neurons in the brain adjust their activity in response to new situations or changes in the environment. The breadth and magnitude of CR impact are enhanced by drawing from motivation science and educational psychology to inform characteristics of the treatment environment and instructional techniques that engage, support, and empower participants to be autonomous learners. Thus, while cognitive skill learning is the primary focus, broader goals of CR may include promoting self-awareness about oneself as a learner, developing self-regulated learning skills, and self-confidence in one's ability to learn and to apply one's skills to pursue valued activities and goals (Medalia et al., 2017). Empirical studies of CR for schizophrenia show that treatment effects extend beyond cognitive gains to impact negative symptoms and quality of life. Based on accumulating evidence, CR is recommended by national and international practice guidelines as a treatment for individuals with schizophrenia with both negative symptoms and cognitive difficulties (APA, 2020; Cella et al., 2023; Galderisi et al., 2021; Galletly et al., 2016; Norman et al., 2017; Vita et al., 2022).

CR is most often conducted as an outpatient service, though it is also used in residential, inpatient, forensic, and other settings. Key components of CR include repeated practice on cognitive exercises, the presence of an active and trained therapist, structured development of cognitive strategies, the use of techniques to improve the transfer of cognitive gains to the real world and instructional strategies that promote motivation to learn (Bowie et al., 2020; Medalia et al., 2017). Specific approaches vary depending on the extent to which they use motivation enhancing instructional techniques, restorative and/or compensatory techniques to improve cognitive ability.

2.1 Restorative and Compensatory Approaches

Restorative techniques employ drill-and-practice on cognitive tasks, designed to activate the neural networks associated with cognitive domains and harness mechanisms underlying neuroplasticity to improve information processing. Exercises are commonly computer-based, accessed through web-based training platforms. Sessions are scheduled at least two to three times weekly (average 2.84 sessions/week; Lejeune et al., 2021) to support learning and maintenance of gains (Barlati et al., 2022) with an average treatment duration ranging from 13.23 (Lejeune et al., 2021) to 15.2 weeks (Vita et al., 2021). Sessions are facilitated by a trained clinician and may be conducted individually or in a group consisting of up to eight participants working simultaneously. A group setting for CR may be preferred over individual sessions given the relative cost effectiveness and potential positive benefits of engaging in a social group on self-efficacy and learning outcomes (Bryce et al., 2018; Contreras et al., 2016; Medalia et al., 2017). Titration of task difficulty and repeated cognitive practice are central elements, which ensure that learning remains challenging, while rewarding success (Bowie et al., 2020). Task difficulty may be modulated by the training platform and/or by the therapist through provision of feedback. CR programs vary in the degree that selection of tasks is personalized to suit each person's cognitive and learning needs.

Compensatory approaches, on the other hand, teach skills and strategies to circumvent a cognitive impairment. Instead of trying to restore a skill with drill and practice, the goal is to develop strategies to compensate for cognitive weaknesses. Compensatory skills can be taught alongside restorative techniques to complement skill practice, although Compensatory Cognitive Training (CCT) is a stand-alone, empirically supported intervention (Twamley et al., 2012). The CCT curriculum, which does not involve computer-based cognitive exercises, targets prospective memory, attention and vigilance, learning and memory, and executive functioning. CCT can be implemented in 12 one-hour individual sessions, or 12 two-hour sessions if done in groups, guided by a trained therapist. Compensatory skills (e.g., using routines to automate tasks, overlearning, self-talk, and self-monitoring while solving problems) are taught and practiced to the point of habit to allow for their routine use in everyday life. Worksheets, in-session practice, and homework support learning and transfer. The skills learned can be applied to any domain of functioning pertinent to a participant's recovery goals such as school, work, social functioning, and independent living.

2.2 Techniques to Promote Generalization

Two therapeutic techniques, strategy coaching and Bridging, are widely used to facilitate use of cognitive skills in everyday life. Strategy coaching during cognitive practice facilitates individuals' metacognitive processing. For example, by reflecting back to the participant their use of cognitive skills and strategies and prompting the use of new strategies for successful task performance, participants learn how to identify and select appropriate strategies, monitor outcomes, and incorporate feedback. Specific strategies may include forming associations, verbal mediation, using visual cues or written prompts, and dividing complex tasks into smaller components. Coaching may also incorporate partnering with participants by modeling skill use, using guided questions to facilitate problem solving, and providing positive feedback to reinforce the process of learning. These treatment elements support task persistence and success, and deepen engagement in the learning process (Reeder et al., 2016; Tsapekos et al., 2017).

Bridging is a group-based discussion that follows individual cognitive practice (Medalia et al., 2017). Participants collectively work on tasks that help bridge the cognitive exercises they do in session with activities in their daily life. Opportunities to place cognitive skill practice within ecologically relevant and personally meaningful contexts reinforce the value of CR, which is important for learning, motivation, and promoting the transfer of cognitive gains from the clinical setting to everyday life.

2.3 Evidence Base for Cognitive Remediation for Negative Symptoms

The efficacy of CR has been established in numerous randomized controlled trials as summarized by meta-analytic studies (Lejeune et al., 2021; McGurk et al., 2007; Wykes et al., 2011) with sustainable medium effect size (ES) improvements for cognition (ES = 0.40) and functional outcomes (ES = 0.43) when CR delivery is conducted by a trained clinician who provides strategy coaching and instructional techniques to promote generalization (Vita et al., 2021). Efficacy studies suggest that the impact of CR on symptom severity favors negative symptom over positive symptom improvement (Lejeune et al., 2021; McGurk et al., 2007; Wykes et al., 2011). Small to moderate effects of CR have been reported on global negative symptoms (Cella et al., 2017; Saperstein et al., 2025) among adults with chronic schizophrenia and for both expressive (blunted affect, alogia) and experiential (avolition/apathy, anhedonia/asociality) symptom subdomains among those early in the course of illness (Ventura et al., 2019). In addition, specific effects of a restorative approach to training working memory have been reported for neural correlates of hedonic processing; working memory for hedonic content and goal-directed behaviors may be critical for treating anhedonia and avolition (Li et al., 2019). Further, CCT, which uses a compensatory approach, has been shown to yield a large effect on negative symptom severity (ES = 0.92) with a moderate beneficial effect on social amotivation and a small beneficial effect on expressive deficits, both associated with improvements in global quality of life (Mahmood et al., 2019).

Together, these data suggest that both restorative and compensatory approaches to cognitive remediation can yield improvements in negative symptoms with significant effects specific to motivation impairment. Importantly, the magnitude of impact is similar to other available pharmacological and behavioral interventions designed to address negative symptoms directly (Barlati et al., 2022; Riehle et al., 2020). Given CR's promising impact on negative symptomatology, there is a need for more research to bolster treatment recommendations guiding the use of CR for motivation impairment as the primary intervention target.

Multiple mechanisms of impact on negative symptoms have been implicated for CR (Saperstein & Medalia, 2012; Saperstein et al., 2025). First, given the overlap between cognitive and negative symptoms (Rund, 1998), one mechanism of impact is through improving specific cognitive skills such as early auditory processing, working memory, problem-solving, planning, and the ability to generate and implement cognitive strategies (Bark et al., 2003; Cella et al., 2017; Farreny et al., 2013; Saperstein et al., 2025). Whereas such skill deficits may result in withdrawal and amotivation, improving these skills and the ability to recruit cognitive resources may facilitate the initiation and completion of planned, goal-directed behaviors. Second, depending on how CR is delivered it may improve motivation, a key component of negative symptoms. Certain instructional techniques enhance intrinsic motivation to autonomously engage in valued goal-directed behaviors (Choi & Medalia, 2010; Saperstein & Medalia, 2016). Further, the use of positive feedback and careful titration of task difficulty may enhance reward sensitivity and perceived competence, thereby addressing apathy, anhedonia, and withdrawal (Cella et al., 2014; Gold et al., 2008; Lee et al., 2017; Li et al., 2019; Saperstein & Medalia, 2012). The CR therapist can play a critical role for inducing these symptom changes. Frequent therapist-participant contact through strategy coaching and learning support may allow for alliance building (Cella & Wykes, 2019), opportunities for individuals to challenge defeatist beliefs (Grant & Beck, 2009), build confidence, and improve self-efficacy (Garrido et al., 2013; Soumet-Leman et al. 2018; Medalia et al., 2017). Helping people with schizophrenia believe that their actions can lead to positive outcomes can motivate individuals toward the initiation of and persistence on goal-oriented tasks, whether in the context of treatment or in applying learned skills in daily life (Cardenas et al., 2013). Thus, by providing positive learning experiences, CR may promote expectations for future success and support motivation and the pursuit of valued activities and recovery goals.

3. Integrated Treatment for Cognition and Motivation

The Neuropsychological and Educational Approach to (Cognitive) Remediation (NEAR) is a specific group-based CR intervention (Medalia et al., 2017). Implementation encompasses all five key components of CR: repeated practice on cognitive exercises, the presence of an active and trained therapist, structured development of cognitive strategies, and use of techniques to improve the transfer of cognitive gains to the real world and instructional techniques to enhance motivation (Bowie et al., 2020; Medalia et al., 2017). NEAR is unique among CR approaches in that it appreciates the intertwining of cognitive and motivational processes within the context of skill learning and is structured with the explicit intent to enhance cognition and motivation simultaneously to maximize outcomes. Two theories figure prominently in the design of NEAR, recognizing that supporting intrinsic motivation is essential for the learning process.

First, self-determination theory (SDT; Ryan & Deci, 2000) guides NEAR practices which promote intrinsic motivation for learning through three elements: (1) fostering positive experiences of *relatedness* through interactions with the therapist and other members of the group, (2) providing opportunities to gain a sense of *competence*, and (3) encouraging *autonomous functioning* in learning environments. Second, expectancy value theory (EVT; Eccles & Wigfield, 2002) informs NEAR practices by emphasizing the roles of *perceived competency*, *program interest*, and *value* as contributing to treatment gains. Similar to what is posited by SDT, an expectation to succeed yields a sense of competency, which predicts effort, engagement, and achievement; those who feel competent are more likely to choose challenging learning tasks and will be more willing to try new ones (Schunk & Zimmerman, 2008). Subjective value appraisals impact the initiation and maintenance of learning behavior. Activities may be valued with respect to how interesting and enjoyable tasks are, how useful they are for meeting goals, and whether attainment of the task goals is considered important. Value appraisals predict behavioral choices to initiate a learning activity and to persist (Schunk et al., 2014). When the value of engaging in a learning task is salient to the individual, and the individual expects to be successful as a learner, behavior that is oriented toward learning is more likely to occur.

Both SDT and EVT principles are instrumental to NEAR from the very beginning of treatment. Enrollment in NEAR always starts with two questions: "What is it you hope to accomplish in the next months?" and "Do you think that improving your attention, memory, or other cognitive skills will help you do that?" These questions provide the framework for cognitive learning that emphasizes the personal value and meaningfulness of one's participation. The intervention is structured as small group sessions that occur two to three times weekly for 60–120 minutes, led by a certified NEAR therapist. Sessions include opportunities for both individualized computer-based learning and noncomputer group-based activities. A menu of cognitive exercises is *personalized*, using shared decision-making to address a participant's cognitive health needs, interests and learning goals. In selecting cognitive exercises, preference is given to those that are *contextualized*, meaning they depict contexts that make the practical utility and link to everyday life activities obvious. *Choice* of activities and learner control within the session foster self-determination and independence. These specific techniques, drawn from educational psychology, support intrinsic motivation, task engagement, and therefore cognitive learning (Cordova & Lepper, 1996). Therapist-guided exercise with feedback offers a supportive context for practicing and applying new skills and strategies; partnering and scaffolding cognitive practice to improve performance builds mastery and promotes perceived self-competency. Observations of task approach combined with strategy coaching builds a metacognitive awareness that reinforces participants' identities as capable learners. Bridging discussions, which promote metacognition and generalization of cognitive gains to valued activities, constitute a key feature of each session (Medalia et al., 2002; Medalia & Freilich, 2008; Medalia et al., 2017).

An international corpus of research provides support for the NEAR approach in improving neurocognitive, social, and occupational outcomes (Bark et al., 2003; Medalia et al., 2000; Medalia et al., 2001; Hodge et al., 2010; Katsumi et al., 2019; Vidarsdottir et al., 2019). Research evaluating potential mechanisms of change and correlates of improvement for NEAR among people with schizophrenia supports the significant role of motivation. Saperstein and colleagues (2020) evaluated cognitive performance, intrinsic motivation, and perceived competency for cognitive training tasks at the beginning and end of 30 NEAR sessions. Greater perceived competency, a key factor in intrinsic motivation, was associated with treatment engagement indicated by a shorter time to treatment completion ($p = 0.0025$); greater intrinsic motivation measured at treatment end-point was associated with greater cognitive change ($p = 0.02$). Another study comparing use of standard drill-and-practice CR techniques with the motivational instructional techniques used in NEAR (e.g., contextualized learning activities) reported that the people with schizophrenia who received the motivational instructional techniques had higher intrinsic motivation levels, reported greater feelings of self-competency, and acquired more cognitive skills (Choi & Medalia, 2010). Further, higher initial intrinsic motivation was associated with greater attendance rates as well as an increased magnitude of generalization to trained and untrained cognitive tasks. Follow-up studies have demonstrated that baseline expectations of success predict learning at both treatment end and at three-month follow up (Choi et al., 2010; Choi & Medalia, 2010). A separate, large multisite randomized controlled trial of pharmacotherapy combined with a modified 30-session NEAR program found that intrinsic motivation was related to the ability to complete the study, as study-end interest/enjoyment, a key factor in intrinsic motivation, was larger in those participants who completed treatment across groups (ES = 0.80) (Kantrowitz et al., 2016).

These empirical studies highlight the critical role of enhancing motivation for promoting cognitive learning and underscore the particular importance of promoting perceived competency and expectations for success through autonomous action. There are strong implications for NEAR's potential impact on negative symptoms, given the central role of amotivation in the negative symptom profile. Across CR approaches, it is recognized that negative symptoms can diminish through modifying dysfunctional attitudes associated with low perceived self-efficacy and anticipated failure in goal-directed tasks (Bowie et al., 2006; Grant & Beck, 2009; Ventura et al., 2014) as well as through improving the cognitive skills that support motivated behavior and psychosocial functioning.

4. Specific Treatments for Motivation

4.1 Motivational Interviewing

Motivational Interviewing (MI) aims to enhance motivation and elicit behavior change. Like NEAR, MI approaches motivation from the perspective of SDT by including key elements of promoting autonomy, facilitating competence, and relatedness (Markland et al., 2005). It has been applied in treating people with schizophrenia for addressing substance use disorders (Wang et al., 2022). More recently, a novel combined Motivational Interviewing and Cognitive Behavioral Therapy (MI-CBT; Reddy et al., 2023) has been developed for treating motivational negative symptoms, adapted from existing MI protocols for schizophrenia and substance use disorders. Sessions focus on building goal-oriented motivation, resolving ambivalence, and establishing commitment toward change while integrating CBT-based skills including cognitive restructuring, behavioral activation, and problem solving. In a randomized controlled trial including 79 participants, those assigned to the 12-session MI-CBT condition demonstrated stronger improvements in motivation compared with a control mindfulness condition that were sustained over a 24-week follow-up period, providing initial evidence for efficacy that warrants additional study. Considering that negative symptoms have been linked to lower rates of service engagement and response (Bucci et al., 2020; Carbon & Correll, 2014; Kukla et al., 2013; MacBeth et al., 2013; Thompson et al., 2011), the remaining body of MI research has focused on its utility for promoting motivation related to treatment adherence, including for cognitive interventions.

Preliminary work has adapted Dual Diagnosis Motivational Interviewing for people with psychosis and substance use disorders to enhance motivation for, adherence to, and benefit from cognitive rehabilitation. Sessions focus on exploring participants' views about their cognitive functioning with personalized feedback based on objective measures of cognitive performance, providing information on how cognition can be improved through cognitive training, and conducting a decisional balance activity to weigh the pros and cons of pursuing a goal and build motivation for change. Collaboration between the participant and therapist yields a change plan for improving cognitive functioning, including the option of participating in a cognitive training intervention. In an initial trial, MI was associated with increased task-specific motivation and higher attendance in a computer-based math training program over treatment as usual (TAU), with session attendance predicted by postintervention motivation levels (Fiszdon et al., 2016). In a second, expanded version of this study, Fiszdon and colleagues (2022) found no significant differences in intent-to-treat analyses between MI and TAU regarding attendance in a full cognitive training course. Analyses were limited, however, by low base rates of treatment participation, and after removing participants from analyses who did not attend any sessions the mean attendance rate was 46% higher for MI compared with TAU. MI was associated with increases in perceived value of training tasks and, to a lesser extent, how enjoyable/interesting they were rated.

4.2 Motivation Skills Training

Motivation Skills Training (MST) is a novel approach, which differs from NEAR and MI by explicitly teaching people how to motivate themselves. MST is derived from the motivation-science literature describing metamotivation, defined as the processes by which individuals identify, monitor, and self-regulate their motivational states. This research literature suggests that people's knowledge, beliefs, and capacity to self-regulate their motivation has a large impact on their ability to initiate and successfully execute goal-directed behaviors. Thus, metamotivation is a novel lens through which to view avolition, defined as a reduction in the initiation of and persistence in goal-directed activities, and the desire to perform such activities. MST is unique because it directly teaches participants the basic tenets of motivation theories, such as SDT and EVT, so that they can develop better awareness and insight into their own motivation and therefore more effectively draw upon skills and strategies to upregulate motivation and change behavior. MST builds upon research indicating that although there is a high prevalence of amotivation/apathy in schizophrenia populations (Kirkpatrick et al., 2006), motivation in individuals with schizophrenia is not a static entity, but rather, a dynamic process that is malleable and amenable to therapeutic intervention (Choi & Medalia, 2010; Medalia & Saperstein, 2011).

MST is designed to be implemented in approximately 14 weekly group 90-minute sessions embedded within existing clinic programs. Each session entails (1) psychoeducation to introduce motivation knowledge and self-regulation skills, (2) individualized goal setting and progress tracking, and (3) group workshopping around skill applications and supports. The group setting fosters collaboration, opportunity for social learning, and supports scalability. Psychoeducation employs in vivo exercises to engage participants in active reflection and discussion of content. For example, participants are prompted to offer definitions and conceptualize determinants of motivation, to identify skills and abilities as personal strengths (e.g., task initiation) or as those they wish to improve (e.g., persistence, motivational self-control). Individualized goal setting and weekly review of goal progress provide the context for identifying what factors are positively or negatively impacting one's motivation and for directly applying motivation knowledge and skills. The intervention utilizes a tool called the "Motivometer," which draws upon the MUSIC® Model of Motivation (Jones, 2009, 2018), a model that incorporates current motivation research and theories into a framework with five components: (1) e**M**powerment, (2) **U**sefulness, (3) **S**uccess, (4) **I**nterest, and (5) **C**aring. *Empowerment* refers to a sense of control and autonomy when doing an activity. *Usefulness* refers to the relevance of a task to a person's life and/or personal goals. *Success* is the perceived sense of competence and perception that they have the ability to succeed in adequately completing the activity. *Interest* refers to the enjoyment and curiosity while doing a task, and *Caring* refers to the belief that social interactions while doing a task will be positive. Throughout MST participants rate and visualize the quantity of their motivation with respect to each motivation component (MUSIC). Sources of motivation are characterized by their quality and rated in terms of their quantity; thoughts and feelings associated with high/low motivation provide clues about sources of motivation and barriers.

Participants learn how to harness the motivation components that are high on the Motivometer and identify those that are rated low; both guide the application of skills and strategies. Capitalizing on positive motivators (e.g., high usefulness) and/or selecting strategies to bolster the motivation components that are undermining goal-directed behavior (e.g., low expectation for success, low interest value) allows individuals to regulate their motivational state and to more effectively approach and persist on challenging tasks. The metamotivation framework, and therefore MST, appreciates that motivation can be impacted by the intertwining of personal, environmental, and/or social factors. All are therefore considered in the conceptualization of motivation deficit and treatment. Treatment of the motivation impairment characteristic of schizophrenia requires consideration of multiple dimensions including the emotional (internal) experiences, cognitive processes, and the interplay between an individual's cognitive and affective processes (e.g., attitudes, expectancies) and social contexts (e.g., stigma, opportunity loss). By addressing amotivation as a key component of negative symptoms, MST has the potential to play a critical role in impacting current functioning and the process of personal recovery.

Although research on MST is in its infancy, two studies to date have provided evidence supporting the rationale for the intervention and its efficacy. In the first study (Hansen et al., 2021) qualitative interviews were conducted with 21 individuals diagnosed with schizophrenia, ages 22–62, receiving outpatient mental health care. Interviews were analyzed using a thematic analysis approach to capture participants' understanding and beliefs about motivation and their capacity to overcome motivational challenges at work or a self-identified upcoming task. Three primary themes emerged. First, the majority of participants (81%) reported a view of motivation as a fixed trait that cannot be changed, and that motivation cannot be increased as a result of effort or persistence. Second, when asked about overcoming motivational challenges, 48% described relying on external rewards for accomplishing tasks, 19% described problem-solving strategies to overcome obstacles, and 33% were unable to describe any approach. Third, the majority of participants (71.4%) thought of motivation as only a pleasurable, positive feeling rather than something that at times may require effort and persistence. The implications for MST are that misperceptions about the malleability of motivation and how motivation can be monitored and upregulated can be directly addressed, and participants can learn how to use both positive *and* negative emotional cues to identify the quantity and quality of their motivation which, in turn, can facilitate the identification of specific self-regulation strategies for accomplishing a particular task or goal.

The results of this study underscore the relevance of targeting motivation *self-regulation* for improving negative symptoms and functional outcomes. Participants who endorsed better self-regulation ability were rated by a clinical interviewer as demonstrating lower avolition ($r = -0.453, p = 0.039$), higher quality of life ($r = 0.54, p = 0.011$), and higher community functioning ($r = 0.394, p = 0.077$). Further, a second study (Hansen et al., 2021) which evaluated the preliminary efficacy of MST in an outpatient sample of 38 adults with serious mental illness indicated significant decreases (improvements) in self-motivation ($Z = -3.15, p = 0.002$) and self-management ($Z = -3.76, p < 0.001$) dysfunction as measured by the Barkley Deficits in Executive Functioning Scale—Short Form (BDEFS-SF). Finally, MST yielded medium effect size improvements in global executive dysfunction (Cohen's $d = 0.47$) and self-reported quality of life ($d = 0.54$). In sum, a focus on metamotivation offers an innovative, promising avenue for treating motivation deficit and psychosocial impairment associated with the negative symptoms of schizophrenia.

5. Future Directions

Psychosocial interventions to address motivation deficits are able to positively impact recovery and quality of life. Yet even as these interventions gain recognition in international treatment guidelines as treatments for negative symptoms, research to refine and improve the treatments is ongoing. Several directions for future investigation are considered below.

1. Dissemination: Lack of clinicians trained in evidence-based CR has constrained implementation and dissemination. More education of clinicians about the importance of addressing cognitive health and the specific instructional techniques to build self-efficacy and motivation is needed. The increasing trend toward online learning, as is offered at www.teachrecovery.com, will hopefully facilitate training of clinicians who can then address the needs of individuals impacted by cognitive and motivation impairment.
2. Technology: CR requires access to technology and the internet. Although the boom in new technologically based interventions has presented opportunity for expanded service delivery options (e.g., via telehealth), there are disparities in access to technology that may constrain uptake (Arlia et al., 2022). Further, additional understanding is needed regarding how such advances may improve accessibility and adherence without sacrificing efficacy outcomes demonstrated in in-person randomized controlled trials.
3. Neuroscience: As neuroscience-informed approaches to measure and enhance neuroplasticity and the neurotransmitter systems underlying reward processing and cognition become more refined, there will be opportunities to personalize motivational and cognitive therapies and enhance treatment effectiveness. Medications to enhance cognition and neuroplasticity are in development and being studied in combination with CR (Horan et al., 2022).
4. Personalization: Both motivational and cognitive interventions are seeking to become more personalized, which provides an opportunity to increase sensitivity to developmental, cultural, and demographic disparities in how deficits present and are reinforced. Consideration of personalization must simultaneously account for scalability to meet the challenges of implementation across large and small systems of care.
5. Acceptability: Sociocultural issues are important exploration areas for maximizing adherence and benefit from psychosocial interventions. As reviewed in this chapter, positive learning experiences, value appraisals, perceived competency, autonomy, and expectations for success are key ingredients for motivation enhancing interventions. These are also subjective experiences, and as such are dynamic and open to social influences including cultural values, competing demands and socioeconomic stressors, as well as stigma and discrimination experiences. Further exploration

of sociocultural influences and client-level values, priorities, and understandings of motivation and cognitive learning is crucial for enhancing service implementation and delivery.

References

American Psychiatric Association. (2020). *The American Psychiatric Association Practice Guideline for the Treatment of Patients with Schizophrenia.* (3rd ed.) American Psychiatric Association Publishing.

Arlia, C., Saperstein, A. M., Meyler, S., Styke, S., & Medalia, A. (2022). Disparities in technology literacy and access negatively impact cognitive remediation scalability. *Schizophrenia Research, 243*, 456–457.

Bark, N., Revheim, N., Huq, F., Khalderov, V., Ganz, Z. W., & Medalia, A. (2003). The impact of cognitive remediation on psychiatric symptoms of schizophrenia. *Schizophrenia Research, 63*(3), 229–235.

Barlati, S., Ariu, C., Ceraso, A., Deste, G., Nibbio, G., & Vita, A. (2022). New strategies to improve cognitive symptoms in schizophrenia. *Psychiatric Care, 8*, 62–80.

Bowie, C. R., Bell, M. D., Fiszdon, J. M., Johannesen, J. K., Lindenmayer, J. P., McGurk, S. R., Medalia, A. A., Penadés, R., Saperstein, A. M., Twamley, E. W., Ueland, T., & Wykes, T. (2020). Cognitive remediation for schizophrenia: An expert working group white paper on core techniques. *Schizophrenia Research, 215*, 49–53.

Bowie, C. R., & Harvey, P. D. (2006). Cognitive deficits and functional outcome in schizophrenia. *Neuropsychiatric Disease and Treatment, 2*(4), 531–536.

Bowie, C. R., Reichenberg, A., Patterson, T. L., Heaton, R. K., & Harvey, P. D. (2006). Determinants of real-world functional performance in schizophrenia subjects: correlations with cognition, functional capacity, and symptoms. *The American journal of psychiatry, 163*(3), 418–425.

Bryce, S., Warren, N., Ponsford, J., Rossell, S., & Lee, S. (2018). Understanding the lived experience of cognitive remediation in schizophrenia: A qualitative comparison with an active control. *Psychiatric Rehabilitation Journal, 41*(4), 302–311.

Bucci, P., Mucci, A., Winter van Rossum, I., Aiello, C., Arango, C., Baandrup, L., Buchanan, R. W., Dazzan, P., Demjaha, A., Díaz-Caneja, C. M., Maria Giordano, G., Glentøj, B. Y., Leucht, S., McGuire, P., Rodriguez-Jimenez, R., Vignapiano, A., Kahn, R. S., & Galderisi, S. (2020). Persistent negative symptoms in recent-onset psychosis: Relationship to treatment response and psychosocial functioning. *European Neuropsychopharmacology: The Journal of the European College of Neuropsychopharmacology, 34*, 76–86.

Carbon, M., & Correll, C. (2014). Thinking and acting beyond the positive: The role of the cognitive and negative symptoms in schizophrenia. *CNS Spectrums, 19*(S1), 35–53.

Cardenas, V., Abel, S., Bowie, C. R., Tiznado, D., Depp, C. A., Patterson, T. L., Jeste, D. V., & Mausbach, B. T. (2013). When functional capacity and real-world functioning converge: The role of self-efficacy. *Schizophrenia Bulletin, 39*(4), 908–916.

Cella, M., Reeder, C., & Wykes, T. (2014). It is all in the factors: Effects of cognitive remediation on symptom dimensions. *Schizophrenia Research, 156*, 60–62.

Cella, M., Preti, A., Edwards, C., Dow, T., & Wykes, T. (2017). Cognitive remediation for negative symptoms of schizophrenia: A network meta-analysis. *Clin Psychol Rev, 52*, 43–51.

Cella, M. & Wykes, T. (2019). The nuts and bolts of Cognitive Remediation: Exploring how different training components relate to cognitive and functional gains. *Schizophrenia Research, 203*, 12–16.

Cella, M., Roberts, S., Pillny, M., Riehle, M., O'Donoghue, B., Lyne, J., Tomlin, P., Valmaggia, L., & Preti, A. (2023). Psychosocial and behavioural interventions for the negative symptoms of schizophrenia: a systematic review of efficacy meta-analyses. *The British Journal of Psychiatry: The Journal of Mental Science, 223*(1), 321–331.

Choi, J., & Medalia, A. (2010). Intrinsic motivation and learning in a schizophrenia spectrum sample. *Schizophrenia Research, 118*(1-3), 12–19.

Choi, J., Fiszdon, J. M., & Medalia, A. (2010). Expectancy-value theory in persistence of learning effects in schizophrenia: role of task value and perceived competency. *Schizophrenia Bulletin*, 36(5), 957–965.

Contreras, N. A., Lee, S., Tan, E. J., Castle, D. J., & Rossell, S. L. (2016). How is cognitive remediation training perceived by people with schizophrenia? A qualitative study examining personal experiences. *Journal of Mental Health, 25*(3), 260–266.

Cordova, D. I., & Lepper, M. R. (1996). Intrinsic motivation and the process of learning: beneficial effects of contextualization, personalization and choice. *Journal of Educational Psychology, 88*, 715–730.

Eccles, J. S., & Wigfield, A. (2002). Motivational beliefs, values, and goals. *Annual Review of Psychology, 53*, 109–132.

Farreny, A., Aguado, J., Ochoa, S., Haro, J. M., & Usall, J. (2013). The role of negative symptoms in the context of cognitive remediation for schizophrenia. *Schizophrenia Research, 150*, 58–63.

Fiszdon, J. M., Kurtz, M. M., Choi, J., Bell, M. D., & Martino, S. (2016). Motivational interviewing to increase cognitive rehabilitation adherence in schizophrenia. *Schizophrenia Bulletin, 42*(2), 327–334.

Fiszdon, J. M., Choi, J., Wang, K., Parente, L. T., Hallinan, S., Burton, E., Bell, M. D., & Martino, S. (2022). Motivational interviewing to enhance psychosocial treatment attendance in people with SMI. *Schizophrenia Research, 246*, 165–171.

Galderisi, S., Mucci, A., Dollfus, S., Nordentoft, M., Falkai, P., Kaiser, S., Giordano, G. M., Vandevelde, A., Nielsen, M. Ø., Glenthøj, L. B., Sabé, M., Pezzella, P., Bitter, I., & Gaebel, W. (2021). EPA guidance on assessment of negative symptoms in schizophrenia. *European Psychiatry: The Journal of the Association of European Psychiatrists, 64*(1), e23.

Galletly, C., Castle, D., Dark, F., Humberstone, V., Jablensky, A., Killackey, E., Kulkarni, J., McGorry, P., Nielssen, O., & Tran, N. (2016). Royal Australian and New Zealand College of Psychiatrists clinical practice guidelines for the management of schizophrenia and related disorders. *The Australian and New Zealand Journal of Psychiatry, 50*(5), 410–472.

Garrido, G., Barrios, M., Penadés, R., Enriquez, M., Garolera, M., Aragay, N., Pajares, M., Vallès, V., Delgado, L., Alberni, J., Faixa, C., & Vendrell, J. M. (2013). Computer-assisted cognitive remediation therapy: cognition, self-esteem and quality of life in schizophrenia. *Schizophrenia Research, 150*(2–3), 563–569.

Gold, J. M., Waltz, J. A., Prentice, K. J., Morris, S. E., & Heerey, E. A. (2008). Reward processing in schizophrenia: a deficit in the representation of value. *Schizophrenia Bulletin, 34*(5), 835–847.

Grant, P. M., & Beck, A. T. (2009). Defeatist beliefs as a mediator of cognitive impairment, negative symptoms, and functioning in schizophrenia. *Schizophrenia Bulletin, 35*(4), 798–806.

Green, M. F., Kern, R. S., & Heaton, R. K. (2004). Longitudinal studies of cognition and functional outcome in schizophrenia: implications for MATRICS. *Schizophrenia Research, 72*, 41–51.

Hansen, M. C., Lynch, D. A., Stefancic, A., & Medalia, A. (2021). Metamotivation in people diagnosed with schizophrenia: A conceptual introduction and qualitative study. *Schizophrenia Research, 243*, 317–321.

Hansen, M. C., Gertmenian, E., Lynch, D., Sardana, S., Herlands, T., & Medalia, A. (2021). Metamotivation therapy: Is it time to focus on metamotivation in severe mental illness? *Journal of Contemporary Psychotherapy, 51*, 295–301.

Hodge, M. A., Siciliano, D., Withey, P., Moss, B., Moore, G., Judd, G., Shores, E. A., & Harris, A. (2010). A randomized controlled trial of cognitive remediation in schizophrenia. *Schizophrenia Bulletin, 36*(2), 419–427.

Horan, W. P., Catalano, L. T., & Green, M. F. (2022). An update on treatment of cognitive impairment associated with schizophrenia. *Current Topics in Behavioral Neurosciences.* 36, 407–436.

Jones, B. D. (2009). Motivating students to engage in learning: The MUSIC model of academic motivation. *International Journal of Teaching and Learning in Higher Education, 21*, 272–285.

Jones, B. D. (2018). *Motivating students by design: Practical strategies for professors* (2nd ed.). CreateSpace.

Kantrowitz, J. T., Sharif, Z., Medalia, A., Keefe, R. S., Harvey, P., Bruder, G., Barch, D. M., Choo, T., Lee, S., & Lieberman, J. A. (2016). A multi-center, rater-blinded, randomized controlled study of auditory processing-focused cognitive remediation combined with open-label lurasidone in patients with schizophrenia and schizoaffective disorder. *Journal of Clinical Psychology, 77*(6), 799–806.

Katsumi, A., Hoshino, H., Fujimoto, S., Yabe, H., Ikebuchi, E., Nakagome, K., & Niwa, S. I. (2019). Effects of cognitive remediation on cognitive and social functions in individuals with schizophrenia. *Neuropsychological Rehabilitation, 29*(9), 1475–1487.

Kirkpatrick, B., Fenton, W. S., Carpenter, W. T., & Marder, S. R. (2006). The NIMH-MATRICS consensus statement on negative symptoms. *Schizophrenia Bulletin, 32*(2), 214–219.

Kukla, M., Davis, L. W., & Lysaker, P. H. (2013). Cognitive behavioral therapy and work outcomes: Correlates of treatment engagement and full and partial success in schizophrenia. *Behavioural and Cognitive Psychotherapy, 42*(5), 577–592.

Lee, H. S., Jang, S. K., Lee, G. Y., Park, S. C., Medalia, A., & Choi, K. H. (2017). Informationally administered reward enhances intrinsic motivation in schizophrenia. *Psychiatry Research, 256*, 290–297.

Lejeune, J. A., Northrop, A., & Kurtz, M. M. (2021). A meta-analysis of cognitive remediation for schizophrenia: Efficacy and the role of participant and treatment factors. *Schizophrenia Bulletin, 47*(4), 997–1006.

Li, X., Chu, M. Y., Lv, Q. Y., Hu, H. X., Li, Z., Yi, Z. H., Wang, J. H., Zhang, J. Y., Lui, S. S. Y., Cheung, E. F. C., Shum, D. H. K., & Chan, R. C. K. (2019). The remediation effects of working memory training in schizophrenia patients with prominent negative symptoms. *Cognitive Neuropsychiatry, 24*(6), 434–453.

MacBeth, A., Gumley, A., Schwannauer, M., & Fisher, R. (2013). Service engagement in first episode psychosis. *The Journal of Nervous and Mental Disease, 201*(5), 359–364.

Mahmood, Z., Clark, J. M. R.,& Twamley, E. W. (2019). Compensatory cognitive training for psychosis: Effects on negative symptom subdomains. *Schizophrenia Research, 204*, 397–400.

Markland, D., Ryan, R. M., Tobin, V. J., & Rollnick, S. (2005). Motivational interviewing and self-determination theory. *Journal of Social and Clinical Psychology, 24*(6), 811–831.

McGurk, S. R., Twamley, E. W., Sitzer, D. I., McHugo, G. J., & Mueser, K.T. (2007). A meta-analysis of cognitive remediation in schizophrenia. *American Journal of Psychiatry, 164*(12), 1791–1802.

Medalia, A., Dorn, H., & Watras-Gans, S. (2000). Treating problem-solving deficits on an acute care psychiatric inpatient unit. *Psychiatry Research, 97*, 79–88.

Medalia, A., & Freilich, B. (2008). The Neuropsychological Educational Approach to Cognitive Remediation (NEAR) Model: Practice principles and outcome studies. *American Journal of Psychiatric Rehabilitation, 11*(2), 123–143.

Medalia, A., Herlands, T., Saperstein, A., & Revheim, N. (2017). *Cognitive remediation for psychological disorders*. Oxford University Press.

Medalia, A., Revheim, N., & Casey, M. (2001). The remediation of problem-solving skills in schizophrenia. *Schizophrenia Bulletin, 27*, 259–267.

Medalia, A., Revheim, N., & Herlands, T. (2002). *Remediation of cognitive deficits in psychiatric outpatients: A clinician's manual*. New York, NY: Montefiore Medical Center.

Medalia, A., & Saperstein, A. (2011). The role of motivation for treatment success. *Schizophrenia Bulletin, 37*, S122–S128.

Norman, R., Lecomte, T., Addington, D., & Anderson, E. (2017). Canadian Treatment Guidelines on Psychosocial Treatment of Schizophrenia in Adults. *Canadian Journal of Psychiatry. Revue Canadienne de Psychiatrie, 62*(9), 617–623.

Reddy, L. F., Glynn, S. M., McGovern, J. E., Sugar, C. A., Reavis, E. A., & Green, M. F. (2023). A novel psychosocial intervention for motivational negative symptoms in schizophrenia: Combined Motivational Interviewing and CBT. *American Journal of Psychiatry, 180*(5), 367–376.

Reeder, C., Pile, V., Crawford, P., Cella, M., Rose, D., Wykes, T., Watson, A., Huddy, V., & Callard, F. (2016). The feasibility and acceptability to service users of CIRCuiTS, a computerized cognitive remediation therapy programme for schizophrenia. *Behavioural and Cognitive Psychotherapy, 44*(3), 288–305.

Riehle, M., Böhl, M. C., Pillny, M., & Lincoln, T. M. (2020). Efficacy of Psychological Treatments for Patients with Schizophrenia and Relevant Negative Symptoms: A Meta-Analysis. *Clinical psychology in Europe, 2*(3), e2899.

Rund, B. R. (1998). A review of longitudinal studies of cognitive functions in schizophrenia patients. *Schizophrenia Bulletin, 24*(3), 425–435.

Ryan, R. M., & Deci, E. L. (2000). Self-determination theory and the facilitation of intrinsic motivation, social development, and well-being. *American Psychologist, 55*, 68–78.

Saperstein, A. M., Lynch, D. A., Qian, M., & Medalia, A. (2020). How does awareness of cognitive impairment impact motivation and treatment outcomes during cognitive remediation for schizophrenia? *Schizophrenia Research, 218*, 70–75.

Saperstein, A. M., & Medalia, A. (2012). The empirical basis for the practice of cognitive remediation for schizophrenia. *Neuropsychiatry, 2*(2), 101–109.

Saperstein, A. M., & Medalia, A. (2016). The Role of Motivation in Cognitive Remediation for People with Schizophrenia. *Current topics in behavioral neurosciences, 27*, 533–546.

Saperstein, A. M., Brennan, R., Qian, M., Javitt, D. C., & Medalia. (2025). Impact of early auditory processing on negative symptom response to cognitive remediation for schizophrenia. *Schizophrenia Bulletin*, sbaf017.

Schunk, D. H., & Zimmerman, B. J. (Eds.). (2008). *Motivation and self-regulated learning: Theory, research, and applications*. Lawrence Erlbaum Associates.

Schunk, D. H., Meece, J. L., & Pintrich, P. R. (2014). *Motivation in education: Theory, research, and applications* (4th ed.). Pearson.

Soumet-Leman, C., Medalia, A., & Erlich, M. D. (2018). Acceptability and perceived effectiveness of cognitive remediation in clinical practice. *Psychiatric Services, 69*(4), 493–494.

Thompson, J., Berk, M., Dean, O., Kohlmann, K., Jeavons, S., Bush, A., & Copolov, D. (2011). Who's left? Symptoms of schizophrenia that predict clinical trial dropout. *Human Psychopharmacology, 26*(8), 609–613.

Tsapekos, D., Taylor, R., & Cella, M. (2017). Feasibility and acceptability of brief cognitive remediation targeting metacognition in acute inpatients with psychosis: A case series. *Neuropsychological Rehabilitation, 29*(3), 361–375.

Twamley, E. W., Vella, L., Burton, C. Z., Heaton, r. K., & Jeste, D. V. (2012). Compensatory cognitive training for psychosis: Effects in a randomized controlled trial. *Journal of Clinical Psychiatry, 73*(9), 1212–1219.

Vidarsdottir, O. G., Roberts, D. L., Twamley, E. W., Gudmundsdottir, B., Sigurdsson, E., & Magnusdottir, B. B. (2019). Integrative cognitive remediation for early psychosis: Results from a randomized controlled trial. *Psychiatry Research, 273*, 690–698.

Ventura, J., Subotnik, K. L., Gretchen-Doorly, D., Casaus, L., Boucher, M., Medalia, A., Bell, M. D., Hellemann, G. S., & Nuechterlein, K. H. (2019). Cognitive remediation can improve negative symptoms and social functioning in first-episode schizophrenia: A randomized controlled trial. *Schizophrenia Research, 203*, 24–31.

Ventura, J., Subotnik, K. L., Ered, A., Gretchen-Doorly, D., Hellemann, G. S., Vaskinn, A., & Nuechterlein, K. H. (2014). The relationship of attitudinal beliefs to negative symptoms, neurocognition, and daily functioning in recent-onset schizophrenia. *Schizophrenia Bulletin, 40*(6), 1308–1318.

Vita, A., Barlati, S., Ceraso, A., Nibbio, G., Ariu, C., Deste, G., & Wykes T. (2021). Effectiveness, core elements, and moderators of response of cognitive remediation for schizophrenia: A systematic review and meta-analysis of randomized clinical trials. *JAMA Psychiatry, 78*(8), 848–858.

Vita, A., Barlati, S., Ceraso, A., Deste, G., Nibbio, G., & Wykes, T. (2022). Acceptability of cognitive remediation for schizophrenia: A systematic review and meta-analysis of randomized controlled trials. *Psychological Medicine, 53*(8), 3661–3671.

Vita, A., Gaebel, W., Mucci, A., Sachs, G., Barlati, S., Giordano, G. M., Nibbio, G., Nordentoft, M., Wykes, T., & Galderisi, S. (2022). European Psychiatric Association guidance on treatment of cognitive impairment in schizophrenia. *European psychiatry: the journal of the Association of European Psychiatrists, 65*(1), e57.

Wang, W., Chun Chau, A. K., Kong, P., Sun, X., & Ho-wai So, S. (2022). Efficacy of motivational interviewing in treating co-occurring psychosis and substance use disorder: A systematic review and meta-analysis. *Journal of Clinical Psychiatry, 83*, 21r13916.

Wykes, T., Huddy, V., Cellard, C., McGurk, S. R., & Czobor, P. (2011). A meta-analysis of cognitive remediation for schizophrenia: Methodology and effect sizes. *American Journal of Psychiatry, 168*(5), 472–485.

17

Social Skills Training for Negative Symptoms

Kim T. Mueser, Daniel Fulford, and Jessica Mow

Clinical pearls

- Social skills training (SST) is an intervention usually provided in a group format that is aimed at teaching more effective interpersonal behaviors and improving social functioning in people with schizophrenia and other serious mental illnesses.
- SST targets specific areas of social functioning depending on the needs and goals of the client population (e.g., friendship and dating, conflict resolution), with corresponding social skills curricula that breaks complex skills down into smaller components.
- Interpersonal skills are systematically taught in SST using a combination of modeling, role playing, feedback, and home practice assignments.
- Research on SST has shown that it is effective at both improving psychosocial functioning and negative symptoms in schizophrenia.
- SST can be provided as a single intervention approach targeting negative symptoms and social functioning, or combined with other treatment approaches such as in family psychoeducation and illness self-management programs.

1. Introduction

Impaired social functioning, including both reduced size of social networks and quality of personal relationships, is a hallmark of schizophrenia that is strongly associated with the negative symptoms of the disorder, especially apathy, avolition, and anhedonia (Pogue-Geile & Harrow, 1985; Sayers et al., 1996; Stouten et al., 2017). Better social functioning in schizophrenia (viz. higher degree of social contacts) is associated with improved overall psychosocial adjustment,

Kim T. Mueser, Daniel Fulford, and Jessica Mow, *Social Skills Training for Negative Symptoms*. In: *Psychosocial Approaches to Negative Symptoms in Psychosis*. Edited by: Tania Lincoln et al., Oxford University Press.
 DOI: 10.1093/oso/9780197676790.003.0017

and is predictive of a better course of the illness (Erickson et al., 1989; J. S. Strauss & Carpenter, 1977). Furthermore, social relationships are an important contributor to quality of life, and a common treatment goal for individuals with the disorder (Ramsay et al., 2011). For these reasons, efforts to improve social functioning have long been a focus of psychosocial treatments for schizophrenia.

One approach to improving social functioning in schizophrenia has been to target social competence, or the person's overall ability or capacity to solve problems and achieve goals, which is comprised of specific social skills. We elaborate further on this model below.

2. Theoretical Background

Social functioning refers to the actual attainment of normative relationships and perceived quality of such relationships. Sufficient quantity and quality of social relationships depend on social competence and skills. *Social competence* is the extent to which an individual has the ability to adjust and thrive in their social environment. *Social skills* are conceptualized as the building blocks of social competence, which are assumed to be learned (or learnable) and not based on traits or other internal processes. They can be broadly defined as the interpersonal skills required to achieve affiliative and instrumental goals (Liberman et al., 1989). By breaking the complex abilities that comprise social competence into smaller, more elemental components, interpersonal skills can be taught through the application of the principles of social learning theory (e.g., modeling skills, behavioral rehearsal, positive and corrective feedback, shaping of successive approximations to desired skill). This approach to systematically teaching skills, or *social skills training*, is one of the oldest and most established psychosocial interventions for schizophrenia (K.T. Mueser et al., 2024), with the earliest trials dating back to the 1970s (Hersen & Bellack, 1976; S. T. Mueser, 1976).

2.1 Social Skills and Negative Symptoms

Three different types of social skill can be distinguished: expressive, social cognitive, and interactive (or reciprocal) (K.T. Mueser et al., 2024). *Expressive skills* are the actual behaviors emitted by someone during a social interaction, which can be broken down into three categories: verbal behaviors, paralinguistic features of speech, and nonverbal behaviors. *Verbal behaviors* are the form, structure, content, and number of words used during communications. For people with schizophrenia, thought disorder symptoms such as idiosyncratic use of words, neologisms, or disorganized syntax are verbal behaviors that can interfere with effective communication. *Paralinguistic features* include characteristics of vocal speech such as volume, pace, intonation, and pitch that are especially important in communicating meaning and emotions during interactions. *Nonverbal behaviors* such as facial expression, eye contact, gestures, posture, body orientation, and proximity to the other person, provide complementary information to vocal characteristics and are vital to conveying feelings to other people. Nonverbal behavioral anomalies in schizophrenia, such as preference for greater interpersonal distance when interacting with others (Holt et al., 2015), may detract from effectively connecting with people in ways other than diminished expressiveness.

Social cognition involves the ability to accurately perceive and process a wide range of socially relevant cues and parameters in different situations (Penn et al., 1997). These include skills such as recognizing others' emotional expressions, understanding unwritten rules and constraints related to specific social contexts, being able to accurately discern others' thoughts and intentions, and being able to formulate reasonable and effective action plans based on the individual's social goals. Social cognitive skills have been shown to mediate the association between impaired cognitive functioning and psychosocial adjustment in schizophrenia (Green et al., 2015). *Interactive skills* involve the "give-and-take" of social encounters, such as the latency of time it takes to respond to another's utterance, the relative time spent talking by two people in a conversation, and the responsivity of partners to the emotional tone and content of what the other person has just said.

Negative symptoms can be defined as reflecting a reduction or relative absence of behaviors, thoughts, feelings, and motivations in schizophrenia that are ordinarily present in individuals without the illness. There has been debate about the specific factor structure of negative symptoms, with the number of factors most often ranging between two (Blanchard & Cohen, 2006; Sayers, et al., 1996) and five (Ahmed, et al., 2022; G. P. Strauss et al., 2018). Negative symptoms, however, can be broadly described as falling into two broad types, including *diminished expressiveness*, such as flattened affect, and *experiential symptoms* such as apathy, anhedonia, and asociality. There is a clear overlap in the diminished expressiveness dimension of negative symptoms and social skill impairments in paralinguistic and nonverbal behaviors that communicate emotion (Bellack et al., 1990; K.T. Mueser et al., 2010). As we discuss further below, there are also associations between experiential negative symptoms and social skills, but no overlap in definitions.

2.2 Social Skills and Social Functioning

Social functioning can be defined as the quantity and quality of social relationships, including the perceived supportiveness and reward or satisfaction with existing connections. The social skills model posits that social competence is based on a set of component response skills (or behavioral repertoires) that are learned or learnable. The model further hypothesizes that problems in social functioning occur when the requisite skills are not in an individual's behavioral repertoire, are not used at the appropriate times, or when the person performs socially inappropriate behaviors (K.T. Mueser et al., 2024).

Of note, the model recognizes that a variety of other factors can interfere with the use of social skills that individuals may nevertheless be capable of. For example, negative mood states such as anxiety or depression may interfere with or reduce the chances of someone using appropriate skills in certain social situations. Similarly, experiential negative symptoms reflecting low levels of social motivation (e.g., apathy, anhedonia, asociality) could result in poor social functioning in an individual due to the non-use of skills that are in their behavioral repertoire. In addition, implicit in the social skills model is the assumption that people have opportunities to improve their social functioning through the use of skills by engaging others in potentially rewarding social relationships. To the extent that environmental constraints reduce social opportunities or outright prevent them, such as in many institutional settings (Wing & Brown, 1979), poor social functioning can be expected regardless of individuals' social skills.

Two lines of evidence provide support for the social skills model of social competence. First, multiple single case designs and randomized controlled trials have shown that individuals can learn and retain social skills using the techniques of social skills training (as described below), and that skills taught in one setting may generalize to other settings (Benton & Schroeder, 1990; Dilk & Bond, 1996). The generalization of social skills can be further enhanced by providing community-based practice of skills (Glynn et al., 2002) or involving naturally supportive individuals in prompting the use of skills in appropriate situations (Tauber et al., 2000).

Second, performance on standardized role play tests of social skill in persons with schizophrenia and other serious mental illnesses is strongly correlated with skills in more naturalistic social interactions (Bellack et al., 1990; K.T. Mueser et al., 1993), suggesting that the ability to use effective social skills in a laboratory test of social competence is related to the actual use of skills in real social interactions. Furthermore, better performance on role play tests in people with schizophrenia is also associated with better social adjustment when rated by independent judges (Bellack et al., 1990; Harvey et al., 2011; K.T. Mueser et al., 1996; Patterson et al., 2001). Thus, individuals who objectively demonstrate a stronger behavioral repertoire of social skills in simulated social interactions may use these skills to achieve greater social functioning in daily life.

2.3 Experiential Negative Symptoms and Social Skills

Similar to research showing a strong association between social skill and social functioning in schizophrenia, negative symptoms are also a potent predictor of psychosocial adjustment (de Winter et al., 2022; Stouten et al., 2017; Weinberg et al., 2009), with the experiential negative symptoms being more important than diminished expressiveness (Sayers et al., 1996). This raises the question of the associations between experiential negative symptoms and social skills.

There is evidence that more severe experiential negative symptoms, such as avolition/amotivation, anhedonia, and asociality, are associated with worse social skills on role play tests (Bellack et al., 1990; Blanchard et al., 2015; K. T. Mueser et al., 1991). The origins and directionality of these associations are unclear, and effects in both directions appear plausible.

A key challenge in understanding directional relationships between negative symptoms and social skills are related to lack of conceptual clarity of how certain negative symptoms are defined, such as asociality. Asociality is more generally defined as declining to engage in social relationships (Carpenter et al., 1988). Some interpret these behaviors as evidence that people with schizophrenia lack the interest in or desire to form interpersonal relationships (i.e., the preference to be alone, as in schizoid personality disorder). In reality, people with schizophrenia endorse high rates of loneliness (Eglit et al., 2018), which reflects a lack of satisfaction with their current relationships, and they report improving relationships as a key treatment goal (Ramsay et al., 2011). This would suggest that, for many, asociality is less a product of low interest and more likely due to other factors, such as limited social skills and social self-efficacy (Grant & Beck, 2009).

Nonetheless, there may at least be a subgroup of individuals with serious mental illness who experience a lack of social interest or drive, consistent with the experience of avolition/amotivation more generally. For these individuals it is reasonable to expect a reduction in the number of social interactions an individual seeks, and hence opportunities to learn relevant skills. Low social drive, and lower investment in social relationships, could also result in a failure to deploy the social skills necessary to engage and sustain the interest of other people during social interactions, both in simulated role play tests and in real life. On the other hand, a history of poor social skills resulting in a lack of social reinforcement could contribute to diminished social drive as individuals reduce their effort to connect with others in order to insulate themselves from further rejection. (See Riehle in this volume for a fuller discussion of this idea.) The poor premorbid social functioning associated with schizophrenia (Zigler & Glick, 1986), and the associations between premorbid functioning and social skills (K.T. Mueser et al., 1990) and negative symptoms (Malla et al., 2002), appear consistent with both of these possible directional effects, but especially the latter direction (i.e., limited social skills leading to reduced social drive), considering the more pathognomonic nature of experiential negative symptoms.

3. Practical Procedure

3.1 Format and Duration

The most common format of SST is a group setting of six to eight members led by two group leaders (Mueser et al., 2024). Group settings are ideal for the delivery of SST because they are both cost-effective and create natural opportunities for group members to observe and practice the social skills being learned. Group members can also provide and receive feedback from multiple people on their performance. The use of two group leaders can create opportunities for additional role-play practice (i.e., through splitting up a large group into smaller sections), and allow for one group leader to focus on group process issues and dynamics while the other leader teaches the skills. SST intervention programs may last anywhere from a few weeks to over a year, depending on the needs of group members, the focus of the intervention, and the resources available. Sessions typically last 45 to 90 minutes and may be held one or more times per week.

The SST procedures were developed to be flexible and modifiable to match the needs of individuals seeking treatment and the resources available within various settings. As such, variables often change depending on the group and setting. For example, if a setting cannot offer group programs, social skills can be taught during individual sessions. Groups may be provided in an open (i.e., new members may join at any time) or closed (i.e., the group consists of the same members throughout the program) format. Additionally, SST can be delivered within both inpatient and outpatient settings.

3.2 Content Focus of SST Programs

SST primarily targets skills within five categories, as described earlier in this chapter: (1) paralinguistic features, (2) nonverbal behavior, (3) verbal content, (4) interactive balance, and (5) social cognition. Each category contains multiple individual skill components. SST groups are sometimes conducted focusing on a specific area of social functioning, such as conversational skills, assertiveness and conflict management, making friends and dating, interacting with health-care professionals, or independent living in the community. Other times SST groups may cover a broad range of different topics, spending several weeks on one topic before going onto the next. For example, in the Helping Older People Experience Success program, which was aimed at improving social and community functioning in older persons with schizophrenia and severe major mood disorders, the one-year SST curriculum covered seven different topic areas: Communicating Effectively, Making and Keeping Friends, Healthy Living, Making the Most of Leisure Time, Using Medications Effectively, and Making the Most of a Health Care Visit (Bartels et al., 2014).

3.3 SST Teaching Methods

Prior to engagement in an SST group one of the leaders meets with each client individually to provide an orientation to the nature of the group, and to explore and identify personal goals the client would like to work on over the course of participating in the group. These goals are routinely followed up, either in group or outside of group (or both), and are revised and updated as needed. Setting and tracking individual goals in SST is important for harnessing individuals' motivation to participate in the group, and helping them understand the relevance of individual skills to their personal goals and lives.

SST is traditionally taught in a standardized series of 10 steps, as outlined in Table 17.1 and summarized below. Step 1 consists of introducing a social skill and discussing with group members how they might find the skill helpful in their lives, thereby generating interest in learning the skill. During Step 2, group leaders explain the components that comprise the skill and how each one relates to the overall skill. Within this step, group leaders can also integrate discussions of the value of the skill components, as well as relevant aspects of social cognition.

The next seven steps involve role playing. Step 3 consists of a role-play in which the group leaders demonstrate effective use of the skill with each other. Following this role-play, group members provide both positive and corrective feedback to the group leaders. Group members are also encouraged to comment on which components of the skill were (or were not) used. Step 4 involves a role-play in which a group member practices the skill with a group leader. Group leaders should take care to prepare thoroughly for Step 4, including specifying the group member's role (i.e., determining a fictional situation and character) and goal (e.g., expressing a positive feeling to the other person) in the role-play. Step 5 consists of group members and leaders providing positive feedback to the group member who participated in the role-play. Importantly, positive feedback

Table 17.1 Steps of Social Skills Training

Step 1: *Establish the rationale for the skill*

- Introduce skill and elicit comments from group about relevance to their lives
- Add additional reasons for value of learning skill

Step 2: *Discuss the steps of the skill*

- Write the steps down so all group members can view (e.g., on a poster)
- Review each of the steps, highlighting why each is important to the skill
- Check for understanding from group members

Step 3: *Model the skill in a role-play and review the role-play with the group members*

- Plan the role-play in advance, keeping it short and simple
- Complete the role-play with two leaders (if possible)
- Elicit positive and corrective feedback from the group members
- Ask group members to evaluate whether steps were used in role-play

Step 4: *Engage a group member in a role-play*

- Ask group member to participate in a role-play
- Plan the role-play in advance keeping it short and simple
- Ask group member questions to be sure they understand the goal
- Instruct remaining group members to observe

Step 5: *Provide positive feedback*

- Elicit positive feedback about group member's skills during role-play
- Encourage specific feedback (e.g., which step of the skill they did well)
- Cut off negative feedback

Step 6: *Provide corrective feedback*

- Elicit comments for how group member could do the skill better next time
- Limit to only one or two suggestions

Step 7: *Engage the group member in another role-play*

- Encourage group member to make one change based on feedback
- Check for understanding
- Complete role-play again with same group member

Step 8: *Provide additional feedback*

- First elicit feedback about the change that was made in role-play
- Elicit additional positive and corrective feedback

Step 9: *Engage other group members in role-plays and provide feedback (as in steps 4–8)*

- Follow steps 4–8 with other group members as time allows

Step 10: *Collaboratively develop home assignments*

- Encourage practice of the skill in real-world and provide rationale
- Ask group members to identify situations in which they could practice skill
- Problem-solve potential barriers (e.g., write down home assignment, set an alarm)

is elicited first to encourage the role-play participant and provide positive reinforcement. Step 6 follows with corrective feedback given by group members and leaders that is framed positively (e.g., "What is one thing that X could do differently to make this role-play even better?"). Only one or two pieces of corrective feedback should be elicited so that the participant is not overwhelmed and can easily integrate the feedback into future use of the skill.

Step 7 involves engaging the same group member in the same role-play again to allow for further practice and to incorporate the feedback. In Step 8, further positive and corrective feedback is elicited from the group. Steps 7 and 8 may repeat again if time allows. During Step 9, other group members engage in role-plays and feedback, repeating Steps 4 through 8 for as many group members as possible. The tenth and final step involves collaboratively developing home assignments for each group member to practice the skill in a real-world setting. Homework assignments are individualized to each participant's circumstances, and potential obstacles are addressed and planned for ahead of time.

4. Evidence Base for Social Skills Training in Schizophrenia

There have been numerous randomized controlled trials of SST for people with schizophrenia or other serious mental illnesses, with four meta-analyses of randomized controlled trials published to date examining negative symptoms as an outcome, all of which reported beneficial effects of skills training (Cella et al., 2023). The first meta-analysis, published in 2008, showed that across 22 controlled studies of SST, there was a large weighted effect on social skills content-mastery, moderate effects for social and daily living skills, community functioning, and negative symptoms, and small effects for other symptoms and relapse/hospitalization (Kurtz & Mueser, 2008). The remaining three meta-analyses focused specifically on the effects of psychosocial interventions on negative symptoms and social functioning. The first of these meta-analyses demonstrated the benefits of SST over other psychosocial interventions in reducing negative symptoms (Turner et al., 2014). This meta-analysis was subsequently expanded upon and showed that SST was superior to both treatment as usual and active comparison interventions in reducing negative symptoms (Turner et al., 2018). In addition, a broader meta-analysis of psychosocial interventions for negative symptoms identified 17 studies of SST (Lutgens et al., 2017), with effects on negative symptoms comparable to studies of CBT, exercise training, and music-based approaches. Effect sizes of SST on negative symptoms were of similar magnitude to those of CBT on positive symptoms.

In terms of potential moderator variables impacting variation in effects of SST on psychosocial functioning, Kurtz and Mueser (2008) identified greater effects among studies with younger sample age, with a shorter duration and intensity of training, and in those that compared SST to a nonactive control condition. Importantly, the effects of SST on negative symptoms were associated with study quality, such that higher quality trials demonstrated a smaller effect on negative symptoms than those of lower quality. It is also important to note that negative symptoms were measured in a variety of ways in these trials, with only some of these studies including direct assessment of socially relevant negative symptoms (e.g., social withdrawal). In their updated meta-analysis, Turner and colleagues (2018) examined subtypes of SST, including cognitive-behavioral and social-cognitive skills training approaches. Although these analyses were generally underpowered, social-cognitive skills training showed some evidence of added benefit for all symptoms relative to the other SST approaches. No specific subtype of SST demonstrated significant benefit for negative symptoms specifically.

5. New Directions

Psychosocial treatment developers and researchers have worked to expand the reach and impact of SST for patients with schizophrenia and other serious mental illnesses (Kopelowicz et al., 2006). Emerging work has focused on a few key areas, including adapting SST for certain settings or methods of delivery, targeting specific drivers of social skills in the context of these treatments, and augmenting SST with other evidence-based treatment approaches.

Special adaptations for improving the generalization of social skills have expanded the reach of SST. For example, with the in-vivo amplified approach, case managers support clients in practicing social skills in real-life settings and scenarios in their communities (Glynn et al., 2002). Others have developed and tested SST programs involving family members, providing opportunities for clients to practice skills and receive feedback in the home setting (Kopelowicz et al., 2003; Moriana et al., 2006). Virtual Reality (VR) and other technology-augmented applications of SST have also recently been developed and tested to increase access and generalizability of the approach (Smith et al., 2022). VR has potential advantages over in-person treatment approaches, including flexibility and controllability in content delivery, with potential lower risk and greater acceptability for those hesitant to engage in group treatments, or otherwise do not have access (Adery et al., 2018). Smartphone-based applications have also been developed that incorporate SST content into digital, standalone interventions for patients with serious mental illness (Fulford et al., 2021).

Targeting specific facets of social behavior, such as drive or interest in engaging with others, could improve the outcomes associated with SST. Another exciting area of potential growth for SST approaches includes targeting social skills for using technology-based communication and networking. Social media platforms such as Facebook and Instagram have become increasingly common places for people to meet and stay in touch, and electronic communication (e.g., messaging, email) is widely used, both in the general population and among people with schizophrenia (Jakubowska et al., 2019; Rekhi et al., 2019). Efforts to enhance the social competence of persons with schizophrenia in their use of social media and electronic communication could improve their skills for connecting with others and forming sustaining relationships, thereby taking full advantage of the advances in technology-based communication.

6. Conclusion

Poor social skills are common in people with schizophrenia and are strongly correlated with the severity of severe negative symptoms and worse social functioning. SST was developed to be a systematic approach to teaching social skills, and multiple meta-analyses of controlled studies have found that it is effective at both reducing negative symptoms and improving psychosocial functioning among people with schizophrenia. There is some evidence that these benefits appear comparable to those of cognitive behavioral therapies for reducing positive symptoms, and that their impact is to be more pronounced for those earlier in the course of illness. What remains relatively unknown is which facets of negative symptoms (i.e., experiential vs. expressive deficits) and social functioning (e.g., perceived quality of interactions, expansion of social support network) are most effectively targeted in SST. Improvements in the development of outcome measures, as well as dismantling and comparative effectiveness studies, should increase our understanding of these impacts in future work.

References

Adery, L. H., Ichinose, M., Torregrossa, L. J., Wade, J., Nichols, H., Bekele, E., Bian, D., Gizdic, A., Granholm, E., Sarkar, N., & Park, S. (2018). The acceptability and feasibility of a novel virtual reality based social skills training game for schizophrenia: Preliminary findings. *Psychiatry Research, 270*, 496–502.

Ahmed, A. O., Kirkpatrick, B., Granholm, E., Rowland, L. M., Barker, P. B., Gold, J. M., Buchanan, R. W., Outram, T., Bernardo, M., García-Portilla, M. P. G., Mane, A., Fernandez-Egea, E., & Strauss, G. P. (2022). Two factors, five factors, or both? External validation studies of negative symptom dimensions in schizophrenia. *Schizophrenia Bulletin, 48*, 620–630.

Bartels, S. J., Pratt, S. I., Mueser, K. T., Forester, B. P., Cather, C., Swain, K., Xie, H., Bird, B., & Feldman, J. (2014). Long-term outcomes of a randomized trial of integrated skills training and preventive healthcare for older adults with serious mental illness. *American Journal of Geriatric Psychiatry, 22*, 1251–1261.

Bellack, A. S., Morrison, R. L., Mueser, K. T., Wade, J. H., & Sayers, S. L. (1990). Role play for assessing the social competence of psychiatric patients. *Psychological Assessment, 2*, 248–255.

Bellack, A. S., Morrison, R. L., Wixted, J. T., & Mueser, K. T. (1990). An analysis of social competence in schizophrenia. *British Journal of Psychiatry, 156*, 809–818.

Benton, M. K., & Schroeder, H. E. (1990). Social skills training with schizophrenics: A meta-analytic evaluation. *Journal of Consulting and Clinical Psychology, 58*, 741–747.

Blanchard, J. J., & Cohen, A. S. (2006). The structure of negative symptoms within schizophrenia: Implications for assessment. *Schizophrenia Bulletin, 32*, 238–245.

Blanchard, J. J., Park, S. G., Catalano, L. T., & Bennett, M. E. (2015). Social affiliation and negative symptoms in schizophrenia: Examining the role of behavioral skills and subjective responding. *Schizophrenia Research, 168*, 491–497.

Carpenter, W. T., Jr., Heinrichs, D. W., & Wagman, A. M. I. (1988). Deficit and nondeficit forms of schizophrenia: The concept. *American Journal of Psychiatry, 145*, 578–583.

Cella, M., Roberts, S., Pillny, M., Riehle, M., O'Donoghue, B., Lyne, J., Tomlin, P., Valmaggia, L., & Preti, A. (2023). Psychosocial and behavioural interventions for the negative symptoms of schizophrenia: a systematic review of efficacy meta-analyses. *British Journal of Psychiatry. 223*(1), 321–331.

de Winter, L., Couwenbergh, C., van Weeghel, J., Hasson-Ohayon, I., Vermeulen, J. M., Mulder, C. L., Boonstra, N., Klaver, K. M., Oud, M., De Haan, L., & Veling, W. (2022). Changes in social functioning over the course of psychotic disorders – A meta-analysis. *Schizophrenia Research, 239*, 55–82.

Dilk, M. N., & Bond, G. R. (1996). Meta-analytic evaluation of skills training research for individuals with severe mental illness. *Journal of Consulting and Clinical Psychology, 64*, 1337–1346.

Eglit, G. M. L., Palmer, B. W., Martin, A. S., Tu, X., & Jeste, D. V. (2018). Loneliness in schizophrenia: Construct clarification, measurement, and clinical relevance. *PLoS ONE, 13*, e0194021.

Erickson, D. H., Beiser, M., Iacono, W. G., Fleming, J. A. E., & Lin, T. (1989). The role of social relationships in the course of first-episode schizophrenia and affective psychosis. *American Journal of Psychiatry, 146*, 1456–1461.

Fulford, D., Gard, D. E., Mueser, K. T., Mote, J., Gill, K., Leung, L., & Mow, J. (2021). Preliminary outcomes of an ecological momentary intervention for social functioning in schizophrenia: Pre-post study of the Motivation and Skills Support (MASS) mobile app. *JMIR Mental Health, 8*, e27475.

Glynn, S. M., Marder, S. R., Liberman, R. P., Blair, K., Wirshing, W. C., Wirshing, D. A., Ross, D., & Mintz, J. (2002). Supplementing clinic-based skills training with manual-based community support sessions: Effects on social adjustment of patients with schizophrenia. *American Journal of Psychiatry, 159*, 829–837.

Grant, P. M., & Beck, A. T. (2009). Defeatist beliefs as a mediator of cognitive impairment, negative symptoms, and functioning in schizophrenia. *Schizophrenia Bulletin, 35*, 798–806.

Green, M. F., Llerena, K., & Kern, R. S. (2015). The "right stuff" revisited: What have we learned about the determinants of daily functioning in schizophrenia? *Schizophrenia Bulletin, 41*, 781–785.

Harvey, P. D., Raykov, T., Twamley, E. W., Vella, L., Heaton, R. K., & Patterson, T. L. (2011). Validating the measurement of real-world functional outcome: Phase I results of the VALERO study. *American Journal of Psychiatry, 268*, 1195–1201.

Hersen, M., & Bellack, A. S. (1976). A multiple-baseline analysis of social-skills training in chronic schizophrenics. *Journal of Applied Behavior Analysis, 9*, 239–245.

Holt, D. J., Boeke, E. A., & Coombs, G. (2015). Abnormalities in personal space and parietal-frontal function in schizophrenia. *Neuroimage Clin, 9*, 233–243.

Jakubowska, A., Kaselionyte, J., Priebe, S., & Giacco, D. (2019). Internet use for social interaction by people with psychosis: A systematic review. *Cyberpsychology, Behavior, and Social Networking, 22*, 336–343.

Kopelowicz, A., Liberman, R. P., & Zarate, R. (2006). Recent advances in social skills training for schizophrenia. *Schizophrenia Bulletin, 32*, S12–S23.

Kopelowicz, A., Zarate, R., Smith, V. G., Mintz, J., & Liberman, R. P. (2003). Disease management in Latinos with schizophrenia: A family-assisted, skills training approach. *Schizophrenia Bulletin, 29*, 211–227.

Kurtz, M. M., & Mueser, K. T. (2008). A meta-analysis of controlled research on social skills training for schizophrenia. *Journal of Consulting and Clinical Psychology, 76*, 491–504.

Liberman, R. P., DeRisi, W. J., & Mueser, K. T. (1989). *Social Skills Training for Psychiatric Patients*. Needham Heights, MA: Allyn & Bacon.

Lutgens, D., Gariepy, G., & Malla, A. (2017). Psychological and psychosocial interventions for negative symptoms in psychosis: systematic review and meta-analysis. *British Journal of Psychiatry, 210*, 324–332.

Malla, A. K., Takhar, J. J., Norman, R. M. G., Manchanda, R., Cortese, L., Haricharan, R., Verdi, M., & Ahmed, R. (2002). Negative symptoms in first episode non-affective psychosis. *Acta Psychiatrica Scandinavica, 105*, 431–439.

Moriana, J. A., Alarcon, E., & Herruzo, J. (2006). In-home psychosocial skills training for patients with schizophrenia. *Psychiatric Services, 57*, 260–262.

Mueser, K. T., Bellack, A. S., Gingerich, S., Agresta, J., & Fulford, D. (2024). *Social Skills Training for Schizophrenia: A Step-by-Step Guide* (Third ed.). New York: Guilford Press.

Mueser, K. T., Bellack, A. S., Morrison, R. L., & Wixted, J. T. (1990). Social competence in schizophrenia: Premorbid adjustment, social skill, and domains of functioning. *Journal of Psychiatric Research, 24*, 51–63.

Mueser, K. T., Bellack, A. S., Wade, J. H., Sayers, S. L., Tierney, A., & Haas, G. (1993). Expressed emotion, social skill, and response to negative affect in schizophrenia. *Journal of Abnormal Psychology, 102*, 339–351.

Mueser, K. T., Doonan, R., Penn, D. L., Blanchard, J. J., Bellack, A. S., Nishith, P., & deLeon, J. (1996). Emotion recognition and social competence in chronic schizophrenia. *Journal of Abnormal Psychology, 105*, 271–275.

Mueser, K. T., Douglas, M. S., Bellack, A. S., & Morrison, R. L. (1991). Assessment of enduring deficit and negative symptom subtypes in schizophrenia. *Schizophrenia Bulletin, 17*, 565–582.

Mueser, K. T., Pratt, S. I., Bartels, S. J., Forester, B., Wolfe, R., & Cather, C. (2010). Neurocognition and social skill in older persons with schizophrenia and major mood disorders: An analysis of gender and diagnosis effects. *Journal of Neurolinguistics, 23*, 297–317.

Mueser, S. T. (1976). *Assertion training for chronic schizophrenics*. Unpublished Dissertation, Rutgers The State University of New Jersey.

Patterson, T. L., Moscona, S., McKibbin, C. L., Davidson, K., & Jeste, D. V. (2001). Social skills performance assessment among older patients with schizophrenia. *Schizophrenia Research, 30*, 351–360.

Penn, D. L., Corrigan, P. W., Bentall, R. P., Racenstein, J. M., & Newman, L. (1997). Social cognition in schizophrenia. *Psychological Bulletin, 121*, 114–132.

Pogue-Geile, M. F., & Harrow, M. (1985). Negative symptoms in schizophrenia: Their longitudinal course and prognostic importance. *Schizophrenia Bulletin, 11*, 427–439.

Ramsay, C. E., Broussard, B., Goulding, S. M., Cristofaro, S., Hall, D., Kaslow, N. J., Killackey, E., Penn, D. P., & Compton, M., T. (2011). Life and treatment goals of individuals hospitalized for first-episode nonaffective psychosis. *Psychiatry Research, 189*, 344–348.

Rekhi, G., Ang, M. S., & Lee, J. (2019). Clinical determinants of social media use in individuals with schizophrenia. *PLoS One, 14*, e0225370.

Sayers, S. L., Curran, P. J., & Mueser, K. T. (1996). Factor structure and construct validity of the Scale for the Assessment of Negative Symptoms. *Psychological Assessment, 8*, 269–280.

Smith, M. J., Smith, J. D., Blajeski, S., Ross, B., Jordan, N., Bell, M. D., McGurk, S., Mueser, K. T., Burke-Miller, J., Oulvey, E. A., Fleming, M. F., Nelson, K., Brown, A., Prestipino, J., Pashka, N., & Razzano, L. A. (2022). An RCT of virtual reality job interview training for persons with serious mental illness in IPS supported employment. *Psychiatric Services, 73*, 1027–1038.

Stouten, L. H., Veling, W., Laan, W., van der Helm, M., & van der Gaag, M. (2017). Psychosocial functioning in first-episode psychosis and associations with neurocognition, social cognition, psychotic and affective symptoms. *Early Intervention in Psychiatry, 11*, 23–36.

Strauss, G. P., Nuñez, A., & Ahmed, A. O. d. (2018). The latent structure of negative symptoms in schizophrenia. *JAMA Psychiatry, 75*, 1271–1279.

Strauss, J. S., & Carpenter, W. T. J. (1977). Prediction of outcome in schizophrenia III. Five-year outcome and its predictors. *Archives of General Psychiatry, 34*, 159–163.

Tauber, R., Wallace, C. J., & Lecomte, T. (2000). Enlisting indigenous community supporters in skills training programs for persons with severe mental illness. *Psychiatric Services, 51*, 1428–1432.

Turner, D. T., McGlanaghy, E., Cuijpers, P., van der Gaag, M., Karyotaki, E., & MacBeth, A. (2018). A meta-analysis of social skills training and related interventions for psychosis. *Schizophrenia Bulletin, 44*, 475–491.

Turner, D. T., van der Gaag, M., Karyotaki, E., & Cuijpers, P. (2014). Psychological interventions for psychosis: A meta-analysis of comparative outcome studies. *American Journal of Psychiatry, 171*, 523–538.

Weinberg, D., Shahar, G., Davidson, L., McGlashan, T. H., & Fennig, S. (2009). Longitudinal associations between negative symptoms and social functioning in schizophrenia: The moderating role of employment status and setting. *Psychiatry, 72*, 370–381.

Wing, J. K., & Brown, G. W. (1979). *Institutionalism and Schizophrenia: A Comparative Study of Three Mental Hospitals*. London: Cambridge University Press.

Zigler, E., & Glick, M. (1986). *A Developmental Approach to Adult Psychopathology*. New York: John Wiley & Sons.

18

The Positive Emotions Program for Schizophrenia (PEPS) as an Affective Intervention for Negative Symptoms

Alexandra Nguyen and Jérôme Favrod

Clinical pearls

- Clinicians can improve patients' ability to feel positive emotions by encouraging them to savor, anticipate, express, and share pleasant experiences.
- Clinicians can help patients change their defeatist beliefs by helping them to imagine more balanced attribution about their failure and to anticipate how alternative conclusions can increase positive expectations about success.
- Clinicians can relate how they overcame their own defeatist beliefs and the effect this had on their performance.
- Clinicians' own descriptions of their pleasant experiences accessible to patients' daily life can demonstrate the skills to feel pleasurable experiences.
- Self-disclosure can contribute to a more egalitarian relationship between professionals and patients and allow the patient to experience another position in the relationship.

1. Theoretical Background of the Intervention

Negative symptoms, including loss of motivation and reduced emotional expression, are correlated with poor patient functioning and quality of life. They also represent a major challenge for family members and professionals who care for patients who endure these symptoms (Galderisi et al., 2021). Negative

Alexandra Nguyen and Jérôme Favrod, *The Positive Emotions Program for Schizophrenia (PEPS) as an Affective Intervention for Negative Symptoms*. In: *Psychosocial Approaches to Negative Symptoms in Psychosis*. Edited by: Tania Lincoln et al., Oxford University Press.
DOI: 10.1093/oso/9780197676790.003.0018

symptoms remain an unmet need in the treatment of people with schizophrenia. Pharmacological treatments have limited ability to improve negative symptoms (Fusar-Poli et al., 2015). Antipsychotic medication improves negative symptoms, but this appears to be limited to secondary negative symptoms in acute patients following improvement in psychotic symptoms (Aleman et al., 2017). Also, meta-analyses suggest that there are no clinically effective psychosocial treatments for primary negative symptoms (Fusar-Poli et al., 2015; Veerman et al., 2017). This is likely related to the high heterogeneity of psychosocial treatments studied and the fact that for many interventions, the effects on negative symptoms have been studied a posteriori. Few interventions have been designed a priori with a theoretical model with the intention of treating primary negative symptoms. The MOtiVation and Enhancement (MOVE) program was designed to address persistent negative symptoms and their functional consequences in individuals with schizophrenia (Velligan et al., 2014). The MOVE program is delivered in the patient's home and in the community and utilizes techniques such as antecedent control, identifying and addressing deficits in anticipatory pleasure, in vivo emotional processing—focusing on identification of the emotion in others and display of one's own emotion, techniques designed to address self-defeating cognitions, and in vivo skill building to address social and instrumental skills deficits. A first study shows a reduction in negative symptoms that occurs with a delayed effect but also a high dropout rate in the experimental group (Velligan et al., 2015).

Recent literature has distinguished between negative symptoms associated with a diminished ability to experience (apathy, anhedonia) and those associated with a diminished ability to express (affective blunting, alogia). The distinction between the two symptom clusters or "syndromes" can allow for a more focused approach to psychosocial intervention development. The diminished-ability-to-experience syndrome tends to be associated with a poorer prognosis than the diminished-ability-to-express syndrome, suggesting that the former is a more severe facet of psychopathology (Strauss et al., 2013). This syndrome is also related to the duration of untreated psychosis, family history of schizophrenia, the patient's employment status during first-episode schizophrenia (Ergul & Ucok, 2015), and has become a challenging target for intervention development.

2. The Development of the Positive Emotions for Schizophrenia Program (PEPS)

The distinction between anticipatory and in-the-moment pleasure in schizophrenia opened the possibility of developing an intervention to reduce anhedonia and apathy (Favrod et al., 2009; Gard et al., 2007). Anticipatory pleasure is related to motivation and goal-directed behaviors, whereas in-the-moment pleasure is associated with satisfaction and satiety. In schizophrenia, studies show that patients do not have a direct impairment of pleasure when participating in a pleasurable activity if measured in the moment (Cohen & Minor, 2010). A systematic review indicated that, compared with healthy subjects, patients with schizophrenia spectrum disorders experience a moderate-sized deficit in anticipatory pleasure, with longer duration of illness, and lower cognitive functioning predicting larger deficits (Hallford & Sharma, 2019). By viewing anhedonia as a deficit in anticipatory pleasure, we conducted an initial pilot study (Favrod et al., 2010), which found that anticipatory pleasure training led to improvements in anhedonia and increased activity. The temporal model of pleasure, proposed by King and others (2013), and the suggestions of Strauss (2013), suggests maximizing positive emotional experiences using techniques developed in the field of affective science (Bryant & Veroff, 2007; Quoidbach et al., 2010) to increase the frequency and duration of positive emotional experiences, enriched this first intervention and added interventions for the maintenance and recall of pleasure. This new intervention was called Positive Emotions for Schizophrenia Program (PEPS) (Nguyen et al., 2016), and was tested in a second pilot study (Favrod et al., 2015). The results of this study indicated that the program leads to improvements in anhedonia and apathy.

3. Practical Procedure

PEPS is a group program that seeks to reduce anhedonia and apathy by increasing the cognitive control of positive emotions. It is an eight-session, one-hour program, delivered using multimedia material (visual and audio) presented as PowerPoint slides projected on a screen. Two characters, Jill and Jack, illustrate the program. Table 18.1 lists the order of the sessions. The groups are composed of five to eight participants. Each session begins with a welcome message and a relaxation or meditation exercise and continues with a focus on questioning defeatist beliefs and searching for an alternative motivating belief. The heart of the session is the skills training, which seeks to help participants anticipate, express behaviorally, savor, and communicate pleasurable experiences. It ends with a homework task for the next session. In the following sessions, the facilitators review the homework assigned at the end of the previous session. Review exercises are facilitated by participants in the last session. The program can be downloaded free from: https://www.seretablir.net/outils-interventions/peps_eng/.

Table 18.1 The Eight PEPS Sessions

Session 1: Changing defeatist beliefs

- Experiencing the effects of positive and negative emotions on behavior
- Identifying the impact of defeatist beliefs on activities of daily living
- Learning strategies to overcome defeatist beliefs

Session 2: Savoring pleasant moments (I)

- Understanding the importance of home exercises
- Learning to deliberately focus attention on the current pleasant experience through the observation of photographs of scenic beauty

Session 3: Emphasizing the behavioral expression of emotions

- Understanding the importance of practicing intersession exercises
- Experiencing that expressing positive emotions through nonverbal behaviors can increase the strength of those emotions, by imitating the expressions produced by pleasant or rewarding activities presented by comedians' pictures

Session 4: Capitalizing on and sharing pleasant moments with others

- Reviewing previous skills
- Learning that to communicate and celebrate positive events with others leads to improved mood, beyond the impact of the positive event itself

Session 5: Savoring pleasant moments (II)

- Deepening strategies for dealing with defeatist beliefs
- Experiencing that the ability to savor can be increased by giving value to the situation at hand

Session 6: Anticipating pleasant moments (I)

- Listing three to four enjoyable activities that one would like to resume, increase or initiate
- Calculating the benefit/cost ratio of these activities
- Learning the ability to anticipate the pleasure of an activity with a positive benefit/cost ratio

Session 7: Anticipating pleasurable moments (II)

- Developing favorable expectations for the future
- Learning to anticipate pleasurable moments by remembering highlights of the best moments of the past

Session 8: Review of all skills

- Reviewing PEPS skills while facilitating the session

PEPS is unique in that it was designed as a collaboration between a clinician and an educator. The pedagogical design of the program is based on Kolb's (Kolb & Kolb 2012) model of experiential learning. This model states that people both prefer and use different strategies to learn. The four major learning strategies described in the model are as follows:

1. *Concrete experience*, which involves consciously participating in an experience or performing a concrete task.
2. *Reflective observation*, which involves reflecting on one's experience and making explicit how a task was performed.
3. *Abstract conceptualization*, which consists of interpreting events by making theoretical connections, guided by both facilitators and the learners themselves.
4. *Active experimentation*, which consists of using a newly learned skill or task acquired in the previous phase in a different situation.

The facilitators take part in the sessions, as other participants, by completing the exercises, sharing their experiences, and carrying out the prescribed tasks. In order to run the group, facilitators undergo a one-day training course on leading PEPS. The training course aims at making potential facilitators aware of their own learning strategies, of their preferred learning strategies, and of the participants' preferred learning strategies in order to take them into account when teaching the skills. All PEPS skills are taught using each of the learning strategies described above. A logo at the top left of each slide indicates the learning strategy used in the exercise.

4. Examples of PEPS Exercises

4.1 Reducing Defeatist Thoughts

Reducing defeatist thoughts is currently considered a necessary ingredient in interventions that aim to reduce negative symptoms (Campellone et al., 2016). Defeatist thoughts may result from the many failures that patients experience in their lives due to functional disabilities. These failures then lead patients to conclude that there is no point in making efforts given that they are not rewarded with success. Therefore, each PEPS session contains an exercise to help participants learn to develop alternatives to defeatist thinking. For example, following a relaxation exercise, our character, Jill, may illustrate a defeatist thought by telling herself that she failed to relax during the exercise and that she was lousy. This negative conclusion may lead her not to continue her attempts to relax in the future. In this case, the task of the group will be to help her develop an alternative belief. Facilitators first guide participants to imagine more balanced attributions about why Jill may have failed to relax. Facilitators will lead the participants to consider what may be related to Jill herself, what may be related to others, and what may be related to the situation; facilitators then help participants come up with alternative conclusions to Jill's belief that "I'm lousy." Examples of responses include: "Just because I don't get it right the first time doesn't mean I'm lousy," "Maybe if I practice, I'll get it right," "Certain areas of my body have relaxed," and "The exercise doesn't work for me, maybe another one will." Finally, facilitators help participants analyze how this new conclusion can increase positive expectations about the success of the activity in a future attempt.

4.2 Savoring Pleasant Experiences

Savoring pleasurable experiences is about becoming aware of the pleasure or positive emotions experienced during an event or activity (Bryant & Veroff, 2007). Difficulty in savoring experiences is associated with negative symptoms in schizophrenia (Cassar et al., 2013). Drinking a cup of coffee in one gulp or eating a meal quickly without taking the time to savor it are examples of this difficulty. Learning to savor is helpful in increasing and integrating pleasure. The exercises in the program that train the participants in this skill invite them to look at a photograph of a pleasant landscape, listen to pleasant music, recall a recent pleasant moment, and then become acutely aware of the pleasure experienced. Facilitators share some of their own experiences in savoring, especially at the beginning of the program, in order to show that it is possible to experience and savor pleasure in the details of everyday life, such as the smile of a passerby on the way to the session, the colors of the sky at sunrise, the taste of jam at breakfast, the smell of coffee, the pleasure of stretching in bed before getting up, or the pleasant sensations during the relaxation exercise. Facilitators should ensure that the experiences shared are accessible to the participants and can be replicated in their daily lives. Facilitators' own descriptions of their experiences and joyful sensations helps participants pay attention to the small pleasures in life and develop a vocabulary to describe them.

Exercises with a photograph are initiated by saying, "Please look at this picture, make a mental note of the things you enjoy about the photograph, and observe how you enjoy them." After each exercise, the participants and facilitators are asked to recount their observations. For example, with the image of a botanical garden, the participants can describe the pleasure of walking through the garden, the desire to explore the forest beyond the bridge, the feeling of peace and quiet, the potential smells of the forest or grass, and the contrast between nature and buildings; they can appreciate the landscaping of the stones on the ground and the covered walkway, admire the trunk of the wisteria, enjoy walking on the bridge and looking out over the water, and so on. Facilitators ask the participants to describe the sensations produced to help them become more aware of them. They can also help participants by sharing their own experiences, thoughts, and sensations when looking at the photograph.

4.3 Expressing Emotions Behaviorally

Exaggerating one's experience of pleasure increases the sensation of pleasure. Behavioral expression is widely used by sports or rock music fans who let their joy explode into frenzy when their star performer approaches the opposing goal, or their favorite band starts a guitar solo. In schizophrenia, behavioral expression is often diminished (Horan et al., 2010; Kring et al., 2011). As a result, the use of behavioral exaggeration is an important strategy for enhancing pleasurable feelings. Facilitators play an important part as role models to support participants in expressing positive emotions such as joy, feelings of achievement, satisfaction, enjoyment of a positive experience, happiness, positive anticipation, and so forth. Facilitators actively support participants in learning to express behaviorally their positive emotions, thereby reducing the feelings of embarrassment that participants may experience when first sharing about pleasurable thoughts, feelings, and behaviors. It is helpful for facilitators to use expressions and gestures when sharing their experiences of enjoyment or anticipating pleasure: for example, rubbing their bellies when describing a food they enjoyed, puffing their chests, and rolling their eyes when recounting a pleasurable sensation, and stomping their feet when describing the excitement of going to their favorite musician's concert.

One of the prescribed exercises in PEPS is to imitate the facial expressions or gestures of actors expressing a positive emotion, projected on the screen for about 10 seconds, and then for each person to describe their own experiences of imitating the facial expression. It is important to give participants time to observe the body sensations that accompany this experience and recount them so that they can become aware of them.

4.4 Sharing Positive Moments

Sharing positive moments involves communicating and celebrating positive events with others. This strategy is associated with improved affect, even beyond the impact of the positive event itself (Lambert et al., 2012). It allows one to relive the experience a second time, and thus, increases the chances of remembering it.

The basic exercise in this session is to tell another participant a positive event and observe the effect on both the teller and the partner. Again, facilitators providing personal examples should ensure that the experiences talked about are accessible to everyone's daily life, such as enjoying a meeting with a friend, listening to a piece of music on the radio, or taking a walk in the park. Participants can also be trained to encourage the people they meet to share their positive moments. For example, they can do it by saying, "That sounded good, tell me more," and listening carefully to what the person says.

4.5 Anticipating Positive Emotions

The above exercises are useful for accessing pleasant activities in one's daily life, and increasing the pleasure of experiencing and remembering pleasant moments. The anticipation of pleasure is a key element of the PEPS program. For pleasure anticipation to serve as a motivational driver, it is important that the ratio of the expected reward (the anticipated pleasure) to the cost of the effort to achieve that reward (or pleasure) is fair. Many people want to start exercising or change their habits but are unable to do so because of the large amount of effort required to achieve the goal. Anticipating pleasurable moments lies in the ability to imagine the nature of the pleasant sensations produced by a future positive event. In this session, participants first make a brief list that includes the following: (a) past pleasant activities they would like to resume; (b) current activities they would like to increase; or (c) new activities they would like to undertake.

The next step is to rate the activities from 0 to 10 in terms of enjoyment and effort: For example, "0" indicates no enjoyment and no effort required, while "10" indicates extreme eagerness to perform the activity and extreme effort required to complete the task. Participants then deduct the effort score from the pleasure score for each activity. Participants are then invited to present their list and discuss it with the group. They are then led to choose and begin the activity that has the best pleasure-effort score. They imagine themselves performing this activity and experiencing, with their five senses, the pleasant sensations that accompany it. After each exercise session, the participants share their experiences. Again, facilitators play an important part as role models and must ensure that participants choose activities that are accessible and feasible. For example, facilitators can use their own difficulties in completing a task by explaining why they fail. They can also explain that some of the resolutions they made were too optimistic, so they chose less ambitious and less effortful activities to motivate themselves, anticipating more of the expected benefits.

4.6 Practicing Between Sessions

Homework or practice exercises are assigned throughout the program at the end of each session to encourage experimentation and practice outside of the group. Participants receive a workbook with useful information to help them remember the session and the exercises to be performed during the intersession, which are an extension of those practiced during the sessions. The facilitators encourage the participants' initiatives; if one of them brings, for example, a photo of a place or a piece of music that they like, the facilitators will positively reinforce the initiative and propose to the participant that they present it during the session. At the beginning of each session, the exercises assigned in the previous session are reviewed and discussed. The facilitators perform the same exercises as the participants to serve as a role model.

5. Evidence from the Literature

An assessor-blind randomized controlled trial (RCT) (Favrod et al., 2019a) sought to establish whether PEPS is clinically effective. The main hypothesis was that, compared with treatment as usual (TAU), eight sessions of PEPS added to TAU would significantly reduce the composite scores for apathy/avolition and anhedonia/asociality of the Scale for the Assessment of Negative Symptoms (SANS). This RCT also tested whether the expected change was sustained at the six-month follow-up. PEPS led to moderate-to-large improvement in the primary outcome of apathy and anhedonia, and SANS composite score, and moderate improvement in the secondary outcomes of anticipatory and consummatory pleasure, as well as social interactions compared with the control group. The effects were maintained at the six-month follow-up for the main outcome. The results indicate that eight sessions of PEPS intervention effectively reduced the diminished capacity to experience pleasure syndrome in a clinical sample of people diagnosed with schizophrenia. A field test (Favrod et al., 2019b) was designed to explore the feasibility of PEPS under natural conditions. The field test was conducted in three expert centers from the French national network of expert centers. The group facilitators were psychiatrists, psychologists, neuropsychologists, and nurses who received the materials and one-day training before leading the intervention. The field test showed a very low attrition rate and an excellent participation rate, indicating that PEPS is acceptable under natural conditions of treatment. After one day of training, the group leaders were able to conduct the program at three different sites, indicating the feasibility of the intervention. The data indicated that participation in PEPS leads to an improvement in negative symptoms and social functioning. A qualitative study (Nguyen et al., 2022a) led to a better understanding of the use and impact of self-disclosure by PEPS facilitators. Thirteen in-depth interviews with PEPS facilitators were conducted and thematically analyzed. Professionals described their personal disclosures as "authentic sharing of lived experiences." From a content point of view, professionals revealed selecting simple events from their personal or professional life, which they found easy to share with participants in the group. The selection criteria for these experiences mainly concerned the therapeutic value anticipated and were formulated in terms of authenticity, perceived usefulness, and relevance to group content. Self-disclosure was viewed as contributing to a more egalitarian relationship between professionals and patients.

Additionally, an online platform to train professionals to lead PEPS for patients with anhedonia was tested: https://e-peps.ch/ (Nguyen et al., 2022b). This study aimed to test clinician's reception of the platform, including its perceived usefulness, as well as investigate whether e-PEPS training improves knowledge about the facilitation of PEPS. Participants were recruited through advertisements. A total of 210 social work and healthcare providers were registered to participate in the study; 185 received access to the platform, and 101 completed the training and post-test assessments. Satisfaction with the training was high. The results showed that the participants' knowledge about PEPS improved significantly, and the skills taught in their personal repertoire increased after the training. The training allowed most clinicians to plan to lead a PEPS group in the year following the training.

6. Outlook/Future Directions

Replication and independent studies are required to verify the validity of the program. Currently, the program's Albanian and Italian versions are freely available on the Internet. In future studies, it would be useful to use assessment instruments such as the Clinical Assessment Interview for Negative Symptoms (CAINS) (Strauss & Gold, 2016) or the Brief Negative Symptom Scale (BNSS) (Mucci et al., 2015) to facilitate comparisons (Riehle et al., 2020). PEPS was built to provide a brief group intervention that is accessible and easy to use. Many patients, however, require a more comprehensive intervention to reduce their negative symptoms. Considering the relatively brief and group-based nature of the intervention, PEPS could be a cost-effective intervention to implement for patients with negative symptoms of schizophrenia as an adjunctive treatment to other psychosocial interventions. We are currently developing a second online training course, developed with peer practitioners in mental health, to use the skills covered in PEPS in the care of patients in everyday situations such as getting out of bed, engaging in social activities, exercising, or enjoying a meal. These efforts are important because dissemination of effective interventions across care settings remains a major challenge in psychiatric care.

References

Aleman, A., Lincoln, T. M., Bruggeman, R., Melle, I., Arends, J., Arango, C., & Knegtering, H. (2017). Treatment of negative symptoms: Where do we stand, and where do we go? *Schizophrenia Research, 186*, 55–62.

Bryant, F. B., & Veroff, J. (2007). *Savoring: A New Model of Positive Experience*. Mahwah, NJ: Lawrence Erlbaum.

Campellone, T. R., Sanchez, A. H., & Kring, A. M. (2016). Defeatist Performance Beliefs, Negative Symptoms, and Functional Outcome in Schizophrenia: A Meta-analytic Review. *Schizophrenia Bulletin, 42*(6), 1343–1352.

Cassar, R., Applegate, E., & Bentall, R. P. (2013). Poor savouring and low self-efficacy are predictors of anhedonia in patients with schizophrenia spectrum disorders. *Psychiatry Research, 210*(3), 830–834.

Cohen, A. S., & Minor, K. S. (2010). Emotional experience in patients with schizophrenia revisited: meta-analysis of laboratory studies. *Schizophrenia Bulletin, 36*(1), 143–150.

Ergul, C., & Ucok, A. (2015). Negative symptom subgroups have different effects on the clinical course of schizophrenia after the first episode: a 24-month follow up study. *European Psychiatry, 30*(1), 14–19.

Favrod, J., Ernst, F., Giuliani, F., & Bonsack, C. (2009). Validation of the Temporal Experience of Pleasure Scale (TEPS) in a French-speaking environment. *Encephale, 35*(3), 241–248.

Favrod, J., Giuliani, F., Ernst, F., & Bonsack, C. (2010). Anticipatory pleasure skills training: a new intervention to reduce anhedonia in schizophrenia. *Perspectives in psychiatric care, 46*(3), 171–181.

Favrod, J., Nguyen, A., Chaix, J., Pellet, J., Frobert, L., Fankhauser, C., ... Bonsack, C. (2019a). Improving Pleasure and Motivation in Schizophrenia: A Randomized Controlled Clinical Trial. *Psychotherapy and psychosomatics, 88*(2), 84–95.

Favrod, J., Nguyen, A., Fankhauser, C., Ismailaj, A., Hasler, J. D., Ringuet, A., ... Bonsack, C. (2015). Positive Emotions Program for Schizophrenia (PEPS): a pilot intervention to reduce anhedonia and apathy. *BMC Psychiatry, 15*, 231.

Favrod, J., Nguyen, A., Tronche, A. M., Blanc, O., Dubreucq, J., Chereau-Boudet, I., ... Llorca, P. M. (2019b). Impact of Positive Emotion Regulation Training on Negative Symptoms and Social Functioning in Schizophrenia: A Field Test. *Frontiers in Psychiatry, 10*(532), 532.

Fusar-Poli, P., Papanastasiou, E., Stahl, D., Rocchetti, M., Carpenter, W., Shergill, S., & McGuire, P. (2015). Treatments of Negative Symptoms in Schizophrenia: Meta-Analysis of 168 Randomized Placebo-Controlled Trials. *Schizophrenia Bulletin, 41*(4), 892–899.

Galderisi, S., Kaiser, S., Bitter, I., Nordentoft, M., Mucci, A., Sabe, M., ... Gaebel, W. (2021). EPA guidance on treatment of negative symptoms in schizophrenia. *European Psychiatry, 64*(1), e21.

Gard, D. E., Kring, A. M., Gard, M. G., Horan, W. P., & Green, M. F. (2007). Anhedonia in schizophrenia: distinctions between anticipatory and consummatory pleasure. *Schizophrenia Research, 93*(1-3), 253–260.

Hallford, D. J., & Sharma, M. K. (2019). Anticipatory pleasure for future experiences in schizophrenia spectrum disorders and major depression: A systematic review and meta-analysis. *British Journal of Clinical Psychology, 58*(4), 357–383.

Horan, W. P., Wynn, J. K., Kring, A. M., Simons, R. F., & Green, M. F. (2010). Electrophysiological correlates of emotional responding in schizophrenia. *Journal of Abnormal Psychology, 119*(1), 18–30.

Kolb, A. Y., & Kolb, D. A. (2012). Experiential Learning Theory. In N. M. Seel (Ed.), *Encyclopedia of the Sciences of Learning* (pp. 1215–1219). Springer US.

Kring, A. M., & Elis, O. (2013). Emotion deficits in people with schizophrenia. *Annual Review of Clinical Psychology, 9*, 409–433.

Kring, A. M., Germans Gard, M., & Gard, D. E. (2011). Emotion deficits in schizophrenia: timing matters. *Journal of Abnormal Psychology, 120*(1), 79–87.

Lambert, N. M., Gwinn, A. M., Baumeister, R. F., Strachman, A., Washburn, I. J., Gable, S. L., & Fincham, F. D. (2012). A boost of positive affect: The perks of sharing positive experiences. *Journal of Social and Personal Relationships, 30*(1), 24–43.

Mucci, A., Galderisi, S., Merlotti, E., Rossi, A., Rocca, P., Bucci, P., ... Italian Network for Research on, P. (2015). The Brief Negative Symptom Scale (BNSS): Independent validation in a large sample of Italian patients with schizophrenia. *European Psychiatry, 30*(5), 641–647.

Nguyen, A., Frobert, L., Ismailaj, A., Monteiro, S., & Favrod, J. (2022a). Qu'est-ce que les professionnels dévoilent d'eux-mêmes dans la relation thérapeutique avec les personnes atteintes de schizophrénie ? *Pratiques Psychologiques, 28*(1), 43–54.

Nguyen, A., Frobert, L., Kollbrunner, A., & Favrod, J. (2022b). An Evaluation of an Online Training Platform for Teaching Positive Emotions for People With Schizophrenia. *Frontiers in Psychiatry, 13*, 798019.

Nguyen, A., Frobert, L., McCluskey, I., Golay, P., Bonsack, C., & Favrod, J. (2016). Development of the Positive Emotions Program for Schizophrenia: An Intervention to Improve Pleasure and Motivation in Schizophrenia. *Frontiers in Psychiatry, 7*, 13.

Quoidbach, J., Berry, E. V., Hansenne, M., & Mikolajczak, M. (2010). Positive emotion regulation and well-being: Comparing the impact of eight savoring and dampening strategies. *Personality and Individual Differences, 49*(5), 368–373.

Riehle, M., Böhl, M. C., Pillny, M., & Lincoln, T. M. (2020). Efficacy of psychological treatments for patients with schizophrenia and relevant negative symptoms: A meta-analysis. *Clinical Psychology in Europe, 2*(3), 1–23.

Strauss, G. P. (2013). Translating basic emotion research into novel psychosocial interventions for anhedonia. *Schizophrenia Bulletin, 39*(4), 737–739.

Strauss, G. P., & Gold, J. M. (2016). A Psychometric Comparison of the Clinical Assessment Interview for Negative Symptoms and the Brief Negative Symptom Scale. *Schizophrenia Bulletin, 42*(6), 1384–1394.

Strauss, G. P., Horan, W. P., Kirkpatrick, B., Fischer, B. A., Keller, W. R., Miski, P., ... Carpenter, W. T., Jr. (2013). Deconstructing negative symptoms of schizophrenia: avolition-apathy and diminished expression clusters predict clinical presentation and functional outcome. *Journal of Psychiatric Research, 47*(6), 783–790.

Veerman, S. R. T., Schulte, P. F. J., & de Haan, L. (2017). Treatment for Negative Symptoms in Schizophrenia: A Comprehensive Review. *Drugs, 77*(13), 1423–1459.

Velligan, D., Maples, N., Roberts, D. L., & Medellin, E. M. (2014). Integrated Psychosocial Treatment for Negative Symptoms. *American Journal of Psychiatric Rehabilitation, 17*(1), 1–19.

Velligan, D., Roberts, D., Mintz, J., Maples, N., Li, X., Medellin, E., & Brown, M. (2015). A randomized pilot study of MOtiVation and Enhancement (MOVE) Training for negative symptoms in schizophrenia. *Schizophrenia Research, 165*(2-3), 175–180.

19

Metacognitive Reflection and Insight Therapy (MERIT)

A metacognitive approach to negative symptoms in psychosis

Paul H. Lysaker, Kelsey Huling and Helena García-Mieres

Clinical pearls

- Metacognitive capacity refers to the ability to notice and think about one's thoughts, the thoughts of others, and one's circumstances, as well as the ability to use this information to pursue meaningful action in the world.
- Metacognitive deficits may contribute to negative symptoms in schizophrenia spectrum disorders and therefore, are a potential treatment target.
- Metacognitive Reflection and Insight Therapy (MERIT) is one form of individual psychotherapy that may address metacognitive deficits and negative symptoms.
- MERIT focuses on helping patients develop an increasingly integrated and coherent sense of their possibilities and psychosocial challenges as well as how to respond to those challenges and possibilities within the flow of life.

1. Introduction

Presently one barrier to developing treatments for negative symptoms is a limited understanding of the processes that may cause negative symptoms to emerge and persist. Thus, it is unclear what might be targeted in order to enhance persons' access to the experience and expression of thoughts, feelings, and desires. One such set of processes that may affect negative symptoms in schizophrenia are alterations in the capacity for metacognition (Huling et al., 2021; Lysaker, Minor et al., 2020). Metacognition refers to the ability to form ideas

Paul H. Lysaker, Kelsey Huling and Helena García-Mieres, *Metacognitive Reflection and Insight Therapy (MERIT)*. In: *Psychosocial Approaches to Negative Symptoms in Psychosis*. Edited by: Tania Lincoln et al.,
Oxford University Press. © Oxford University Press (2025). DOI: 10.1093/oso/9780197676790.003.0019

about oneself, others, and one's responses to emerging life challenges (Semerari et al., 2003). It has been proposed that difficulties in metacognitive capacity, then, may lead to persistent negative symptoms when they interfere with persons abilities to recognize and express thoughts, feelings, and desires (Lysaker, Hasson-Ohayon et al., 2021). In this chapter we will explore this model and focus on its particular implications for treatment. We will first explore the construct of metacognition and research supporting its associations with negative symptoms in schizophrenia spectrum disorders. We next focus on one particular psychotherapy approach, which seeks to enhance metacognitive capacity, Metacognitive Reflection and Insight Therapy (MERIT; Lysaker & Klion, 2017).

2. Metacognitive Capacity and Negative Symptoms in Schizophrenia Spectrum Disorders

Across psychological research, the construct of "metacognition" has been used to refer to persons' ability to think about their thoughts, feelings and wishes, which then allows them to decide how to respond to life's events (Flavell, 1979; Hasson-Ohayon et al., 2020). Broadly, metacognitive processes involve a spectrum of activities that include ideas about specific things one thinks and feels, general tendencies of how one thinks and feels, and specific and general thoughts about oneself and others as unique persons (Moritz & Lysaker, 2018).

Research on the subjective experience of schizophrenia spectrum disorders has proposed an integrative model of metacognition. In this model, the multiple facets of metacognition are conceptualized as interacting in a way that allows persons to have availability to a sense of themselves and others as unique beings in the world in a given moment (Lysaker & Hasson-Ohayon, 2021). Metacognitive processes allow persons to recognize specific experiences, understand the relationship of those experiences to other experiences, and to form larger ideas about oneself on the basis of how their thoughts and feelings are related to one another both presently and across time. In the integrative model, this is possible because the interaction of metacognitive activities focuses not just on the self, but also separately on others, one's larger communities, and one's perception of and response to the challenges and possibilities that fluidly emerge in life. This capacity for metacognition is understood as multidetermined and supported by a broad range of psychological, social, and biological processes. These include one's psychosocial history, current attachments, and psychosocial opportunities, as well as the neural systems that allow for the encoding, integration of, and reflection upon information within the flow of life.

Any number of compromises in the psychological, social, or biological processes which support metacognition can lead to decrements in metacognitive capacity, which will then be manifest as a relatively fragmented and less cohesive sense of self and others (Lysaker, Cheli et al., 2021). The integrative model proposes that deficits in metacognitive capacity may help explain a broad range of disturbances in behavior, cognition, and emotion found in psychopathology (Lysaker & Lysaker, 2020). Importantly, metacognition is not merely proposed as a cause or consequence of symptoms of a given disorder, but as a node in a network that impacts how symptoms and other forms of cognition influence one another (Hasson-Ohayon et al., 2018; Lysaker, Kukla et al., 2020).

Turning to negative symptoms in schizophrenia, this model has made several direct hypotheses. First, metacognitive deficits might impair one's ability to perceive how different discrete experiences are related to one another as part of an emotional reaction or a wish for something. For example, one might not see how warmth in one's face, rapid heartbeat, and a particular thought are signs of wanting attention from a particular person. More broadly, the motivation to pursue any given course of action is determined by the meaning that action might hold. For example, one person might be willing to make significant sacrifices in order to reach a goal, whereas another person may not, simply because people place different levels of importance or meaning on different things. With metacognitive deficits, a person may lose a larger sense of themselves, and therefore, no longer have a sense of what is worth pursuing or making sacrifices for, resulting in experiential negative symptoms related to lack of volition and motivation. In parallel, deficits in metacognition may also erode one's sense of what is possible for them in the world, resulting not just in the loss of motivation to pursue a given goal, but to even see that goal, again appearing as avolition or abulia. Further, with greater metacognitive deficits and a more fragmented sense of self and others, a person may lose a sense of their larger place in the social world, leaving them with a relatively weaker sense of what they should express to others resulting in expressive negative symptoms (c.f. Lysaker, Minor et al., 2020).

Research supporting these hypotheses includes cross-sectional findings demonstrating a link between graver deficits in metacognitive capacity and more severe negative symptoms (e.g. Lysaker et al., 2005; Lysaker, Chernov et al., 2020; Trauelsen et al., 2016). Further, prospective longitudinal research has reported that poorer metacognitive function predicts severe negative symptoms in the future even after controlling for initial levels of negative symptoms (Austin et al., 2019; Faith et al., 2020; Hamm et al., 2012; Lysaker et al., 2015; McLeod et al., 2014). García-Mieres, Lundin, and colleagues (2020) have suggested that deficits in metacognition and abnormalities in higher-order language structures may interact with disorganization symptoms resulting in diminished emotional expression in schizophrenia. This is consistent with other studies that have found higher levels of negative symptoms to be related to impoverished self-concept in people with schizophrenia (Cicero et al., 2016; García-Mieres, Villaplana et al., 2020; Hesse et al., 2015).

3. The Metacognitive Model in the Treatment of Negative Symptoms in Schizophrenia Spectrum Disorders

The theoretical integrated model of metacognition has informed the development of a treatment intervention: Metacognitive Reflection and Insight Therapy (MERIT; Lysaker & Klion, 2017). Overall, MERIT seeks to promote recovery by assisting people with significant psychiatric and psychosocial challenges to make sense of their experiences and decide how to respond meaningfully to these experiences (both in terms of their challenges and potentials) as they evolve. The aim of MERIT is to promote an increasingly integrated sense self-and-others and one's actions in the world, ultimately culminating in self-management and community membership. Following the metaphor of physical therapy in which patients, regardless of the acuity of their condition, develop increasing levels of movement and function as they engage in exercises that match their abilities, in MERIT, metacognitive capacity is believed to increase over time through reflection about oneself, others, and their actions in the world, at levels that match their maximal metacognitive capacity (Lysaker, Kukla et al., 2020).

Importantly, the reflections that take place in MERIT, take place between the therapist and patient, as they work together jointly to make meaning of the challenges the patient experiences, as well as develop potential responses to those challenges. As such, the therapist in MERIT is not teaching patients a skill or educating them about something that they should attempt to execute. There is no prescribed content. Therapists and patients may jointly decide that the patient should try to undertake a particular activity, but that is something that occurs organically and collaboratively, as a shared sense of meaning is made and determined ahead of time. What is prescribed in MERIT are measurable therapist behaviors that seek to promote patients' abilities to think about themselves, others, and their actions in the world. Referred to as elements, each is an activity in which the therapist and patient can think jointly about the patients' sense of themselves, others, and their actions in the broader context of a discussion about the challenges and possibilities the patient faces. Each element reflects behaviors applicable to patients with differing levels of acuity, needs, and goals.

There are eight elements divided into three classes: content, process, and superordinate. The *content* elements begin with shared attention to the patient's agenda or their underlying wishes and desires. Element One includes opportunities to acknowledge the patient's wishes about the session, which could be within or outside of awareness, as well as contradictory, complimentary, and unrelated wishes. Element Two calls for the therapist to attempt to share their own thoughts and reactions in a way that sustains and does not inhibit dialogue. Element Three requires therapists to elicit and think with patients about actual events described in narrative form, while Element Four calls for there to be opportunities for recognizing and thinking about the psychological challenges the patient encounters.

The *process* elements begin with Element Five, which calls for opportunities for shared consideration of the therapeutic relationship as the larger structure within which reflection within the session takes place. Element Six calls for offering chances to think about the potentially positive, negative, or neutral impact of the session. The final two *superordinate* elements (Elements Seven and Eight) call for and require that therapists offer opportunities for reflection which match the patient's current metacognitive capacity for thinking about themselves or others as measured by the Self-reflectivity and Awareness of the Other subscales on the Metacognition Assessment Sale—Abbreviated (MAS-A; Lysaker & Dimaggio, 2014), as well as thinking about psychosocial challenges and how they are responding to them as measured with the MAS-A Mastery subscale. Detailed descriptions of how interventions are matched to metacognitive capacity have been provided elsewhere (Lysaker, Gagen, et al., 2020; Lysaker & Klion, 2017).

To date the evidence to support MERIT is still accumulating. Two randomized controlled studies have reported good levels of feasibility and acceptability with meaningful gains noted in the targeted outcomes of metacognition and insight respectively (de Jong et al., 2019; Vohs et al., 2018). Several open trials have similarly reported good levels of feasibility and acceptability as well as clinically meaningful improvements (de Jong et al., 2016; Lavi Rotenberg et al., 2021; Minor et al. 2021). Considering the perspective of patients who have received MERIT, qualitative studies have affirmed that patients report positive experiences with MERIT describing, in their own words, growth in the ability to make sense and respond to what is emerging in their lives (de Jong et al., 2020; Kukla et al., 2021; Lysaker et al., 2015). Similarly, single case studies while not a measure of the effectiveness of the treatment, have offered ample reports that this treatment can be adapted to patients with very different clinical needs, across diverse real world clinical settings, and in response to changing treatment parameters such as those provided by COVID-19 (e.g. Cohen-Chazani et al., 2021; Faith et al., 2022; Dmitryeva et al., 2021; Hamm & Lysaker, 2018). Finally, other interventions that follow the MERIT model of treatment are showing promising results. A randomized controlled study of a metacognition-oriented social skills training in prolonged psychosis evidenced improvement in social functioning and targeted outcomes of metacognition (Inchausti, et al., 2018).

4. A Case Illustration

4.1 Presenting Problem and Patient Background

The patient in this case will be referred to as Gordan. His name and all identifying information have been systematically disguised for the purposes of confidentiality. Gordan is a white male in his late thirties living in a residential treatment program for persons with a history of substance use and homelessness. He has never been married, has no children, and has never experienced significant legal problems. He was raised by his father who was widowed early in Gordan's childhood. He is the youngest of four siblings, whom he reports he was never very close with emotionally. He described his father as caring at times but often distracted by conflicts with women he dated after the death of Gordan's mother. Gordan reported that several of his father's girlfriends were physically abusive to him during this period. His father and siblings were still living at the time he began therapy. There is a family history of alcohol abuse and depression but no other forms of mental illness.

Throughout childhood, Gordan was a below average student and appeared to be of low average intelligence. He reports he had acquaintances while growing up but never a best friend or circle of close friends. His attendance at school was inconsistent, and he reports he often snuck out of school to smoke marijuana. He was not involved in any extracurricular activities, though he noted that as a hobby he liked to draw. While he identifies as heterosexual, he never dated, nor could he recall a romantic interest during childhood or adolescence.

Gordan left high school before graduation and obtained his GED. After this, he worked part time in a grocery store and enlisted in the Army. In the Army he noted forming some casual friendships, which mainly revolved around smoking marijuana. He reports some disciplinary issues related to being unable to focus upon and complete simple tasks and was discharged after two years. He returned to his hometown and struggled to secure a stable job for several years, often leaving or being laid off after a few months. He did not date during this time, although he noted forming some casual social connections, again around cannabis use. He experienced his first episode of psychosis during this period in which he reported visual and auditory hallucinations, disorganized behavior, as well as gross withdrawal and general levels of near complete inactivity, often not leaving his apartment or bathing for long periods of time. There were several inpatient hospitalizations, after which he was placed on disability income. At this time, he accepted he had been addicted to marijuana and ceased all use of that or any other drug or substance. In the following years he became increasingly withdrawn, and his lack of active self-care eventually culminated in becoming homeless.

4.2 Case Conceptualization

At the start of MERIT, Gordan fully met criteria for schizophrenia for over a decade. He was prescribed an atypical antipsychotic, which he thought was useful but offered no specifics other than "it makes me stable." Since his initial hospitalization, his positive symptoms had rapidly diminished to the point where he reported only occasional auditory hallucinations of single muffled words. By contrast, his experience of negative symptoms progressed over time. He presented with severe levels of flat affect; even when reporting painful life events. Gordan was furthermore quite withdrawn socially and only interacted with others for practical reasons, expressing little interest in others or reporting pleasure from these interactions. He also displayed significant levels of avolition; reporting little to no intrinsic motivation from day to day. His motor movements and speech were also notably slow and retarded in pace.

Gordan's metacognitive capacity was assessed using the Metacognition Assessment Scale—Abbreviated as noted above (MAS-A; Lysaker, Minor et al., 2020). On the MAS-A Self-Reflectivity subscale, he could identify that various mental activities were occurring in his own mind, including memories, desires, and thoughts. He was unable, however, to identify nuanced states of emotion and could only describe events as "ok" or "bad." With regard to his scores on the Understanding the Mind of the Other subscale, Gordan was aware that others had their own mental activities, but struggled to form a sense of the different mental activities or emotions others might have. In terms of the Decentration subscale, Gordan was unable to take the perspective of others or to think about others pursuing different things in their lives for their own reasons. Finally, in terms of the Mastery subscale, Gordan seemed to have little to no sense of having any plausible psychological problem. He could say he had a mental illness but could not say more about that other than to use vague labels.

4.3 Course of Treatment

The psychotherapy described here was conducted in an outpatient clinic over the course of two to three years. There were no changes in medication or hospitalizations over the course of the therapy. Additionally, Gordan engaged in supportive group psychotherapy as well as a 12-Step program for persons recovering from drug addiction outside of his MERIT sessions. Sessions lasted 50 minutes and occurred once per week. His attendance was consistent even though initially he could not articulate a reason why he wanted psychotherapy, other than that he enjoyed the trip to the clinic. He was polite but withdrawn. As noted above, he expressed little to no emotion in session and often sat in silence, appearing to experience few thoughts. An exploration of the course of therapy and the associated interventions will be described according to each of the eight elements of MERIT.

4.3.1 Element 1: The Patient's Agenda

The first element of MERIT calls for opportunities to notice and think about what the patient is looking for in any given session in order to promote an experience of oneself as an active agent in treatment. As the therapist wondered aloud about what Gordan wanted to get out of treatment, Gordan would generally say he did not know and then become quiet and withdrawn. If asked directly, sometimes he would say he was waiting for the therapist to tell him what to do, though, he couldn't offer anything pertaining to what advice or direction might be most helpful.

Observing Gordan's behavior, the therapist accepted the confusion but also noted moments in session, particularly when the therapist was sharing his thoughts, that Gordan appeared uncomfortable. This led to the establishment of an initial agenda, namely that Gordan did not want to feel uncomfortable and that it was safer to be "the man of granite." As this was explored, it emerged slowly that feeling nothing was the only bearable alternative to believing others were "looking down" upon him and thinking him "defective."

Over time, Gordan began slowly sharing more memories of his life, and it became clearer that being "numb" protected him from feeling pain or anger, which he feared he could not control and would completely overwhelm him. Thus, "not falling apart" was identified as an agenda item. "Falling apart" was further discussed as a state in which the few thoughts and feelings he could perceive would be lost in chaos.

As therapy further progressed, Gordan became more talkative and shared his experiences of others neglecting his needs and also having the sense that others blamed him for his struggles in life. He noted feeling he was destined to be on the "outside" of any fulfilling social activities and so his being "the man of granite" protected him from what he thought was inevitable rejection. Notably within the MERIT framework, what can be observed here is Gordan thinking about himself and jointly forming ideas about himself in the moment.

4.3.2 Element 2: Insertion of the Therapist's Mind

In this MERIT element, the therapist is tasked with sharing their own thoughts as objects that can then be reflected on within dialogue. This proved to be quite a challenge with Gordan. Often when the therapist shared a thought or reaction, such as a recent social experience with his family or a future aspiration, Gordan would either quickly agree and fall silent or say nothing and lapse into a state in which he appeared disconnected and relatively unresponsive to the therapist.

The therapist's response to this was to offer fewer, simpler thoughts but also to preface them by asking permission to share what he was thinking. The therapist also often asked if sharing his thoughts in a given moment might be helpful or if it was better for him to listen for a while longer. Importantly, this allowed for Gordan and the therapist to jointly recognize that the therapist's thoughts interfered with Gordan's own thinking. Gordan was able to say he often was unsure what the therapist was getting after and that this caused him to lose his train of thought completely. With time, Gordan was able to increasingly accept and use the therapist's comments to scaffold his own, as well as think about his reactions in the moment to those thoughts and help the therapist understand what was helpful for him. From the MERIT perspective, this was seen as allowing Gordan again to think about himself, beyond someone looking for something (as in the first element), but as someone reacting to the thoughts of another person.

4.3.3 Element 3: Narrative Episodes

The third element of MERIT requires the therapist to elicit and promote thoughtful consideration about narrative episodes or sequences of events that have unfolded across the patient's life. This allows for joint reflection about the patient as a unique and complex being in the world, with their own sense of purpose and relationship to others. Initially, Gordan struggled to recall events from his life. He could offer abstractions such as school was "boring" or a meeting was "stupid." He struggled, however, to freely describe events including things leading up to those events, who else was involved, and what happened after. He appeared overall disconnected from any sense of a life story and a world inhabited by others. If asked about his "story," he said he didn't know. If asked about specific events, they were also barren. For example, he could recall that after the military he briefly attended a trade school, but how he chose that school, what happened when he enrolled, or how he decided to leave were all left blank in his mind.

The therapist's response here was to accept Gordan's fragmented accounts and refrain from making connections for him or repeatedly ask for more details. The therapist allowed space, for both himself and Gordan, to sit with the feeling of being deeply confused and uncertain about what had happened to Gordan across his life. With time and practice, Gordan expressed a deeper interest in his own history and multiple narratives began to emerge in a more nuanced, shared understanding of himself as the main character in his life story.

4.3.4 Element 4: The Psychological Problem

The fourth element of MERIT progressed alongside the third element. As noted above, initially Gordan could not identify any significant challenges he faced outside of interacting with people he did not like. As stories emerged within the treatment, however, Gordan and his therapist jointly found a range of themes, which clearly coalesced into a set of reoccurring psychological challenges Gordan faced. In addition to identifying these themes or challenges, the therapist and Gordon also explored how he experienced these problems and what their history had been across his life.

The psychological problems were varied, though two particularly poignant themes emerged. The first was feeling "cheated." He described multiple narratives in which it seemed as though others had what they needed, but Gordan was excluded and could only watch from the outside without any chance of being invited in. A second theme or problem was he found his emotions unmanageable. He linked this to the death of his mother, as well as a cause of his previous drug use and withdrawal from the world. As noted above, being "the man of granite" was better than being "obliterated." From the MERIT perspective, the point was not that Gordan arrived at a correct account of his life or set of specific problems, but that he was actively thinking about himself, others, and his actions in the world, in the context of seeking to direct his own life and belong somewhere.

4.3.5 Element 5: Reflecting on Interpersonal Processes

In the fifth element, the goal is to foster joint reflection upon the interpersonal processes and dynamics within session. Initially, this proved to be difficult given that Gordan could at most report that he didn't know or felt nothing about the therapist. He indeed seemed overwhelmed and unable to comment on the relationship that was occurring with the therapist.

One path that allowed these considerations to begin, however, was the reflection that the therapist's thoughts were disruptive for him. This enabled an early reflection that the therapist was another person who was not listening to him or giving him what he needed. He was unable to articulate what he needed but could note when the therapist did something he did not want. With time, this grew into a clearer portrait of the therapist as a "truant officer," or someone who was firm, highly critical, and disinterested. This slowly evolved as the dyad reflected upon these perceptions into a full picture Gordon had of the therapist; that of a well-meaning but overwhelming person, who was unlikely to remain attentive to Gordan's needs, similar to his perception of his father while growing up. This picture continued to evolve to include the belief that the therapist was someone who could potentially understand something Gordon might express, allowing for emotional expression to become more meaningful. Through the lens of MERIT, a key outcome of these discussions was not only improvement in the therapeutic alliance, but just as importantly, an indication of Gordan's ability to see the relationship as something he could think about as separate from himself and therefore reflect upon.

4.3.6 Element 6: Change within the Session

In parallel with the fifth element, Gordan found it almost impossible to understand what the therapist meant when he asked, "How did this conversation go for you today?" or find meaning in reflections like, "Today it seemed something in you changed as we talked . . . did you notice that too?" He generally appeared confused and merely stated, "I'm fine."

With time, Gordan started to feel frustrated by not knowing and felt pressured by the question. This allowed for a reflection that one perception or experience of the session was a sense of pressure. This naturally opened the door to wonder what might relieve that pressure and why sharing his thoughts provoked this feeling. Related to this, he noted that one source of this pressure might be an overarching struggle in "finding words."

As therapy progressed, Gordan began noting sessions helped him feel less anger and tension, which at times provided contentment in place of resentment. When asked how that might have happened, he noted being surprised and formed the idea that relationships across his life had never led to contentment, and that he found something in these conversations which was validating in ways that went against his long-standing idea of how relationships work.

4.3.7 Element 7: Stimulating Self-Reflectivity and Understanding the Mind of the Other

Following assessment of metacognitive capacity using the MAS-A, initial therapist reflections and comments offered Gordan an opportunity to think first about the different contents he found in his mind. This included noticing: "You have a thought about your going back to school . . . " or "You have a memory of your mother." As Gordan began to reflect more on the occurrences in his mind, he provided increasingly detailed narratives about his life. These narratives often allowed for evidence that he could notice emotions and at times even doubt his thoughts. These, reflected in higher rating on the MAS-A, led to therapist comments that invited Gordan to think about emotions and his changing opinions about things.

Similar to self-reflectivity, Gordon began with a very limited ability to form ideas of other people. He was aware that other people had their own thoughts but could not form ideas about different mental activities that might be taking place within their minds. The therapist focused interventions on wondering about discrete mental activities that others might be having within Gordon's narratives and emphasized sharing the contents of his own mind. This seemed to lead to metacognitive growth, with Gordan being able to begin thinking about emotions others might be having.

4.3.8 Element 8: Stimulating Psychological Mastery

In the last element of MERIT, the assessment of Gordan's level of mastery called for initial interventions that first stimulated the awareness of a psychosocial challenge. This laid the path for reflection about feeling helpless when facing problems, such as being overwhelmed by emotions or feeling excluded. This led him to think about the potential of turning to others for support during such times. Again, interventions were offered that matched Gordon's capacity for mastery. Through the lens of MERIT, gains were observed in Gordan's ability to think about his actions in the world in response to the challenges he faced.

5. Outcomes

Following the treatment described above, Gordon has continued to have contact with the therapist but at a decreased rate generally dictated by his needs. Concerning this course of therapy, he reflected that this was something that had been surprising to him, because it led him to move away from a state of numbness toward the ability to experience emotions without the threat of negative consequence. He noted this did not necessarily lead him to being a more content or happy person because with awareness came more pain. Nevertheless, this new state was desirable as he was becoming someone more in charge of his life who could then pursue things that were meaningful to him.

In terms of measurable outcome, therapist assessment revealed the following changes in metacognitive capacity as assessed with the MAS-A. Self-reflectivity began with a score of 2.5 and ended at 4.5 (possible total score is 9). Awareness of the Other began at 2 and ended at 3.5 (possible total score of 7). Decentration began at 0 and ended at 1.5 (total possible score of 3). Finally, Mastery began at 1 and ended with a score of 4 (total possible score of 9). Together these were summed separately such that his total score moved from a score of 5 to a score of 13.5, reflecting Gordan's ability to form an increasingly integrated and less fragmented sense of self, others, and his actions in the world. Similar gains were noted in negative symptoms. While he initially presented with moderately severe levels of blunted affect, avolition, anhedonia, motor retardation, and lack of social interest, by the end of therapy these symptoms all fell in the mild range, except blunted affect, which fell in the minimal range. From a recovery standpoint, we observed Gordan become increasingly able to form a coherent narrative of his challenges and possibilities in life, and an ability to better manage his actions independently, while also feeling more connected to the community.

6. Conclusions

Research has suggested that metacognitive deficits may cause or sustain negative symptoms in schizophrenia. In this paper we have presented an illustration of a treatment designed to address metacognition that may have in part successfully addressed negative symptoms. These observations are consistent with other case work reporting how MERIT may target negative symptoms in prolonged schizophrenia (George & Buck, 2018; van Donkersgoed et al., 2016).This is also consistent with past work suggesting that MERIT may offer approaches to helping patients with particularly complex clinical presentations, often thought to have a poor prognosis (Hamm & Lysaker, 2018). Although the results of this one case study are promising, there are limitations. Findings of one case study may not generalize to other symptom presentations. Observations here were done by the therapist and thus not blinded. Randomized and clinical trials are needed in particular with persons with enduring negative symptoms. Other work is called for comparing this treatment to other emerging cognitive, interpersonal, and metacognitively oriented therapies as presented elsewhere in this volume.

References

Austin, S. F., Lysaker, P. H., Jansen, J. E., Trauelsen, A. M., Pedersen, M. B., Simonsen, E., Nielsen, H-G. L., Pedersen, M. B., Haahr, U. H., & Simonsen, E. (2019). Metacognitive capacity and negative symptoms in first episode psychosis: Evidence of a prospective relationship over a 3-year follow-up. *Journal of Experimental Psychopathology, 10*, 1–11.

Cicero, D. C., Martin, E. A., Becker, T. M., & Kerns, J. G. (2016). Decreased self-concept clarity in people with schizophrenia. *The Journal of Nervous and Mental Disease, 204*(2), 142–147.

Cohen-Chazani Y, Lysaker PH, Roe & Hasson-Ohayon I (2021). Metacognitive reflection and insight therapy in an inpatient setting: Transforming messianism to a coherent mission *Journal of Clinical Psychology*. 77(8), 1836–1850.

Dmitryeva N., Chernov N, Kostyuk G & Lysaker PH. (2021). Utilizing MERIT to promote recovery in Schizotypal Personality Disorder: An illustrative case study. Journal of Clinical Psychology. 77(8), 1798–1806.

Faith, L. A., Zou, D. S., & Kukla, M. (2022). Metacognitive Reflection and Insight Therapy (MERIT) Delivered Virtually During the COVID-19 Pandemic: An Illustration of Two Cases. *Journal of contemporary psychotherapy*, 53(1), 71–79.

Faith, L. A., Lecomte, T., Corbiere, M., Francoeur, A., Hach Labelle, C., & Lysaker, P.H. (2020). Metacognition is uniquely related to concurrent and prospective assessments of negative symptoms independent of verbal memory in serious mental illness. *Journal of Nervous and Mental Disease, 208*(11), 837–842.

Flavell, J. H. (1979). Metacognition and cognitive monitoring: A new area of cognitive-developmental inquiry. *American Psychologist, 34*, 906–911.

García-Mieres, H., Villaplana, A., López-Carrilero, R., Grasa, E., Barajas, A., Pousa, E., Feixas, G., & Ochoa, S. (2020). The role of personal identity on positive and negative symptoms in psychosis: A study using the repertory grid technique. *Schizophrenia Bulletin, 46*(3), 572–580.

García-Mieres, H., Lundin, N., Minor, K., Dimaggio, G., Cheli, S., & Lysaker, P. H. (2020). A cognitive model of diminished expression in schizophrenia: the interface of metacognition, cognitive impairment and language disturbances. *Journal of Psychiatric Research, 131*, 169–176.

George, S. E., & Buck, K. D. (2018). Metacognitive reflection and insight therapy for persons with severe negative symptoms of schizophrenia. *American Journal of Psychotherapy, 71(4)*, 135–144.

Hamm. J., & Lysaker, P. H. (2018). Integrative metacognitive psychotherapy for serious mental illness: Applications to diverse clinical needs and its processes that promote recovery. *American Journal of Psychotherapy.* 71(4), 122–127.

Hamm, J. A., Renard, S. B., Fogley, R. L., Leonhardt, B. L., Dimaggio, G., Buck, K. D., & Lysaker, P. H. (2012). Metacognition and social cognition in schizophrenia: Stability and relationship to concurrent and prospective symptom assessments. *Journal of* Clinical Psychology, 68(12), 1303–1312.

Hasson-Ohayon, I., Goldzweig, G., Lavi-Rotenberg, A., Luther, L., & Lysaker, P. H. (2018). The centrality of cognitive symptoms and metacognition within the interacting network of symptoms, neurocognition, social cognition and metacognition in schizophrenia. *Schizophrenia Research, 202*, 260–266.

Hasson-Ohayon, I., Gumley, A., McLeod, H., & Lysaker, P. H. (2020). Metacognition and intersubjectivity: Reconsidering their relationship following advances from the study of persons with psychosis. *Frontiers, 11*, 567.

Hesse, K., Kriston, L., Wittorf, A., Herrlich, J., Wölwer, W., & Klingberg, S. (2015). Longitudinal relations between symptoms, neurocognition, and self-concept in schizophrenia. *Frontiers in Psychology, 6*, 917.

Huling, K., Lysaker, P. H., Faith, L., & García-Mieres, H. (2021). Addressing negative symptoms in schizophrenia through Metacognitive Reflection and Insight Therapy: An illustrated case study. Quaderni di Psicoterapia Cognitiva, 48, 36–58.

Inchausti, F., García-Poveda, N. V., Ballesteros-Prados, A., Ortuño-Sierra, J., Sánchez-Reales, S., Prado-Abril, J., Aldaz-Armendáriz, J. A., Mole, J., Dimaggio, G., Ottavi, P., & Fonseca-Pedrero, E. (2018). The Effects of Metacognition-Oriented Social Skills Training on Psychosocial Outcome in Schizophrenia-Spectrum Disorders: A Randomized Controlled Trial. *Schizophrenia bulletin, 44*(6), 1235–1244.

de Jong, S, Donkersgoed RJM, Aleman A, van der Gaag M, Wunderink L, Arends J, Lysaker PH & Pijnenborg G.H.M (2016). The practical implications of Metacognitive psychotherapy in psychosis: Findings from a pilot study. *Journal of Nervous and Mental Disease* 204(9):713–716.

de Jong S, Hasson-Ohayon I, van Donkersgoed R, Aleman A, Pijnenborg GHM. (2020). A qualitative evaluation of the effects of Metacognitive Reflection and Insight Therapy: "Living more consciously." Psychology and Psychotherapy. 93(2):223–240.

de Jong Jong S, van Donkersgoed RJM., Timmerman ME, aan het Rot M, Wunderink L, Arends JM. van der Gaag, Aleman A, Lysaker PH, Pijnenborg, GHM. (2019). Metacognitive reflection and insight therapy (MERIT) for patients with schizophrenia. *Psychological Medicine. 49*(2), 303–313.

Kukla, M., Arellano-Bravo, C., & Lysaker, P. H. (2021). "I'd Be A Completely Different Person if I Hadn't Gone to Therapy": A Qualitative Study of Metacognitive Therapy and Recovery Outcomes in Adults with Schizophrenia. *Psychiatry, 85*(3), 259–269. Advance online publication.

Lavi-Rotenberg, A., Eran Bar-Kalifa, E., de Jong, S., Ben-Dor, L., Lysaker, P.H. & Hasson-Ohayon I. (2021). Elements that enhance therapeutic alliance and short-term outcomes in Metacognitive Reflection and Insight Therapy: A session by session assessment. *Journal of Psychiatric Rehabilitation. 43*(4), 318–326.

Lysaker, P. H., Carcione, A., Dimaggio, G., Johannesen, J. K., Nicolo, G., Procacci, M., & Semerari, A. (2005). Metacognition amidst narratives of self and illness in schizophrenia:

Associations with neurocognition, symptoms, insight and quality of life. *Acta Psychiatrica Scandinavica, 112*, 64–71.

Lysaker, P. H., Cheli, S., Dimaggio, G., Buck, B., Bonfils, K., Huling, K., Wiesepape, C., & Lysaker, J. T. (2021). Metacognition, social cognition, and mentalizing in psychosis: Are these distinct constructs when it comes to subjective experience or are we just splitting hairs? *BMC Psychiatry, 21*, 329.

Lysaker, P. H., Chernov, N., Moiseeva, T., Sozinova, M., Dmitryeva, N., Alyoshin, V., Faith, L. A., Karpenko, O., & Kostyuk, G. (2020). Contrasting metacognitive profiles and their association with negative symptoms in groups with schizophrenia, early psychosis and depression in a Russian sample. *Psychiatry Research, 291*, 113–177.

Lysaker, P. H., & Dimaggio, G. (2014). Metacognitive capacities for reflection in schizophrenia: Implications for developing treatments. *Schizophrenia Bulletin, 40*(3), 487–491.

Lysaker, P. H., Gagen, E. C., Klion, R., Zalzala, A. B., Vohs, J., Faith, L. A., Leonhardt, B. L., Hamm, J. A., & Hasson-Ohayon, I. (2020). Metacognitive Reflection and Insight Therapy: A recovery-oriented treatment approach for psychosis. *Psychology Research and Behavior Management, 13*, 331–341.

Lysaker, P. H., & Hasson-Ohayon, I. (2021). Metacognition in psychosis: A renewed path to understanding of core disturbances and recovery-oriented treatment. *World Psychiatry, 20*(3), 359–361.

Lysaker, P. H., Hasson-Ohayon, I., Wiesepape, C., Huling, K., Musselman, A., & Lysaker, J. T. (2021). Social dysfunction in psychosis is more than a matter of misperception: Advances from the study of metacognition. *Frontiers in Psychology, 12*, 723952

Lysaker, P. H., & Klion, R. (2017) Recovery, Meaning-making, and Severe Mental Illness: A Comprehensive Guide to Metacognitive Reflection and Insight Therapy. Routledge.

Lysaker, P. H., Kukla, M., Dubreucq, J., Gumley, A., Mcleod, H., Vohs, J. L., Buck, K. D., Minor, K. S., Luther, L., Leonhardt, B. L., Belanger, E. A., Popolo, R., & Dimaggio, G. (2015). Metacognitive deficits predict future levels of negative symptoms in schizophrenia controlling for neurocognition, affect recognition, and self-expectation of goal attainment. *Schizophrenia Research, 168*, 267–272.

Lysaker, P. H., Kukla, M., Leonhardt, B. L., Hamm, J. A., Schnackenberg-Martin, A., Zalzala A. B., Gagen, E. C., & Hasson-Ohayon, I. (2020). Meaning, integration, and the self in serious mental illness: Implications of research in metacognition for psychiatric rehabilitation. *Journal of Psychiatric Rehabilitation, 43*(4), 275–283.

Lysaker, P. H., & Lysaker, J. T. (2020). Disturbances in dialogue and metacognition: A renewed way to understand and respond to alterations in self-experience in psychosis. *Theory and Psychology, 31*(3), 335–354.

Lysaker, P. H., Minor, K. S., Lysaker, J. T., Hasson-Ohayon, I., Bonfils, K., Hochheiser, J., & Vohs, J. L. (2020). Metacognitive function and fragmentation in schizophrenia: Relationship to cognition, self-experience and developing treatments. *Schizophrenia Research: Cognition, 19*, 1–9.

Minor, K., Marggraf, M, P., Davis, B. J., Mickens, J. L., Beaudette, D.M., Robbins, M. L., Buck, K. D., Wiehe, S. E. & Lysaker, P. H. (2021) Personalizing Interventions Using Real-World Interactions: Improving Symptoms and Social Functioning in Schizophrenia with Tailored Metacognitive Therapy. *Journal of Consulting and Clinical Psychology*, 90(1), 18–28.

McLeod, H. J., Gumley, A. I., Macbeth, A., Schwannauer, M., & Lysaker, P. H. (2014). Metacognitive functioning predicts positive and negative symptoms over 12 months in first episode psychosis. *Journal of Psychiatric Research, 54*, 109–115.

Moritz, S., & Lysaker, P. H. (2018) Metacognition – what did James H. Flavell really say and the implications for the conceptualization and design of metacognitive interventions in schizophrenia. *Schizophrenia Research, 201*, 20–26.

Semerari, A., Carcione, A., Dimaggio, G., Falcone, M., Nicolo, G., Procaci, M., & Alleva, G. (2003). How to evaluate metacognitive function in psychotherapy? The metacognition assessment scale and its applications. *Clinical Psychology & Psychotherapy, 10* (4), 238–261.

Trauelsen, A. M., Gumley, A., Jansen, J. E., Pedersen, M. B., Nielsen, H. G., Trier, C. H., Haahr, U. H., & Simonsen, E. (2016). Metacognition in first-episode psychosis and its association with positive and negative symptom profiles. *Psychiatry Research*, *238*, 14–23.

van Donkersgoed, R. J. M., de Jong, S., & Pijnenborg, G. H. M. (2016). Metacognitive reflection and insight therapy (MERIT) with a patient with persistent negative symptoms. *Journal of Contemporary Psychotherapy*, *46*, 245–253.

Vohs, J. L., Leonhardt, B. L., James, A. V., Francis, M. M., Breier, A., Mehdiyoun, N., Visco, A. C. & Lysaker, P. H. (2018). Metacognitive Reflection and Insight Therapy for Early Psychosis: A preliminary study of a novel integrative psychotherapy. *Schizophrenia Research*, *195*, 428–433.

20
Mindfulness and Negative Symptoms

Kerem Böge and Pamela Jacobsen

"It's like, being mindful wipes the fog from your glasses, you know, on a steamy day or something, you know, on a rainy day"

Participant quoted in Dennick et al. (2013)

"So, to realize that they [the symptoms] are only part of more in me. That I am not always just my symptoms that I can let go. (...) I am much more besides my symptoms.

Participant quoted in Böge et al. (2020)

Clinical pearls:

- Mindfulness for psychosis may effectively target negative symptoms of psychosis through reducing experiential avoidance, upregulating positive emotions, and modifying deficits in mental imagery.
- Mindfulness for psychosis has been shown to be safe and effective when delivered according to best practice guidelines and by practitioners with appropriate mindfulness training and supervision.
- Recommended adaptations for people with negative symptoms include reduced length of practices (e.g., five to ten minutes), frequent guidance using concrete language, smaller group sizes, and explicit reference to psychotic symptoms that may arise during practice.
- A full range of mindfulness practices can be used in this population, including the body scan, mindfulness of the breath, and mindful movement. Practices can be tailored to meet the needs of the individual client as well as the clinical setting and mode of delivery (e.g., in-person or online, in a group or individually).

Kerem Böge and Pamela Jacobsen, *Mindfulness and Negative Symptoms*. In: *Psychosocial Approaches to Negative Symptoms in Psychosis*. Edited by: Tania Lincoln et al., Oxford University Press. © Oxford University Press (2025). DOI: 10.1093/oso/9780197676790.003.0020

1. Theoretical Background of the Intervention

Cognitive-behavioral models of psychosis (Freeman et al., 2002; Garety et al., 2001; Morrison, 2001) have thus far predominantly focused on explaining the development and maintenance of positive symptoms rather than negative symptoms. Likewise, models of mindfulness for psychosis first focused on how people relate to and respond to positive symptoms such as intrusive voices or paranoid thoughts (Chadwick et al., 2005). These mindfulness models, however, can also be applied to understanding how maladaptive responses such as suppression and rumination could also explain aspects of negative symptoms; for example, by social withdrawal and emotional flattening emerging because of an avoidant coping style.

The first theoretical model of mindfulness for psychosis was adapted from existing models of mindfulness for other mental health difficulties, most prominently to reduce risk of relapse in people experiencing recurrent depressive episodes (Kuyken et al., 2015). In Mindfulness Based Cognitive Therapy (MBCT) for depression, the key process that is targeted by the development of mindfulness skills is the recognition of and skillful disengagement from patterns of negative thought that characterize relapse (Segal et al., 2013). Likewise, the model of mindfulness for psychosis (Chadwick et al., 2005) proposes that a mindful response to distressing psychotic experiences, such as voices or paranoid thoughts, might offer a more adaptive alternative to habitual ways of responding that perpetuate distress based on experiential avoidance (e.g., pushing voices away). Targeting experiential avoidance is also a key part of acceptance-based approaches, such as Acceptance and Commitment Therapy (ACT), which have also been adapted for psychosis (Johns et al., 2016).

Mindfulness-based approaches for psychosis are theoretically consistent with traditional Cognitive Behavioral Therapy for Psychosis (CBTp). This is because the shared goal across both approaches is to reduce distress and impairment associated with symptoms, rather than to get rid of the symptoms themselves. The treatment effect is therefore achieved through modification of the relationship people have with their internal experiences, rather than changing the form or content of the experiences themselves. People with distressing psychosis often struggle to cope with distressing voices or beliefs, and frequently get trapped in cycles of either trying to avoid their experiences or getting lost in battling against them (Falloon & Talbot, 1981; Howard et al., 2013; Johns et al., 2002; Rassin & van der Heiden, 2007). Over time this can lead to considerable distress and impairment to functioning, which may also manifest in the development of negative symptoms. For example, someone may experience a loss of interest and pleasure in previously enjoyed activities because they have become so focused on trying to control or fight with their symptoms. Poverty of speech may arise as cognitive resources are depleted by on-going internal battles with voices. A person may display reduced facial expressiveness and a flattening of emotional tone as experiential avoidance blocks the experience of both positive *and* negative emotions.

Mindfulness offers an alternative way of being with psychotic experiences, by bringing nonjudgmental awareness to these experiences, acceptance of the present moment, and a letting go of struggling or fighting against experiences. This may bring benefits in terms of reducing distress and impairment associated with both positive and negative symptoms. For example, by increasing people's emotional responsiveness and ability to interact in social situations, this should counteract the tendency to avoid and withdraw from others as is so often seen in people experiencing prominent negative symptoms in psychosis.

The use of mindfulness for psychosis was considered quite a radical approach at the time it was first investigated and remained so many years on (Böge et al., 2021). There had historically been concerns that meditation techniques might be unsafe to use with people experiencing psychotic symptoms, or with those considered at risk of experiencing a psychotic episode. This was partly based on isolated case-study evidence of reported psychotic or manic episodes associated with intensive meditation retreats (of varying schools of meditation). However, none of the meditation retreats described in these case studies would be typical of a mindfulness-based intervention delivered within a healthcare setting. The retreats typically included additional risk factors for development of a mental health crisis such as sleep deprivation, food restriction, and extreme social isolation (i.e., no talking or eye contact for 18 hours a day for two weeks; Walsh & Roche, 1979). It is also possible that people beginning to experience a mental health crisis sought out retreats in response to their deteriorating mental state, rather than the meditation retreat itself being the causal factor. Concerns about mindfulness for psychosis can also arise from a misunderstanding of the goals of a mindfulness practice; for example, that if the intention is to "focus on" voices or paranoid thoughts, this could cause an exacerbation in their intensity or frequency. However, the goal of a mindfulness practice is to turn intentionally toward whatever is *already present*—there is no inducement or creation of any symptoms, but instead an opportunity to cultivate an alternative response style to constant avoidance or struggle, which may be perpetuating distress.

Qualitative studies of people's experiences of taking part in mindfulness for psychosis groups have provided important information on the key therapeutic processes and mechanisms. A grounded theory study of 16 people who had taken part in a UK mindfulness for psychosis group found that people reported relating differently to psychosis through three main processes (Abba et al., 2008).

There were: (1) decentering from voices, thoughts, and images; (2) making skillful choices in responding; and (3) reclaiming power and a sense of the self apart from "psychosis." A later qualitative study was conducted in Germany with 27 people who had taken part in a mindfulness group program as part of their inpatient care (Böge et al., 2020). The findings similarly showed that people described developing core skills in detaching/decentering from voices, thoughts, and images, and cultivating an attitude of openness and nonjudgment. Alongside a reduction in distress, people also reported increases in the experience of positive emotions such as joy after doing a mindfulness course, and improvements in cognition including a greater ability to concentrate, and improved imagination and creativity.

These qualitative findings are important, because they provide an initial source of empirical data with which to evaluate possible mechanisms for mindfulness to improve negative symptoms in psychosis. Jansen and colleagues (2020) proposed some possible theoretical pathways including the benefits of a behavioral component (e.g., behavioral activation through simply attending a group), increasing positive emotions and reducing deficits in anticipatory pleasure, and improving skills in decentering and metacognitive awareness. A difficulty in regulating positive emotions (i.e., having the skills to change the nature, frequency, and intensity of positive emotions) may underlie symptoms including apathy, anhedonia, and social withdrawal. Carl and colleagues (2013) suggest that mindfulness-based interventions are credible treatment strategies for targeting difficulties in regulating positive emotions, through attentional training (e.g., correcting deficits in attending to positive stimuli) and response modulation (i.e., abilities in up-regulating or down-regulating positive emotions).

Another key deficit that may be modified by mindfulness interventions is a difficulty in generating vivid mental imagery. This may partly underlie problems with accurate predictions of anticipatory pleasure (i.e., a sense of looking forward to something that is expected to be enjoyable). It is well-documented that there is a disconnect in schizophrenia between anticipatory and consummatory pleasure, in that people do enjoy things once they have done them, but underestimate in advance how pleasurable they will find them (Edwards et al., 2018; Edwards et al., 2015). A difficulty in mental imagery may contribute to this gap between predicted and actual enjoyment. That is, if people find it difficult to generate vivid projections of future events with rich sensory detail (e.g., difficulty imagining the smell and taste of a meal at a planned restaurant outing), they will be less likely to anticipate the pleasure of the activity. The link between impaired mental imagery and negative symptoms is supported by previous studies, using a variety of experimental methods (Blackwell, 2019). Mindfulness interventions may help to improve the vividness and richness of mental imagery, through attentional training and improving sensory awareness (e.g., noticing smells, tastes, and tactile sensations). Therefore, mindfulness may help reduce negative symptoms in psychosis through several plausible theoretical mechanisms.

2. Practical Procedures of Mindfulness-Based Interventions

Mindfulness for psychosis interventions has been delivered in a variety of ways, including in group format (Chadwick et al., 2009; Chadwick et al., 2005), as an individually delivered therapy (Jacobsen et al., 2020), with variable requirements for home practice (Jacobsen et al., 2022), and also adapted for online delivery (Ellett et al., 2022). Mindfulness for psychosis has been evaluated and implemented in a variety of clinical settings, including as part of routine clinical care in the community (Jacobsen et al., 2019; Ting et al., 2020) and inpatient services (Böge et al., 2021; Jacobsen et al., 2011; Jacobsen et al., 2020; Millar et al., 2020).

The original Chadwick protocol for mindfulness for psychosis was delivered as an in-person group therapy of six weekly 1.5-hour sessions. Each group session included two 10-minute guided sitting meditations per session, with teacher-led enquiry after each in-session practice (Chadwick et al., 2009; Chadwick et al., 2005). Participants were invited to practice at home between sessions, with the use of audio recordings, but this was not a requirement and much less emphasis was placed on this compared to Mindfulness Based Cognitive Therapy (MBCT) protocols. The range of mindfulness practices used in mindfulness for psychosis has expanded since Chadwick's first studies, and includes the full range of core practices (e.g., body scan, mindful movement, and mindfulness of the breath (Böge et al., 2021; Jacobsen et al., 2020). There is now considerable heterogeneity in how mindfulness for psychosis has been delivered in terms of format, length of sessions, and duration of intervention. There are core components, however, which are important for fidelity as a mindfulness-based intervention, including the development of a new decentered relationship with internal experience, and the cultivation of greater attentional, emotional, and behavioral control through experiential practice with teacher-led inquiry. Using the metaphor of a weaving loom, Crane and colleagues (2017) refer to these core components as the "warp thread" that provides the fixed, vertical structure of the cloth. The "weft thread," by contrast, runs across the warp thread, making each tapestry unique in texture, color, and pattern. For mindfulness for psychosis, the "weft threads" include shorter meditations (around 10 minutes), more frequent guidance and avoiding long silences, and including explicit reference to psychotic symptoms that may arise during the practices, such as voices or paranoid thoughts.

A typical mindfulness of the breath practice would begin with grounding in the body through an invitation to turn toward bodily sensations associated with how a person is sitting. Mindfulness for psychosis groups delivered in health-care settings have generally kept things simple by having people sit in chairs to avoid the need for special equipment such as mats, cushions, or meditation stools. However, a person may sit in whatever position works best for them. Assuming a person or group is sitting in chairs, the first invitation would be to uncross the arms and legs and place both feet on the floor. This introduces a deliberate change in posture, which helps embody a person's intention for the meditation practice, that is, to pay attention in the present moment. A comfortable, upright position is suggested to embody "falling awake" rather than falling asleep. Any position in which someone might reasonably fall asleep is to be avoided (e.g., having people sink back into chairs with head back and eyes closed), especially as this may inadvertently convey a message that the goal of the practice is to achieve a state of relaxation. It is very important that the mindfulness teacher conveys a consistent, embodied message that the goal is to achieve a state of *compassionate awareness*, not to get relaxed, or to try to create an empty or blank mind. A few words around setting intentions can be helpful at this point to explicitly acknowledge goals that may arise in the mind (e.g., *I must be really focused for the whole 10 minutes*) and encouraging participants to just notice these as transient mental events rather than attaching to them and buying into them. Guidance should be given that a person may either close their eyes or keep a soft gaze on the floor in front of them if they prefer to keep their eyes open. Giving options around eye gaze is particularly important for people who may be used to maintaining a high level of vigilance in their daily lives due to worries about safety and vulnerability to harm. The mindfulness teacher's voice as well as other auditory cues (e.g., using bells or a singing bowl) can be used to mark the end and beginning of the practice, as well as providing a grounding anchor throughout the practice.

As the mindfulness practice starts, people are invited to begin the process of connecting with the present moment by turning awareness toward the physical sensations arising from the contact between their body and the outside world; for example, the soles of the feet on the floor. Noticing sensations in the soles of the feet, allowing them to come and go in their own time, without trying to fix or change things, serve as a way to practice this skill on a fairly neutral focus of awareness. This way of relating to other internal experiences can then be applied to more challenging internal experiences such as critical voices, distressing thoughts, or aversive emotions. The meditation may then proceed with a mini body-scan, guiding awareness up from the soles of the feet, through the body all the way to the crown of the head. An invitation can then be given to gather awareness around the sensations of breathing, wherever these are most comfortable and noticeable for people, such as at the tip of the nostrils, the rise and fall of the chest, or down in the stomach and diaphragm. The focus is on feeling the breath, rather than thinking *about* the breath, or controlling or changing the breath in any way. It is important therefore not to give any instructions which might imply a need to change the breath, such as breathing more deeply or slowly—the invitation is just to notice however the body is already breathing from a decentered observer stance. As with all other mindfulness-based therapies, guidance is given throughout on working with the wandering mind (i.e., just noticing when the mind has wandered away, and bringing it gently back to the intended focus of awareness). Specific guidance is also given on working with psychotic symptoms that may arise, such as voices or paranoid thoughts. Their presence in current-moment awareness is noted without trying to push them away or ignore them, and people are invited to simply observe them and let them come and go in their own time, as with other internal experiences.

In addition to mindfulness practices, mindfulness for psychosis protocols have also incorporated other treatment elements. These include psychoeducation about psychosis (e.g., Chien et al., 2017) and defusion exercises and metaphors in Acceptance and Commitment Therapy (ACT) (e.g., Gaudiano & Herbert, 2006; Shawyer et al., 2012; Spidel et al., 2018). For example, the Passengers on the Bus metaphor (https://youtu.be/Z29ptSuoWRc) is used to express several key ideas within ACT, including the concept of defusion, whereby thoughts, emotions, and bodily sensations are "passengers" on the bus (representing the self) and therefore distinct from the self, rather than being fully fused with it. ACT for psychosis groups have included innovative ways of using this metaphor within sessions, such as having participants physically "act out" the Passengers on the Bus exercise by having them role-play the driver and passengers on the bus (Johns et al., 2016). The driver and the passengers can repeat the exercise using different approaches; for example, the passengers being rowdy and disruptive and the driver stopping to remonstrate with them (fight/struggle scenario) versus the driver welcoming the passengers on the bus and thanking them for their comments, but not getting drawn off course (openness/acceptance scenario). These approaches can be seen as complementary to the process of skill development in responding differently to internal experiences, whether this is through a sitting meditation, or by acting out a metaphor in a group exercise. A reduction in experiential avoidance achieved by increased willingness to accept and "be with" moment-by-moment experience may be beneficial in improving negative symptoms by reducing emotional flattening as discussed earlier.

Although as mentioned earlier, there historically have been concerns about using meditation practices with people with psychosis, or those considered vulnerable to experiencing psychosis, the empirical data from clinical studies shows that it is safe and acceptable when delivered in line with these adaptations, and by a suitably qualified mindfulness teacher. As with all psychological therapies, however, it is important that any associated harms are properly recorded and monitored both in clinical trials and routine clinical practice (Ellett & Chadwick, 2021).

3. Evidence-Base for Mindfulness-Based Interventions in Psychosis

Mindfulness for psychosis is still an emerging field of research. In the first published uncontrolled pilot study, which was conducted in the United Kingdom, 10 outpatients with distressing psychosis participated in mindfulness groups consisting of six sessions (Chadwick et al., 2005). The pilot results were promising in terms of reported increases in pre-post measures of well-being and functioning. Moreover, individuals showed improvements in mindfulness over the course of the group, and group members rated mindfulness as an important overall group process along with universality and mutual support. Negative symptoms were not specifically assessed in this initial pilot study, nor in two follow-up randomized controlled trials (Chadwick et al., 2009; Chadwick et al., 2016). Following this early work, mindfulness for psychosis has been further adapted and evaluated in larger scale randomized controlled trials across the world including the United States, Hong Kong, Spain, Australia, and Canada. Increased attention has been paid to the assessment of negative symptoms, with more trials now including outcome measures such as the PANSS (Positive and Negative Syndrome Scale; Kay et al., 1987) which assess both positive and negative psychotic symptoms. More than 10 meta-analyses and systematic reviews of mindfulness and acceptance-based approaches have been conducted to date indicating a high level of clinical and research interest in this growing field (Aust & Bradshaw, 2017; Chai et al., 2022; Cramer et al., 2016; Hodann-Caudevilla et al., 2020; Jansen et al., 2020; Khoury et al., 2013; Lam & Chien, 2016; Liu et al., 2021; Louise et al., 2018; Sabe et al., 2019; Tao et al., 2021; Yip et al., 2022).

Interpreting the overall evidence base from the available meta-analytic data should be approached with caution, because there are multiple sources of heterogeneity between trials, meaning that they are not always necessarily comparing like with like. Sources of heterogeneity include treatment protocols, home practice requirements, trial settings, the characteristics of the clinical populations, and whether acceptance-based approaches such as ACT and Compassion Focused Therapy (CFT) are included in the reviews. Where the results of mindfulness- and acceptance-based trials have been synthesized together, this has made it more challenging to precisely distinguish the specific effect of different approaches. For example, acceptance-based approaches may have little requirement for formal mindfulness meditation within each session or as home practice. This has led to the increasing use of subgroup analyses, whereby studies are grouped together in smaller categories to better specify which approaches may have significant effects on which outcomes. In this section, we will mainly focus on the available evidence from mindfulness for psychosis trials on negative symptoms, which include mindfulness practices with teacher-led inquiry as a core part of each therapy session.

Two of the existing meta-analyses in the field focus specifically on negative symptoms (Chai et al., 2022; Sabe et al., 2019). The Sabe and colleagues (2019) review included all "mind-body therapies" for schizophrenia, including yoga and tai-chi as well as mindfulness for psychosis. Different groups of therapy were meta-analyzed separately so as to reduce heterogeneity for the reasons discussed above. For the three mindfulness for psychosis trials included in the review (Chien et al., 2017; Lee, 2019; Lopez-Navarro, Del Canto, et al., 2015), the results of the meta-analysis showed evidence of efficacy in reducing negative symptoms (as measured by the PANSS) from pre-post treatment, with a medium effect size (SMD = −0.45; [95% CI: −0.67, −0.23]). A later review by Chai and colleagues (2022) also reported beneficial effects of mindfulness for psychosis on negative symptoms (SMD = −0.96 [95% CI: −1.50, 0.43]). Their review similarly included a range of treatment approaches including mind-body therapies (e.g., yoga), acceptance-based therapies, and mindfulness for psychosis, and the sub-group analysis for mindfulness interventions included data from eight trials (Chien et al., 2017; Huang et al., 2018; Lee, 2019; Lopez-Navarro, Canto, et al., 2015; Wang et al., 2021; Wang et al., 2016; Wang et al., 2019; Xu et al., 2018). It is notable that for this most recent meta-analysis, seven out of the eight trials were conducted in mainland China, Hong Kong and/or Taiwan, with the one remaining trial from Spain (Lopez-Navarro, Canto, et al., 2015). This likely arises because the mindfulness trials in China mainly focus on adapted approaches known as Mindfulness-Based Psychoeducation Programs (MBPP) or Mindfulness-Based Psychoeducation Group Program (MPGP). These programs have a strong focus on rehabilitation for patients with more chronic difficulties, hence they are more likely to include measures of negative symptoms as trial outcomes. The findings of these negative-symptom focused meta-analyses are also consistent with two other meta-analyses published around the same time, which included data on a wider range of outcomes, but also reported meta-analyses separately for measures of negative psychotic symptoms (Hodann-Caudevilla et al., 2020; Jansen et al., 2020).

Separating out the synthesis of outcome data across different therapeutic approaches in meta-analyses is particularly important for determining mechanisms of effectiveness, as these may differ across different approaches. For example, as discussed earlier in this chapter, we may hypothesize that a reduction in experiential avoidance is one of the mechanisms by which negative symptoms can be effectively targeted in mindfulness-based approaches. Therefore, we would expect treatment protocols with a heavy emphasis on formal mindfulness practice, both in- and between-session, which help participants to cultivate this skill, to show better treatment outcomes in terms of impact on negative symptoms. This is, in fact, consistent with what the data are currently showing, as there is evidence of effectiveness of mindfulness for psychosis on negative symptoms (Chai et al., 2022; Hodann-Caudevilla et al., 2020; Jansen et al., 2020; Sabe et al., 2019) but not for acceptance-based therapies (Cramer et al., 2016; Jansen et al., 2020). The Cramer et al. (2016) meta-analysis synthesized data from three ACT trials (Gaudiano & Herbert, 2006; Shawyer et al., 2012; White et al., 2011) and found no evidence for an effect on negative symptoms (SMD= −0.27, [95% CI: −0.72, 0.17]). The later Jansen et al. (2020) review synthesized data from these same three studies, in addition to including the results of a subsequent larger ACT trial (Shawyer et al., 2017) with the overall body of evidence pointing to an even smaller effect size, which was not statistically significant (SMD= − 0.03 [95% CI: −0.31, 0.25]).

4. Future Research Directions

In summary, the theoretical basis of the mechanisms of action of mindfulness for psychosis clearly suggest several plausible routes for impact on negative symptoms, including via up-regulation of positive emotions and improved vividness of mental imagery. Although the literature on the effectiveness of mindfulness for psychosis has grown significantly since the first pilot trials were published, currently the main barrier to knowing more about the potential impact on negative symptoms is that many trials so far have not measured it. The exception to this is a family of trials conducted in China, Hong Kong, and Taiwan focusing on an adapted version of mindfulness for psychosis incorporating psychoeducation and psychiatric rehabilitation alongside formal meditation practice for people with chronic difficulties experiencing high levels of functional impairment. The effect of mindfulness for negative symptoms in other clinical settings and populations, such as people in first-episode/early intervention services or community mental health teams, is currently unknown because the available trials so far have not included measures of negative symptoms. The key recommendation at present therefore is for future trials to include measures of negative symptoms, as well as process measures so that hypothesized mediators of treatment effect can be tested out (e.g., mental imagery).

It is important that the selection of trial outcomes is done in collaboration with both clinicians, researchers, and people with lived experience of psychosis. The mindfulness for psychosis field so far has included examples of good practice in participatory research and the involvement of people with lived experience in developing therapy protocols and conducting research (Böge et al., 2021). It is also interesting to note that the current evidence for the efficacy of mindfulness for psychosis on negative symptoms is based mainly on trials using the PANSS (Positive and Negative Syndrome Scale; Kay et al., 1987). The PANSS includes items on blunted affect, social withdrawal, and lack of spontaneity in conversation. Future studies could also include newer scales such as the BNSS (Brief Negative Symptom Scale; Kirkpatrick et al., 2011), which covers five categories of negative symptoms (anhedonia, asociality, avolition, blunted affect, and alogia) mapping onto two factors, which are Motivation-Pleasure (MAP) and Emotional Expressivity (EE). A more fine-grained assessment of negative symptoms using a broader range of assessment tools would help elucidate more precisely which facets of negative symptoms may be most effectively targeted by mindfulness-based approaches.

Overall, there is an emerging field of research and clinical practice in mindfulness for persons with psychosis, which shows promise in developing into a novel and modern evidence-based psychological therapy specifically for negative symptoms. People with a diagnosis of psychosis and schizophrenia remain one of the most highly stigmatized and marginalized groups of people in society. Therefore, it is perhaps no surprise that there is a desire for change in this group of patients, and they are expressing a desire for "feeling heard," "feeling safe," and "reconnecting," especially in an age of increasing busyness and disconnection. Mindfulness may be one way, among many others, which for some people is a coherent way of enhancing interpersonal resonance, searching for reconnection with oneself and one's environment, and building rapport with others.

References

Abba, N., Chadwick, P., & Stevenson, C. (2008). Responding mindfully to distressing psychosis: A grounded theory analysis. *Psychotherapy Research, 18*(1), 77–87.

Aust, J., & Bradshaw, T. (2017). Mindfulness interventions for psychosis: a systematic review of the literature. *Journal of Psychiatric and Mental Health Nursing, 24*(1), 69–83.

Blackwell, S. E. (2019). Mental imagery: From basic research to clinical practice. *Journal of Psychotherapy Integration, 29*, 235–247.

Böge, K., Hahne, I., Bergmann, N., Wingenfeld, K., Zierhut, M., Thomas, N., Ta, T. M. T., Bajbouj, M., & Hahn, E. (2021). Mindfulness-based group therapy for in-patients with schizophrenia spectrum disorders – Feasibility, acceptability, and preliminary outcomes of a rater-blinded randomized controlled trial [Article]. *Schizophrenia Research, 228*, 134–144.

Böge, K., Karadza, A., Fuchs, L. M., Ehlen, F., Ta, T. M. T., Thomas, N., Bajbouj, M., & Hahn, E. (2020). Mindfulness-Based Interventions for In-Patients With Schizophrenia Spectrum Disorders – A Qualitative Approach [Article]. *Front Psychiatry, 11*, Article 600.

Böge, K., Thomas, N., & Jacobsen, P. (2021). Is mindfulness for psychosis harmful? Deconstructing a myth [Review]. *British Journal of Psychiatry, 218*(2), 71–72.

Carl, J. R., Soskin, D. P., Kerns, C., & Barlow, D. H. (2013). Positive emotion regulation in emotional disorders: A theoretical review. *Clinical Psychology Review, 33*(3), 343–360.

Chadwick, P., Hughes, S., Russell, D., Russell, I., & Dagnan, D. (2009). Mindfulness Groups for Distressing Voices and Paranoia: A Replication and Randomized Feasibility Trial. *Behavioural and Cognitive Psychotherapy, 37*(4), 403–412.

Chadwick, P., Strauss, C., Jones, A.-M., Kingdon, D., Ellett, L., Dannahy, L., & Hayward, M. (2016). Group mindfulness-based intervention for distressing voices: A pragmatic randomised controlled trial. *Schizophrenia Research, 175*(1–3), 168–173.

Chadwick, P., Taylor, K. N., & Abba, N. (2005). Mindfulness groups for people with psychosis. *Behavioural and Cognitive Psychotherapy, 33*(3), 351–359.

Chai, J., Xiao, X., An, N., Liu, F., Liu, S., Hu, N., Yang, Y., Cui, Y., & Li, Y. (2022). Efficacy of Mindfulness-Based Interventions for Negative Symptoms in Patients Diagnosed with Schizophrenia: a Meta-analysis [Article]. *Mindfulness, 13*(8), 2069–2081.

Chien, W. T., Bressington, D., Yip, A., & Karatzias, T. (2017). An international multi-site, randomized controlled trial of a mindfulness-based psychoeducation group programme for people with schizophrenia. *Psychological Medicine, 47*(12), 2081–2096.

Cramer, H., Lauche, R., Haller, H., Langhorst, J., & Dobos, G. (2016). Mindfulness- and Acceptance-based Interventions for Psychosis: A Systematic Review and Meta-analysis. *Global Advances in Health and Medicine, 5*(1), 30–43.

Crane, R. S., Brewer, J., Feldman, C., Kabat-Zinn, J., Santorelli, S., Williams, J. M. G., & Kuyken, W. (2017). What defines mindfulness-based programs? The warp and the weft. *Psychological Medicine, 47*(6), 990–999.

Dennick, L., Fox, A. P., & Walter-Brice, A. (2013). Mindfulness groups for people experiencing distressing psychosis: An interpretative phenomenological analysis. *Mental Health Review Journal, 18*, 32–43.

Edwards, C. J., Cella, M., Emsley, R., Tarrier, N., & Wykes, T. H. M. (2018). Exploring the relationship between the anticipation and experience of pleasure in people with schizophrenia: An experience sampling study. *Schizophrenia Research, 202*, 72–79.

Edwards, C. J., Cella, M., Tarrier, N., & Wykes, T. (2015). Predicting the future in schizophrenia: The discrepancy between anticipatory and consummatory pleasure. *Psychiatry Research, 229*(1-2), 462–469.

Ellett, L., & Chadwick, P. (2021). Recommendations for monitoring and reporting harm in mindfulness for psychosis research [Review]. *British Journal of Psychiatry, 19*(6), 629–631.

Ellett, L., Dannahy, L., & Chadwick, P. (2022). Engagement, clinical outcomes and therapeutic process in online mindfulness for psychosis groups delivered in routine care. *Psychology and Psychotherapy: Theory, Research and Practice.*

Falloon, I. R. H., & Talbot, R. E. (1981). Persistent Auditory Hallucinations - Coping Mechanisms and Implications for Management. *Psychological Medicine, 11*(2), 329–339.

Freeman, D., Garety, P. A., Kuipers, E., Fowler, D., & Bebbington, P. E. (2002). A cognitive model of persecutory delusions. *British Journal of Clinical Psychology, 41*, 331–347.

Garety, P. A., Kuipers, E., Fowler, D., Freeman, D., & Bebbington, P. E. (2001). A cognitive model of the positive symptoms of psychosis. *Psychological Medicine, 31*(2), 189–195.

Gaudiano, B. A., & Herbert, J. D. (2006). Acute treatment of inpatients with psychotic symptoms using Acceptance and Commitment Therapy: Pilot results. *Behaviour Research and Therapy, 44*(3), 415–437.

Hodann-Caudevilla, R. M., Díaz-Silveira, C., Burgos-Julián, F. A., & Santed, M. A. (2020). Mindfulness-based interventions for people with schizophrenia: A systematic review and meta-analysis [Review]. *International Journal of Environmental Research and Public Health, 17*(13), 1–18, Article 4690.

Howard, A., Forsyth, A., Spencer, H., Young, E. W., & Turkington, D. (2013). Do voice hearers naturally use focusing and metacognitive coping techniques? *Psychosis-Psychological Social and Integrative Approaches, 5*(2), 119–126.

Huang, S., Cao, X., & Shen, C. (2018). The influence of mindfulness training on social function of inpatients with schizophrenia. *Shanghai Nursing, 18*(6), 21–24.

Jacobsen, P., Choksi, T., Sawyer, K., Maximen, C., Harding, E., & Richardson, M. (2022). Home practice in mindfulness-based interventions for psychosis groups: a systematic review and qualitative study [Article]. *BMC Psychology, 10*(1), Article 9.

Jacobsen, P., Morris, E., Johns, L., & Hodkinson, K. (2011). Mindfulness Groups for Psychosis; Key Issues for Implementation on an Inpatient Unit. *Behavioural and Cognitive Psychotherapy, 39*(3), 349–353.

Jacobsen, P., Peters, E., Robinson, E. J., & Chadwick, P. (2020). Mindfulness-based crisis interventions (MBCI) for psychosis within acute inpatient psychiatric settings; a feasibility randomised controlled trial. *Bmc Psychiatry, 20*(1), 193.

Jacobsen, P., Richardson, M., Harding, E., & Chadwick, P. (2019). Mindfulness for Psychosis Groups; Within-Session Effects on Stress and Symptom-Related Distress in Routine Community Care. *Behavioural and Cognitive Psychotherapy, 47*(4), 421–430.

Jansen, J. E., Gleeson, J., Bendall, S., Rice, S., & Alvarez-Jimenez, M. (2020). Acceptance- and mindfulness-based interventions for persons with psychosis: A systematic review and meta-analysis. *Schizophrenia Research, 215*, 25–37.

Johns, L., Oliver, J. E., Khondoker, M., Byrne, M., Jolley, S., Wykes, T., Joseph, C., Butler, L., Craig, T., & Morris, E. M. (2016). The feasibility and acceptability of a brief Acceptance and Commitment Therapy (ACT) group intervention for people with psychosis: The 'ACT for life' study. *Journal of Behavior Therapy and Experimental Psychiatry, 50*, 257–263.

Johns, L. C., Hemsley, D., & Kuipers, E. (2002). A comparison of auditory hallucinations in a psychiatric and non-psychiatric group. *British Journal of Clinical Psychology, 41*(1), 81–86.

Kay, S. R., Fiszbein, A., & Opler, L. A. (1987). The Positive and Negative Syndrome Scale (PANSS) for Schizophrenia. *Schizophrenia Bulletin, 13*(2), 261–276.

Khoury, B., Lecomte, T., Gaudiano, B. A., & Paquin, K. (2013). Mindfulness interventions for psychosis: A meta-analysis. *Schizophrenia Research, 150*(1), 176–184.

Kirkpatrick, B., Strauss, G. P., Nguyen, L., Fischer, B. A., Daniel, D. G., Cienfuegos, A., & Marder, S. R. (2011). The Brief Negative Symptom Scale: Psychometric properties. *Schizophrenia Bulletin, 37*(2), 300–305.

Kuyken, W., Hayes, R., Barrett, B., Byng, R., Dalgleish, T., Kessler, D., Lewis, G., Watkins, E., Brejcha, C., Cardy, J., Causley, A., Cowderoy, S., Evans, A., Gradinger, F., Kaur, S., Lanham, P., Morant, N., Richards, J., Shah, P., Sutton, H., Vicary, R., Weaver, A., Wilks, J., Williams, M., Taylor, R. S., & Byford, S. (2015). Effectiveness and cost-effectiveness of mindfulness-based cognitive therapy compared with maintenance antidepressant treatment in the prevention of depressive relapse or recurrence (PREVENT): A randomised controlled trial. *The Lancet, 386*(9988), 63–73.

Lam, A. H. Y., & Chien, W. T. (2016). The effectiveness of mindfulness-based intervention for people with schizophrenia: a systematic review. *Neuropsychiatry, 6*(5), 208.

Lee, K. H. (2019). A randomized controlled trial of mindfulness in patients with schizophrenia. *Psychiatry Research, 275*, 137–142.

Liu, Y.-C., Li, I.-L., & Hsiao, F.-H. (2021). Effectiveness of mindfulness-based intervention on psychotic symptoms for patients with schizophrenia: A meta-analysis of randomized controlled trials. *Journal of Advanced Nursing, 77*(6), 2565–2580.

Lopez-Navarro, E., Canto, C., Belber, M., Mayol, A., Fernandez-Alonso, O., Lluis, J., Munar, E., & Chadwick, P. (2015). Mindfulness improves psychological quality of life in community-based patients with severe mental health problems: A pilot randomized clinical trial. *Schizophrenia Research, 168*(1–2), 530–536.

Lopez-Navarro, E., Del Canto, C., Belber, M., Mayol, A., Fernandez-Alonso, O., Lluis, J., Munar, E., & Chadwick, P. (2015). Mindfulness improves psychological quality of life in community-based patients with severe mental health problems: A pilot randomized clinical trial. *Schizophrenia Research, 168*(1–2), 530–536.

Louise, S., Fitzpatrick, M., Strauss, C., Rossell, S. L., & Thomas, N. (2018). Mindfulness- and acceptance-based interventions for psychosis: Our current understanding and a meta-analysis. *Schizophrenia Research, 192*, 57–63.

Millar, A., Tip, L., Lennon, R., Macinnes, M., Michalska, B., Lawrie, S. M., & Schwannauer, M. (2020). The introduction of mindfulness groups to a psychiatric rehabilitation in-patient setting: a feasibility study. *Bmc Psychiatry, 20*(1), 322.

Morrison, A. P. (2001). The interpretation of intrusions in psychosis: an integrative cognitive approach to hallucinations and delusions. *Behav Cogn Psychother, 29*(3), 257–276.

Rassin, E., & van der Heiden, S. (2007). Swearing voices: An experimental investigation of the suppression of hostile hallucinations. *Behavioural and Cognitive Psychotherapy, 35*(3), 355–360.

Sabe, M., Sentissi, O., & Kaiser, S. (2019). Meditation-based mind-body therapies for negative symptoms of schizophrenia: Systematic review of randomized controlled trials and meta-analysis [Review]. *Schizophrenia Research, 212*, 15–25.

Segal, Z. V., Williams, J. M. G., & Teasdale, J. D. (2013). *Mindfulness-based cognitive therapy for depression* (2nd ed.). Guilford Press.

Shawyer, F., Farhall, J., Mackinnon, A., Trauer, T., Sims, E., Ratcliff, K., Larner, C., Thomas, N., Castle, D., Mullen, P., & Copolov, D. (2012). A randomised controlled trial of acceptance-based cognitive behavioural therapy for command hallucinations in psychotic disorders. *Behaviour Research and Therapy, 50*(2), 110–121.

Shawyer, F., Farhall, J., Thomas, N., Hayes, S. C., Gallop, R., Copolov, D., & Castle, D. J. (2017). Acceptance and commitment therapy for psychosis: Randomised controlled trial. *British Journal of Psychiatry, 210*(2), 140–148.

Spidel, A., Lecomte, T., Kealy, D., & Daigneault, I. (2018). Acceptance and commitment therapy for psychosis and trauma: Improvement in psychiatric symptoms, emotion regulation, and treatment compliance following a brief group intervention. *Psychology and Psychotherapy: Theory, Research and Practice, 91*(2), 248–261.

Tao, T. J., Hui, C. L. M., Lam, B. S. T., Ho, E. C. N., Hui, P. W. M., Suen, Y. N., Lin, J. J., Tong, A. C. Y., Lee, E. H. M., Chan, S. K. W., Chang, W. C., & Chen, E. Y. H. (2021). Mindfulness meditation for Chinese patients with psychosis: A systematic review and meta-analysis. *Schizophrenia Research, 237*, 103–114.

Ting, K. T., Tam, W., & Jacobsen, P. (2020). Mindfulness for psychosis groups; description and preliminary evaluation of a novel routine care pathway in Hong Kong. *International Journal of Mental Health Systems, 14*(1), 81.

Walsh, R., & Roche, L. (1979). Precipitation of acute psychotic episodes by intensive meditation in individuals with a history of schizophrenia. *American Journal of Psychiatry, 136*(8), 1085–1086.

Wang, L., Mao, Y., & Ye, D. (2021). Mindfulness-based therapy combined with risperidone treatment for emotional disorder in schizophrenic patients during the recovery period. *Chinese Journal of Primary Medicine and Pharmacy, 12*, 686–689.

Wang, L. Q., Chien, W. T., Yip, L. K., & Karatzias, T. (2016). A randomized controlled trial of a mindfulness-based intervention program for people with schizophrenia: 6-month follow-up. *Neuropsychiatric Disease and Treatment, 12*, 3097–3110.

Wang, X., Wen, M., Huang, H., & Jiang, Y. (2019). Effect of mindfulness psychological intervention on medication compliance and relapse in convalescent schizophrenia. *China Medicine and Pharmacy*, *9*(23), 278–281.

White, R., Gumley, A., McTaggart, J., Rattrie, L., McConville, D., Cleare, S., & Mitchell, G. (2011). A feasibility study of Acceptance and Commitment Therapy for emotional dysfunction following psychosis. *Behaviour Research and Therapy*, *49*(12), 901–907.

Xu, S., Xie, J., Peng, L., Fu, C., Li, M., & Xiong, J. (2018). Effects of mindfulness psychological intervention on emotional experience and attentional control of convalescent soldiers with schizophrenia. *Journal of the Third Military Medical University*, *40*(17), 1527–1532.

Yip, A. L. K., Karatzias, T., & Chien, W. T. (2022). Mindfulness-based interventions for non-affective psychosis: a comprehensive systematic review and meta-analysis [Article]. *Annals of Medicine*, *54*(1), 2340–2353.

21

Negative Symptoms in Clinical High-Risk Populations

Psychological and Social Approaches for Clinicians and Researchers

Trevor F. Williams, Danielle N. Pratt, Sydney H. James, and Vijay A. Mittal

Clinical pearls

- Negative symptoms are often present in those at clinical high risk (CHR) for psychosis, who experience attenuated positive symptoms of psychosis.
- Research on treatments for negative symptoms in CHR individuals is in an early stage and treatments for attenuated positive symptoms do not improve negative symptoms.
- Preliminary evidence suggests several intervention strategies that may be useful in this population, such as incorporating family members, using third-wave cognitive behavioral approaches (e.g., mindfulness), and designing interventions to be engaging to youth.

1. Background

Individuals with psychosis spectrum disorders often experience a symptom development pattern characterized by the emergence of subtle, and then increasingly distracting and impairing positive symptoms prior to the development of a formal psychotic disorder. These emerging, or attenuated, positive symptoms are generally less formed (e.g., shadows moving in peripheral vision vs. well-defined person), characterized by lower conviction, and have less functional impact relative to psychotic disorders (McGlashan et al., 2010). The period of attenuated symptoms before conversion to psychosis is considered "prodromal," and researchers and clinicians describe individuals who may be in the prodrome as at clinical high risk for psychosis (CHR; Woods et al., 2009).

Trevor F. Williams et al. *Negative Symptoms in Clinical High-Risk Populations*. In: *Psychosocial Approaches to Negative Symptoms in Psychosis*. Edited by: Tania Lincoln et al., Oxford University Press. © Oxford University Press (2025). DOI: 10.1093/oso/9780197676790.003.0021

Ongoing research aims to hone the ability to predict which CHR individuals are most likely to develop psychosis spectrum disorders and deploy preventive interventions, which decrease the likelihood of developing psychosis and improve functional outcomes (Fusar-Poli et al., 2019). It is also important, however, to note that the majority of CHR individuals do not transition (many show persistent symptoms while some exhibit remission), but still represent a help-seeking population characterized by symptoms accompanying considerable distress and disability.

Although this period is typically defined by attenuated positive symptoms, there is evidence that negative symptoms may also emerge at this stage and may be important to understanding outcomes in this group (Addington et al., 2015; Anderson et al., 2021; Schlosser et al., 2015). Several studies have documented that higher negative symptoms at initial presentation predict a higher likelihood of conversion to a psychosis spectrum disorder, with the persistence (vs. improvement) over time of negative symptoms potentially further heightening this risk (Carrión et al., 2016; Zhang et al., 2019). Negative symptoms have also been linked to pathogenic mechanisms underlying the emerging disorder (Bernard et al., 2014; Dean et al., 2015; Mittal et al., 2014). Furthermore, as noted, although not all CHR individuals develop psychotic disorders (i.e., only 15% to 30%; Gold et al., 2020), functional impairments related to negative symptoms may persist outside of full psychosis (social, work, etc.; Addington et al., 2019). These findings parallel the importance of negative symptoms in psychosis spectrum disorders (Harvey, 2013); however, there are unique difficulties conceptualizing and measuring negative symptoms in CHR individuals that must be considered before discussing treatment approaches.

2. Describing and Assessing Negative Symptoms

Research on negative symptoms in CHR individuals has only recently accelerated and many early studies focus on outdated conceptual models of negative symptoms (Strauss et al., 2020). In the last few years, there have been calls to advance more modern conceptual models and develop better assessment instruments, based on developments in the psychosis literature (Pelletier-Baldelli et al., 2017). Specifically, a 2005 NIMH-sponsored consensus conference on schizophrenia treatment concluded that there are at least five primary negative symptom domains: anhedonia, avolition, asociality, alogia, and blunted affect

(Kirkpatrick et al., 2006). Per (Strauss & Cohen, 2017), *anhedonia* is a reduction in positive emotion intensity and/or frequency of pleasurable activities; *avolition* reflects reduced desire, initiation, and persistence in goal-directed activities; *asociality* involves few social interactions and decreased desire for close relationships; *alogia* is marked by reduced speech quantity and spontaneous elaboration; and *blunted affect* is indicated by reduced nonverbal emotional expression and bodily gesture. New research in CHR samples suggests the validity of this five symptom model in the CHR population (Azis et al., 2019; Chang et al., 2021) and has resulted in the recently developed Negative Symptom Inventory-Psychosis Risk (NSI-PR) structured clinical interview (Pelletier-Baldelli et al., 2017). This interview continues to be refined, but currently has 11 items that cut across these five primary negative symptom domains, which are rated based on past week symptoms and aim to be relevant to this age group (e.g., social media items). In addition, the measure contains items that separate inner experience from behavior and consummatory from anticipatory pleasure, which may be important for identifying the mechanisms underlying negative symptoms (Strauss et al., 2020). For more on assessing negative symptoms, see Chapter 10 (Kring, Weittenhiller, & Cogan).

One ongoing challenge to conceptualizing and measuring negative symptoms in CHR individuals relates to the high prevalence of comorbid internalizing disorders (depression, anxiety, eating disorders, etc.) that phenomenologically overlap with negative symptoms (Gupta et al., 2021). The impact of comorbid symptoms may be understood in terms of the primary versus secondary negative symptom distinction. This distinction was introduced to differentiate symptoms that are more intrinsic to psychosis spectrum disorders and psychosis risk (primary) and those symptoms that are caused by factors other than the risk state itself (e.g., paranoia, anxiety, disorganization, medication). One study in a CHR sample found that anxiety and depression accounted for substantial variance in negative symptom rating scales, which were common in this sample (Gupta et al., 2021). Similarly, a study of 509 CHR individuals found that 73% had a comorbid Axis I disorder (e.g., 40% with a comorbid depressive disorder) and that the presence of comorbid diagnoses was associated with more severe negative symptoms, specifically avolition and apathy (Fusar-Poli et al., 2014). Other studies have found similar rates of comorbidity in CHR individuals and correlations with negative symptoms (Addington et al., 2017; Kuhney et al., 2021; McAusland et al., 2017). Such findings are consistent with reviews of diagnostic criteria, indicating that many disorders have symptoms and features that descriptively overlap with negative symptoms, albeit with potentially different underlying mechanisms (Strauss & Cohen, 2017).

3. Treatments for Negative Symptoms

As noted above, research on negative symptoms in CHR individuals is still in an early stage. Nonetheless, a variety of preliminary evidence has emerged regarding treatments that may be promising. Broadly, treatments have taken one of two approaches: (1) translating existing psychosis spectrum disorder treatments for use in CHR individuals; and (2) developing new treatments aimed to be more relevant to the unique needs of this population. Meta-analyses indicate that there is little evidence that one intervention strategy is favorable to others in this population (Davies et al., 2018) and that many interventions focused on positive symptoms do not necessarily improve negative symptoms in CHR individuals (Devoe et al., 2018). Nonetheless, individual studies provide hope that interventions, especially those with a personalized treatment approach, can be effective in this population (McGorry et al., 2021). Below we review interventions with promising evidence and more briefly note treatments that appear ineffective or inconclusive in efficacy. In the process, we aim to consider these interventions from the perspective of the five-domain model of negative symptoms described in the preceding section and highlight details on practical implementation to the extent possible. Interventions with positive evidence are summarized in Table 21.1.

3.1 Psychosocial Interventions Adapted from the Schizophrenia Literature

Most psychosocial interventions researched in CHR individuals have been adapted from the schizophrenia literature, with minimal modifications. Notably, most of these interventions, and CHR treatment research more generally, are focused on reducing positive symptoms and risk of conversion to a psychosis spectrum disorder. Among the adapted psychosocial intervention trials that have examined negative symptoms in CHR individuals, many had small sample sizes, few were specifically designed to target negative symptoms, and none have been found to have an impact at the meta-analytic level (Devoe et al., 2018). Notably, cognitive behavioral therapy (CBT) for psychosis, though potentially efficacious in other respects—such as preventing conversion (Hutton & Taylor, 2014; Ising et al., 2016; Zheng et al., 2022) and reducing attenuated positive symptoms (Zheng et al., 2022)—does not appear to improve negative symptoms any more than supportive therapy or treatment as usual (Addington et al., 2011; Ising et al., 2016). Furthermore, there is mixed evidence that cognitive remediation efforts improve negative symptoms (Devoe et al., 2018). Despite this, some directions look promising and provide hope for alleviating negative symptoms for CHR youth.

Table 21.1 Summary of Treatments with Positive Evidence

Name	Description	Findings	Citation
Adapted from psychosis literature			
Group and Family based CBT (GF-CBT)	Individual therapy, skills group, and 15-week family CBT skills group that seeks to 1) increase family support, 2) help the family cope, and 3) teach skills to family members.	Reductions in overall negative symptoms	Landa et al., 2016
Family-aided Assertive Community Treatment (FACT)	Treatment includes family psychoeducation, supported education and employment, community treatment, and psychotropic medication.	Reductions in overall negative symptoms	McFarlane et al., 2015
Developed for CHR individuals			
MOMENTUM	2-month online intervention. Treatment includes social media component and self-guided modules. Seeks to enhance well-being, promote positive interpersonal connections, and foster self-efficacy.	Improvement in outcomes relevant to asociality, as well as potentially anhedonia and avolition.	(Alvarez-Jimenez et al., 2018)
Cognitive for Learning and Understanding Everyday Social Situations (CLUES)	Treatment incorporates cognitive exercises, social-cognitive groups, value identification, mindfulness, and individual coaching. Improvements in social functioning and social cognition were demonstrated.	Improvements in outcomes relevant to asociality	Friedman-Yakoobian et al., 2020

Continued

Table 21.1 *Continued*

Name	Description	Findings	Citation
Mindfulness and Compassion Group Program (MAC-P)	8-week program that includes symptom psychoeducation and lessons on mindfulness and compassion toward self and others.	Reduction in overall, negative symptoms, as well as potentially improvements in outcomes relevant to anhedonia and asociality	Hickey et al., 2021
Theatre Improvisation Training to Promote Social Cognition (TIPS)	18-week group sessions that incorporated CBT principles into collaborative improvisation and acting exercises.	Reduction in overall negative symptoms	Tang et al., 2020
Interventions for Secondary Negative Symptoms			
Acceptance and Commitment Therapy in Daily Life (ACT-DL)	8-week program that includes manualized sessions based on ACT for psychosis including psychoeducation and six ACT core processes. After each session, participants were prompted 8 times for three days after each session for their mood, symptoms, activities, and were given exercises to practice as well as to use when needed.	Reduction in overall negative symptoms	Myin-Germeys et al., 2022
Community-oriented family-based intervention	Treatment is focused on the importance of stress reduction for the client, the role of family conflict in the client's stress, and the importance of family support for the client.	Positive effects on depression, hopelessness, anxiety, quality of life, and functioning	Grano et al., 2014; Grano et al., 2009

Note: Further detail can be found on these treatments in the text.

In contrast to traditional CBT approaches, a comprehensive Group and Family Based CBT program (GF-CBT) has shown promise for reducing *overall* negative symptoms in a small trial of CHR individuals ($N = 6$; Landa et al., 2016). This 15-week program supplements traditional CBT (i.e., individual therapy and a skills group) with a weekly family CBT skills group that teaches the family to implement skills to bolster gains beyond the program, increase familial support for the CHR individual, and help the family cope with their own distress (Landa et al., 2016). CBT skills taught in this program include changing negative thought patterns, normalizing symptomatology, and reducing cognitive biases (such as jumping to conclusions; Landa et al., 2016). It may be that family-based therapies in general provide added benefit for the treatment of negative symptoms. A program called Family-Aided Assertive Community Treatment (FACT), which incorporates a psychoeducational multifamily group therapy, assertive community treatment, supported education and employment, and psychotropic medication, decreased *overall* negative symptoms compared to a lower risk sample (with equal negative symptoms at baseline) receiving community care (McFarlane et al., 2015). Negative symptoms also improved for a sample receiving 18 sessions of Family-Focused Therapy for CHR individuals (FFT-CHR) involving psychoeducation, stress management, and training in communication and problem solving (Miklowitz et al., 2014). Negative symptoms also improved, however, for the control group who were given a three-session family psychoeducation program about symptom prevention (Miklowitz et al., 2014), indicating that family involvement may be the important aspect; an update on this intervention with a larger sample and a longer follow-up interval is expected soon (Miklowitz et al., 2021). Given the similarities across these interventions of family involvement, increased support, and psychoeducation, these three principles may be particularly important for treating negative symptoms in CHR individuals.

There are other promising interventions that have alleviated negative symptoms in psychotic disorders that either have not been tried yet for CHR individuals or are at the beginning stages. The preceding chapters of this section overview many such interventions, including CBT that is more targeted toward negative symptoms (Chapter 14; van der Gaag) and recovery oriented cognitive therapy (Chapter 15; Inverso & Grant); here, we briefly highlight several others. One promising group of interventions are third wave psychotherapies, such as Acceptance and Commitment Therapy (ACT). One study found that a new protocol called ACT in Daily Life (ACT-DL) reduced *overall* negative symptoms compared to treatment as usual (Myin-Germeys et al., 2022). In this protocol, participants received eight sessions of manualized ACT for psychosis and used an Ecological Momentary Interventions application to record mood and symptoms, as well as provide ACT exercises (Myin-Germeys et al., 2022).

Additionally, Cognitive Behavioral Social Skills Training has been shown to be effective at reducing negative symptoms in those with schizophrenia (Granholm et al., 2014), and this is just beginning to be assessed in CHR individuals (Addington et al., 2021). Further, nonpsychotherapeutic interventions may have promise for alleviating negative symptoms in CHR individuals. For one, participating in yoga appears to reduce negative symptoms in women with early psychosis (Lin et al., 2015). Thus there is hope that interventions from the schizophrenia literature may provide guidance for treating negative symptoms in CHR individuals.

3.2 Psychosocial Interventions Developed for CHR Individuals

Aside from adapting existing treatments from the schizophrenia literature, some work has aimed to develop interventions specifically designed to treat negative symptoms and their functional outcomes in CHR individuals. A strength of such an approach is that it may be better positioned to consider the nuanced developmental context and other unique features of the CHR population. Thus, although most studies of psychosocial interventions specifically developed to treat negative symptoms in CHR individuals are preliminary, their specific methods may indicate useful tools for this population. Below, we review a selection of such emerging treatments that are tailored to CHR individuals.

Most interventions developed focus specifically on social functioning and thus are most directly relevant to the *asociality* domain of negative symptoms, though in many cases change in negative symptoms was not directly measured. A small pilot study (N = 14 CHR, no control) was recently completed for the MOMENTUM intervention, which found improvements in social functioning, social support, mindfulness, personal strengths use, and well-being; such outcomes are relevant to not only *asociality*, but potentially *anhedonia* and *avolition* negative symptom domains (Alvarez-Jimenez et al., 2018). The MOMENTUM intervention draws upon mindfulness, strengths-based, and Self-Determination Theories, and is administered over two months in an online format with a social media component and self-guided modules. The intervention techniques are designed to enhance subject well-being (mindfulness exercises), identify personal strengths, and foster positive interpersonal connections (e.g., responding to positive news). Another recent study was conducted on Cognition for Learning and for Understanding Everyday Social Situations (CLUES), which combines elements of Cognitive Enhancement Therapy for schizophrenia (cognitive exercises, social-cognitive groups, and individual coaching) and Acceptance and Commitment Therapy (value identification, mindfulness). A small randomized control trial on 38 CHR participants with poor social functioning (20 CLUES,

18 ACT control intervention) found that CHR individuals in CLUES showed greater improvements in social functioning and social cognition measures over six months of intervention (Friedman-Yakoobian et al., 2020). Another small pilot study (N = 17 mixed CHR and first episode psychosis, no control group) examined an eight session mindfulness and compassion group program (MAC-P), which focused on psychoeducation, mindfulness, and compassion toward self and others (Hickey et al., 2021). This study found significant improvements in *overall* negative symptoms, depression (potentially *anhedonia*), and a variety of social functioning measures (*asociality*). Finally, Theatre Improvisation Training to Promote Social Cognition (TIPS) was developed for CHR individuals and is designed to improve negative symptoms, social functioning, and social cognition. Across 18, two-hour sessions, TIPS focuses on collaborative improvisation exercises that emphasize social skills and efficacy, which are complemented by cognitive behavioral therapy-style homework. An initial nonrandomized control trial found that CHR participants receiving the intervention (N − 26) improved *overall* negative symptoms and functioning, relative to matched CHR controls (N = 26; Tang et al., 2020).

Notably, many of the findings regarding novel CHR psychosocial interventions that may impact negative symptoms are preliminary, involving small samples or lacking adequate control groups. Nonetheless, these studies suggest the value of focusing on the consequences of negative symptoms for social functioning, as well as novel approaches that may be engaging to adolescents and young adults.

3.3 Psychosocial Interventions for Secondary Sources of Negative Symptoms

Based on the literature in schizophrenia that suggests that negative symptoms may be responsive to treatments directed at the symptom source (Fusar-Poli et al., 2015; Kirscher et al., 2017) and that some individuals experience negative symptoms caused by comorbidity conditions (e.g., secondary source negative symptoms), it is important to consider treatments of common comorbid conditions in CHR individuals (e.g., anxiety disorders). Indeed, Gupta and colleagues (2021) suggest the potential value of cognitive behavioral therapy as a means for treating secondary negative symptoms caused by comorbid disorders. Beyond this, there may be overlap in treatment mechanisms across primary and secondary negative symptom treatments. For instance, defeatist performance beliefs were originally a focus of depression treatment, but have also become an important treatment target in negative symptom treatments for schizophrenia (Campellone et al., 2016; Granholm et al., 2014). More broadly, this suggests that treatments focusing on comorbid conditions may substantially improve functional outcomes relevant to negative symptoms in CHR individuals, regardless of mechanism.

Indeed, research in adolescent CHR populations has found beneficial effects of community-oriented family-based interventions on depression, hopelessness, and functioning (Granö et al., 2014, 2016) as well as improvements in anxiety and quality of life (Granö et al., 2009). These community-oriented family-based interventions involved (1) helping the clients reduce stress, (2) discussing the role of family conflict in the client's stress, and (3) emphasizing the importance of family support in the client's life. Another study that examined family interventions in the CHR population compared family-focused therapy (FFT) to family psychoeducational treatment (FPT) and found reduced depressive symptoms in CHR adolescents in both groups (Rinne et al., 2021). Interestingly, in addition to the above noted reduction in negative symptoms, the Landa and colleagues (2016) study on GF-CBT also revealed improvements in depression, though this was in a small sample. This is consistent with possible overlap in depression and negative symptom treatment approaches (Campellone et al., 2016). Overall, these studies suggest that including the family unit in treatment with CHR adolescents may be beneficial in reducing symptomatology in these individuals.

Regarding individual treatment modalities in the CHR population, one study found that individuals who received heart rate variability biofeedback treatment experienced significant reductions in dysphoric mood and improvements in distress tolerance over a four-week period (McAusland & Addington, 2018). Although reductions in anxiety were not significant, there was a trend toward improvement at post-treatment (McAusland & Addington, 2018). CBT for treating depression, anxiety, and related disorders have not been directly examined in CHR samples; however, the vast literature on these treatments and preliminary findings of efficacy in schizophrenia samples suggests that it is reasonable to believe that that CBT would be efficacious for treating comorbid conditions in CHR individuals (Butler et al., 2006; Michail et al., 2017). Inasmuch as treatment research with this population is still in its infancy, it may be advantageous for clinicians to use the conceptualization of the client and their clinical judgment in tandem with treatment research findings to guide treatment decisions.

4. Conclusions and Future Directions

Overall, CHR negative symptom treatment development and evaluation is in an early stage. Treatments that have shown promise for positive symptoms (CBT, antipsychotics, etc.) generally do not appear to be beneficial for treating negative symptoms in CHR individuals (Devoe et al., 2018). Nonetheless, as documented in the preceding sections, preliminary evidence for a variety of promising interventions for negative symptoms have emerged. In this final section, we critically appraise the overall state of this evidence and make recommendations for further work.

A review of meta-analyses by (Addington, et al., 2019) points to a variety of limitations in the existing CHR treatment literature. One that is particularly relevant to negative symptoms is that intervention trials have not specifically targeted CHR individuals with negative symptoms, which is problematic given the heterogeneity of this population. Most all CHR individuals experience attenuated positive symptoms, but not all of them have negative symptoms and thus limit the power of existing studies to detect improvement. It would thus be beneficial for future work to follow the lead of (Friedman-Yakoobian et al., 2020), recruiting individuals with symptoms or functional deficits that are relevant to the aims of the intervention being examined. Relatedly, another limitation of existing studies is that most studies assessed negative symptoms with a negative symptom total score, as well as using outdated measures and conceptual models (Strauss et al., 2020). More refined measurement may demonstrate that some interventions target specific negative symptom domains (e.g., asociality) more so than others and also may be useful for identifying whether improvements are specific to primary or secondary negative symptoms.

Beyond these limitations, there are some promising themes that cut across interventions and modalities, which may indicate general treatment principles. A number of interventions appear to be achieving success through explicitly including family members. This is a developmentally sensitive adaptation for this population, as many CHR individuals are minors or strongly tied to their family (e.g., live at home). Another theme that emerged in several successful interventions is the inclusion of varied third-wave CBT techniques, most notably mindfulness. It may be that mindfulness and related interventions hold unique value for addressing symptoms in this population. Finally, many of these interventions made strong attempts to engage CHR individuals, through social media interfaces, games, social groups, and even performance art. Appealing to adolescents and young adults, who may have complex feelings regarding their at-risk status and experiences of positive symptoms is a challenging issue (DeLuca et al., 2021), such that these additions may actually be of great importance if they spark engagement in this population. These promising themes represent relatively low-risk interventions that may augment existing treatments. Nonetheless, further research is needed to confirm that these themes from promising interventions are truly important mechanisms that can be deployed as treatment principles.

References

Addington, J., Devoe, D., & Santesteban-Echarri, O. (2019). Multidisciplinary Treatment for Individuals at Clinical High Risk of Developing Psychosis. *Current Treatment Options in Pediatrics, 6*, 1–16.

Addington, J., Epstein, I., Liu, L., French, P., Boydell, K. M., & Zipursky, R. B. (2011). A randomized controlled trial of cognitive behavioral therapy for individuals at clinical high risk of psychosis. *Schizophrenia Research, 125*(1), 54–61.

Addington, J., Liu, L., Buchy, L., Cadenhead, K. S., Cannon, T. D., Cornblatt, B. A., Perkins, D. O., Seidman, L. J., Tsuang, M. T., Walker, E. F., Woods, S. W., Bearden, C. E., Mathalon, D. H., & McGlashan, T. H. (2015). North American Prodrome Longitudinal Study (NAPLS 2): The Prodromal Symptoms. *The Journal of Nervous and Mental Disease, 203*(5), 328–335.

Addington, J., Liu, L., Santesteban-Echarri, O., Brummitt, K., Braun, A., Cadenhead, K. S., Cornblatt, B. A., Holden, J. L., & Granholm, E. (2021). Cognitive behavioural social skills training: Methods of a randomized controlled trial for youth at risk of psychosis. *Early Intervention in Psychiatry, 15*(6), 1626–1636.

Addington, J., Piskulic, D., Liu, L., Lockwood, J., Cadenhead, K. S., Cannon, T. D., Cornblatt, B. A., McGlashan, T. H., Perkins, D. O., Seidman, L. J., Tsuang, M. T., Walker, E. F., Bearden, C. E., Mathalon, D. H., & Woods, S. W. (2017). Comorbid diagnoses for youth at clinical high risk of psychosis. *Schizophrenia Research, 190*, 90–95.

Addington, J., Stowkowy, J., Liu, L., Cadenhead, K. S., Cannon, T. D., Cornblatt, B. A., McGlashan, T. H., Perkins, D. O., Seidman, L. J., Tsuang, M. T., Walker, E. F., Bearden, C. E., Mathalon, D. H., Santesteban-Echarri, O., & Woods, S. W. (2019). Clinical and functional characteristics of youth at clinical high-risk for psychosis who do not transition to psychosis. *Psychological Medicine, 49*(10), 1670–1677.

Alvarez-Jimenez, M., Gleeson, J. F., Bendall, S., Penn, D. L., Yung, A. R., Ryan, R. M., Eleftheriadis, D., D'Alfonso, S., Rice, S., Miles, C., Russon, P., Lederman, R., Chambers, R., Gonzalez-Blanch, C., Lim, M. H., Killackey, E., McGorry, P. D., & Nelson, B. (2018). Enhancing social functioning in young people at Ultra High Risk (UHR) for psychosis: A pilot study of a novel strengths and mindfulness-based online social therapy. *Schizophrenia Research, 202*, 369–377.

Anderson, Z., Gupta, T., Revelle, W., Haase, C. M., & Mittal, V. A. (2021). Alterations in Emotional Diversity Correspond With Increased Severity of Attenuated Positive and Negative Symptoms in the Clinical High-Risk Syndrome. *Frontiers in Psychiatry, 12*, 755027.

Azis, M., Strauss, G. P., Walker, E., Revelle, W., Zinbarg, R., & Mittal, V. (2019). Factor Analysis of Negative Symptom Items in the Structured Interview for Prodromal Syndromes. *Schizophrenia Bulletin, 45*(5), 1042–1050.

Bernard, J. A., Dean, D. J., Kent, J. S., Orr, J. M., Pelletier-Baldelli, A., Lunsford-Avery, J. R., Gupta, T., & Mittal, V. A. (2014). Cerebellar networks in individuals at ultra high-risk of psychosis: Impact on postural sway and symptom severity. *Human Brain Mapping, 35*(8), 4064–4078.

Butler, A. C., Chapman, J. E., Forman, E. M., & Beck, A. T. (2006). The empirical status of cognitive-behavioral therapy: A review of meta-analyses. *Clinical Psychology Review, 26*(1), 17–31.

Campellone, T. R., Sanchez, A. H., & Kring, A. M. (2016). Defeatist Performance Beliefs, Negative Symptoms, and Functional Outcome in Schizophrenia: A Meta-analytic Review. *Schizophrenia Bulletin, 42*(6), 1343–1352.

Carrión, R. E., Demmin, D., Auther, A. M., McLaughlin, D., Olsen, R., Lencz, T., Correll, C. U., & Cornblatt, B. A. (2016). Duration of attenuated positive and negative symptoms in individuals at clinical high risk: Associations with risk of conversion to psychosis and functional outcome. *Journal of Psychiatric Research, 81*, 95–101.

Chang, W. C., Strauss, G. P., Ahmed, A. O., Wong, S. C. Y., Chan, J. K. N., Lee, E. H. M., Chan, S. K. W., Hui, C. L. M., James, S. H., Chapman, H. C., & Chen, E. Y. H. (2021). The Latent Structure of Negative Symptoms in Individuals with Attenuated Psychosis Syndrome and Early Psychosis: Support for the 5 Consensus Domains. *Schizophrenia Bulletin, 47*(2), 386–394.

Davies, C., Cipriani, A., Ioannidis, J. P. A., Radua, J., Stahl, D., Provenzani, U., McGuire, P., & Fusar-Poli, P. (2018). Lack of evidence to favor specific preventive interventions in psychosis: A network meta-analysis. *World Psychiatry, 17*(2), 196–209.

Dean, D. J., Kent, J. S., Bernard, J. A., Orr, J. M., Gupta, T., Pelletier-Baldelli, A., Carol, E. E., & Mittal, V. A. (2015). Increased Postural Sway Predicts Negative Symptom Progression in Youth at Ultrahigh Risk for Psychosis. *Schizophrenia Research, 162*(0), 86–89.

DeLuca, J. S., Akouri-Shan, L., Jay, S. Y., Redman, S. L., Petti, E., Lucksted, A., Rouhakhtar, P. R., Klaunig, M. J., Edwards, S. M., Reeves, G. M., & Schiffman, J. (2021). Predictors of internalized mental health stigma in a help-seeking sample of youth: The roles of psychosis-spectrum symptoms and family functioning. *Journal of Abnormal Psychology, 130*(6), 587–593.

Devoe, D. J., Peterson, A., & Addington, J. (2018). Negative Symptom Interventions in Youth at Risk of Psychosis: A Systematic Review and Network Meta-analysis. *Schizophrenia Bulletin, 44*(4), 807–823.

Friedman-Yakoobian, M, S., Parrish, E. M., Eack, S. M., & Keshavan, M. S. (2022). Neurocognitive and social cognitive training for youth at clinical high risk (CHR) for psychosis: A randomized controlled feasibility trial. *Schizophrenia Research, 243*, 302–306.

Fusar-Poli, P., Frascarelli, M., Valmaggia, L., Byrne, M., Stahl, D., Rocchetti, M., Codjoe, L. Weinberg, L., Tognin, S., Xenaki, L., & McGuire, P. (2015). Antidepressant, antipsychotic and psychological interventions in subjects at high clinical risk for psychosis: OASIS 6-year naturalistic study. *Psycholigical Medicine, 45*(6), 1327–1339.

Fusar-Poli, P., Nelson, B., Valmaggia, L., Yung, A. R., & McGuire, P. K. (2014). Comorbid Depressive and Anxiety Disorders in 509 Individuals With an At-Risk Mental State: Impact on Psychopathology and Transition to Psychosis. *Schizophrenia Bulletin, 40*(1), 120–131.

Fusar-Poli, P., Sullivan, S. A., Shah, J. L., & Uhlhaas, P. J. (2019). Improving the Detection of Individuals at Clinical Risk for Psychosis in the Community, Primary and Secondary Care: An Integrated Evidence-Based Approach. *Frontiers in Psychiatry, 10*, 774.

Gold, J. M., Corlett, P. R., Strauss, G. P., Schiffman, J., Ellman, L. M., Walker, E. F., Powers, A. R., Woods, S. W., Waltz, J. A., Silverstein, S. M., & Mittal, V. A. (2020). Enhancing Psychosis Risk Prediction Through Computational Cognitive Neuroscience. *Schizophrenia Bulletin, 46*(6), 1346–1352.

Granholm, E., Holden, J., Link, P. C., & McQuaid, J. R. (2014). Randomized Clinical Trial of Cognitive Behavioral Social Skills Training for Schizophrenia: Improvement in Functioning and Experiential Negative Symptoms. *Journal of Consulting and Clinical Psychology, 82*(6), 1173–1185.

Granö, N., Karjalainen, M., Anto, J., Itkonen, A., Edlund, V., & Roine, M. (2009). Intervention to improve level of overall functioning and mental condition of adolescents at high risk of developing first-episode psychosis in Finland. *Early Intervention in Psychiatry, 3*(2), 94–98.

Granö, N., Karjalainen, M., Edlund, V., Saari, E., Itkonen, A., Anto, J., & Roine, M. (2014). Changes in depression, anxiety and hopelessness symptoms during family- and community-oriented intervention for help-seeking adolescents and adolescents at risk of psychosis. *Nordic Journal of Psychiatry, 68*(2), 93–99.

Granö, N., Karjalainen, M., Ranta, K., Lindgren, M., Roine, M., & Therman, S. (2016). Community-oriented family-based intervention superior to standard treatment in improving depression, hopelessness and functioning among adolescents with any psychosis-risk symptoms. *Psychiatry Research, 237*, 9–16.

Gupta, T., Strauss, G. P., Cowan, H. R., Pelletier-Baldelli, A., Ellman, L. M., Schiffman, J., & Mittal, V. A. (2021). Secondary Sources of Negative Symptoms in Those Meeting Criteria for a Clinical High-Risk Syndrome. *Biological Psychiatry Global Open Science, 1*(3), 210–218.

Harvey, P. D. (2013). Assessment of everyday functioning in schizophrenia: Implications for treatments aimed at negative symptoms. *Schizophrenia Research, 150*(2), 353–355.

Hickey, T., Nelson, B., Enticott, J., & Meadows, G. (2021). The MAC-P program: A pilot study of a mindfulness and compassion program for youth with psychotic experiences. *Early Intervention in Psychiatry, 15*(5), 1326–1334.

Hutton, P., & Taylor, P. J. (2014). Cognitive behavioural therapy for psychosis prevention: A systematic review and meta-analysis. *Psychological Medicine, 44*(3), 449–468.

Ising, H. K., Kraan, T. C., Rietdijk, J., Dragt, S., Klaassen, R. M. C., Boonstra, N., Nieman, D. H., Willebrands-Mendrik, M., van den Berg, D. P. G., Linszen, D. H., Wunderink, L., Veling, W., Smit, F., & van der Gaag, M. (2016). Four-Year Follow-up of Cognitive Behavioral Therapy in Persons at Ultra-High Risk for Developing Psychosis: The Dutch Early Detection Intervention Evaluation (EDIE-NL) Trial. *Schizophrenia Bulletin, 42*(5), 1243–1252.

Kirkpatrick, B., Fenton, W. S., Carpenter, W. T., Jr., & Marder, S. R. (2006). The NIMH-MATRICS Consensus Statement on Negative Symptoms. *Schizophrenia Bulletin, 32*(2), 214–219.

Kirschner, M., Aleman, A., & Kaiser, S. (2017). Secondary negative symptoms-A review of mechanisms, assessment and treatment. *Schizophrenia Research, 186*, 29–38.

Kuhney, F. S., Damme, K. S. F., Pelletier-Baldelli, A., Chun, C., Ellman, L. M., Schiffman, J., & Mittal, V. A. (2021). Prevalence and Functional Consequences of Social Anxiety in Individuals at Clinical High-Risk for Psychosis: Perspective from a Community Sample Comparison. *Schizophrenia Bulletin Open, 2*(1), sgab025.

Landa, Y., Mueser, K. T., Wyka, K. E., Shreck, E., Jespersen, R., Jacobs, M. A., Griffin, K. W., van der Gaag, M., Reyna, V. F., Beck, A. T., Silbersweig, D. A., & Walkup, J. T. (2016). Development of a group and family-based cognitive behavioral therapy program for youth at risk for psychosis. *Early Intervention in Psychiatry, 10*(6), 511–521.

Lin, J., Chan, S. K., Lee, E. H., Chang, W. C., Tse, M., Su, W. W., Sham, P., Hui, C. L., Joe, G., Chan, C. L., Khong, P. L., So, K. F., Honer, W. G., & Chen, E. Y. (2015). Aerobic exercise and yoga improve neurocognitive function in women with early psychosis. *Npj Schizophrenia, 1*(1), 1–7.

McAusland, L., & Addington, J. (2018). Biofeedback to treat anxiety in young people at clinical high risk for developing psychosis. *Early Intervention in Psychiatry, 12*(4), 694–701.

McAusland, L., Buchy, L., Cadenhead, K. S., Cannon, T. D., Cornblatt, B. A., Heinssen, R., McGlashan, T. H., Perkins, D. O., Seidman, L. J., Tsuang, M. T., Walker, E. F., Woods, S. W., Bearden, C. E., Mathalon, D. H., & Addington, J. (2017). Anxiety in youth at clinical high risk for psychosis. *Early Intervention in Psychiatry, 11*(6), 480–487.

McFarlane, W. R., Levin, B., Travis, L., Lucas, F. L., Lynch, S., Verdi, M., Williams, D., Adelsheim, S., Calkins, R., Carter, C. S., Cornblatt, B., Taylor, S. F., Auther, A. M., McFarland, B., Melton, R., Migliorati, M., Niendam, T., Ragland, J. D., Sale, T., … Spring, E. (2015). Clinical and Functional Outcomes After 2 Years in the Early Detection and Intervention for the Prevention of Psychosis Multisite Effectiveness Trial. *Schizophrenia Bulletin, 41*(1), 30–43.

McGlashan, T., Walsh, B., & Woods, S. (2010). *The Psychosis-Risk Syndrome: Handbook for Diagnosis and Follow-Up*. Oxford University Press, USA.

McGorry, P. D., Mei, C., Hartmann, J., Yung, A. R., & Nelson, B. (2021). Intervention strategies for ultra-high risk for psychosis: Progress in delaying the onset and reducing the impact of first-episode psychosis. *Schizophrenia Research, 228*, 344–356.

Michail, M., Birchwood, M., & Tait, L. (2017). Systematic Review of Cognitive-Behavioural Therapy for Social Anxiety Disorder in Psychosis. *Brain Sciences, 7*(5), 45.

Miklowitz, D. J., Addington, J. M., O'Brien, M. P., Denenny, D. M., Weintraub, M. J., Zinberg, J. L., Mathalon, D. H., Cornblatt, B. A., Friedman-Yakoobian, M. S., Stone, W. S., Cadenhead, K. S., Woods, S. W., Sugar, C. A., Cannon, T. D., & Bearden, C. E. (2021). Family-focused therapy for individuals at high clinical risk for psychosis: A confirmatory efficacy trial. *Early Intervention in Psychiatry, 16*(6), 632–642.

Miklowitz, D. J., O'Brien, M. P., Schlosser, D. A., Addington, J., Candan, K. A., Marshall, C., Domingues, I., Walsh, B. C., Zinberg, J. L., De Silva, S. D., Friedman-Yakoobian, M., & Cannon, T. D. (2014). Family-focused treatment for adolescents and young adults at high risk for psychosis: Results of a randomized trial. *Journal of the American Academy of Child and Adolescent Psychiatry, 53*(8), 848–858.

Mittal, V. A., Dean, D. J., Bernard, J. A., Orr, J. M., Pelletier-Baldelli, A., Carol, E. E., Gupta, T., Turner, J., Leopold, D. R., Robustelli, B. L., & Millman, Z. B. (2014). Neurological Soft Signs Predict Abnormal Cerebellar-Thalamic Tract Development and Negative Symptoms in Adolescents at High Risk for Psychosis: A Longitudinal Perspective. *Schizophrenia Bulletin, 40*(6), 1204–1215.

Myin-Germeys, I., van Aubel, E., Vaessen, T., Steinhart, H., Klippel, A., Lafit, G., Viechtbauer, W., Batink, T., van Winkel, R., van der Gaag, M., van Amelsvoort, T., Marcelis, M., Schirmbeck, F., de Haan, L., & Reininghaus, U. (2022). Efficacy of Acceptance and Commitment Therapy in Daily Life in Early Psychosis: Results from the Multi-Center INTERACT Randomized Controlled Trial. *Psychotherapy and Psychosomatics, 91*(6), 1–13.

Pelletier-Baldelli, A., Strauss, G. P., Visser, K. H., & Mittal, V. A. (2017). Initial development and preliminary psychometric properties of the Prodromal Inventory of Negative Symptoms (PINS). *Schizophrenia Research, 189*, 43–49.

Rinne, G. R., O'Brien, M. P., Miklowitz, D. J., Addington, J. M., & Cannon, T. D. (2021). Depression, family interaction and family intervention in adolescents at clinical-high risk for psychosis. *Early Intervention in Psychiatry, 15*(2), 360–366.

Schlosser, D. A., Campellone, T. R., Biagianti, B., Delucchi, K. L., Gard, D. E., Fulford, D., Stuart, B. K., Fisher, M., Loewy, R. L., & Vinogradov, S. (2015). Modeling the role of negative symptoms in determining social functioning in individuals at clinical high risk of psychosis. *Schizophrenia Research, 169*(1-3), 204–208.

Strauss, G. P., & Cohen, A. S. (2017). A Transdiagnostic Review of Negative Symptom Phenomenology and Etiology. *Schizophrenia Bulletin, 43*(4), 712–719.

Strauss, G. P., Pelletier-Baldelli, A., Visser, K. F., Walker, E. F., & Mittal, V. A. (2020). A review of negative symptom assessment strategies in youth at clinical high-risk for psychosis. *Schizophrenia Research, 222*, 104–112.

Tang, S. X., Seelaus, K. H., Moore, T. M., Taylor, J., Moog, C., O'Connor, D., Burkholder, M., Kohler, C. G., Grant, P. M., Eliash, D., Calkins, M. E., Gur, R. E., & Gur, R. C. (2020). Theatre improvisation training to promote social cognition: A novel recovery-oriented intervention for youths at clinical risk for psychosis. *Early Intervention in Psychiatry, 14*(2), 163–171.

Woods, S. W., Addington, J., Cadenhead, K. S., Cannon, T. D., Cornblatt, B. A., Heinssen, R., Perkins, D. O., Seidman, L. J., Tsuang, M. T., Walker, E. F., & McGlashan, T. H. (2009). Validity of the Prodromal Risk Syndrome for First Psychosis: Findings from the North American Prodrome Longitudinal Study. *Schizophrenia Bulletin, 35*(5), 894–908.

Zhang, T., Xu, L., Tang, Y., Li, H., Tang, X., Cui, H., Wei, Y., Wang, Y., Hu, Q., Liu, X., Li, C., Lu, Z., McCarley, R. W., Seidman, L. J., Wang, J., & Group, on behalf of the S. (ShangHai A. R. for P. S. (2019). Prediction of psychosis in prodrome: Development and validation of a simple, personalized risk calculator. *Psychological Medicine, 49*(12), 1990–1998.

Zheng, Y., Xu, T., Zhu, Y., Li, C., Wang, J., Livingstone, S., & Zhang, T. (2022). Cognitive Behavioral Therapy for Prodromal Stage of Psychosis – Outcomes for Transition, Functioning, Distress, and Quality of Life: A Systematic Review and Meta-analysis. *Schizophrenia Bulletin, 48*(1), 8–19.

Index

For the benefit of digital users, indexed terms that span two pages (e.g., 52–53) may, on occasion, appear on only one of those pages.

Tables, figures, and boxes are indicated by an italic *t*, *f*, or *b*.